Divided Britain

Divided Britain

Second Edition

Ray Hudson
and
Allan M. Williams

JOHN WILEY & SONS

Chichester · New York · Brisbane · Toronto · Singapore

First Edition   1989
Second Edition   1995

Copyright © 1989, 1995 R. Hudson and A. Williams
Published in 1995 by John Wiley & Sons Ltd,
                        Baffins Lane, Chichester,
                        West Sussex PO19 1UD, England
                        Telephone   National Chichester (01243) 779777
                                          International (+44) 1243 779777

Other Wiley Editorial Offices

John Wiley & Sons, Inc., 605 Third Avenue,
Nev York, NY 10158–0012, USA

Jacaranda Wiley Ltd, 33 Park Road, Milton,
Queensland 4064, Australia

John Wiley & Sons (Canada) Ltd, 22 Worcester Road,
Rexdale, Ontario M9W 1LI, Canada

John Wiley & Sons (SEA) Pte Ltd, 37 Jalan Pemimpin #05–04,
Block B, Union Industrial Building, Singapore 2057

Library of Congress Cataloging-in-Publication Data

Hudson, Raymond.
   Divided Britain / by Ray Hudson and Allan M. Williams. — 2nd ed.
      p.   cm.
   Includes bibliographical references (p.   ) and index.
   ISBN 0-471-95204-4
      1. Great Britain—Social conditions—1945-   2. Great Britain—
   Economic conditions—1945-   3. Equality—Great Britain—
History—20th century.   I. Williams, Allan W.   II. Title.
HN385.5.H84   1994
306'.0941'0904—dc20   94-30675
                                                              CIP

British Library Cataloguing in Publication Data

A catalogue record for this book is available from the British Library

ISBN 0-471-95204-4

Typeset in 10/12pt Times by Mathematical Composition Setters Ltd, Salisbury, Wiltshire
Printed and bound in Great Britain by Biddles Ltd, Guildford and King's Lynn

Contents

List of tables   viii

List of figures   xi

Preface to the first edition   xiii

Preface to the second edition   xv

1   A Divided realm? Conceptualising the divisions   1
   1.1 Introduction: contemporary divisions in historical context   1
   1.2 Conceptualising social structure: division and fragmentation   4
   1.3 Conceptualising the state: regulation and social cohesion   17
   1.4 An outline   25

2   State strategies and economic change: the UK in a divided world   26
   2.1 Introduction   26
   2.2 One Nation political strategies, 1944–75   28
   2.3 Two Nations political strategies, 1975–93   36

3   Divided by class I: wealth and income   50
   3.1 Introduction: class, income and wealth   50
   3.2 Who owns the land? Land, wealth and incomes   55
   3.3 Who owns the companies? Capital, share-ownership, wealth
      and incomes   62
   3.4 Working for a wage: wage labour and money incomes   75
   3.5 On the dole   89

4   Divided by class II: consumption and life-styles   97
   4.1 Introduction: class, consumption and life-styles   97
   4.2 Class and education   99
   4.3 Class, health and health care   107
   4.4 Class, tenure and housing   111
   4.5 Class, consumption and life-styles   118
   4.6 Class and party politics   125

5 Divided by gender   133
   5.1 Gender relationships in historical context: One Nation versus
       Two Nations politics   133
   5.2 Men and women in the labour market   135
   5.3 His and her schooling: the gendering of educational access
       and opportunities   155
   5.4 Women in the domestic sphere: consumption, housing and
       leisure   161
   5.5 Men, women and political power   172
   5.6 Reprise: the 'doll's house' still stands   175

6 Divided by race   177
   6.1 The division begins: immigration and the UK   177
   6.2 Race, employment and income   182
   6.3 Education and race   193
   6.4 Race and housing: living in separate worlds?   199
   6.5 Race, politics and civil society   209

7 Divided by region   218
   7.1 Introduction: where you live matters   218
   7.2 Unemployment, employment and incomes in the North and
       in the South   220
   7.3 Consumption, life-styles and living conditions in the North
       and South   235
   7.4 Party politics: voting in the North and the South   243
   7.5 The political construction of regional inequalities in the UK
       in the 1980s and 1990s   245
   7.6 Conclusions: the UK's map of regional divisions   248

8 Divided within regions   249
   8.1 Introduction: landscapes of disadvantage   249
   8.2 Restructuring local economies   253
   8.3 Housing: tenure and intra-regional locational access   257
   8.4 Intra-regional differences: worlds apart within regions   262
   8.5 Where you live matters   268

9 Divided and divided   270
   9.1 Introduction   270
   9.2 Multiple deprivation and areas of multiple deprivation   272
   9.3 Multiple deprivation and state policies: remedies and gestures   285

10 Divided forever and for ever?   295
   10.1 Introduction   295
   10.2 The immediate future   295

10.3 Medium-term political alternatives?   300
10.4 So is the UK divided for ever?   303

References   305

Index   316

Tables

1.1 The UK international context: indicators of social and economic change in the 1980s   20
2.1 Indicators of UK national economic performance in the 1980s and 1990s   46
3.1 Distribution of income, UK, 1976−85   51
3.2 Distribution of wealth in Great Britain, adults over 18 (percentage), 1971−89   52
3.3 Pension fund investment: asset mix and geographical distribution   66
3.4 The UK's share of inward investment in industrial countries, 1971−89   66
3.5 Executives holding share options, 1987   71
3.6 The main beneficiaries of London Weekend Television's share scheme   72
3.7 Management buy-outs, 1967−91   72
3.8 Britain's shareholder profile, 1983−87   73
3.9 Changes in employees in employment, 1979−91, thousands seasonally adjusted   76
3.10 Job generation by company size, 1987−90   78
3.11 Small firm growth 1963−86 (firms employing 1−99 people)   78
3.12 Persons economically active, by socio-economic group, 1981   80
3.13 Occupational analysis of persons in employment by SOC major groups, spring 1991   80
3.14 Occupational change, 1984−91   81
3.15 Change in earnings for occupational groups, 1973−86   82
3.16 Remuneration of company executives and senior managers, 1979−89   83
3.17 The highest paid company directors in the UK, 1988   84
3.18 Directors' and executives' salary increases, 1988−89   84
3.19 Temporary and second jobs, 1984−91   87
3.20 Unemployment rates by occupation, 1979−92   92
4.1 Social class of UK candidates accepted for universities (percentages), 1979−84   102

4.2	Educational background of the UK's industrial leaders, 1979–89	104
4.3	Mortgage arrears, 1992–93	117
4.4	Household ownership of selected consumer durables, 1979–90	119
4.5	Consumer durables and relations to social class, 1990	120
4.6	Household expenditure: by socio-economic group of head, 1991	122
4.7	Expenditure on selected leisure items in 1985 by gross normal weekly income of household	123
4.8	Voting by trade union members in general elections, 1964–87	128
4.9	Voting by occupational class	128
5.1	Women's economic activities, Great Britain, 1973–91	137
5.2	Economic activity rates for women with and without dependent children, 1973–91	139
5.3	Women civil servants, 1982 and 1987	140
5.4	Women's earnings as a percentage of men's earnings in 1970–92	145
5.5	Male/female wage differentials in the EC, 1991	147
5.6	Levels of pay and hours for men and women, 1987 (1991)	148
5.7	Pensions: the gendering of occupational schemes, 1991	149
5.8	Unemployment by sex and duration in 1987 and 1993	154
5.9	School-leavers' highest qualification, by sex, 1970/71 to 1989–90	156
5.10	Highest qualifications attained by men and women, 1990–91	158
5.11	Men's and women's earnings and qualifications in the UK, 1991	161
5.12	Household division of labour in Great Britain, 1984	165
5.13	Men's and women's use of time in a typical week, 1985–92	167
5.14	Men's and women's housing tenure, 1985	170
5.15	Women candidates in general elections, 1918–92	173
5.16	Women in national governments in the European Union	174
6.1	Occupation by ethnic group and sex, 1971–86	183
6.2	Gross earnings by race and age, 1982	188
6.3	Unemployment rates by gender and race, 1984 and 1990	189
6.4	Highest qualification level by sex and ethnic group in 1984–86 (1988–90)	195
6.5	The housing tenures of ethnic groups in 1982 and 1987–90	201
6.6	Housing conditions of ethnic households in 1982	202
8.1	Manufacturing decline in urban areas in Great Britain, 1960–78	254
8.2	Urban–rural employment changes in Great Britain, 1981–89	256
8.3	Housing characteristics of inner- and outer-urban areas in England and Wales, 1981	259

8.4   Population change, 1971–88, and employment change,
       1981–87, by types of local authority districts   263
9.1   The experience of disadvantage in the UK in 1975   273
9.2   Vulnerability to multiple disadvantage, 1975   274
9.3   Multiple deprivation in London in 1981   281
9.4   Multiple deprivation in Scotland in the late 1970s   282
9.5   The patterns of poverty, 1983–91   291

Figures

1.1   General government expenditure as a percentage of GDP, UK
1891–1991   22

2.1   Gross profit shares of UK manufacturing and services,
1966–76   33

2.2   UK unemployment rates, 1966–92   41

2.3   UK share of world trade in manufactures, 1966–93   44

2.4   UK M0 monetary base, 1980–91   47

3.1   Major landholdings of the Cadogan and Grosvenor estates in
central London   57

3.2   Nominal and real agricultural land prices, 1960–92   59

3.3   Overseas investment in UK property, 1980–92   61

3.4   Who owns company shares, 1963–84?   63

3.5   Labour productivity in manufacturing, 1979–87   77

3.6   Unemployment in the UK   90

4.1   Per capita disposable income and consumer expenditure,
1948–91   98

5.1   Male and female economic activity rates, 1951–91   136

5.2   Percentage of employees working part-time, by industrial
division, 1992   144

5.3   Women's earnings as percentage of men's   146

5.4   How wages councils lost their influence   153

5.5   Subject choice in higher education, 1991–92   159

6.1   Immigration to the UK, 1950–82   178

6.2   Ethnic minority groups as a percentage of the total population,
1991   207

7.1   Standard regional boundaries   219

7.2   Regional unemployment rates (annual average percentages),
1979–93   221

7.3   Net civilian migration (thousands), 1981–91   222

7.4   Total employment change (percentage), 1979–91   223

7.5   Part-time employment change (percentage), 1979–91   224

7.6   Manufacturing employment change (percentage), 1979–91   225

7.7   Capacity utilisation in manufacturing, 1989   226

7.8   Capacity utilisation in manufacturing, 1992   227

7.9   New firm formation, 1981–89   229
7.10   Industrial militancy, 1991   230
7.11   Average weekly household incomes, 1980–81 and 1990–91   231
7.12   Popular capitalism, 1990   232
7.13   Government spending per capita on selected cash benefits,
       1988–89   233
7.14   Government spending on unemployment benefits, 1988–89   234
7.15   New dwelling price increases, 1981–89   236
7.16   Changes in dwelling prices, all dwellings, 1989–92   238
7.17   Household car ownership, 1981 and 1990   240
7.18   Educational attainment, 1990/91   243
7.19   Conservative Party support, 1987 General Election   245
8.1   The UK regional policy map, 1979 and 1993   250
8.2   Unemployment rate by county, January 1993   251
8.3   Household disposable income, 1990   265
9.1   Parliamentary constituencies with high levels of urban
       deprivation   278
9.2   London Docklands in crisis, 1992   290
9.3   Long-term unemployment, London boroughs, January 1993   293

Preface to first edition

In 1985 Prince Charles spoke publicly about his fears of the United Kingdom becoming a 'divided realm'. In this, he was no more than reflecting the feelings that many others had expressed, some publicly, others privately, about growing divisions within the UK in the 1980s and the dangers to social cohesion that they contained. Nevertheless, we believe this royal intervention in the public debate to be a significant one. Indeed, our original title for the book simply was 'The Divided Realm'. As this clearly did not have the same connotations for others as it did for us, we altered the title to the present one. But the book is still infused with the spirit of the divided realm, even if this is no longer its title.

There is no doubt that divisions within the UK, on a wide variety of dimensions, have deepened in the 1980s, though at the same time in other respects the gap has narrowed. The pattern of change, then, has often been a complex one, so that the UK is differently divided, as well as more deeply divided, in 1989 than it was in 1979. There is a tendency to attribute all this simply to the effects of Thatcherite policies. By implication, a reversal of these policies would produce a less divided Britain. In passing, however, we would argue that a combination of Thatcherite politics and changes in the global political economy preclude any easy return − perhaps any return at all − to consensus policies of the type that characterised the three decades prior to Mrs Thatcher.

Accepting this latter caveat, this is fine as far as it goes. But it neglects the fact that for a very long period before Mrs Thatcher became Prime Minister, the UK had in fact been a deeply divided and profoundly unequal society. The transition from feudalism to capitalism had laid the basis for the most fundamental transformation in the structure of divisions within the UK (although significant feudal traces remain today, as we show). Moreover, within the last couple of centuries the lineaments of division within a predominantly capitalist UK have changed in significant ways, as class structures have altered, gender divisions have been redefined, ethnic divisions have been created, and spatial divisions have been recast in various moulds. The state has often been integrally involved in such changes as the form, content and extent of its own involvement have varied. Perhaps the central point is that as a capitalist society the UK is − and *must* be − divided on class lines. Any attempt to deny this is based on a misunderstanding of capitalism or represents an attempt to mystify the fundamental basis on which capitalist societies are constituted. Divisions via gender, place and race are related to – but are not reducible to – those of class, but they are not necessary in the same structural sense as those of class. Divisions and the inequality that flows from them are thus built into the way in which UK society is constituted.

What we therefore seek to do in this book is to explore the interplay between these various ingrained dimensions of division in UK society – class, gender, place and race – and the specific politics of Thatcherism. We would argue that it is only by locating Mrs Thatcher's divided realm in the historical context of the creation and reproduction of divisions within the UK that both Thatcherite policies and their effects can be properly understood. Thatcherism is as much symptomatic of such divisions, as it is a cause of them.

In what follows, we use the terms (Great) Britain and United Kingdom synonymously, unless we make it specifically clear that the former excludes Northern Ireland. This is not intended as a slight to the inhabitants of the latter area, but is simply a way of introducing some variety in terminology.

Finally, in this Preface we wish to acknowledge various forms of advice and help in producing this book: to the numerous individuals who persuaded us to change the title; to Catherine Reed, Elizabeth Pearson and Tracy Reeves for typing various drafts of the text; to Terry Bacon for drawing the maps and figures; to Mark Cohen, for his initial advice and support, and with our best wishes for the future; and finally, but not least, to Iain Stevenson, for his positive response to the text and for a speed of production that is quite remarkable! As ever, however, the usual disclaimers apply: the shortcomings in what follows are ours alone.

Ray Hudson, Durham
Allan M. Williams, Exeter
April 1989

Preface to second edition

The first edition of this book had a quite specific purpose – to document the ways in which, and degree to which, the UK had become a more unequal society in the first decade of Mrs Thatcher's premiership. It explored the extent to which the magnitude and character of inequality in the 1980s was a product of the specific political economy of Thatcherism, the extent to which such inequality reflected deeper structural cleavage planes in UK society, and the extent to which Thatcherism was itself a response to the failure of earlier political strategies to deal with deep-seated structural weaknesses in the UK economy. At the time, in 1989, Mrs Thatcher seemed to be in an impregnable position, at the height of her power within the Conservative Party and a figure of great seniority and authority on the world's political stage.

In the five years that have elapsed since the first edition was published, there have been some significant changes within the UK. One of these, of course, is that Mrs Thatcher is no longer Prime Minister – and one of the safer predictions that we made in the first edition was that at some point she would have to cease to occupy this office. One of the questions that we posed then, however, was the extent to which Thatcherism would outlive Mrs Thatcher (p. 219) and this remains a valid question. As the economic boom of the late 1980s was succeeded by a deep and lasting recession in the 1990s, Mrs Thatcher was ditched by a Conservative Party fearful of its electoral prospects and in many ways against all the odds, her successor as Party Leader and Prime Minister, Mr Major, led the Conservatives to a fourth consecutive success in the 1992 general election. The extent to which Majorism represents a continuation of Thatcherism, or in fact constitutes a break with it, remains an open question. While the rhetoric may have softened, amid Prime Ministerial references to the 'classless society', social divisions and inequality have continued to deepen.

One of the aims of this edition, therefore, is to bring up-to-date the documentation of the main ways in which the UK remains a deeply divided society – along the cleavage planes of class, gender, race and place, and their various interactions. As well as revising material in the first edition, we have added a completely new chapter on intra-regional divisions. This is for two reasons. First, it reflects a recognition of the way in which the pattern of spatial inequality became more complicated as regional divisions were in some ways narrowed while other spatial divides sharpened in the recession of the 1990s. Secondly, it is an acknowledgement of the fact that we have in any case had too little to say about intra-regional, urban and rural variation in the first edi-tion as the focus of debate about spatial inequality in the 1980s came to focus so heavily on the 'North–South' divide.

As well as the up-dating and expansion of the account of the dimensions of inequalities, however, we have had a second objective in this second edition. This is to put the last fifteen years, and the expansion and re-working of inequality throughout this period of Conservative rule, into a broader his-torical perspective. This has involved fuller consideration of two aspects. The first is to locate this period more comprehensively in relation to a systematic periodisation of structural economic change and the changing pattern of social inequalities in the post-war period. When there have been critical junctures, potential crisis points at which the dominant social order and the pattern of inequalities that are integrally a part of this might have been challenged, the pressures have been contained with – as in the 1984/5 miners' strike – state power deployed, if need be in a very visible way, to deal with 'the enemies within' as well as those without. This capacity to contain pressures for radical change raises important questions, both about the past and about prospects for the future.

Acknowledging this, therefore, secondly we seek to locate the changing pat-terns of inequality within the UK in terms of theorisations of the structures of divisions within the UK and of the role of the state in regulating economy and society to enable a divided realm nonetheless to reproduce itself for most of the time in a more or less non-problematic way. In order to consider such issues more fully, we have replaced the original introductory chapter by two new and expanded ones. This also serves to place the reproduction of social relationships more fully in the context of the changing role of the UK in the international economic and political order.

Finally, as before acknowledgements of help from a number of people, which has been crucial in producing this edition: to Joan Dresser at Durham for sorting out the text from a succession of discs in varied formats: to Terry Bacon at Exeter for drawing and re-drawing the figures; and to Iain Stevenson at John Wiley and Sons for his continuing editorial encouragement and for-bearance. As before, most of the discussion as to what should go into this volume took place over the 'phone; we must, however, extend a special word of thanks to Richard Munton in the Department of Geography at UCL for providing us with a room to meet in a location that is approximately equidis-tant between Durham and Exeter; these meetings were an invaluable supple-ment to a succession of long telephone conversations about the process of revision. It is debatable whether we should thank BT or whether BT should thank us for a boost to corporate profits.

Ray Hudson, Durham
Allan M. Williams, Exeter
July 1994

1

A divided realm? Conceptualising the divisions

1.1 Introduction: contemporary divisions in historical context

The 1980s were commonly seen as a decade of unprecedented deepening and widening of divisions in UK society. But poverty and inequality were by no means specific to the 1980s and 1990s. There is a copious nineteenth-century literature, both fictional and factual, which chronicles the extent of social inequalities. Social commentators, such as Booth and Rowntree, and novelists, such as Dickens, have left a rich record of the prevalence of poverty and inequality in imperial Great Britain. But the most salient of these accounts in the context of characterising the UK in the 1980s was Disraeli, with his notion of the Two Nations. Clearly the Thatcherite appeals for a return to 'Victorian values' had their darker side.

At the same time, it is not difficult to make the case that, on average, the UK in the 1980s and the early 1990s was a prosperous society, certainly in comparison to most of the rest of the world (for example, see World Bank 1992); or to demonstrate statistically that the admittedly mythical average UK citizen was certainly amongst the world's most materially affluent (see, for instance, the data presented in the official government publication *Britain 1989*). The surge in prosperity from the mid- to the late 1980s was real, even if in large part it was no more than a consequence of the severity of the early 1980s recession ... which at some point had to end (unless the UK economy really had entered irreversible terminal decline). If the 1979 Conservative general election victory came on the back of the winter of discontent, and that in 1983 on the crest of a jingoistic post-Falklands war wave, then that in 1987 was firmly grounded in the post-1985 recovery and associated consumer boom. It was followed by a fourth successive victory in 1992 based on promises of renewed growth and recovery from the deep and long recession of the previous couple of years.

The ignominious withdrawal from the European exchange rate mechanism (ERM), just six months after the 1992 election, only served to confirm that recovery remained a forlorn hope as gross domestic product per caput in the UK fell to around 95 per cent of the European Community average. Whilst still an affluent country compared to most of the world, the UK was slipping down the first division league table in a way that again raised profound fears of irreversible decline (Table 1.1). Registered unemployment again rose to 3 million while the public sector borrowing requirement and the balance of payments deficit simultaneously rose to record levels. The claim that there had been a decisive transformation in national economic performance in the 1980s was no longer tenable.

Nevertheless, whilst the second half of the 1980s witnessed a consumer boom of sorts, it was starkly apparent that the benefits were not being equitably distributed, socially or spatially, within the UK. As the Child Poverty Action Group declared in 1985 'Britain is divided into different worlds by extremes of wealth, income and prospects. In north and south there is a widening gap between rich and poor, men and women, black and white, sick and healthy, employed and unemployed'. In short it was as easy, and as valid, to paint a picture of a deeply divided realm – a phrase used in 1985 by Prince Charles as he voiced his fears about the future of his kingdom – as it was to depict the UK as a prosperous society in the 1980s. As slump succeeded boom in the early 1990s many of these inequalities were further magnified.

We would not wish to argue that the absolute levels of generalised poverty recorded by Booth, Rowntree and others in the nineteenth century are to be found in the contemporary UK. The sight of people sleeping in cardboard boxes in doorways on the streets of London and most other major cities suggests that some direct parallels can be found. More generally, however, the conditions experienced by the millions of people living in the UK in the 1980s and 1990s at below supplementary benefit levels cannot be equated with those of the inhabitants of east London, as graphically described by Charles Booth. But poverty is a relative as well as an absolute condition; it is not to be judged simply in terms of the ability of people to feed, clothe and physiologically reproduce themselves. The concept of relative poverty can be defined in terms of an inability to participate in the consumption of material and non-material goods and activities to the level that is regarded as the expected minimum standard of living in a particular time and place; in other words it is a form of social exclusion. It is one measure of the depth of the structural problems that blight the UK's economy, as well as the political legacy of Thatcherism in the 1980s, that by 1993 the Conservative government had embarked on a campaign to lower citizens' expectations as to what they might expect from the state in terms of welfare rights, public sector services and pensions. It is no coincidence that it is the most vulnerable and disadvantaged within society who will be most severely affected by this further erosion of an already emaciated welfare state. Seen in this perspective, these inhabitants of the UK who, in the 1980s, continued to live in the least desirable of Disraeli's 'Two Nations', experienced real and meaningful poverty, with lives blighted by manifold deprivations in what remains a real and not just metaphorical world. Moreover, they continue to do so in the 1990s. More than ever in an era of mass advertising proclaiming the virtues of conspicuous designer consumption, the have-nots are only too frequently reminded of that which they do not have.

One name – Thatcher – and its associated ideological trappings and policies is particularly closely linked with growing inequality during the 1980s. Although we do not subscribe to a personality cult interpretation of history, the policies pursued by her governments have undeniably left their imprint on the UK. Margaret Thatcher and the Conservative Party were elected to government in 1979 on a radically reforming platform, which emphasised the need for enterprise, efficiency and freedom, with little more than a fleeting backward glance at equity and justice. It is worth recalling Mrs Thatcher's words, borrowed from St Francis, as she entered No. 10 Downing Street on Friday, May 4, 1979:

> Where there is discord may we bring harmony. Where there is error may we bring truth. Where there is doubt may we bring certainty. Where there is despair may we bring hope.

These are undoubtedly fine words and sentiments. Reality, however, turned out to be very different. By the end of Mrs Thatcher's tenancy of No. 10 Downing Street, the benefits of this sort of freedom had been enjoyed by that minority, albeit a substantial one, who were the principal beneficiaries of Thatcherism. But the realities of freedom had become only too clear to a growing number of the UK's population in markedly different ways – a freedom to become unemployed, and to experience poverty with all the costs and deprivations that this entails. For many people this represented an uncomfortable end to old certainties; many of the rights and securities that citizens had come to take for granted in the previous decades of 'One Nation' politics were systematically dismantled and discarded. This was a deliberate part of the Thatcherite political project as it sought to break, irrevocably, the mould of the post-war settlement within the UK. In doing so, it dramatically redefined the breadth and depth of inequalities and remoulded the contours of inequality within an increasingly divided realm. It is this growing polarisation that we seek to place in context, describe and account for in this book.

By way of conclusion to this introductory section, we would emphasise three points. Firstly, it is certainly the case that inequalities persisted throughout the post-war period of 'One Nation' politics. It is, however, vital to relate the expansion of inequality in the 1980s and 1990s to the specific and distinctive political strategy of Thatcherism and its post-Thatcherite successor, Majorism; burgeoning inequality was a deliberate consequence of the Thatcherite 'Two Nations' strategy, in strong contrast to the intent of the previous 40 years of 'One Nation' politics. Despite Mr Major's proclaimed intent to produce a classless society, the policies of his government are no less divisive than those of his predecessor. This 'Two Nations' strategy harked back to nineteenth-century concerns about freedom, enterprise and individual and family rather than societal responsibility. It was, however, articulated in specific ways to the condition of the UK in the 1980s and early 1990s, in the context of the long-run international decline of the UK economy and the crises of the post-war settlement, Keynesianism and the welfare state. Growing inequality was not an accidental but a deliberate effect of policy, expressed in diverse and manifest ways in relation to class, gender, race and place. To begin to comprehend this, we need, secondly, to specify the dimensions of social structure around which divisions form and are expressed and the ways in which those relate to one another. Thirdly, we need to understand the social institutions and processes through which an inherently economically crisis-prone and socially fissiparous society 'holds together' and is, most of the time, more or less non-problematically reproduced. In particular, we need to pay particular attention to the regulatory role of the state.

1.2   Conceptualising social structure: division and fragmentation

Whilst class undeniably remains the main structural axis of capitalist societies, it is by no means the only dimension of social structure and differentiation. Furthermore, over the last few years there has been a significant change in the way in which some social scientists have conceptualised class, a shift that is also related to a relative de-emphasis of class as an explanatory variable. Thrift (1992, 10) suggests that work on class has become increasingly cultural and is now seen as one of a number of different structuring forces in society and 'not necessarily the most prominent one'. Gender, ethnicity and location are also recognised as important dimensions of social division in an increasingly plural civil society. In addition, there are those who would suggest that variables such as age or, more controversially, divisions of labour (on the latter, see Sayer and Walker 1992) have a causal effect in structuring society and generating differentiation.

In recent years, then, there has been both a partial reconceptualisation of class and a de-emphasis of its significance in social differentiation. Thrift (1992, 17), for instance, argues that 'no-one now believes that class is the be all and end-all of social life or that social life, culture and politics are necessarily organised along class lines'. It is, of course, debatable whether anyone ever really did believe that everything was reducible to class in the way that is implied here. Whilst acknowledging Thrift's point, we would none the less want to insist on the crucial pivotal role – indeed the primacy – of class as a structural dimension of differentiation within capitalist societies.

Nevertheless, teasing out the precise significance of class, gender, ethnicity and so on is problematic. As Sayer and Walker (1992, 13–15) emphasise, it is impossible to close off one structure and observe the unambiguous effects of its operations. As a consequence, 'we cannot expect societies to break neatly along the fault lines of class, gender. ... While the structural cleavages, like continental plates, run deep and grind mercilessly, they nevertheless turn and twist against one another, against circumstance, against the willful intransigence of human beings, and against their own internal contradictions.' Analysing social structure and the relations between agency and structure is, therefore, a challenging theoretical and empirical task.

1.2.1 The UK as a Class Society

1.2.1.1 Divided by class: but how?

The conceptualisation of class, and the assessment of the significance of class as a dimension of social structuration, have re-emerged as one of the most controversial and intense areas of contemporary social scientific discourse. Disputes over the theorisation of class are not, however, new. There has, for example, been a long-running debate between adherents of, broadly speaking, Marxian and Weberian views about class. The current variety of theoretical positions cannot be easily reduced to one of these alternatives, not least because other ways of thinking about class have grown in importance. Consequently, contemporary theorists tend to blend strands drawn from a variety of theoretical positions (see, for example, Giddens 1981, 1984; Urry 1981; Wright 1985, 1989).

Our theoretical point of departure is Marx's identification of the decisive class structural relation between capital and labour as lying at the heart of capitalist societies. This is, above all, an asymmetrical relation in terms of power. Members of the working class have to work for a wage in order to live whilst capitalists reap the rewards of their labour. It is, however, important to appreciate that this two-class conceptualisation represents a powerful abstraction, constructed to reveal the inner dynamism and the pivotal class structural relationship of capitalism. But – and this is a very important but – any particular capitalist society, such as that of the UK, is constructed around more complex and nuanced sets of class relationships than just a dichotomous direct antagonism between capital and labour. To put the point another way, the existence of capital and labour as a fundamental structural class relationship does not mean that the principal social actors are always, or even often, the sole and unified collective representatives of these interests. The interplay between agency and structure, and the diverse forms of defining and representing class interests, mean that actual capitalist societies are much more complex and complicated than the two-class model.

What are the implications of this in the conceptualisation of class structure and relations in the UK? Two points can be made at this stage. First, the transition from feudalism to capitalism in the UK did not result in the eradication of all traces of pre-capitalist social relationships. Significant 'relictual' relationships, especially in terms of landownership and landed property and the social practices associated with these, persist to this day. Moreover, the initial development and subsequent evolution of industrial capitalism were often shaped in decisive ways by the feudal heritage, not least in the ways in which 'carboniferous capitalism' developed on the coalfields (for example, see Beynon and Austrin 1993). More generally, there is considerable validity in the view that capitalism was established in the UK in a strangely compromised form (for example, see Nairn 1977).

Secondly, within capitalist societies the simple dichotomy between capital and labour influences but by no means determines class formation. It is rather like peeling an onion from the inside, beginning from the fundamental class structural relationship at the core and gradually working outwards, layer by layer, to the skin on the surface, revealing the complexities of the web of class relations in the process.

There are a number of dimensions to this complexity. Firstly, there are divisions within the bourgeoisie, the owners of capital. These are made and remade as a continuing process. There are conflicts between capital in the financial and manufacturing sectors; there are conflicts between branches within these sectors, for example between steel and electronics; and there are conflicts between companies in the same branch of the economy − for example, in chemicals between ICI, BASF and Bayer. Moreover, these particular forms of intra-class conflict are far from static. As Taylor (1992, 34) has noted, in the 1980s Thatcherism was 'revolutionary' in intra-class terms as it mounted an attack upon one part of the traditional etablishment whilst promoting the interests of another.

There are also divisions amongst those who work for a wage, both between and within the working class and the middle class. The relative sizes of the working class and middle class, and indeed the criteria by which they might be specified and defined, are matters of some debate. These inter- and intra-class divisions are generally defined on the bases of industry, occupation and so on. More recently and more contentiously, it has been suggested (notably by Sayer and Walker 1992) that these are most appropriately thought of not in terms of inter- and intra-class cleavages but as differences attributable to various divisions of labour. In so far as this involves more than semantic differences, we would emphasise that these are intra-class differences.

The growth and changing composition of the middle class is perhaps the most contentious issue in recent theoretical debates (for example, see Abercrombie and Urry 1983; Goldthorpe 1982; Scase 1982; Wright 1978, 1985, 1989). For one thing, the 'old' middle class − the *petite bourgeoisie* − has not disappeared. There are still many people who are self-employed, or who are owners of small enterprises who do not employ wage labour. Similarly, there are still many owners of small firms who still do so. This old middle class has not only persisted but, in some respects, has grown and some of the reasons for this are explored more fully in Chapter 3.

There has also been further growth in the new middle class which some, following Renner, define as a service class (see Urry 1986). This expansion is linked to two rather different processes: first, the growing size and significance of major private sector companies and, second, the growth of state involvement in both economy and society. As capital has become increasingly centralised in a relatively small number of firms, a separation emerged between the owners and managers of capital. The former derive incomes from profits, rents and dividends while the latter are paid a salary, albeit often a very large one, and exercise control without ownership. This change was closely tied to the growth of institutional share ownership in the UK. The second source of growth of this new middle class was grounded in the considerable post-war expansion of the welfare state (see Gough 1979; Corrigan 1984). This resulted in an increasing number of professional employees (in education, health, social services, local and central government, etc.) who were reliant on the state for their incomes and livelihood.

There is a further point that is of particular significance in relation to recent labour market changes in the UK. The growth in unemployment, and in particular of long-term, more or less permanent unemployment, has raised important theoretical issues as to the relationship of this group of non-working working class to those who are still in work. Not least, the existence of such a pool of unemployed people has become both a structural feature of the labour market and at the same time influenced broader patterns of labour market structuration and segmentation. One theoretical response has been to conceptualise it as part of the underclass (see Morris 1993), a surplus population permanently excluded from the formal segment of the labour market and reliant on state transfer payments as a means of subsistence. Borrowing a concept from Pugliese (1985), devised in a very different context, such people have become clients of the welfare state and, moreover, one that has been drastically cut back over the last 15 years. It says much about the developmental trajectory of economy and society in the UK over this period that such concepts, devised originally to be applied to agricultural workers in the Mezzogiorno, are appropriate for describing its social structure.

There is one final point to be made at this stage. There has also been some limited growth in property ownership amongst the lower-middle and working classes. Some of this has been direct, mainly through house purchase, in part reflecting the representation of owner occupation as the 'natural' and preferred housing tenure in the policies of both Labour and Conservative governments from the 1950s (see Hudson and Williams 1986, 31–37). One result of this bipartisan policy, which showered tax advantages on house purchasers and owners, is that owner occupation has become the majority tenure amongst the skilled manual fraction of the working class. This process was extended further by the sale of local authority houses to sitting tenants in the 1980s. Purchase of a house simultaneously provided a home and a place in which to live, and the prospects of capital gain as a result of future appreciation of prices. A further important effect relates to intergenerational transfers of wealth and its implications for people's perceptions of their class position. Whether individuals or households own or rent their homes conditions whether they – and perhaps more importantly their children – have shared in the redistribution of wealth that followed from spiralling property prices in the 1970s and 1980s. Even so, as the slump in the housing market in the early 1990s forcibly demonstrated, this is a contingent rather than a guaranteed route to the accumulation of wealth.

There have been other important changes in the ownership of wealth that have implications for class formation. Over most of the twentieth century individual share ownership has declined in the UK. More recently, the promotion of share ownership, via the tax benefits of personal equity plans and personal pension plans, and, especially, via the privatisation of former state-owned companies, became an important element in Mrs Thatcher's 'popular capitalism', a project which deliberately sought to restructure class relations in the UK and which continues as part of Majorism. This – discussed more fully in Chapter 3 – remains much less important for many people, however, than 'indirect' share ownership via their participation in pension schemes, which have increasingly been provided privately through major institutional investors. In this way, pensioners' future incomes come to depend on the investment decisions of fund managers. As the Stock Market crash of October 1987 showed, this is not necessarily a secure future.

The full implications of such changes in property ownership for changes in patterns of class relations remain to be determined. The generalisation of owner occupation, along with the more recent thin veneer of rising share ownership, has, however, undeniably had a profound influence on many aspects of traditional working-class values and behaviour. A particularly striking example of this is to be seen in voting behaviour in the 1980s. Whilst the working class as a whole largely continued to vote for the Labour Party, some sections of it came to give substantial electoral support to the Conservatives during that decade and on into the early 1990s (see Johnston et al. 1988). Examples such as these lead us to argue that many aspects of behaviour bear no simple linear relationship to class differences, though class certainly spills over to shape such behaviour in a determinate though not deterministic way.

1.2.1.2 *Analysing Class in the UK*

Classes in the UK are not static and unchanging entities. Their composition and pattern have changed within structural limits set by the character of an evolving capitalism. In the half century since the end of the Second World

War, the characteristics of both the working class and middle class have been moulded and remoulded. Partly because of this dynamism, there are unavoidable problems in the theoretical specification of class and the delineation of class boundaries. This is precisely why there has been such a lively debate on these issues, although this has raised questions rather than resolving them in an agreed consensus. It also reflects the fact that debates about class are unavoidably political as well as theoretical.

There is also a further problem. This is the correspondence – or rather lack of it – between theoretical categories and available empirical data. Much of the official data available from sources such as the Census of Population refer to socio-economic groups (SEGs) which, at best, only partially correspond to the theoretical categories of class. If, for example, we consider all those within a given occupational group (on which SEGs are based), such as electrician, it will contain members of different classes: wage labourers; the self-employed; capitalist employers. Nevertheless, many social scientists, as well as government statisticians, would accept that classes delimited in terms of occupational groupings are as reasonable a definition as one can produce from readily available data. Further complications arise when defining the class positions of those who do not work for a wage, or of households in which there is more than one wage earner. Is it reasonable to allocate wives or husbands to the occupational class of their spouses? An empirical investigation of class divisions in the UK cannot avoid such problems but at least we can be aware of their existence and implications.

1.2.2 Beyond class: conceptualising the other cleavages in the divided realm

Class, as a structural relationship, still remains the key to interpreting differential access to money, power and life chances. We are not, however, arguing that variables such as consumption patterns, electoral behaviour or political beliefs can be derived in any simplistic and deterministic manner from the class structure of the UK (see Marshall et al. 1988). There are cleavages within structurally defined classes in terms of life-style, incomes and wealth that themselves often partially serve to delineate subjective understandings of class. Moreover, in recent years there has been an increasing recognition that class is not the only dimension on which UK society is divided. Events such as the Falklands War and inner-city riots in the UK in their differing ways helped ensure that issues of race and nationalism rose to the forefront of political and popular discourses. The election of Mrs Thatcher as the UK's first female Prime Minister, and a number of equal pay disputes, likewise ensured that gender was never far from the headlines. In different ways, then, gender, race and place were recognised as sources of structural inequality and disadvantage, in part as a theoretical response to some of the practices of the 1980s.

Moreover, one of the impressive features of the political scene in the last two decades has been the efforts of ethnic minorities, women and particular areas to gain greater recognition of these inequalities and their implications; in other words, in contributing to their own destinies – even if their successes have been very uneven. In seeking to advance their causes, these groups have helped reshape class divisions as well as reinforcing the importance of non-class cleavages within UK society.

Recognising the existence of these other dimensions of social division raises acute theoretical problems. In particular, how are gender, race, and place to be related both to class (in a non-reductionist way that does not simply reduce them to its passive by-products) and to one another so as to retain some sense of the multiple over-determination of people's behaviour. This has been associated with important changes in the theorisation of class itself as well as of the links between class and non-class dimensions. The point may be illustrated in relation to analyses of the links between gender and class. Thrift (1992, 9 – emphasis added) argues that, by the end of the 1980s, Hartmann's (1978) approach, which saw women's oppression as a product of the articulation of class and gender, had been 'discredited ... and replaced by an approach which stressed notions of culture and subjectivity ... [and] the social construction of gender and sexuality'.

It is, however, important not to forget that gender relations have a material basis that, in capitalist societies, is grounded in the social relations of capital (see Allen 1982). What is at issue is not just a question of the cultural representation of class and gender relations. Also at issue is the material basis of that which is being so represented. This is not to deny the existence of patriarchy as a source of power/domination by men over women. The key theoretical question, however, is understanding the ways in which patriarchy relates to class (see for example, ten Tusscher 1986).

Patriarchy does not constitute a set of absolute and invariant relationships; their form varies between societies. However, certain general tendencies are common to all capitalist societies; these centre on domestic work, paid work, the role of the state and the culture of male dominance (Walby 1986). Gender inequalities have been shaped by changes in each of these, as well as by their interrelationships.

The prominence of women in domestic labour is central to the reproduction of labour power, both via child bearing and rearing and providing household services to partners and working children. Although essential to the reproduction of labour power, this work is unwaged. Women are also under economic and cultural pressure to combine the role of wife and mother with that of paid employee. This alone weakens their labour market position but in addition there are patriarchal relationships in the workplace. Women's access to paid work is socially filtered, not least because there are many forms of informal discrimination in recruitment, promotion and redundancies (see Chapter 5). There are no simple outcomes from the dual roles that women occupy in domestic and paid labour. Instead there are many forms of the gender division of labour and there are strong but varied tensions between the two roles. Another element in the social construction of patriarchy is the state, which is both capitalist and patriarchal. This is evident with respect to policies concerned with women's role in the reproduction of labour power. Considerable material benefits (tax allowances, housing benefits, etc.) as well as ideological support have been provided for the household form in which women provide unpaid domestic service for men, that is the family. Finally, there is also a deeply rooted culture of male dominance, reinforced in different ways by processes of socialisation, education and, at times, by male violence. None of these relationships individually constitutes an adequate explanation of gendered inequalities in the UK. Instead, they are interrelated and mutually reinforcing.

Gendered inequalities also interact with those generated through other social relationships, not least with class. The outcome is not a single model of inequality for all men and women. Educational opportunities, the availability of assistance with domestic chores and discrimination in the workplace affect working- and middle-class women differently. Therefore, whilst gender inequalities exist within particular classes, the experiences which working- and middle-class women have of disadvantage are different.

Traditional class analyses have largely ignored issues of gender. Married women are seen as marginal to the occupational structure of society and their class position is determined by that of the bread-winning (male) household head. Some commentators argue that there is not even a conceptual problem in those instances where women have waged employment, for this is likely to be intermittent, limited and conditioned by the class context in which it occurs (Goldthorpe 1983). Such a view is unsatisfactory because it ignores women's unpaid work in the household, growing male unemployment, and the fact that women are developing longer employment careers, shorter breaks for child rearing and generally greater labour market participation. This does not mean that women's class position can be inferred simply from their occupational experiences. Patriarchy and class are interdependent not independent. They are shaped by and help to shape women's specific participation in the labour force. As Marshall et al (1988, 73) argue, 'class structures, and the market processes behind them are ... "gendered"'.

There are also important points to be be made in relation to links between class and race and ethnicity. It is clear that differences in ethnicity are important in social structuration but whilst these are not reducible to class differences neither are they unrelated to class relations. The existence of significant ethnic minorities in some of the UK's cities reflects a demand for certain sorts of wage labour that were met in the past via international migration. Moreover this migration was decisively shaped by the UK's imperial past and the distinctive structure of the class relations in which this was cast.

There are at least three different views of the relationship between class and race in UK society. A 'class' based view stresses the interrelated disadvantages of the working class and, more specifically, of the underclass. It is recognised that non-white people disproportionately form part of this class mainly by virtue of the jobs they hold or lack. Although they have some additional disadvantages resulting from racism, they share many class disadvantages with the white working class. In contrast, a 'race' based view stresses that white racism keeps ethnic minorities locked into the bottom rungs of the social hierarchy. This can be extended to the view that the non-white population forms an underclass below the white working class (Rex and Tomlinson 1979). In terms of employment there may be some overlap between the white and non-white working class, but non-whites are far more likely to be found in the dirtiest and lowest paid jobs. To this extent there are segmented but not exclusive labour markets. The imperial legacy of the inferior status of non-white people in the colonial system also contributes to formation of this underlcass.

A third view, with which we concur, is that class and race are intertwined. The economic and social structures of the UK produce disadvantaged positions in the class structure, whilst racism ensures that non-white people occupy a disproportionate number of these (Abercrombie and Warde 1988). This was the view of the 1975 White Paper (Cmnd 6234) on racial discrimination, which stressed that non white people may have 'a special dimension to their problems to the extent that the factor of racial discrimination multiplies and accentuates the disadvantages which are shared in part with others'. This does not mean that there is some mechanistic allocation of individuals to particular economic and social roles. After all the term 'non-white' is being used in this instance to describe people from several continents with very different histories, languages and cultures. This is reflected, for instance, in the higher status, better paid jobs and lower unemployment of the Indian and Afro-Asian communities compared to the Pakistani, Bangladeshi and Afro-Carribean communities (Policy Studies Institute 1993). Given that there are also varying experiences within these ethnic groups, it is clear that there is no simple association between class and ethnicity.

Finally, there are interrelationships between gendered and racialised inequalities. For example, patriarchy has different meanings amongst different ethnic groups, not least because the family can be relatively less important as a locale for exploitation for black women, if only because it has often been significant as a bastion against racism. Black women do of course suffer from gender inequalities, but their experience of them is different from that of white women. Consideration of location necessarily adds another dimension to the analytical framework. In the case of location, the issues are rather more complicated. In this instance it is a question of how class, gender and race relate to one another in place and of the ways in which these relations differ or are similar between places (see, for example, Beynon and Hudson 1993; Hudson 1993).

Whilst the substantive issues of the relationships between inequality and gender, race and location are reviewed separately in later chapters, some brief introductory comments are appropriate at this point.

1.2.2.1   Gender: disadvantaged women

In some respects, there has been a narrowing of the social gap between men and women in the post-war UK. More women have entered the wage labour force. There have also been advances in the legal recognition of the rights of women and in anti-discrimination legislation. Consequently – as a late 1980s TV programme expressed it – women have come 'out of the doll's house'. It would be more accurate to state that some women are in the process of coming out.

Despite the progress, there continue to be glaring inequalities in the types of job to which men and women gain access. Women may be coming out of the doll's house but few are penetrating the male-constructed glass ceiling in the labour market. Few women have attained positions of power and influence in highly remunerated jobs. This affects women's incomes, their independence and, more generally, their capacities to control their lives. Indeed, men and women have still not achieved equality in the eyes of the law, let alone in terms of social practices. There are significant differences in retirement ages and access to state pensions, and the policies of many occupational pension schemes are gendered. It is only very recently – in 1991 – that there has been equality in the taxation treatment of men and women. Not all the differences are tilted in favour of men, but the majority are.

Even if all legal and formal barriers to equality had been removed, considerable informal ones would remain. Some of society's most powerful regulatory mechanisms are grounded in the relations of civil society and the family. Socially constructed expectations as to the roles of mothers and wives still largely determine the domestic division of labour in many households – for example, who does what jobs in the home, or who stays at home to care for children. This socially constructed gender division of labour severely circumscribes the range of opportunities open to women. It affects career and employment prospects as well as access to services and leisure activities.

In the 1980s and 1990s Conservative governments launched a sustained ideological campaign centred on the virtues of Victorian family life. The aims were to promote greater reliance on the family – essentially women in their roles as carers – rather than the state to support dependants, unemployed teenagers and the sick or elderly. This was an explicit attempt further to confine married women to unpaid domestic labour in the home. It sat uneasily with the stress that the same governments placed upon enhancing individual freedom as it has tended to place greater demands on women in their socially constructed role as carers. These demands seem certain to increase further in the future, especially as the Two Nations squeeze on public expenditure is extended, and welfare provision is reduced, in an attempt to reduce the public sector borrowing requirement from the level it had reached in 1993.

1.2.2.2   *Race: disadvantaged minorities*

Perhaps the most dramatic manifestation of the significance of racial divides in the UK in the 1980s was the violent civil disturbances on the streets of many major cities. Whilst not necessarily all race riots, they were undoubtedly linked to the grievances of the young black and Asian residents of these areas. They were symptomatic of the deep mistrust which exists between many black and Asian people and the police, and of their alienation from white society. Formal discrimination has largely been made illegal but black and Asian people still tend to do less well in educational attainment, and in housing and labour markets. They are also disadvantaged in access to public services such as health care − somewhat ironically, in view of the dependence of the National Health Service in many parts of the country on doctors and nurses with black or brown skins. Furthermore, whilst formal discrimination may be illegal, racial prejudices − often deeply rooted − still remain. The election, on a blatantly racist manifesto, of a representative of the British National Party − the successor to the infamous National Front − in a local government election on the Isle of Dogs in London's East End in September 1993 was a sharp reminder of the salience of racial prejudice in at least some parts of the UK. A more persistent reminder is the almost daily incidence of racist violence in many large cities.

Inner-city disturbances are also symptomatic of changes produced by deep-seated structural processes generating multiple inequalities that have become concentrated within particular locations in the cities. Moreover, it is important to remember that the costs this imposes are not only borne by ethnic minorities but also by parts of the poor white working (and non-working) class. The inner-cities and outer estates are peopled by deprived black and white people and youths of all races were prominent in the riots in Brixton, Toxteth and elsewhere in the 1980s. It is, therefore, − as we stressed earlier − both incorrect and dangerously misleading to equate the urban underclass with members of the black and brown inner city population, though they undoubtedly form a prominent part of this underclass. Conversely, there are many individual examples of successful individuals from ethnic minorities. There are frequent references to the success of Asian small business people. More visibly, individuals such as Frank Bruno, Lennox Lewis, Lenny Henry and Joan Armatrading have all in their own way achieved great success. The issue with race, as with gender, however, is not whether individuals can succeed despite the system, but whether there are structural inequalities inscribed in society which systematically disadvantage particular categories of people.

1.2.2.3 Location: disadvantaged places

The same point can be made with regard to locational differences. The significance of living in particular parts of cities has already been alluded to in the previous section but the most publicised and statistically well-documented spatial cleavage in the UK in the 1980s was not intra-urban but interregional: the 'North–South Divide'. In the same way as not all women and all black people are poor and disadvantaged, so too there are both areas of deprivation in the South and pockets of affluence in the North. There is, however, no denying the significance of this broad regional divide. Whilst the gulf narrowed in some respects in the early 1990s, in the preceding decade there was a burgeoning gap between these two parts of the UK. Perhaps the most poignant expression of this were the 'Tebbit Specials', the early Monday morning and late Friday evening trains bringing workers from places such as Liverpool and Middlesbrough to and from the London job market. These were unemployed workers who could not find work in their home areas but could not afford London house prices. They therefore became long-distance commuters, living in the cheapest possible lodgings or sleeping on-site in London. It has been estimated that there were some 10 000 such 'industrial gypsies' (Hogarth and Daniel 1989).

A broad regional division in voting behaviour, with the North tending to vote Labour and the South more likely to vote Conservative, has been a recurrent feature of the post-war period. One of the most prominent manifestations of growing regional inequality in the 1980s was a further polarisation in voting patterns. The South became even more of a Conservative heartland whilst in the North rejection of the Conservative Party reached new levels. The rejection of Thatcherism was especially marked in the Celtic fringes. In Scotland, in particular, it was associated with a resurgence of nationalist politics and sentiment, based on the proposition that the Conservatives had no mandate to rule in Scotland. These nationalist and separatist sentiments are certainly not the creation of Thatcherism but Thatcherite policies breathed fresh life (as in the Govan by-election) into a political cause that seemed to have foundered in the late 1970s. The renewed nationalist demands in Scotland, along with the continued failure to find a political solution to the problems of Northern Ireland, raised profound constitutional questions about the future – a United Kingdom or a Divided Realm ?

As the magnitude of regional inequalities narrowed in the early 1990s because of the disproportionate impacts of national recession on the South East, so too the maps of spatial inequalities and voting patterns became more complicated. One very visible expression of this was the government's new map of areas eligible for regional policy assistance, which belatedly appeared in the summer of 1993. The seemingly interminable delay that preceded its publication was indicative of the bitter struggle to achieve or retain assisted area status in a deeply depressed national economy. Places in the South East, such as Brighton and Southend, part of the Conservatives' electoral heartland, previously regarded as prosperous and impervious to the threats of economic downturn, clamoured to win assisted area status. There was fierce competition both amongst areas in the South and between them and localities elsewhere in the more traditionally problematic regions of the North − not least coalfield communities devastated by further colliery closures as a result of the Government's preparation of the coal industry for privatisation. Moreover, in these circumstances, contrasts between urban and rural areas, between conurbations and small market towns and villages, and between locations within the conurbations and major urban areas assumed a much greater significance. The relationship between residential location, labour market conditions and life-styles became both more complex and of greater practical significance. As a result, the map of spatial inequalities in the 1990s promised to be a more complicated one than had been seen in preceding decades.

1.2.2.4   *Reprise*

Theorising the relationships between the different dimensions of social structure and division remains a difficult task, and there is certainly no consensus as to how best to resolve the issues that it raises. On the other hand, the preceding comments serve to remind us that the UK is indeed divided in many different ways and that this is of immense practical importance, especially to the people who live on the disadvantaged side of such divides. There are, of course, other cleavages in addition to those considered above. Age, for example, is of growing importance as a dimension of social division, not least because of increasing frailty as more people live longer in the context of decreasing levels of welfare state provision.

There are those who have argued that class has become less salient as a dimension of social cleavage as classes have fragmented more along lines of gender, race and location. Sectional interests within the major structurally defined classes have further undermined the analytic usefulness of class categories. Conflict over the distribution of resources − such as health care, housing or jobs − has become intersectional rather than inter-class. We recognise that there is indeed a more complex anatomy of divisions but reject the rejection of the primacy of class.

Class is not and never has been the only basis of social structuration and division within the UK. A person's life chances and life-style are not just determined by class, but whilst class does not have a simplistic deterministic influence, it does have a powerful determinate one. The precise nature of the opportunities open to a black working-class girl in London are clearly very different from those of a white working-class boy living in Glasgow. Nevertheless, they are both powerfully affected by the fact of having been born into the working class rather than the middle class or the bourgeoisie. This conditions the range of opportunities open to them and also, very probably, the expectations that their parents and teachers, but above all they themselves, have about the sort of future life that they can expect. In short, while class is not the only dimension of social structure and division, and other non-class dimensions are not reducible to it, it does none the less impinge strongly on and interact with them. Delineating the character and extent of inequality on each of these dimensions, and assessing the ways in which patterns of inequality altered in the 1980s and early 1990s, as compared to earlier years, is a major objective of this book.

Despite evident deep social divisions, it nevertheless remains the case that economy and society in the UK have been reproduced, albeit occasionally in highly contested ways, over a long period of time. The instability and inequality inherent to capitalism have been held within limits that are considered acceptable to a sufficiently large proportion of the population to allow life to proceed 'as normal'. Potential moments of crisis that threaten to rupture these boundary conditions have been contained. Whilst the regulatory relations and mechanisms that underpin this are in part located within civil society, the state has also played a central role in ensuring societal reproduction. It is to a preliminary consideration of state involvement and activity that we now turn.

1.3 Conceptualising the state: regulation and social cohesion

1.3.1 Some general considerations

There are a variety of competing theoretical perspectives on the state (see, for example, Held 1983). Given the general theoretical stance to the analysis of social structure outlined above, however, we will confine ourselves to brief consideration of some recent theories that take their point of departure from Marxian political economy. This debate has its origins in an exchange between Miliband (1969) and Poulantzas (1975, 1978). For Miliband, the state was conceived as acting at the behest of class interests which are located, constituted and organised outside of the state system, in the economy or civil society. In summary, it is seen as the instrument of the ruling class. For Poulantzas, the state was seen to act in the interests of capital because of constraints imposed on its mode and scope of operations by the wider structures of social and economic power. This is essentially a structuralist view of the state.

There is an element of truth in both approaches. The state is certainly an institutional and organisational ensemble, with its own powers and resources, but these are not equally available to all social forces. There is marked social selectivity in who has privileged access to the powers and resources of the state. In addition, these social forces are not fully constituted outside of the state for they are also partially formed and organised through state agencies and structures. The resources that the state can deploy, for example, result in it becoming an arena for social struggle. At the same time, the form of this struggle is moulded by the institutional and organisational forms of the state itself. Equally, both of these approaches have weaknesses. Both ultimately reduce political to economic power. Moreover, each lies at opposite poles of a false dichotomy. Instrumentalist accounts allocate primacy to the voluntaristic agency of social forces at the expense of their structural conditions. Structuralist accounts assert the primacy of social structures over individual or collective agency, reducing people to the status of cultural dopes who are mere bearers of structures.

A more nuanced and sophisticated understanding of the capitalist state must recognise that the state is a social force in its own right. State policies do not simply reflect the dynamic of the economy or civil society. Such an approach must, therefore, also explore the linkages between agency and structure, taking into account the differential power and resources available to individuals and groups seeking to pursue their interests through the state. Moreover, it is also necessary to encapsulate two seemingly incompatible propositions. Firstly, that capitalist societies are inherently and unavoidably crisis prone and, secondly, that for most of the time such societies are more or less non-problematically reproduced. Furthermore, they are reproduced as national societies within the territories of national states, so that there is a strong territoriality to the mode of operation of the state. This necessarily extends both to the intra-national and to the international levels.

The state therefore plays a – indeed, the – key role in social reproduction, although it is by no means the only regulatory institution and mechanism. Moreover, reflecting the multidimensional character of capitalist societies, and the variety of interests represented within them, the state has to tackle a complex agenda. Externally, this involves regulating relationships with other national states, embryonic supranational states (such as the European Union) and extra-state organisations (such as multinational companies). The fact that national states exist as part of an international state system has important constraining effects. As Taylor (1992, 41) argues, referring to the movements of long waves, the world economy is enabling and constraining; governing politicians create their country's version of the dominant growth model within particular phases in the evolution of the world economy. Whilst acknowledging the significance of these wider constraints, it is important not to slip into a reductionist position which reduces national strategies to the effects of the global swings of long waves. It is necessary to explain why there are national specificities and why these take the forms that they do. National uniqueness as well as international interdependence is important in this regard.

Internally, the state must seek to balance competing claims over accumulation strategies and economic growth trajectories, and equity and social justice in the distribution of the benefits and costs of growth. As capitalist societies have become more complex, the balance of issues on the agenda that the state sets for itself or has set for it by other social forces has altered. A recent example of this is the way that ecological issues have assumed greater prominence in the priorities of many advanced capitalist states. There have also been significant changes in the ways in which states approach their roles of crisis avoidance and crisis management in order to try to guarantee relatively long periods of economic prosperity and social stability. The contrast between the UK and USA, West Germany and Sweden, and Japan in the 1980s provides a striking example of the different ways in which national state strategies can develop in response to the same global economic and political environment.

One of the potentially more promising approaches to theorising the state in these terms is that developed by the French Regulation School (for example, see Lipietz 1986; Dunford 1990). It advocates an approach which privileges neither production nor reproduction but which emphasises the correspondence between regimes of accumulation and modes of regulation necessary for the stability of a social system. A regime of accumulation refers to a relatively stable aggregate relationship between production and consumption. This stability over time implies some correspondence between changes in consumption and the life-styles and living conditions of those working for a wage and those in production itself – for example, in terms of rising consumption levels and changing labour productivity. Mode of regulation refers to the regulatory mechanisms, the body of beliefs, habits, laws and norms, that are consistent with and supportive of a regime of accumulation and which, in fact, make it possible. Not all combinations of regime of accumulation and mode of regulation are feasible, however. Recognition of this directs attention to the complex relations – political practices, social norms and cultural forms – which allow the highly dynamic and unstable capitalist system to function, at least for a period, in a relatively coherent and stable fashion (Mayer 1992, 266). The state clearly has a crucial role to play in all this. It both ensures that changes in conditions of production and consumption are consistent and compatible with one another (via taxation and income redistribution policies, for example) and that the mode of regulation is itself successfully reproduced (for example, through educational and health policies).

It is important to remember, however, that state involvement in economy and society does not necessarily abolish crisis tendencies but rather internalises them within the state itself and its mode of operation. This is particularly so with the transition from a liberal to an interventionist mode of state operation (Habermas 1975; Offe 1975). A liberal mode of state involvement sets the parameters within which the law of value operates within a particular state territory and through which the more or less visible hand of the market functions as a resource allocation mechanism. An interventionist mode of state involvement goes beyond this with policies that supplement or replace rather than merely facilitate market mechanisms; for example, via nationalising key sectors of industry or taking on responsibility for educational and health care provision. Whilst the immediate proximate motives for this major qualitative

Table 1.1 The UK international context: indicators of social and economic change in the 1980s

	France	Germany	Japan	UK	USA	All OECD
The position in 1990						
GDP per caput 1990 ($)	19 490	22 320	25 430	16 100	21 790	20 170
Energy consumption per caput 1990 (kilos, oil equivalent)	3 845	3 491	3 563	3 646	7 822	5 179
International currency reserves expressed as months of import coverage	2.4	2.8	2.6	1.3	2.9	3.1
Changes (percentages) over the period 1980–90 (annual average)						
Annual % growth rate, gross domestic investment (1980–90)	2.6	2.4	5.7	6.4	4.4	4.3
Annual % growth rate, GDP (1980–90 average)	2.2	2.1	4.1	3.1	3.4	3.1
Annual % growth rate, manufacturing output (1980–90, average)	0.2	0.9	5.3	4.8	n.a.	4.2

Source: World Bank (1992)

extension in the scope of state activities vary, in the final analysis it is because they are no longer profitable (or sufficiently profitable) to attract private capital. None the less, they are seen as goods and services that 'have' to be provided, for economic, political or social reasons, as the boundary between private and public sector provision is redrawn (see Hudson 1986). Defined in this way, all national states in the advanced capitalist world are now interventionist, although to varying degrees. The issue, in the UK as elsewhere, is the extent and forms of intervention and the political projects and strategies which inform intervention.

The fact that the state takes on responsibility for the provision of vital goods and services does not, however, abolish the economic crisis tendency that necessitated this. Production of these goods and services does not become economically non-problematic simply by virtue of being taken over by the state. The underlying crisis can, in the fullness of time, emerge in different forms, either within the operations of the state itself, or within civil society. Three forms of such crisis are of relevance here. Rationality crises arise as a consequence of the fact that there are competing pressures seeking to shape the course of state action; for example, those of efficiency versus equity. Should, for example, public services be organised so as to minimise cost of delivery or maximise use of the services? As a result of such pressures, there can be, and often are, unintended effects as well as − or instead of − those outcomes that state involvement was intended to produce. Legitimation crises may emerge, or at least be threatened, as a result of this chronic gap between actual and intended outcomes. In some circumstances this can even lead to a challenge to the authority of the state itself, and so to the dominant pattern of social relationships represented through that state - as, for example, in Italy in the early 1990s. This leads the state to seek out strategies to reassert the legitimacy of its actions.

There may be yet another complication, however. In some circumstances, the state may have to try to deal with the internalised economic contradictions more directly if these re-emerge in the form of a fiscal crisis. This is an altogether trickier operation in crisis avoidance and management but one that must be attempted; otherwise, there is a risk that a much more generalised economic crisis could be triggered, for example, through the wider impacts of burgeoning state borrowing or public expenditure. One state response in such circumstances is to redefine the extent and form of state activities and reduce the resources needed to sustain them. The boundaries between state and market, between public and private sectors, can be redrawn to reduce as well as to extend the scope of state involvement in economic and social life. Pulling in the boundaries of state involvement involves redrawing the public–private sector divide and recommodifying more of the provision of services such as education and health whilst introducing pseudo-profitability efficiency criteria into the remainder of public sector industry and services.

Such moments of redefinition of the balance of regulatory mechanisms, which may or may not herald the transition to a new regime of accumulation and mode of regulation, sometimes mark significant turning points in developmental trajectories. Whether this actually has been the case can, of course, only be known ex-post and not ex-ante. The general implication is nevertheless clear: crises will appear in different forms as the content, form and style of state policies and politics vary. Theoretically, therefore, we would not expect the policies and political strategies characteristic of any feasible combination of regime of accumulation and mode of regulation to be a seamless web. Equally, we would not expect any particular party political strategy to be such a web. We would, however, expect the paradoxes and inconsistencies to be more apparent and visible in those moments of transition from an old to a new combination, in those periods of seeking out new feasible combinations.

1.3.2 The state in the UK: some introductory remarks

The significance of the state in the regulation of social and economic life, as indicated by measures such as public expenditure as a proportion of gross domestic product, grew seemingly inexorably over the post-war period until it reached a peak at almost 44 per cent in the mid-1970s (see Hudson and Williams 1986, 42−49). It then declined sharply to less than 37 per cent but, despite the anti-statist rhetoric of Thatcherism, rose and hovered around a level of 40 per cent before again rising to around 45 per cent in the early 1990s (Figure 1.1). There was increased spending in some sectors, notably unemployment but also law and order, defence − prior to *glasnost* and *perestroika* in the former USSR − and some forms of urban policy. This offset severe cuts

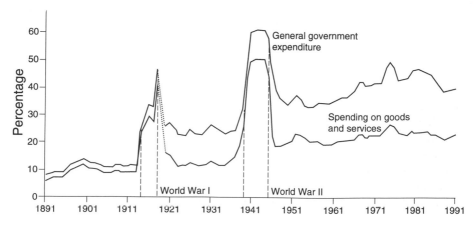

Figure 1.1 General government expenditure as a percentage of GDP, UK 1891−1991 (GDP adjusted to take account of change to community charge)

Source: HM Treasury; Central Statistical Office

in others, such as public sector housing, nationalised industries and regional policy. Nevertheless, as emphasised above, the state is not some monolithic instrument, unproblematically serving the interests of capital or guaranteeing the smooth reproduction of society. For example, the struggle within the UK state between the Treasury and other central government departments over the level and allocation of public expenditure has been a recurrent feature of central government policy-making over many decades. Moreover, policy formation reflects much more than just an internal debate within the apparatus of the state itself. Decision-making is the outcome of interactions between elected representatives, usually acting along party lines (but less evident since the 1992 general election), the permanent bureaucracies of the state apparatuses themselves, and pressure groups and other interested parties.

Since the UK's entry to the European Community in 1973, the process of decision making has been further complicated; relationships with an embryonic supranational state add a European dimension to state policy formation. In part this derives from legislation at European Community level, in part from supranational regulation of, and limits upon, national state competence in policy formation and implementation, in respect of both consumption (e.g. health and environmental standards) and production (e.g. on the form and extent of subsidies). This has become a source of increasing friction in the 1980s and 1990s as the governments of Mrs Thatcher and Mr Major have sought – at least publicly – to resist the deepening integration of the Community and growing supranational regulation from Brussels (see Williams 1991). For example, there has been strong resistance from successive governments to Community social policy initiatives, such as those defining higher norms on working conditions. These run counter to national government objectives of privatising parts of public services and retaining the UK's attraction to multinational capital through the availability of cheap, flexible and compliant labour. There has equally been opposition to Community initiatives with respect to competition in formerly state dominated sectors, state procurement and merger controls.

As well as the complications that arise 'from above', there are also others that arise 'from below' (see Kolinsky 1981). Within the UK, as elsewhere, the state is of necessity organised as a series of different agencies, at national, regional and local levels. Each has powers and resources available to it and there is a continuing struggle to influence the allocation of these between different interest groups and areas. This territorial distribution of state powers and resources is partly a matter of functional efficiency, partly a matter of retaining popular consent for and the legitimacy of state involvement. These goals are pursued by decentralising – or at least seeming to decentralise – power and resources so that control over them is – or at least appears to be – nearer to those who are most directly affected by the activities of different state agencies (see Hudson and Plum 1986).

One of the characteristic features of the 1980s and 1990s in the UK was a restructuring of the state, a process of centralisation that removed powers and resources from local to central government level. At the same time, government increasingly concentrated decision making in quangos (quasi-autonomous non-governmental organisations), dominated by non-elected people, many of whom were political appointees with a strong pro-government bias. Quangos became more important precisely because of the centralisation of power in central government departments. By 1992 there were 1412 quangos, with 114 000 board members and staff. They had control of budgets totalling £14 billion, of which £10.5 billion was taxpayers' money, and took decisions affecting wide areas of public services. The 'quangocracy' accounted for no less than 20 per cent of government spending in 1992/93 and had grown by 20 per cent since 1979. This was despite Conservative electoral promises to cut back quangos so as to help restore local democracy. As Professor John Stewart put it: 'Britain is increasingly governed locally by Westminster appointees, who can in no sense be regarded as locally accountable. Indeed, the public does not know who these people are. It is government by the unknown and the unknowable' (cited in the *Independent on Sunday*, 28 March 1993).

There is also a complex relationship between party political allegiance and social class and the other main dimensions of social structure. Neither the Conservative nor Labour Party is exclusively the representative of one social class, though they both have class affiliations. Nevertheless, the relationships between the trade unions and the Labour Party and (big) business interests and the Conservative Party, and the ways in which these have shaped central governments' policies, have been and remain a significant political issue. The debate in the Labour Party in the 1990s about the need to distance the Party policy-making process from trade union influence is one clear expression of this. It is also the case that there are complex relationships between the main pressure and interest groups and differences of class, gender and ethnicity. Some, such as the Country Landowners Association or the Child Poverty Action Group, have clear class affiliations whilst others, such as the Consumers' Association, have a fairly broad social basis.

Nevertheless, whilst the struggle to control, or at least influence, the activities of the state may not always be conducted along overtly class lines, the outcomes of implementing many state policies have clear class implications. The same point can be made about the differential effects of state policies in relation to gender or ethnicity. Policies for taxation and income distribution, or the balance between public and private sector provision of services, impact in varying ways on different social groups and areas, though not only as intended.

One of the most notable features of the UK over much of the post-war period is that the struggle over the state was confined within relatively narrow limits. For some 30 years, until the latter part of the 1970s, there was a marked consensus on 'One Nation' politics. Certainly there were differences in emphasis in the policies of Conservative and Labour governments but these were circumscribed within relatively tight limits defining the boundaries to permissible state policies. In particular, there was consensus on the desirability of and necessity for an inclusive and universalist welfare state, providing educational and health care and a welfare system to address the needs of the less fortunate members of society. Subsequently, this approach came under severe attack as the politics of Thatcherism became constructed around a 'Two Nations' approach that was deliberately divisive in its impacts. Majorism has largely pursued the same political goals, whilst jettisoning some of the provocative rhetoric of its predecessor. Analysing the implications of this major reorientation in state policies and political strategies on inequality within the UK is a major objective of this book.

1.4 An outline

In the next chapter, we develop an interpretation of the changing character of state strategies towards economy and society within the UK in the post-war period. We also examine the implications of this in terms of tendencies in national social and economic change, where relevant placing these in broader comparative international context. Succeeding chapters then examine the pattern of divisions in the UK around the major dimensions of class, gender, race and place. Although we have stressed the impossibility of neatly closing off the effects of one set of structural influences from those of the others, the available data come in forms which necessitate this approach of treating each major dimension of division separately. We do, however, attempt to consider their interactions. Finally, we seek to draw some conclusions about the future anatomy of inequality within the UK, based on our analyses of present patterns and the processes through which these came about.

2

State strategies and economic change: the UK in a divided world

2.1 Introduction

In the previous chapter we suggested that a regulationist approach offered a promising way of understanding both how potentially crisis-prone capitalist societies were reproduced and, at the same time, how the character of such societies altered over time but within the parameters that defined them as capitalist. Nevertheless, it left open important questions to do with how societies move from one feasible combination of regime of accumulation and mode of regulation to another. There is certainly no ex-ante predetermined developmental sequence along which a society must inevitably proceed. Such trajectories of change must be discovered and constructed as part of the process of change itself.

There are also problems of periodisation concerning where to draw the boundaries between one developmental phase and another, and of the theoretical basis in which this delimitation of distinctive phases is grounded. To what extent are significant shifts in economy and society in the UK to be interpreted as a mere reflection of general structural shifts in capitalism, to what extent are they regarded as an effect of UK-specific political strategies, and to what extent are they most appropriately seen as a product of the mutual determination of specific and general processes? Partly this is a matter of specifying the criteria to be used; for example, a periodisation primarily based upon state policy shifts would not necessarily coincide with one based upon turning points in the national economy. This is a familiar problem (which geographers will recognise in relation to regionalisation) as different questions focus attention on different criteria and produce different answers.

Periodisation is not just a matter of simple chronological sequence, however. A periodisation orders actions and events in terms of multiple time horizons; it also classifies them into stages according to their conjunctural implications (as specific combinations of constraints and opportunities) for different social forces (Jessop et. al. 1988, 41). Both of these procedures involve consideration of the ways in which actions and events are generated as the complex result of multiple determinations. They therefore necessarily operate within an explanatory framework as well as simultaneously providing a basis for a complex narrative. Clearly a sophisticated periodisation defined in these terms would make demands for a breadth and depth of data that are beyond the scope of this study.

Nevertheless, it is necessary at least to sketch out the anatomy of such a periodisation. One of our concerns is to delineate the extent to which inequality in the UK has become magnified in recent years and to investigate the extent to which this was a direct or indirect consequence, a deliberate or inadvertent effect, of the political economy of Thatcherism in the 1980s and its legacy in the 1990s. This requires that we locate the links between inequality and political strategy in the last decade and a half in the broader historical context of such relationships within the UK. It is our contention that Thatcherism did represent a sharp qualitative break with previous political strategies in terms − *inter alia* − of its attitudes towards inequality. In order to understand how and why it did so, however, requires some consideration of the limits which preceding approaches to policy formation encountered.

To establish this broader context, we draw on the work of Jessop et al. (1988, 17−18), who situate the demise of previous political approaches and the consequent rise of Thatcherism in terms of a threefold periodisation. Firstly, over the long term, these shifts must be related to the long *durée* of the mode of economic growth in the UK; they have to be seen in relation to the long-run decline of the UK economy over the last century. Secondly, over the medium term, the emergence of Thatcherism must be related to the political-economic dynamic of the post-war settlement. This involves consideration of the emerging crisis of the specific form of the UK's insertion into the international political-economic order after 1945. In addition, it requires analysis of the associated social democratic mode of political and social regulation within the UK, the limits to which could no longer be concealed or contained by the mid-1970s. Thirdly, over the shorter term, it must be situated in relation to the changing political scene over the last 15 or 20 years, and the organic crisis of UK society that once again became acute in the mid-1970s as a direct consequence of these limits being reached and, arguably, breached. We will have relatively little to say about the first of these dimensions of change here (although see Hudson and Williams 1986, 2−12) but the second and third will be considered much more fully.

It is, however, important to appreciate that the emergence of Thatcherism was not just a reaction to past failures but was also a putative project for the future which − crucially in terms of our interests here − had heightened levels of inequality built into it. Seen in this light, the Thatcherite project was seeking to prepare the ground for new modes of growth and regulation. These were supposedly more in tune with current changes in contemporary capitalism, such as the alleged transitions from organised to disorganised capitalism

(Lash and Urry 1987) or from Fordism to flexible accumulation (Harvey 1988). We will return to these questions about the future in the final chapter. For the remainder of this chapter, however, we will concentrate on further elaborating the changing political economy of the UK in the post-war period (drawing on previous studies: see Hudson and Williams 1986; Hudson 1989a). We will focus upon state strategies for growth and regulation and the ways in which these were linked both to the UK's changing place in the global political-economic order, and to patterns of inequality within the UK. This analysis is set within a broad framework that contrasts One Nation with Two Nations political strategies.

2.2 One Nation political strategies, 1944–75

2.2.1 *Version I: full employment and welfare state policies, 1944–62*

We begin with a question: why is 1944 seen as a key turning point? This year can be seen as a watershed, the transitional moment towards a much more interventionist mode of state involvement in economy and society in the UK. Of course, there were faint signs of such a transition in the inter-war years, as the old regime of accumulation and mode of regulation encountered deep crises. But it was the publication of the highly influential White Paper on employment policy (Cmnd 6577) that most clearly signalled a decisive political shift towards a new regime of accumulation and mode of regulation. The new approach was centred around – indeed predicated upon – state guarantees of 'full employment' and a significant qualitative extension in the scope of state activity. This encompassed economic planning, and direct involvement in production (via the nationalisation of key industries) and reproduction (via the creation of a welfare state, symbolised above all in the creation of the National Health Service). At one level, the emergence of One Nation politics can be seen as intended to demonstrate to those who had fought in and otherwise helped to win the war that their sacrifices had not been in vain. The message was clear: the poverty and misery of the inter-war years were not to be repeated. It remained to be seen how this message would be received by the population and how it would translate into party political electoral contests in a peacetime environment. The significance of memories of inter-war unemployment was soon confirmed in the 1945 general election, when the electorate rejected Churchill's Conservative Party and returned a Labour government, seemingly committed to a radically reforming programme.

The 1944 White Paper thus heralded the emergence of three decades of One Nation political strategies, with their emphasis, at least in terms of intention if not always outcome, on an inclusive universalism centred around full employment and the welfare state. Nevertheless, there were definite limits to the scope of radical reform and it is important to acknowledge this, without denying the significance of Labour's socially progressive reformist package. Whilst it addressed, to a degree, issues of class inequalities, via its commitment to 'full employment' and welfare state provision, it had little explicit to say about other dimensions of inequality. Issues of race and gender inequalities, for example, were not on the agenda. Although the major expansion in immigration from the New Commonwealth was not to occur until the next decade, there were already significant ethnic minority groups in the UK as a result of previous waves of immigration; yet there were no measures to address inequalities generated by racial discrimination or racialised access to opportunities. Equally, whilst women would benefit from the creation of a universalist welfare state, there was no recognition that the narrowing of gender inequalities might require more specific measures. Whatever gains may have accrued to women from the recasting of occupational divisions of labour during the war years were subsequently stalled rather than enhanced. It was to be another two decades before such issues began to be addressed with any degree of seriousness by the state.

In the second half of the 1940s, issues other than inequalities were dominating the political agenda. By 1948 the limits to economic 'planning' had already been reached, as 'planning' was transformed to accommodate externally oriented capitalist interests, state crisis management tactics and Treasury hostility to increasing public expenditure (Rowthorne 1983, 66). The government's response to a national economic crisis in 1947 was selectively to restrict public expenditure and shift the emphasis in industrial production to import substitution and export growth. Given the priority still attached to defence spending (accounting for 7 per cent of GNP in 1948), the cuts fell disproportionately heavily on the nascent welfare state and programmes such as education, health and housing. Sterling's devaluation against the dollar in 1949 reflected both the government's commitment to domestic industrial production and its unwillingness to seek to guarantee this by stronger interventionist planning. Instead, measures such as wage restrictions were introduced to try to preserve the competitive advantage conferred by devaluation, passing the costs of this on to the working class. Clearly there were definite limits to the new post-war approach, even in terms of its own reformist agenda.

Within these externally imposed and self-imposed external constraints, the One Nation project was implemented. The economic policy shifts initiated from 1948 ushered in the era of 'Butskellite' policies which were to dominate until 1962 (Keegan 1984, 20–24). Conservative governments, between 1951 and 1962, accepted many of the policy changes introduced after 1945. Most of the nationalisations of basic industries were not challenged because they were seen as vital to national economic recovery and there was little prospect of their attracting new private capital. The only instances of denationalisation — road transport and steel — were in industries in which there were prospects of profits (Brown 1962). They also endorsed the creation of the welfare state and commitments to full employment, although the means of attaining these goals altered somewhat. Equally, whilst the commitment to state housing provision remained intact, there was a perceptible shift in emphasis in the 1950s. At the start of the decade the state was seen as the main provider of new housing but, within a few years, its role was seen more as providing housing for those in need and unable to purchase a house in a society in which owner occupation came to be seen as the 'natural' tenure (see Gray 1976; Short 1982).

The emphasis on restraining public expenditure growth strengthened during the 1950s – it only rose from 21.5 to 22.3 per cent of GDP between 1950 and 1960 (Brown and Sherriff 1979). A dramatic cut-back in military spending meant that this could be done without sacrificing the welfare state, workers' wages or industry's profits – at least for a time. Maintaining full employment – or, more accurately, male full employment (this gender bias was present from the outset) – increasingly came to depend upon 'fine tuning' of the economy, regulating domestic demand via changing taxation levels.

For much of the 1950s, Butskellite policies seemingly produced the desired results. The economy grew strongly, in a non-inflationary way. Industrial output expanded sharply, although manufacturing output did fall as a percentage of GDP as a result of even more rapid growth in other sectors. Moreover, profitability was restored in manufacturing whilst investment recovered strongly in comparison with the inter war period. Full employment conditions prevailed, and growing labour demands could only be met by a combination of rising female activity rates and immigration from Ireland and the New Commonwealth. Associated with this, there was something of a consumer boom in the second half of the decade. Mass consumerism was becoming a reality as working-class living standards rose. As Harold Macmillan put it pithily at a garden fête in Bedford in 1957, in a way that recognised that rising average living standards were not necessarily eliminating social inequalities: 'Let us be frank about it. Most of our people have never had it so good.' The critical word here is 'most', for neither the state nor the market had proved able to universalise the benefits of economic growth or the consumer boom.

By the end of the decade, however, several paradoxes were appearing in the relation of government policies to national economic performance. Successive 'stop–go' cycles, in part a product of regional imbalances in the economy, were having deleterious effects on manufacturing investment and economic modernisation. Furthermore, whilst national output growth rates were impressive, compared to the inter-war years, they paled in comparison with most of the UK's main international competitors (Hudson et al. 1984, 80–82; Williams 1987). No fundamental modernisation of the economy was taking place on a scale comparable to that in Japan or West Germany, for example. As a result, the UK's share of world manufacturing output and trade began to fall more sharply in the 1950s. Its share in world trade in invisibles and private services also fell sharply in the second half of the 1950s, while the balance-of-payments position became increasingly fragile and sterling crises became endemic (see Hudson and Williams 1986, 2–7). Rowthorne (1983, 67) rightly suggests that by the end of the 1950s 'on all fronts, British capitalism was in difficulties'. It seemed that a post-war golden age had been achieved in the UK in the 1950s, based on the discovery of a very specific combination of regime of accumulation and mode of regulation, which enabled the interests of capital, labour and the state to be satisfied simultaneously. Those who believed that these very special circumstances would continue indefinitely were living in a fool's paradise (Rowthorne 1983, 66). There was evidence of another fool's paradise in perceptions of the UK's position in the international economic and political order. A belief that the UK had a special relationship with the USA, and a refusal to come to terms with the ending of the UK's imperial role, were reflected in events such as the débâcle over Suez and rejection of the emergent European Economic Community.

2.2.2 *Version II: modernisation and welfare state policies, 1962–75*

The year 1962 marks another important turning point. This ushered in significant changes which altered not the aims of One Nation politics but rather the content, and to some degree, the form of state policies and institutional mechanisms through which these goals were pursued. Around 1962 the Conservative government began markedly to change its ideology and practices as it sought to promote faster economic growth, sustain full employment and improve international competitiveness. The immediate motives for this were short term and electoral but the significance of the changes was deeper and longer-lasting. The essence of the new approach was the creation of a tripartite corporatism involving the government, big industrial companies and the trade unions. This provided an environment in which major companies could invest with confidence whilst trade unions moderated their wage demands as part of the price of maintaining full employment. Government, as its part of the bargain, would selectively and significantly increase public expenditure; this would underwrite the restructuring of industrial capital and guarantee the expanded reproduction of the welfare state (see Hudson and Williams 1986, 19–24 and 43–48). The replacement of a Conservative with a Labour government in 1964 gave fresh impetus to this enhanced interventionist approach, both via further restructuring of the state apparatus itself and significant policy extensions and innovations. This was the case in terms of state provision of educational and health services, for example, but it was especially so in terms of indicative economic planning, culminating in the publication of the National Plan (Department of Economic Affairs 1965).

The subsequent rapid abandonment of the Plan both signalled the high point of indicative planning and sharply revealed the limits to the government's capacity to shape a fundamental restructuring of industrial production within the national territory. Mounting and severe external pressures on sterling led to the introduction of deflationary measures in 1966, involving reining in planned public expenditure increases and jettisoning the economic growth targets that were integral to the Plan. Thus the overriding importance attached by government to preserving sterling's international exchange rate necessitated tackling balance-of-payments problems via the abandonment of modernisation policies. Severely deflationary domestic policies were also adopted in an attempt to curb domestic consumption and boost exports.

As it happened, deflation proved insufficient to cope with pressures on both the balance of payments and sterling, which was devalued in 1967. Abandoning the attempt at coherently 'planned' industrial modernisation also implied continuing deterioration in the international competitiveness of UK manufacturing. In recognition of this, the government continued, in a pragmatic and more or less *ad hoc* fashion, to seek ways of modernising manufacturing by more incremental policy and institutional changes, such as through the activities of the Industrial Reorganisation Corporation. Such activities were, however, always confined within parameters dictated by external pressures and interests. Devaluation did offer opportunities to some sections of manufacturing capital in terms of import substitution and/or export growth. Crucially, however, as in the late 1940s, the government attempted to preserve these competitive advantages by the imposition of an incomes policy, pushing the costs of recovery on to the wage-earning classes. This was significant, politically, in relation to a Conservative victory in the 1970 general election.

The new Conservative government remained committed to the social democratic aims of the One Nation project but, initially, switched more to market forces as an economic steering mechanism. This experiment, with the benefit of hindsight, can in many ways be seen to prefigure the Two Nations project of Thatcherism. It was, however, rapidly abandoned in the (in)famous policy U-turn back to the strongest forms of interventionist economic policies yet seen in the UK. This was confirmed unambiguously in the 1972 Industry Act. Like its Labour predecessor, however, Mr Heath's government came unstuck over its policies towards incomes control and the trade unions. It lost the February 1974 general election but not before it had signalled an historical reorientation of the UK's external policies as, belatedly, the UK secured accession to the European Community in 1973. Echoing events a decade earlier, the new Labour government initially sought to pursue stronger interventionist economic policies but was soon forced into a radical change of direction by external pressures. The 1973–74 oil price rises intensified both recessionary tendencies in the international economy and inflationary ones in the domestic economy, forcing a radical redefinition of the government's political philosophy and economic policies. It abandoned the commitment to full (male) employment and had a growing preoccupation with tackling inflation as annual wage settlements of 30 per cent or more were reported as 'becoming normal' in 1975 (Shanks 1977, 75). This heralded the beginning of the end of the One Nation project and helped sow the seeds of its Two Nations successor, which was revealed in fully blown form in the Thatcher era.

Despite over a decade of attempts at modernisation, especially of manufacturing, by the mid-1970s the UK economy had slid into a condition of crisis. This was especially so in terms of manufacturing, for whilst the rate of profit had held up in services, that in manufacturing collapsed between the mid-1960s and mid-1970s (see Figure 2.1). Growth in industrial production and manufacturing output lagged behind that in other countries, especially after 1966 (Rowthorne 1983, 69). Manufacturing investment per capita and labour productivity growth in manufacturing likewise remained well below the levels recorded in other major manufacturing countries (Brown and Sheriff 1979, 247–251). Whilst an improvement on past performance in the UK, it was insufficient to prevent its share of world industrial exports falling still further.

This period had also seen a restructuring of the state itself in an attempt to facilitate the desired transformation of the economy. This had been true both at central and local government levels: new central government departments and institutions such as the Departments of Economic Affairs and of the Environment had been created, and local government had been reformed so as to produce more cost efficient service delivery and a local land use planning system which would be more closely tailored to the needs of a modern economy. Furthermore, in the absence of a regional tier within the state apparatus, attempts were made to implement policies intended to produce

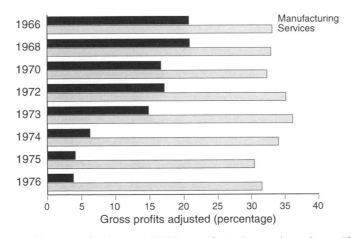

Figure 2.1 Gross profit shares of UK manufacturing and services, 1966–76.
Gross profit shares are less stock appreciation; as proportions of net output. Gross profits of manufacturing include trading surpluses of public corporations; gross profits of services include 'other income' plus rent. Capital consumption deducted from gross profits. Services include distributive trades, insurance, banking, etc. and other services

Source: based on data in Brown and Sheriff (1979, p. 251)

balanced regional growth via new forms of co-operation and collaboration between central and local government.

Despite all this, the national economy continued to stutter along and to slide down the international economic order. Pressures for new forms of state policy initiatives therefore grew. It also became clear that new policies which were necessary to attempt to restore conditions of growth and accumulation in the domestic economy could no longer be made compatible with the social policy commitments of the welfare state within a One Nation political project. Increasingly, public sector provision of housing and of educational, health and social services came under pressure, in two ways: via private sector provision and by incorporating pseudo-market criteria into the remainder of the public services sector. Abandoning the One Nation project clearly carried risks, not just at a party political and electoral level, but more profoundly in the dangers of triggering a legitimation crisis that challenged the authority of the state. On the other hand, not to run this risk might entail a still greater one: an irreversible crisis of accumulation, precipitating a massive flight of capital. This would drain the state of its resource base via taxation on monetary incomes of various forms and make the UK a no-go area for major capitalist investment.

2.2.3 Reprise: One Nation politics in retrospect

The government's policy responses to economic crisis in the late 1940s represented the first instance of what was to become a recurrent theme of One Nation politics: that is, 'stop–go' economic policies. The switch from go to stop generally came in response to international pressures as the UK's position in the international economic order deteriorated. Indeed, it has been suggested that the external aspects of the post-war settlement were the dominant factors influencing the political and economic developmental trajectory of the UK. As Jessop et al. (1988, 164) have argued, 'the cross-party state sponsored commitment to Churchillism was perhaps the dominant level of the post-war state strategy. . . . This consensus around Keynesianism, international liberalisation and Atlanticism was as significant for what it precluded as for what it included: above all it ruled out any serious attempt by the state to co-ordinate a domestically focused strategy for industrial regeneration.' This is a revealing conclusion for it invalidates any attempt to represent this first part of the post-war period in the UK as one of a Fordist regime of accumulation, centred around a state-managed strategy of intensive accumulation within the national territory, and redistributive policies to raise levels of mass consumption in line with the productivity gains of mass production (see, for example, Dunford and Perrons 1986). The UK's regime of accumulation over the post-war period of One Nation politics was at best a deformed version of a Fordist regime; as Lipietz (1986, 30) has rightly remarked, 'Britain, because of the resistant strength of its working class and the weight of its finance capital, which is too internationalised to be given over to this internal revolution [of intensive accumulation] has partially missed the boat of Fordism.' The same point is made in different ways by Nairn (1977), Ingham (1982) and Rowthorne (1983). Moreover, if the first three decades were not Fordist, it raises questions as to the sense in which what came afterwards can be represented as Post-Fordist; this issue is taken up below.

In summary, the state policy responses to national economic crisis which were formulated in the late 1940s clearly signalled a continuing privileging of international economic, diplomatic and military interests over those of the domestic requirements of a growth-oriented social democracy. This commitment was shared by the largest power blocs within both major political parties and remained a constant feature of the three decades of One Nation politics. Seen in this light, and viewed comparatively, the fundamental causes of the UK's continuing relative economic decline since 1945 are twofold: firstly, the continuing dominance of international and/or financial capitalist interests over those of production within the national territory for the domestic market; secondly, the burdens imposed on the national economy by the global pretensions of the UK state in its post-imperial phase. The interaction of these two sets of processes has resulted in a distinctive combination of multinationalisation and contraction of the national industrial base, to the point where some even question whether it is sensible to talk of a national economy (see Radice 1984). At the same time, it has led to commercial and financial capital strengthening their positions in the economy. As a result, their capacity to exert structural constraints over alternative state policies has increased, precisely because of their power to determine the terms on which government debt and/or any negative foreign balances are funded (Jessop et al. 1988, 165).

From one point of view, then, this era of One Nation politics was, seemingly paradoxically, characterised by its fostering of divisions between different fractions of capital and capitalist interests. From another perspective, however, One Nation politics was distinguished – indeed defined – by continuing political commitments to an inclusive society, in which all the members shared to a degree in its material and immaterial benefits. There was no question of abandoning the welfare state as a mechanism for progressive income redistribution and for ensuring access to key services, more or less irrespective of capacity to pay for them. It is undeniably true that the actual, as opposed to the intended, redistributional effects of educational and health policies were often regressive rather than progressive. In part, this was because inequality was primarily seen in terms of differential class access to power and resources whilst accepting that there were very strict limits as to the scope for any really radical attack on class divisions. In prioritising class to this extent, however, it also tended to ignore other dimensions of inequality such as gender and race, both in themselves and in terms of their relationships to class inequalities. But the era of One Nation politics was nevertheless marked by political responses to the discovery of such unintended outcomes; there were attempts to find fresh institutional or legislative ways of meeting the original socially progressive goals. As a result, these other dimensions of inequality were increasingly explicitly addressed. This involved both new legislation, as for example, over race relations, and new policy initiatives, such as the area-based policies of the 1960s that sought to combat locationally concentrated multiple deprivation within the UK's major cities. There was a belief that it would be morally desirable and politically possible to deal with such issues via finding appropriate forms of state policy response in a civilised modern society.

The question that was looming ever more prominently by the mid-1970s, however, was whether these commitments could be maintained in an era of deepening national economic crisis. The question that was to be firmly on the agenda by the end of the 1970s was whether it was in fact desirable to seek to narrow such inequalities or whether they should be encouraged as the motor of national economic recovery in a Two Nations state that embraced not a society but a collection of competitive and potentially antagonistic individuals.

2.3   Two Nations political strategies, 1975–93

2.3.1   Seeking to reconcile the irreconcilable: the Labour government, disinflation policies and the abandonment of full employment, 1975–79

The April 1975 Budget was an event of considerable significance. It confirmed that the government's economic strategy now centred on restraining the growth of public expenditure, cuts in real wages and rising unemployment as deliberate, albeit reluctant, policy choices. Domestic deflation to improve the balance-of-payments position was seen as unavoidable, given the 1972 decision to adopt a floating sterling exchange rate. The 1975 Budget proposals, along with the correct forecast that their implementation would push registered unemployment above 1 million, clearly meant jettisoning the key plank of the One Nation project. Yet again the interests of international capital took precedence over those of jobs and production in the policy calculus of the state. Whilst some claim that the Labour government was 'blown off course' by pressures imposed by the IMF in 1976, it had chosen to alter course sharply prior to that point (Bosanquet 1980), thereby decisively altering the terrain for the debate about economic policy. At an ideological level, for understandable electoral and party political reasons, the Labour government continued to proclaim its commitment to the welfare state but the second half of the 1970s saw severe cuts in public sector educational, health and housing provision (see, for example, Townsend 1980; Short 1982).

Although the government cut public expenditure – both in terms of slowing planned rates of increase and in absolute levels – private sector investment did not fill the vacated space, thereby thwarting government intentions as to the route to economic recovery. Its revised policy for the 'regeneration of British industry', based on a revived corporatist approach to industrial policy, failed to produce its intended results. There was at best a weak and patchy recovery in manufacturing output, which by 1979 still stood well below the level of 1973–74. Labour productivity grew very slowly, especially compared to other countries, a result of continuing low levels of new fixed capital investment. Increasing productivity differentials were the key reason for falling international competitiveness. Manufacturing employment continued to decline as companies shed labour as part of a restructuring of production within the UK, switched production abroad, went bankrupt or switched capital out of manufacturing. In aggregate, though, the economy recovered rather more steadily. There was a variety of reasons for this: in part, it was because of the impacts of EC membership boosting the agricultural sector, and because of the effects of the 1973–74 energy crisis on domestic energy production. A more important factor, however, was strong growth in services, especially financial ones. Overall, though, the UK remained in a weak economic position.

Although the government's revised economic policies failed to produce their intended effects, they did generate some important unintended ones. For a time, the Government successfully converted its social contract with the trade unions into a restrictive incomes policy. Once again, the costs of attempted industrial regeneration were to be borne by the working class. Average real wages fell by 8 per cent between 1975 and 1977 (Ormerod 1980, 59), helping some recovery in profitability. Subsequently, increasing frustration with real wage cuts and rising unemployment led to widespread rank-and-file militancy, especially in parts of the public services sector. The revived UK corporatist model was pushed to its sustainable limits, and then beyond them, in the face of persistent and severe international pressures on the national government's room for manoeuvre in policy formation. The collapse of the social contract in the 'winter of discontent' was an important conjunctural factor in Mrs Thatcher's victory in the 1979 general election but it was also symptomatic of a deeper shift in the relationships between state, economy and society. The succeeding decade of Thatcherism was to make the 1970s seem like the good old days to many of those who opposed the policies of the 1970s.

2.3.2 Thatcherism, 1979–90

There is now a voluminous literature that seek to define Thatcherism. Typically, commentators seek to specify those characteristics that mark out Thatcherism as a distinctive political-economic strategy (see, for example, Gamble 1983; Jessop et al. 1988). How should we define Thatcherism? This is not an easy question to answer for Thatcherism was an evolving approach which tactically altered its policy emphases as it fought a series of wars of position in a changing political and economic environment. An initial list of defining and seemingly enduring characteristics might include claims – though, as we show below, not always sustainable ones – about:

(1) 'Sound money' – mastering inflation via control of the money supply and, if need be, by high interest rates.
(2) Cutting and altering the composition of public expenditure, intentionally away from regional and industrial aid and welfare state expenditures towards defence and law and order and, unintentionally, towards unemployment and social security expenditure – although some would dispute whether these latter changes were in fact unintentional; at the same time, increasing restrictions were imposed on the capacity of local authorities to pursue their own spending and borrowing policies.
(3) Privatisation as the mirror image of cutting back the public sector, creating space into which an enterprise culture could develop. This was to be further encouraged by extending the scope of the property-owning democracy via the subsidised sale of parts of the public sector housing stock to sitting tenants and via the sale of shares in newly privatised companies at extremely generous prices. At the same time, pseudo-profitability efficiency criteria were introduced into the commercialised rump of the public sector, whilst notions of public service as their guiding rationale became increasingly subservient to the rhetoric of being responsive to customers and led by the market.
(4) Market deregulation to allow more or less unfettered scope for market forces to act as the resource allocation mechanism, both for private sector companies and the remainder of the public sector. This has been associated with encouraging and facilitating the internationalisation of capital and the national economy, via enhanced inward and outward investment, and above all with promoting the City of London as a major global financial centre via the Big Bang of deregulation of financial markets. Somewhat paradoxically, it has also involved seeking to promote the birth and growth of indigenous small firms.
(5) Trade union reform and a marked reduction in the perceived powers of the unions (via legislation, direct state action and mass unemployment). This, along with a growth in coercive government training schemes, has been seen as a way of enhancing 'flexibility' in the labour market and in working practices in a way that furthers the interests of capital.

Defined in this way, how radical a break with the past was Thatcherism? Certainly over the long *durée*, it harked back to themes and emphases that characterised the nineteenth century. In relation to the more immediate past, it is clear that the emphases on anti-inflation policies and cutting public expenditure and the scope of the public sector were not new. Moreover, there was selectivity in radically breaking with the past; activities such as agriculture and nuclear power, for example, continued to be protected from the harsh winds of free market competition. Some of the claimed radical breaks with the past also proved to be temporary; monetary policy, for example, became very lax in the period 1987–89, whilst public expenditure stubbornly failed to fall as a percentage of national output. There were more radical and sustained departures, such as market deregulation, and the assaults on trade unionism and local government's powers and resources. None the less, in terms of a balance sheet, it could be argued that the continuities with the past were at least as prominent as the radical rupture. Nevertheless, to see things only in terms of such a listing of distinctive dimensions is to miss much of the point about what made Thatcherism so radically different. This related both to the way in which these different elements of the programme were combined and also to the particularly distinctive and abrasive character of Mrs Thatcher's own political style. The Thatcherite project was above all else an attempt radically and irrevocably to redefine the relationships between the state, economy and society and to break out of the old social democratic consensus of One Nation politics. Whereas state intervention and regulation were formerly seen as a – if not the – solution to economic and social problems in the UK, they had now come to be seen as the problem. The problem, in Mrs Thatcher's deeply pejorative phrase, was 'the nanny state'.

The Thatcherite project was not, however, a seamless web, involving the implementation of a carefully and logically thought through plan of political action. In contrast, it evolved incrementally, as a result of a series of tactical manœuvres and positional battles. Not least, this was because the policies that it initially began to implement following the 1979 general election had been devised whilst in opposition in the 1970s. In that sense, they had, at least in part, been overtaken by subsequent events, both within and outside the UK. The initial package of economic policies exacerbated rather than ameliorated the problems of national economic performance and this generated considerable pressures to change them, not least within sections of the Conservative Party and its business supporters. The subsequent policy changes and sequence of victories and occasional retreats and defeats was, however, always informed by a sense of longer-term strategic purpose in terms of redrawing the contours of economy and society. There were and are, however, significant social groups and forces which sought and seek to preserve these contours, or at least to modify them. This has meant that there has been resistance to the Thatcherite project which further contributed to its uneven progress.

Intertwined with the pursuit of the longer-term objective was, of necessity, a more immediate concern with electoral success. Particularly during her first two administrations, Mrs Thatcher displayed an acute populist instinct as to which issues and policies to pursue, which vested interests to challenge and which to ignore or neglect, in the pursuit of victory in the polling booths. Thus the various defining elements of the Thatcherite approach have been given differential emphases at varying times. An evolving Thatcherism thus contained elements of both stasis and change. This shifting character may be one reason why Thatcherism has never become hegemonic. All the survey evidence points to steadily declining national levels of popular support, suggesting that Thatcherism was seeking to change deeply embedded values and societal norms in ways that raised fears and suspicion amongst the UK's citizens. Whilst it may not have become hegemonic, however, there is no doubt that Thatcherism has certainly been dominant.

In broad terms, the Thatcherite years may be divided into two broad periods (see Jessop et al. 1988; Jessop 1989): the rise and consolidation of Thatcherism before 1986, and the rise and fall of radical Thatcherism after that date. The subsequent post-Mrs Thatcher period of Majorism is probably best thought of as one of the partial decomposition of Thatcherism (accompanied by a softening of the rhetoric), although it is as yet too early to pass definitive judgement on this.

2.3.2.1 Phase I: the consolidation of Thatcherism

Gamble (1983, 222) correctly observes that the first Thatcher government was distinguished from its predecessors in that its 'electoral ideology, far from being discarded having served its purpose, formed the basis of the economic programme that the government intended to implement'. This remained the position, despite significant opposition from sections of both capital and the Conservative Party to key elements of the programme. Following the 1979 general election, therefore, the main emphasis in economic policy was on tight monetarist policies and efforts to reduce public expenditure. By the 1981 Budget, however, this strategy was in disarray on most fronts, though inflation and interest rates had begun to fall (Gamble 1983, 129). The price of implementing severely deflationary policies in a context of international recession was to provoke a major economic crisis in the UK, of much greater severity than that experienced by any of its major rivals. Deindustrialisation was rampant and registered unemployment rose for a time to over 3 million (see Townsend 1983; also Figure 2.2).

By the 1982 Budget the monetary component of the medium-term financial strategy (MTFS) was visibly disintegrating as concern over the political costs of unemployment led to a relaxation of monetary targets. This in turn led to enhanced pressures to adhere to the fiscal part of the MTFS and reduce both public expenditure and government borrowing. Both continued to rise, however, as widespread cuts in regional and industrial aid, and in nationalised industry and welfare state spending, failed to compensate for growing expenditure as a result of an ageing population, planned growth in defence spending and unplanned growth as a result of burgeoning unemployment. The government's general strategy and specific policies – on issues such as monetary control, fiscal fine-tuning and the sterling exchange rate – simply exacerbated existing economic problems. As a result, it created new forms of the familiar

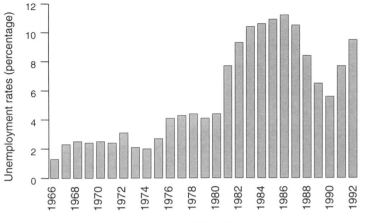

Figure 2.2 UK unemployment rates, 1966–92, second quarter of each year, seasonally adjusted

Source: CSO, *Economic Trends Annual Supplement*, 1993 edn, London: HMSO

'stop–go' cycle so prevalent throughout the One Nation era that Thatcherism was so intent on destroying.

It says much for the tactical acumen of Mrs Thatcher and her advisers that, despite all this, the government none the less swept to another landslide victory in the 1983 general election. For example, the government backed away from a potentially risky confrontation with the National Union of Mineworkers in 1982; it preferred to wait until it had carefully prepared its own plans, and coal stocks had been built up, for a struggle to the bitter end in 1984/85. Whether as a result of luck or judgement, the major reason for the government's electoral success in June 1983 was the wave of jingoistic and nationalistic fervour that swept through the country during and after the Falklands/Malvinas war (see Barnett 1982). Once again, Mrs Thatcher showed a fine sense of political finesse in making the most of the populist opportunities that this provided. Having won the war against the 'enemy without', the government then turned on the 'enemy within'. Legislative reductions to the rights of trade unions and the national steel strike of 1980 became a mere prelude to what was clearly intended to be the decisive moment: that is, the deeply symbolic defeat of the National Union of Mineworkers (NUM). The political message was crystal clear: if the NUM could be crushed, then trade unionism, as conventionally understood over the long period of One Nation politics, was no longer viable. For that reason, the government could not afford to be defeated and committed vast resources to ensuring the defeat of the strike (see Beynon 1985).

The government also increasingly came to see privatisation as a central element of its overall strategy, one that had the advantage of furthering the simultaneous pursuit of a number of objectives. At one level, the mounting proceeds from privatisations such as those of British Telecom created room for manœuvre for the government in relation to its economic policies. Privatisation proceeds allowed it to push on with cutting direct taxation. Nevertheless, reductions in direct taxes were counter-balanced by less publicised increases in indirect taxation, not indexing thresholds for income tax allowances in line with inflation, and increasing National Insurance contributions, so that for most people the total burden of taxation rose rather than fell. This approach allowed the government to leave the politically sensitive tax breaks of its supporters untouched; in particular, tax relief on mortgages. This was untouchable during the years in which Mrs Thatcher was Prime Minister, despite the fact that it is perhaps the single biggest distortion to the operation of market forces in the UK. This was not just a case of helping secure the support of traditional Conservative voters. Even more so, it was about keeping those recent converts to the cause of Thatcherism, won over as a result of policies to sell council houses to sitting tenants at handsome discounts. This was very important electorally (if not ideologically) in detaching a fraction of the skilled working class from support for the Labour Party. This was especially so in the remains of the manufacturing heartlands of the Midlands as these people were persuaded to return Conservative rather than Labour MPs to Westminster. At the same time, there were central government's restrictions on local authorities' house-building activities and, particularly, on their capacity to invest the proceeds of council house sales in replenishing the public sector stock. This effectively forced other people to become owner occupiers, to rent from the private sector, or, for an increasing number, to join the ranks of the homeless.

From 1983, however, evidence of a more general and sustained economic recovery became increasingly visible – though, one might reasonably argue, to a large extent this was no more than a reflection of the depths of recession in the economy in the early 1980s. In these circumstances, there was a growing discussion within the Conservative Party, partly with an eye to the best tactical approach to the next general election, as to how best to proceed in policy terms. But much more was at issue than just this. For this debate was also about long-term and strategic issues and in particular the necessity to push through the Thatcherite revolution to its historical and logical conclusion, to ensure that change was taken to the point at which the mould of One Nation politics had been irrevocably and irreparably broken.

2.3.2.2 *Phase II: the rise and fall of radical Thatcherism*

The radical Thatcherite project was publicly launched, in a blaze of publicity, at the 1986 Conservative Party Conference. Responding to the potential electoral damage that might be wreaked by unbridled market forces, and the potential threat of market research designer socialism (Jessop et al. 1990, 85), the radical tendency sought to both refine and redefine the Thatcherite project. This was to be achieved via a selective reworking of themes that had been visible in the first half of the 1980s. Above all, the hopes of radical Thatcherism rested upon developing and confirming the 'enterprise culture' and 'popular capitalism' as a hegemonic alternative to the Keynesian welfare state based on full employment and inclusive social democracy. Increasing inequality and social polarisation was thus an integral and central part of the reshaped project. At the same time the emphasis upon entrepreneurialism and popular capitalism was intended to legitimise this shift to an unambiguously Two Nations strategy.

A central element in this search for legitimation was the way in which 'individual freedom' took on markedly different connotations as part of the Thatcherite project. For freedom was a central concept within the post-war settlement which had set the parameters within which the One Nation approach evolved. Although imprecisely defined, it clearly embraced both freedoms to and freedoms from. For example, freedom from hunger and unemployment were seen to be as important as freedom to belong to trade unions, or political parties, and to criticise government. The Thatcherite view of freedom is both more narrowly and more precisely defined. Grounded in the views of Hayek (1988), it is a belief that government interference is the fundamental cause of the diminution of true freedom. Freedom therefore is seen as the right of citizens to make their own decisions about how to live their lives.

These philosophical premises became translated by Mrs Thatcher's governments into a radical programme of selective state deintervention and disengagement from the provision of goods and services and deregulation of the private sector. Strands of this were already visible prior to 1986 – for example, in terms of council house sales and privatisation. It was after 1985, however, that such elements took on new and added significance. The 'enterprise culture' and 'popular capitalism' became the central unifying threads of policy, with an influence that was felt widely across the whole spectrum of economic and social policies. The privatisation programme boomed (as a consequence creating further scope for radical taxation policy changes) whilst there was an explosion of measures to encourage new small firm formation and entrepreneurship. The intention of such changes was to extend the emphasis on self-help and self-reliance beyond housing provision to an increasing reliance on the provision of self-employment. These changes became personified in and symbolised by images of Essex men and women and the rise of the Yuppies.

Changes to the taxation structure and the introduction of new tax breaks were, in like fashion, intended to increase private sector provision of pensions and of educational and health services. Such services became increasingly, but selectively, purchased by individual consumers through the market rather than provided by the state as of right to citizens. Alternatively, reflecting the influence of appeals to Victorian values, care of the elderly and sick was again to be internalised, in a gender-selective fashion, within the household. Whether by increased family involvement or market provision, however, state involvement in the provision of these various services was to be reduced further. Moreover, within the remaining public service sector provision of such services, the same themes of 'freedom' and 'choice' found a resonance in the reforms of education and health care introduced in the late 1980s to allow state schools to opt out and patients to choose their doctor. Transport provision too was increasingly pushed towards individual mobility via increased car ownership as public transport provision was restricted as a prelude to privatisation, which in turn led to cuts in levels of service provision in many areas.

This radical Thatcherite project was far from unproblematic and it soon encountered resistance not only from its opponents inside and outside Parliament but also from some sections of Conservative Party supporters. They began to be adversely affected by aspects of its implementation, which served to undermine some of the political and social bases of support for the project. For example, cuts in public services such as transport increasingly affected middle-class commuters in the South East, whilst growing use of private cars had a range of environmental consequences that also often impacted directly in the Conservative heartlands; these were to become increasingly difficult to square with a growing government commitment to environmental protection. More fundamentally, however, the radical project ran up against the constraint of the structural problems of the UK economy. For whilst claiming to address and even resolve these, in fact the second phase of Thatcherism if anything exacerbated them. The balance of available evidence weighed very

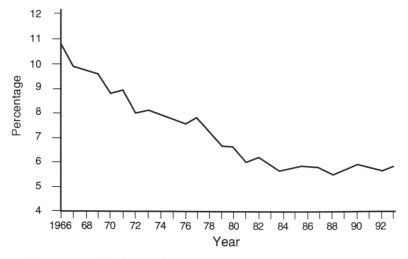

Figure 2.3 UK share of world trade in manufactures, 1966–93

Source: *Barclays Review*, November 1993

heavily against the claims of a successful radical supply-side revolution which has prepared the ground for a root and branch resurgence of the UK economy.

The evidence may be summarised as follows. Firstly, there has been a continuing failure of manufacturing industry, with a continuing fall in the UK's share of world manufacturing exports and a growing balance-of-payments deficit (see Figure 2.3). As Jessop et al. (1990, 86) have put it, comparing the Thatcherite years to the preceding part of the post-war period, 'nothing much has changed here under Thatcherism'. Secondly, whilst gross investment in services rose rapidly, that in manufacturing increased much more slowly and from a very depressed level during the 1980s. Thirdly, between 1979 and 1986, facilitated by the removal of controls on capital export, the UK's 40 largest manufacturing firms cut employment in the UK by 415 000 but increased it elsewhere by 125 000. More generally, increased direct foreign investment by firms from across the whole spectrum of the economy meant that the UK had the greatest stock of direct foreign investment relative to GDP of any of the major capitalist economies. Fourthly, whilst there was a much smaller counter-flow of inward investment in manufacturing to the UK by multinationals based elsewhere, this was largely in low wage labour-intensive assembly and sub-assembly operations (see Table 2.1). Indeed, such inward investment, especially from Japan, was seen by the Thatcher governments as having a key transformative role in the reshaping of industrial relations and working practices (see, for example, Garrahan and Stewart 1992; Hudson 1992). This links to a fifth point: that such domestic manufacturing investment as did take place was primarily deployed as part of low-wage, 'flexible labour' strategies rather than on highly skilled work in high-technology operations.

More generally, in fact, the labour market was becoming still more deeply segmented, characterised by a growth in low wages and jobs with poor skill levels. Although there was some well-publicised growth in highly remunerated positions in financial services, mainly associated with the City of London, most of the new jobs in the services sector were part-time, poorly paid and with little skill content. Such labour market restructuring was closely linked to further changes in the UK's position in the international economic order. This juxtaposed further deindustrialisation with a growing specialisation in financial services. At the same time, inward flows of international tourists became of growing significance to the national economy as tourism became the fastest growing sector in terms of employment creation. The growing importance of such tourist flows suggested a future as a gigantic post-industrial heritage park rather than as a revived industrial power of global significance.

If the project failed to deliver the promised transformation of the productive base of the UK economy, it also encountered serious difficulties on other fronts. Financial deregulation considerably increased the amount of credit and debt in the economy, following the abandonment of broad money supply

Table 2.1 Indicators of UK national economic performance in the 1980s and 1990s

	1980	1981	1982	1983	1984	1985	1986	1987	1988	1989	1990	1991
Balance of payment (£m., current balance)	1 843	6 748	4 649	3 765	1 798	2 790	66	- 4 682	- 16 179	- 21 726	- 17 029	- 6 321
Public sector borrowing requirement (£m.)*	2 159	8 631	8 904	9 678	10 134	5 622	3 559	- 3 406	- 14 657	- 7 932	- 457	13 728
Inflation rate (retail prices index)†	18.4	13.0	12.0	4.9	5.1	5.0	5.5	3.9	3.3	7.5	7.7	9.0
Consumer credit (total outstanding, £m.)	n.a.	n.a.	15 450	15 905	18 820	22 229	26 069	30 150	36 174	42 544	48 404	52 579
Overseas investment in the UK (£m.)	5 786	3 189	3 016	5 087	1 107	14 279	18 018	28 984	27 570	33 170	23 910	28 627
Investment overseas from the UK (£m.)	8 175	10 474	11 656	12 768	15 789	25 203	33 955	14 076	32 183	57 001	25 397	41 169
Investment in manufacturing in the domestic economy (£m.)	5 786	6 154	6 417	6 714	8 321	10 118	9 731	10 814	12 281	14 281	14 328	12 678
Output per person employed, manufacturing (1985 = 100)	76.9	79.5	84.8	91.9	97.0	100.0	103.5	109.8	116.2	120.8	121.9	122.5
Output per person employed, whole economy (1985 = 100)	87.3	89.4	96.7	96.9	97.3	100.0	103.7	106.6	107.9	107.5	107.5	108.0
Employees in employment (m.)	22.9	21.9	21.4	21.1	21.2	21.4	21.4	21.6	22.3	22.7	22.9	22.2
Employees in employment in manufacturing (m.)						5.4	5.2	5.2	5.2	5.2	5.1	4.8
Self-employed (m.)	2.0	2.1	2.2	2.2	2.5	2.6	2.6	2.9	3.0	3.3	3.3	3.1
Work-related goverment training schemes (000's)				16	175	176	226	311	343	462	423	343
Unemployed (registered, m.)	1.3	2.2	2.5	2.9	2.9	3.0	3.1	2.8	2.3	1.8	1.6	

* In each case refers to financial year beginning in this calendar year
† Refers to the percentage rate of increase in January each year compared to previous January
Source: CSO, various dates, *Annual Abstract of Statistics*, HMSO. CSO, various dates, *Economic Trends Annual Supplement*, HMSO

targets in 1986 and narrow ones in 1988 (see Figure 2.4; also *Barclays Review* May 1989, 7). This not only forced the government to push up interest rates counter to its own anti-inflationary strategy but unambiguously signalled the death and burial of monetarism which only a few years earlier had seemed so central to Thatcherism. The Stock Market collapse in 1987 and fears of this sliding into a 1930s-style slump, allied to a concern not to let sterling appreciate too much against the Deutschmark after it was pegged to the German currency, led the government to lower interest rates at a time when there was 'apparently excessive growth of money and credit [with] annual increases of over twenty percent' (*Barclays Review* November 1987, 7). The growing expansion of financial services sharply increased this sector's claims on a fragile productive economy, although the crisis of the Lloyd's insurance business in the early 1990s was to provide a sharp reminder of the potential risks involved in reliance upon such financial services. At the same time, strongly growing consumer demand resulted in increasing imports and balance-of-payments problems.

These tendencies were given further sharp impetus by the 1987 and 1988 Budgets, which radically and regressively redistributed some £6.0 billion of tax cuts; £4.7 billion of these benefited the most affluent 1 per cent of tax payers, a rich minority of 210 000 members of the population, heavily concentrated in the South East. The effects of this were further to stimulate a consumption boom that was heavily dependent on the growth of credit and personal indebtedness and stoke up severe inflationary pressures, above all in housing markets. New loans for housing alone exceeded £40 billion in 1988, both increasing inflationary pressures and diverting potential investment from more productive uses. This in turn exacerbated external pressures on the economy as the balance-of-payments position deteriorated sharply, reaching an annual current account deficit of over £20 billion by 1989 (see Table 2.1). These pressures resulted in a sharp reversal in interest rate policy, with rates soaring to reach 15 per cent in 1989 and remaining there. This above all else induced a deep and lasting recession in the national economy. High interest rates were translated into burgeoning mortgage payments, a spectacular crash in housing and property markets that was particularly severe in London and the

Figure 2.4 UK M0 monetary base, 1980–91

Source: *Barclays Review*, November 1986 and 1992

South East, falling domestic demand for many consumer goods and further contraction of the manufacturing sector. Unemployment once again began to increase rapidly, further increasing pressures on public expenditure and reinforcing the spectre of a fiscal crisis for the state.

The difficulties facing the manufacturing sector in export markets were not helped by the decision to join the ERM at a high rate against the Deutschmark, following some years of unofficially shadowing it, and an increasingly generalised global recession. Despite – or because of – this tale of woe, external pressures grew to the point at which they could no longer be sustained as speculation against sterling forced its devaluation and retreat from the ERM in October 1992. This, however, simply served to highlight and intensify divisions within the Conservative Party over Europe as Mr Major continued to refuse to accept the Social Chapter within the Maastricht Treaty. By then, however, Mrs Thatcher herself had already gone to another place as pressures from Conservative Members of Parliament, fearful of losing their seats in the next general election, had forced her to resign in November 1990.

2.3.3   Conclusions: Majorism – or decomposing Thatcherism?

The replacement of Mrs Thatcher with Mr Major as leader of the Conservative Party and Prime Minister raised important issues for Thatcherism post-Thatcher and for the future of the Two Nations project. For a change of personnel did nothing to dispel the contradictions and structural weaknesses in the economy which precipitated Mrs Thatcher's fall from grace. The continuing problems over the balance of payments were compounded by a rapid reversal in the position over the government's own finances and the public sector borrowing requirement as the economy continued to bump along on the bottom of the longest recession in the post-war period. In the short term, these pressures on public expenditure were compounded by increased spending prior to the 1992 general elction. Over the longer term, such pressures were intensified as a result of continuing high levels of unemployment as well as demographic changes that translated into a growing requirement for expenditure on state pensions and on education and, especially, health services. Not least, this pressure grew because the government initially refused to countenance increases in income tax and direct taxation as a way of raising revenue, at a time when its other revenue-raising options – such as further privatisations – were becoming increasingly scarce. Moreover, the effects of recession had reduced its corporate tax base. The government's response to this shortfall of revenue was to seek to cut costs via a public sector pay freeze in 1993 and 1994 and the further contracting out of central and local government services in an attempt to rein in public expenditure increases.

Mr Major's government was becoming increasingly boxed in as a result of its own actions and attitudes and the Thatcherite legacy that it inherited. Not least, this included a sizeable rump of unreconstructed Thatcherite MPs. It soon became reduced to shuffling its members between jobs, notably after the ritual sacrifice of Mr Lamont from his post as Chancellor of the Exchequer. Even so, Mr. Lamont left a legacy of a final Budget in 1993 which contained significant increases in National Insurance contributions and indirect taxes, most notably the extension of VAT to domestic consumers of gas and electricity. The effect of these taxation increases will be sharply regressive, falling hardest on those who are already the most disadvantaged. Such measures represent one response to the problems of funding governmental spending. These problems are symptomatic of a deeper malaise, however, and such tax increases are a poor substitute for policy initiatives to tackle underlying problems of economic decline and social inequality that continue to plague the Divided Realm in the 1990s.

It is difficult to escape the conclusion that radical Thatcherism is decomposing and giving way to something else — which might be Thatcherism post-Thatcher or may be something different that could, for want of a better term, be denoted as Majorism. But if Majorism exists, it differs from Thatcherism in little but presentational style across a broad range of policy issues. Certainly, as Mrs Thatcher made clear following the 1993 Conservative Party Conference, she saw Thatcherism alive and well in government policies — albeit after a period when the government had strayed from the true path of its Thatcherite inheritance. If the policies of Mr Major are most appropriately thought of as a new phase of Thatcherism, however, they are not so much a new recharged offensive form as an exhausted defensive one (Jessop et al. 1990, 102). This new phase represents one of consolidation but one in which the government's room for both economic and political manœuvring has become much more restricted. It is, of course, economically hemmed in by the failures of past Thatcherite policies to engender a supply-side revolution and constructively restructure the productive basis of the national economy. It is, however, also hemmed in politically by the different interests within the Conservative Party and by its small Parliamentary majority. Economic policies that the government, its advisers and international financial markets see as necessary are anathema to many Conservative MPs. Not least, this is because they would adversely effect core sections of their constituency supporters, with obvious electoral risks.

3

Divided by class I: wealth and income

3.1 Introduction: class, income and wealth

Capitalist societies are inevitably characterised by inequalities between classes in income and wealth, although the precise form of these depends upon social and political conditions specific to particular societies. Such inequalities have been endemic in the UK since capitalism became established there. During the inter-war years, mass unemployment and poverty led to growing concern about the social and economic consequences of these inequalities. Such inequalities were accepted as an unavoidable consequence of capitalist class relations but political pressures grew for the state to confine these within 'acceptable' limits. Following some redistribution from rich to poor in the immediate post-war years, the next three decades were ones of relative stability in the distribution of income with a slight tendency to reduced income inequalities. Growing equality in pre-tax personal incomes between 1949 and 1977 largely involved a redistribution within the top 30 per cent of income earners, away from the top 10 per cent and particularly the top 1 per cent (whose share of incomes more than halved) (see Abercrombie and Warde 1988).An important reason why income inequalities remained substantially unaltered is that the proportions of tax paid at different income levels above the bottom 20 per cent of the population (who received most of their income in state benefit payments) varied little.Any progressive tendency in direct taxation was largely cancelled out by the effects of indirect taxation. This is indicative of the redistributive limits to One Nation politics.

In contrast, in the 1980s income inequalities widened as the Two Nations project, with its celebration of growing inequality intimately linked to a more deeply segmented labour market, gathered pace (Table 3.1). This process began under the preceding Labour government but accelerated sharply as Conservative policies on taxation and benefits then became sharply regressive. The share of the top 20 per cent (and especially that of the top 1 and 5 per cent) increased whilst that of the bottom 60 per cent fell. The magnitude of inequalities was less for disposable and post-tax incomes, reflecting some continuing redistributive element in government taxation policies. Further taxation

Table 3.1 Distribution of income, UK, 1976–85. Percentage-share of national total

	Quintile groups of households				
	Bottom fifth	Next fifth	Middle fifth	Next fifth	Top fifth
Equivalised original income					
1977	4	10	18	26	43
1979	2	10	18	27	43
1981	3	9	17	26	46
1983	3	8	17	26	47
1985	2	7	17	27	47
1988	2	7	16	25	50
Equivalised disposable income					
1977	10	14	18	23	36
1979	9	13	18	23	36
1981	9	13	17	23	38
1983	10	13	17	23	38
1985	9	13	17	23	38
1988	8	11	16	23	42
Equivalised post-tax income					
1977	9	14	17	23	37
1979	10	13	18	23	37
1981	9	13	17	22	39
1983	9	13	17	22	39
1985	9	13	17	23	39
1988	7	11	16	22	44

Notes:
Original income comes from various sources such as wages and dividends
Disposable income is defined as original income plus benefits and less direct taxes
Post-tax income is defined as disposable income adjusted for the effects of indirect taxes
Source: CSO (1992)

changes introduced after 1985, particularly in the March 1988 Budget, further cut the top rate of income tax to 40 per cent. A subsequent reduction in the basic rate of tax to 20 per cent on the first £2000 of earned income did little to ameliorate the magnitudes of inequality. This was particularly so as further increases in National Insurance contributions and value added tax in the 1990s emphasised the regressive switch from direct income tax to indirect taxes as the Major government struggled to cope with the legacy of the economic policies of the 1980s. The net effect of taxation changes, both indirect and direct, since

Table 3.2 Distribution of wealth in Great Britain, adults over 18 (percentage), 1971–89

	1971	1976	1979	1981	1985	1986	1989
Marketable wealth							
Percentage owned by most							
wealthy x% of population:							
1% of	31	21	22	18	20	18	18
5%	52	38	40	36	40	36	38
10%	65	50	54	50	54	50	53
50%	97	92	95	92	93	90	94
Marketable wealth plus occupational and state pension rights							
Percentage owned by most							
wealthy x% of population:							
1% of	21	12	13	10	11	10	11
5%	37	24	25	23	25	23	26
10%	49	34	35	33	36	34	38
25%	69–72	54	56–69	55	57–60	57	62
50%	85–89	78	79–93	78	81–85	81	83
Marketable wealth less the value of dwellings							
Percentage owned by most							
wealthy x% of population:							
1% of	n.a.	29	n.a.	26	n.a.	25	28
5%	n.a.	47	n.a.	45	n.a.	46	53
10%	n.a.	57	n.a.	56	n.a.	58	66
25%	n.a.	73	n.a.	74	n.a.	75	81
50%	n.a.	88	n.a.	87	n.a.	89	94

Note: 'Marketable wealth' refers to assets such as houses or shares that could be sold. Assets such as pension schemes will yield a future income but cannot be sold
Source: CSO (various dates)

1979 has therefore been further to increase inequalities whilst the overall burden of personal taxation has risen.

The growing concentration of income amongst the top 20 per cent has been paralleled by growing poverty at the other end of the scale. From 1960 to 1977 it is estimated that around 2 million people were, at any one time, living below the government's own supplementary benefit level (the officially defined level of inadequate income). By 1981 this had risen to 2.6 million. In 1983 there were an estimated 8.6 million people living at or below the supplementary benefit level, an increase of 43 per cent since 1979. By 1988–89, the Child Poverty Action Group estimated that between 11 and 12 million people were living at or below the government income support level. Using a different definition of poverty, based on a measure of a minimum standard of living widely agreed among the population, Mack and Lansley (1985) suggest that there were between 6 and 12 million poor people in Britain in the 1980s, of whom 2.6 million faced intense poverty. These include a disproportionate representation of the unemployed, the disabled, one-parent families and the elderly retired. Since the incomes of many of these groups depend directly on state benefit payments, the creation of increased poverty for many is as much a product of government policies as is increased affluence for others. Whereas a two-child family in the bottom 20 per cent of the income distribution experienced a 6 per cent decrease in income (including benefits) between 1979 and 1985, a two-child family in the top 20 per cent had a 9 per cent increase. Figures such as these led Mr Malcolm Wicks, Director of the Policy Studies Centre, succinctly to sum up the position: 'the poor are getting poorer and the rich are getting richer' (cited in the *Financial Times*, 4 January 1988).

In many ways, inequalities in wealth are related to but are more deeply entrenched and extensive than those in income. By wealth, we mean the assets that people own, either as money or in forms that can be converted to money (such as houses). Over the last 50 years or so, there has apparently been a marked redistribution of wealth; for example, the share of the top 1 per cent fell from 55 per cent in 1938 to 32 per cent in 1972. This was largely a redistribution within the top 20 per cent however; over the same period their share only fell from 91 to 85 per cent. This pattern continued throughout the 1970s (Table 3.2). Although the share of the top 1 per cent declined further, by the end of that decade the least wealthy 50 per cent of the population had only increased its share of marketable wealth from 3 to 6 per cent. Including occupational and state pensions lessens the inequalities in marketable wealth but by no means removes them. Inequalities in wealth have largely stabilised in the 1980s; 1 per cent of the population still owned 18 per cent of marketable wealth and 5 per cent owned 38 per cent of it in 1989. A more favourable tax regime has been created since 1979, making it easier for the wealthy to preserve their assets within their families. The continuing redistribution of wealth within the top quarter of the population partly reflects the strategies of the wealthy to set up trusts or distribute assets amongst members of their families prior to death, precisely to avoid the higher taxes payable on death.

How then are recent trends in income and wealth inequalities to be interpreted? To some extent, changes in the distribution of wealth and incomes from the late 1940s to the late 1970s resulted from the redistributive taxation policies which were central to One Nation politics. It is indicative of the limits to these reformist policies that the distribution of income and wealth changed so little. To the 'economic evangelicals' (Keegan 1984) of the new right, however, the class compromises around which the post-war consensus was built caused the UK's economic decline. In contrast to its predecessors, from 1979 the new government deliberately set out to widen income inequalities as an integral part of the Two Nations project. In particular, it reduced higher tax rates and the burden on those with high incomes. A more divided society was central to regenerating the economy via creating an 'enterprise culture' that rewarded success and punished failure via policies such as cuts in benefits for those without paid work.

The causes of the reversal of previous weak trends towards a more equal distribution of income and wealth therefore lie in the specific Two Nations politics of Thatcherism. Moreover, once wealth in the form of house ownership is discounted, the dominance of the wealthiest 1 per cent, 5 per cent and 10 per cent of the population in terms of other forms of wealth is sharply reinforced. This points to the significance of growing owner occupation in maintaining a degree of stability in the distribution of wealth, counteracting a growing concentration of other forms of wealth, especially during the 1980s. Nevertheless, the large minority which was unable to become owner occupiers was excluded from these benefits. This is indicative of the way in which the changes initiated in the 1980s took effect in a society where the distribution of income and wealth was already markedly uneven.

There are clear relationships between forms of property ownership, sources of money income and size of incomes. For most people, ownership of wealth is minimal. For most of those for whom it is more substantial, it is held in forms that relate to individuals' and households' consumption patterns: for example, the houses they live in, bank and building society deposits or insurance policies to provide future income. Ownership of wealth in these forms largely depends upon money earned through wage labour, though income levels and the conditions under which they are earned vary greatly both between and within classes (not least, in terms of differences in gender and race). An important change for some, undoubtedly, is the one-off inflow of money from the inheritance of parental homes. In addition, a minority of wage earners have acquired small amounts of share capital in private (usually privatised) companies which provide marginal unearned income. For another and smaller minority, however, concentrated ownership of wealth provides access to very considerable unearned income in the form of dividends, profits and rents from money invested in government stocks, shares or land.

In summary, then, access to different forms and amounts of income and wealth is related (though not reducible) to class relations. To simplify matters for the moment, we can suggest that:

(1) for a few, rents provide a source of money income (often related to the persistence of landownership from an earlier feudal era);
(2) for a few, profits provide a source of income because of their ownership of property as industrial capital;
(3) for a minority, who are self-employed, money income depends upon their ability to sell goods or services produced by their own labour;
(4) for most people, whether categorised as working or 'middle' class, wages form the main source of money income upon which they depend;
(5) for many people, some of whom are unemployed and others of whom for various reasons are too young or too old to form part of the wage labour force, state payments form the main source of money incomes. Many of these people form part of an increasingly – and multiply – disadvantaged underclass.

We consider each of these groups, which were differentially affected by the transition from One to Two Nations politics, in turn.

3.2 Who owns the land? Land, wealth and incomes

Perhaps the most surprising aspect of the contemporary pattern of landowner-ship is the extent to which traces of pre-capitalist ownership persist (Massey and Catalano, 1978). The Crown estate, the monarchy, the Church of England and the universities (principally Oxbridge) remain important property and land owners. The commercial property portfolio of the Church Commis-sioners was estimated to be worth in excess of £1.5 billion in 1990, producing an annual income of around £140 million (*Financial Times*, 7 April 1990). Even more striking, despite a sustained decline in their holdings, is that over 31 per cent of land is owned by the aristocracy. Other non-titled individuals own over 19 per cent of land.

Different categories of landowners have differing reasons for owning land. For many, owning a small piece of land is simply a condition for living in a particular house. For non-financial companies, landholdings are typically a necessary condition for carrying out their main economic activities (although selling sites in urban areas has often proved extremely profitable for them). For many other individuals and organisations, however, landholdings are themselves a major sources of income via rents or profits.

3.2.1 Major private owners

Some big private estates result from the activities of successful capitalists who, having made their fortunes, wished to mimic the life-style of the landed aristocracy. These range from *nouveau riche* industrialists in the nineteenth century to another generation of *nouveau riche* industrialists, property developers and popular entertainers and sports personalities in the second half of the twentieth. In part, this has involved a transfer of land from the aristocracy. Yet despite reductions, with capital transfer taxes leading to a break-up of some estates and the shrinking of others, the aristocracy remain very significant private owners of land. Two-thirds of the landed nobility in England and Wales, just over 200 families, own at least 5000 acres each; in Scotland, retention of large estates by the nobility is, if anything, stronger.

Twenty-six aristocrats have combined holdings of over 1 million acres. About a third of the peerage, some 350 lords, still own enough land to provide a significant element in their income; about one-half combine their landed estates with active business interests whilst the other half live off their land alone. Consequently, an entirely land-dependent group still exists. Moreover, the surge in land prices has more than compensated for shrinking acreages, especially for those with major holdings of urban land.

By the late 1970s very substantial landowners like Lords Leicester, Rosebery and Sefton were once again amongst Britain's wealthiest individuals, as they had been a century before. The largest aristocratic landowner in Scotland is the Duke of Buccleuch (277 000 acres), whilst the largest in England is the Duke of Northumberland (90 786 acres); the two families are, of course, linked through marriage. When Hugh Algernon Percy, tenth Duke of Northumberland, died in 1988, he was succeeded as eleventh Duke by Lord Harry Percy, who thus became the latest in a long line whose family have held land ever since a remote ancestor was granted estates for services to William the Conqueror. His estates include more than 80 000 acres in Northumberland, administered from the ancestral home in Alnwick Castle; this yields a variety of forms of income from tenanted farms, farms in hand, villages, stretches of moorland, parkland, grouse moor and rivers. In the past it also yielded huge returns from royalty payments on coal to his predecessors. He also owns 3 500 acres of rolling farm, forest and downland in Surrey, along with Syon House and the 200–acre Syon Park by the Thames in west London.

Other dukes also remain major landowners, mostly of rural land but with some very valuable urban holdings. The Duke of Westminster, for example, has extensive urban holdings of prime land in London and other towns (held of course in family trusts); these include most of Oxford Street, Mayfair and Belgravia. He also owns agricultural land in England and estates in Scotland (see Figure 3.1). The Queen personally is also a major landowner, with the 47 000 acres of the Balmoral and Sandringham estates. Landownership on this scale provides access to considerable monetary incomes.

Incomes from landholdings take various forms. Rents are derived from a variety of urban functions and from the profits of farmers, or more recently from expenditure by the wealthy on leisure activities such as grouse shoots and salmon fishing. Any threat to these rental incomes may be fiercely

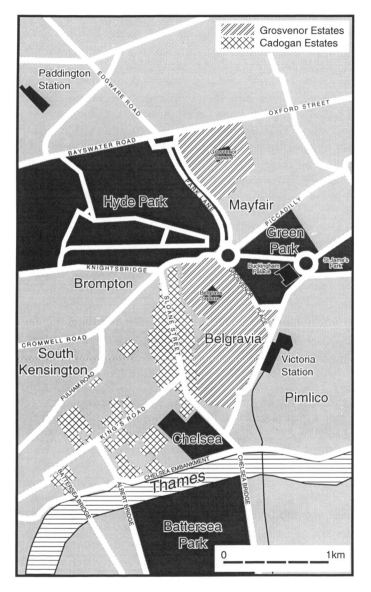

Figure 3.1 Major landholdings of the Cadogan and Grosvenor estates in central London

resisted, as the resignation of the Duke of Westminster from the Conservative Party in 1993 over proposed changes to leasehold law made abundantly clear. Profits are derived from farming and forestry, especially since 1945, in response to the inducements of state grants and subsidised prices (but recently threatened by reform of the European Community's Common Agricultural Policy). At the same time the aristocracy has diversified its sources of income away from land in the narrow sense. Many – some from economic necessity – cashed in on the leisure boom, opening the doors of their stately homes to the public. Great houses and their contents have become attractions that people will pay to see. Often these developments have been linked to the activities of the National Trust, which therefore preserved a fraction of the aristocracy and a particular definition of the national heritage. In some cases, taking advantage of the growth in leisure has involved innovations that have little to do with history. Longleat Wild Life Park illustrates this tendency.

Another group of landowners, also originating in the pre-capitalist era, is the landed gentry, a uniquely British phenomenon. It ranges from yeoman farmers, to the titled nobility. In the mid-1980s about 1000 families in the landed gentry owned 1000 or more acres each, with another 500 families each owning a few hundred acres.They remain heavily reliant upon income from their estates but there have been important changes in the way in which land generates money for them. They have gradually moved from reliance upon rents to dependence upon profits from owner-occupied farming, changing from landowners who also produce to agricultural producers who also own land. Moreover, since 1945 they have tended to adopt a more 'economic' approach towards landownership; not least, sales of land have often provided an alternative source of money.

In some respects, the transformation of part of the landed gentry overlaps the third main group of private landowners: owner-occupier farmers. For them, landownership is central. It usually represents the bulk of their invested capital and land-based production is likely to be their sole economic interest. Acquisition of more land is usually the simplest means (however difficult) of expanding production. Nevertheless, there is evidence that for all big farmers, non-farm sources of income have become increasingly important. For example, for the largest 12 per cent of farms, non-farm income accounted for between one-third and one-half of total income between 1977/88 and 1985/86 (Ministry of Agriculture, Fisheries and Food 1988).

Owner-occupied farming increased markedly after 1945, partly because of state support for agriculture. In 1908, 88 per cent of farm holdings were rented; this then fell to 60 per cent in 1950, 50 per cent in 1960, 30 per cent in 1976 and 28 per cent in 1987 (*Financial Times*, 28 September 1989). Conversely, the proportion of owner-occupied holdings rose but most of them were small. For example, by 1960, about 80 per cent had less than 100 acres. By 1987, the smallest 40 per cent of holdings had an average size of only 32 acres or 12 hectares (Ministry of Agriculture, Fisheries and Food 1988) whilst by 1990 the smallest 42 per cent averaged only 27 acres or 11 hectares.But size is not the main feature distinguishing this group from the nobility and gentry. Fundamentally, such farmers are industrial capitalists for whom land is essential to production. Many employ wage labourers. Many, however, only employ such labour on a part-time or casual basis. Others are wholly reliant upon their own and/or family labour and more accurately are conceptualised as self-employed. Indeed, small farmers, too, are increasingly becoming less reliant on their farming activities: by 1987 almost half of Britain's farmers were part-time, farmed less than 35 acres, and earned much more from jobs off the farm than from farming itself (Ministry of Agriculture, Fisheries and Food 1988). A later study (*Financial Times*, 22 October 1991) suggested that the smallest 42 per cent of farms yielded an average farm income of £300 in 1988 and £200 in 1989, compared to off-farm incomes of £12 000 and £13 500 respectively. Clearly there is an increasing divergence between these and larger farmers in the significance of land to their income.

In one sense, however, all owner-occupier farmers have seen a great increase in their wealth as land price increased (see Figure 3.2). Nominal agricultural land prices rose more or less steadily until the end of the 1980s, though in real terms they fell sharply and more or less steadily after 1979. In the 1970s agricultural land values rose steeply as a result of European Community price support and demand from financial institutions. By the 1980s, pressures to reform the Common Agricultural Policy were mounting whilst such land became increasingly less attractive to large institutional owners (*Financial Times*, 16 April 1993). In the 1990s the implications of the crisis in the Lloyd's insurance business led to 'names' putting land on the market.

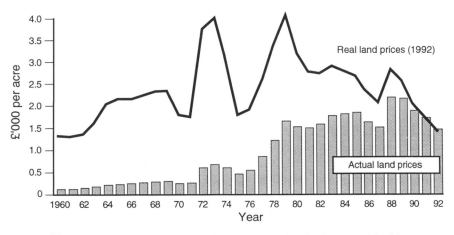

Figure 3.2 Nominal and real agricultural land prices, 1960–92

Source: *Financial Times*, 16 April 1993

Nevertheless, in the 1970s ownership of 1800 or more acres of land made hundreds of farmers into paper millionaires. As agricultural land prices escalated in the 1980s, the acreage necessary to create a millionaire fell. Selling 2 or 3 acres for residential development in the right place was itself sufficient to raise a million pounds. For example, estate agents Strutt and Parker pointed out that the 7500 new houses zoned in the Berkshire Structure Plan in 1988 equated to around 750 acres for building sites at £500 000 per acre. The resulting £375 million would be shared amongst those who owned this formerly agricultural land. As the agents commented: 'The money has to go somewhere' (cited in *Financial Times*, 11 January, 1989).

For small owner-occupier farmers who wished to expand, however, escalating land prices caused problems. In these circumstances, the rational capitalist solution of selling an existing holding at inflated prices became a more attractive proposition. This further helped reduce the number of small owner-occupied units and farmers. This was especially so as the taxation system made it attractive for those who had sold land at very high prices for non-agricultural use to reinvest the proceeds in agricultural land or in forestry schemes. In this way, capital gains tax is deferred. Thus a farmer selling 10 acres of land at £500 000 per acre could be in a position to buy a 2000 acre estate with cash to spare (*Financial Times*, 16 May 1989).This taxation arrangement helped reinforce a long-term trend which had seen the size distribution of agricultural holdings become increasingly skewed and the number of agricultural holdings fall from almost 380 000 in 1960 (Ministry of Agriculture, Fisheries and Food 1988) to 240 000 in 1990 (*Financial Times*, 22 October 1991).

3.2.2 Institutions as landowners

Some institutions have long histories as landowners, such as the Oxbridge universities (160 000 acres) and the Church of England (170 000 acres). Rents from land are an important element in their income whilst the land itself represents a considerable accumulation of wealth. Since 1945 established organisations such as the National Trust have become important landowners (over 400 000 acres), as a result of gifts or purchases. More recently, other institutions have become significant landowners. Financial institutions – life insurance companies and pension funds – became important landowners from the 1960s, in large part due to the 1965 Finance Act. In the 1960s and early 1970s, this mainly involved small acreages of highly priced urban land; rising rents provided income and, because of the method of calculating land values (as capitalised rents), also translated into spiralling paper wealth. Following the property market slump of the early 1970s, the financial institutions sought to diversify their holdings into rural land. As early as 1973, they purchased 28 per cent of all agricultural land that came on the market, a trend that subsequently continued. By the latter part of the 1980s and early 1990s, however, this trend was reversed as these institutions increasingly sold their agricultural landholdings. For example, British Coal's pension fund disposed of 11 500 acres in 1990, Guardian Royal Exchange sold off 22 500 acres of East Anglian farmland in 1991 and Postel sought to dispose of 7,745 acres in Hampshire and Wiltshire in 1993. In all, City of London financial institutions sold off around 250 000 acres of farmland between 1986 and 1991 (see *Financial Times*, 25 May 1991 and 10 April 1993). Indeed, the general slump in land and property markets, allied to the depreciation of sterling against other major currencies, notably the Deutschmark, saw a surge in overseas investment in the UK property market, especially in 1989 and 1990 (see Figure 3.3). As a result, some rental income from property in the UK is being transferred to owners in other countries.

Property companies have become increasingly linked to financial institutions. By 1973 insurance companies and pension funds owned almost one-quarter of the share capital of property companies. Property companies specialise in land: their economic activity consists almost exclusively in purchasing and/or developing land or property in order to collect rental incomes. Their activities are essentially speculative. Consequently they provide opportunities for a few individuals to amass great personal wealth very quickly. For

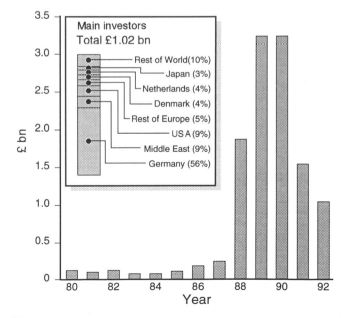

Figure 3.3 Overseas investment in UK property, 1980–92

Source: *Financial Times*, 12 March 1993

example, Harry Hyams, one of the more (in)famous property developers, was credited, at the height of the property boom of the early 1970s, with a personal fortune of between £500 million and £1000 million. During the 1980s the privatisation policies forcing sales of land by local authorities and nationalised industries such as British Rail, created fresh spaces in which these speculative property companies could operate.

Landownership is an important source of wealth and income. It has a wider social significance, however, that is important in relation to class. Some owners regard land purely and simply as a route to rents or profits. For others this is not the case. Many small farmers feel a strong bond to 'their' land (whether owned or rented). The landed aristocracy and gentry are also often deeply attached to particular pieces of land which hold a deep symbolic value for them. Ownership of specific tracts of land also helps define the status of particular social groups and delineates the social relationships around which life in the countryside revolves – though perhaps this was more true of the 1950s than the 1990s. Ownership of specific areas of land helped define the 'traditional' social order in the countryside by virtue of the status that it conferred upon the gentry and aristocracy. Reflecting this, landownership became a status symbol for successful urban bourgeois, seeking to mimic the life-styles of the landed aristocracy. This persistent, if socially changing, group of influential rural landowners helped shape the conservative character of much of the post-war planning system, designed to prevent or contain change.

3.3   Who owns the companies? Capital, share ownership, wealth and incomes

As the foundation of private enterprise capitalism, company shareholdings are crucially important; thus ownership of the companies is a politically sensitive issue in capitalist societies. Sustained debates as to the merits of privatisation and nationalisation, and over multinational companies undermining national governments' economic strategies, bear testimony to this. Ownership of these companies is equally crucial in structuring links between class, power and income and is, therefore, central to understanding inequality.

3.3.1   *Individual or institutional share ownership? Share ownership and corporate control*

Broadly speaking, the twentieth century has seen a change from personal to institutional shareholding in the UK. Personal shareholding was dominant until the early years of the century. As late as 1963, personal ownership of shares still stood at almost 59 per cent. Since then it has fallen substantially to 37 per cent in 1975 and to 20 per cent in 1992, despite the growth in numbers

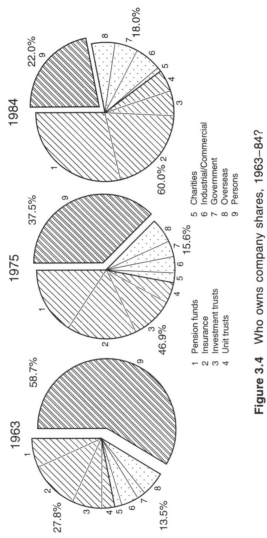

Figure 3.4 Who owns company shares, 1963–84?

Source: *Financial Times*, 11 January 1986

1 Pension funds
2 Insurance
3 Investment trusts
4 Unit trusts
5 Charities
6 Industrial/Commercial
7 Government
8 Overseas
9 Persons

of individuals owning shares. The break-up of personal and family share-holdings created space for a reconcentration of share holdings via the growth of institutional shareownership: from 21 per cent in 1957, to 47 per cent in 1975 and 60 per cent in 1984 (Figure 3.4) and 1990. This has involved financial institutions, such as unit trusts, mobilising the small savings of millions of people (see Minns 1980). For many others the decisions have been taken for them by pension fund managers, responsible for the funds of occupational pension schemes and, increasingly, for individuals' personal pension plans. In this sense very many people have become involuntary and indirect shareholders.

There has undoubtedly been a dilution of family control over private companies. Many of the remaining family participants in such companies became passive 'rentier' shareholders, content to withdraw from active control over corporate strategies and to draw their unearned incomes in the form of dividends, etc. Many continue to do so. There is equally no doubt that growing institutional share ownership has been associated with growing centralisation of control and concentration of output in a small number of major conglomerates that have become increasingly internationalised. It has not, however, led to any generalised real democratic control of the management of such large companies. Small firms (and their owners) have by no means disappeared – quite the contrary – but the strategic significance of transnationals in determining the trajectory of national economies has increased enormously.

For some, the growth of major transnational conglomerates, with a less concentrated pattern of share ownership, was interpreted as bringing a more diffuse distribution of power and control. This supposedly heralded the demise of buccaneering figures such as 'Tiny' Rowland, with his personal 12 per cent stake in Lonrho. To some extent, this is true but it is important not to overstate the point. For example, the growing internationalisation of the economy helped create space for entrepreneurs such as Richard Branson, Robert Maxwell, Rupert Murdoch and Alan Sugar to increase the scale and variety of their activities. Private share ownership may have fallen but it remains highly concentrated amongst a small number of powerful individuals and families: in 1975, the top 1 per cent of wealth holders held 54 per cent of all privately owned shares (see, for example, Rubinstein 1981). Little has changed since.

It is, then, important not to underestimate the continuing significance of either personal and family control or of the entrepreneurial capitalists. What is remarkable is that family control and influence remain so pervasive – with active family control in 29 per cent of the largest 250 companies in 1976, compared to 44 per cent in 1904. This indicates the continuing existence of a small group of individuals and families which possesses enormous power and derives great monetary incomes and wealth from company profits.

In some cases, continuing personal or family control depends upon majority or total shareholding. Companies such as Barings, Littlewoods and

Rothschilds are 100 per cent family-owned. In some — Pilkington, Marley and Mercury Securities — family share ownership was less than 10 per cent. In others exclusive control was achieved with minority shareholdings. Dispersed institutional shareholdings have created the space for what Scott (1986) terms controlling 'constellations of interest' to emerge. These are based on minority shareholdings and complex interconnections between the largest enterprises. By 1976, 100 of the largest 250 UK firms were controlled by such 'constellations of interest'. There has been a growing concentration in strategic decision-making power precisely because of this trend. We would agree with Scott (1986, 96) that: 'the growth of "institutional shareholding" has resulted in the rise to dominance of a relatively small group of enterprises involved in fund management. Clearing banks, merchant banks, insurers and investment groups, together with a handful of large industrial pension schemes, have achieved a virtual monopoly over the mobilization of capital'.

This 'monopoly' over key investment and disinvestment decisions lies not only with a small group of companies but with a very few key decision-makers within them. The senior investment executives of the 10 largest investment institutions control around £100 billion of investment — some 25 per cent of the share valuation of the London Stock Market and 10 per cent of national gross domestic product (*Independent on Sunday*, 10 February 1992). Moreover there are considerable links between these key 'controllers'. Several pivotal merchant banks and investment groups remain under family control. Thus a very small élite take decisions that, directly and indirectly, affect the (earned and unearned) incomes of the great majority of the population.

The criteria on which these investment and disinvestment decisions are taken are, therefore, critically important. Pension fund managers, for example, are legally obliged to seek the maximum rate of return on their investments to maximise returns to those drawing pensions. Despite some revival in profits in the UK, this led to further internationalisation of their investments in the 1980s (see Table 3.3). Their success in this was reflected in booming profits and contributions 'holidays' (periods when contributions were waived) for some pension funds in the second half of the 1980s. There is a clear conflict between seeking to maximise the incomes of pensioners (or at least some of them, as class differences affect which pensioners benefit from the activities of these companies) and the numbers of jobs, and the wages and conditions attached to them, in the UK.

Growing foreign investment by pension funds in the 1980s was not simply a UK-specific 'Thatcher effect'. It also reflected broader global tendencies of deregulation and internationalisation, though ones that Thatcherism helped set in train and encouraged. Moreover, there is a long history of foreign investment by UK capital and investment in the UK by foreign capital. This was historically related to the UK's imperial role. Since 1979, however, the scale of these activities has increased, with an expansion of overseas investment and of foreign investment in the UK in direct response to government policies.

Table 3.3 Pension fund investment: asset mix and geographical distribution

	% of total			
	1979	1984	1987	1989
UK equities	44	47	54	53
Overseas equities	6	16	14	21
UK bonds	23	17	10	6
Overseas bonds	—	—	1	2
UK property	22	13	9	9
Overseas property	—	—	1	1
Other	5	7	11	8

Source: *Financial Times*, 19 March 1990

Investment abroad by UK-based banks, finance houses and manufacturing concerns soared after 1979, especially in the USA, whilst there was a smaller inflow of multinational investment into the UK. A survey of investment patterns in 1988 by the KPMG international accountancy firm, revealed that investment outside the UK by UK-based companies was still increasing. It greatly exceeded, both absolutely and relatively, international investment by the UK's main competitors – Japan, West Germany, the USA, France (reported in the *Financial Times*, 13 March 1989).

This growing two-way movement of capital was seen by Mrs Thatcher's government as central to the Two Nations project and as important in reinforcing the role of the City of London as a global banking and financial centre. Underpinned by high interest and sterling exchange rates, and encouraged by the restructuring of financial markets driven by the catalyst of the 'Big Bang', foreign capital flowed in. This was also seen as central to 'solving' the problems of manufacturing in the UK and the UK's share of inward investment in industrial countries rose rapidly in both absolute and relative terms (Table 3.4). In particular, inward direct investment by Japanese

Table 3.4 The UK's share of inward investment in industrial countries, 1971–89

	1971–80	1981–84	1985–87	1988–89
Total ($bn)	16.7	30.4	56.2	127.0
of which (%)				
UK	29.7	13.2	15.0	18.0
EC (excluding UK)	31.8	25.1	22.3	27.8
Non-EC	38.5	62.7	62.7	54.2

Source: OECD (cited in *Independent on Sunday*, 10 February 1991)

capital was intended to engender new working practices and increased productivity. Nevertheless, whilst there are well-publicised examples of Japanese companies establishing new flexible working practices via careful recruitment on greenfield sites (see Hudson 1992), there are substantial limits to the extent to which their example has been or can be successfully followed in existing factories (Income Data Services 1990).

The converse of facilitating the flow of foreign transnational investment into the UK was that UK companies became free to locate abroad in search of greater profits. In turn, these could be repatriated to help alleviate pressures on the balance of payments once the visible account slid into deficit, especially as North Sea oil revenues declined. For others, however, an increasingly deregulated, open and internationalised economy posed problems rather than offered solutions; profits were repatriated from the UK, technological dependence deepened, and more jobs and wages became dependent upon decisions by 'foreign' transnationals.

It is perhaps too early to reach a conclusive judgement as to the merits of the Thatcherite strategy. The burgeoning balance-of-payments deficit from mid-1988 (well before any major decline in North Sea oil production), growing import penetration and falling competitiveness of exports raised serious question marks about its effectiveness, even in its own terms, during Mrs Thatcher's premiership. The re-emergence of these problems, along with an immanent fiscal crisis of the state, in the 1990s cast considerable doubt on the value of the economic legacy of the 1980s. What is less debatable is that growing international capital flows have implications as to where unearned incomes arise, how and between whom they are distributed, for the income levels of those reliant upon pension fund performance, and for opportunities for waged work in the UK. A growing number of companies and individuals are dependent upon a very small number of key decision-makers for the forms and levels of their money incomes. These key decision-makers are thus influential in the creation and remoulding of inequalities.

3.3.2   Big firms, small firms and their owners

An important part of the Two Nations political strategy of radical Thatcherism was, partially and selectively, to reverse previous trends towards big companies and institutional ownership. This was to be achieved via the encouragement of new small firms and mass share ownership as part of a new enterprise culture. Although the economy has increasingly been dominated by 'big' companies, small firms and their owners, though reduced in importance, have not disappeared. Nurturing them was central to the political economy of Thatcherism via policies to encourage the formation and growth of small firms. Specific initiatives, such as the Enterprise Allowance Scheme, and changes in taxation, were introduced to encourage this.

The *petite bourgeoisie* has important ideological effects, if only because it is the custodian of certain 'core' capitalist values. Proprietors tend to emphasise the desirability of the market, personal ownership and profit as rational resource allocation mechanisms. This is reflected politically by right-wing parties which, in turn, shape the parameters of political debate, and so the core elements of the political culture. The *petite bourgeoisie*, however, is also a very heterogeneous group. Scase (1982), for example, points out that it is composed of minor landlords, small capitalists and the self-employed. Curran et al. (1987) stress that the self-employed are not small business owners without, as yet, employees but are involved in the economy in different ways. Such differences have implications for their class positions and also for how they obtain their incomes. Undoubtedly, creating an 'enterprise culture' is a project that simultaneously involves economic and class restructuring within the UK. It also has related gender and racial implications, for example in the emergence of a largely male Asian fraction of the self-employed and *petite bourgeoisie*. But the very heterogeneity of the *mélange* of groupings which comprise the *petite bourgeoisie* imply that it is not obvious what promoting 'small firms' would in practice mean in terms of the restructuring of social relationships.

Against this background, we consider some empirical evidence about small firms and the *petite bourgeoisie*. In 1980 about 5 per cent of the population were self-employed workers (mostly non-professionals) and 2 per cent were small-business owners (employing 1−24 employees). Small-business owners and the non-professional self-employed were drawn from a narrow range of social backgrounds. There is considerable intergenerational transfer of small firms and sources of self-employment. Moreover, manufacturing was conspicuous by its absence from the activities of both small-business owners and the self-employed. Services of various types were by far the dominant areas of activity (although there are significant numbers of small businesses and of the self-employed in agriculture: see pp. 58−60). This situation markedly contrasts with claims that technologically sophisticated manufacturing forms the core of the small firm sector.

To what extent have more and new sorts of small firms sprung up in the 1980s and 1990s? This is not an easy question definitively to answer, for government statistics do not provide an up-to-date picture of self-employment. Data from the *Labour Force Survey* estimate growth as follows: 1981−83, 51 000; 1983−84, 275 000; 1984−85, 115 000; 1985−86, 17 000. This led to suggestions that there was a 'one-off' burst of growth in 1983−85, as an adjustment to the new political economy of Thatcherism, with self-employment levelling out at around 2.6 million people, 11 per cent of the labour force. By 1991, the number of self-employed had further risen to 3.3 million − slightly down from the peak 1990 figure − but representing 13 per cent of the labour force. Much of the post-1985 growth was associated with transport (reflecting deregulation), construction (a booming housing market) and various services, such as hairdressing and dry cleaning. The policies of Two Nations politics have, therefore, in many ways reinforced existing patterns of small firm growth rather than radically altered them.

Claims that a new spirit of enterprise has transformed the economy should be treated with considerable scepticism. Some government policies do encourage small firm formation and growth. Others, however, such as high interest rates, contributed to the existing difficulties of small firm survival, let alone growth. As yet, at least, the evidence does not suggest a dramatic revival and expansion into new innovative activities of the *petite bourgeoisie* in the UK in the 1980s and 1990s. Rather it suggests limited growth of a restricted range of occupations in various service sector activities, providing low monetary incomes both to employees of small firms, their employers and the self-employed alike.

There are good reasons for questioning the sort of economy that such small firms growth produces and for believing that it is unlikely to become very different in future. The concentration of small firms and self-employment into particular segments of the service sector is not accidental; rather it is structured by the niches into which they are able to fit within the economy. There are definite relations between big and small capitals which structure the activities and sectors of the economy to which the latter are confined. The 'independence', 'autonomy' and 'glamour' provided by becoming a small business owner are, typically, more illusory than real. This positive up-beat – and gendered – image is epitomised in TV advertisements about a bank helping small businesses as he exchanges the keys of the company Porsche for independence whilst she does the same later. Many small businesses are set up in response to the terms and conditions of employment in big business or as a defensive response to the reality or threat of unemployment, encouraged by government policies such as the Enterprise Allowance Scheme.

In this sense, the 1980s may have witnessed a broadening of the social base of new small firm owners, reducing the importance of inherited wealth as the criterion for becoming a small business person. These small firms are typically established in marginalised sectors of the economy where the monetary rewards are modest. Indeed, maximising income may not be the prime motivation for setting up such businesses. In most cases, a small business is part of an individual or household survival strategy, and one that has definite limits to it, even though it promises great wealth for some. As mounting bankruptcies and company failures in the recession of the early 1990s dramatically revealed, however, the risks attached to becoming one of the new class of entrepreneurs could be very great. Business failures more than doubled between 1989 and 1991 to 49 000. No less than two thirds of the 46 000 failures in the first nine months of 1992 were bankruptcies of individuals acting as sole traders or in partnerships (*Financial Times*, 20 October 1992). Although the economic impact of small firms may be marginal, there are considerable ideological effects which made the promotion of independent, self-reliant small businesses central to the Two Nations political project of radical Thatcherism. It remains to be seen if these will survive the wave of bankruptcies of the early 1990s.

Encouraging the growth of mass share ownership and reversing the trends of previous decades – a decline from 2.5 million individual shareholders in the 1950s to 1.75 million in 1981 – is another important element in this project. Both Mrs Thatcher's and Mr Major's governments set out via legislation and privatisation (offering shares at very attractive prices) to alter the climate for individual shareholding. As with so many aspects of Thatcherism, however, the seeds for this were sown by the preceding Labour government, as a result of the Lib–Lab pact in 1977–78. The Liberals secured the introduction of profit-sharing legislation with tax incentives, as part of their price for supporting Mr Callaghan's government.

The succeeding Conservative government rapidly reinforced this initial breakthrough with various schemes to widen further employee share ownership. In 1980 it granted tax incentives to a save as you earn employee share option scheme and, in 1984, introduced an executive share option scheme. The introduction of the personal equity plan (PEP) scheme at the beginning of 1987 represented a further mechanism to try to 'deepen' wider share ownership. Up to £2400 per annum could initially be invested and, subject to a short qualifying period, no tax is payable on reinvested dividends, or capital gains. The annual limit was later raised to £7000, equally split between individual shares and unit trusts. By September 1987, 200 000 people had taken out PEPs, investing £350 million – an average of £1750. By the end of March 1991 PEPs to the value of £3.88 billion had been taken out by 1 470 000 individuals – an average of £2640 (Board of Inland Revenue 1992). It is again mostly those who are already relatively wealthy who take advantage of such schemes. In an attempt further to broaden the base of share ownership, employee share ownership plans (ESOPs) were introduced in 1988, but again with limited effect.

As well as these specific measures, more general tax changes encouraged increased individual share ownership by the more wealthy: for example, cutting the top rate of income tax from 83 to 60 per cent and then to 40 per cent; abolishing the 15 per cent investment income surcharge; and halving the rate of stamp duty to 1 per cent. As a result of introducing inflation adjustment for capital gains tax, and increasing the tax threshold sixfold, only the wealthiest or most successful shareholders now pay it. However, the government's privatisation programme has played the decisive role in its attempt to promote mass share ownership and not just a revival of personal shareholding amongst the affluent middle and upper classes. This becomes clear if we examine changes in patterns of personal shareholding.

The 1984 share option scheme increased shareholding by senior managers and company executives, allowing companies to offer them options worth up to four times their salary. Any resultant gains are liable only to capital transfer tax, not income tax, provided the beneficiaries wait three years before exercising their options. Subsequent transition changes reduced these advantages somewhat but did little to slow the growth of this scheme. By March 1991 there were almost 4800 discretionary share option schemes in existence (*Financial Times*, 22 October 1992). A majority of senior executives participated in such schemes. For comparison, in over 11 years, only 840 profit-sharing schemes were introduced and in over nine years only 800 save as you earn schemes were taken up. The combined 1989 value of profit sharing schemes (£1.5 billion) and SAYE Option Schemes (£3.6 billion) was less than that of the discretionary share option schemes (£5.9 billion), whilst the latter was concentrated in a much smaller number of individuals (*Financial Times*, 4 May 1989). Growing shareholding amongst senior managers as well as board directors, especially in bigger companies (Table 3.5), has resulted in a growing reliance upon a share of profits rather than merely their (often considerable) wages for their monetary incomes. Between 1988 and 1991, for example, the average value per employee of shares distributed via executive option schemes was around £20 000 whilst that of all-employee SAYE schemes was around £2000. These newly acquired options are not without some risk, as the October 1987 Stock Market crash revealed. Even so, the potential gains, for some, are enormous. Sir Ralph Halpern, Chairman of the Burton Group, exercised options on 545 000 shares at 21p – making a £1.6 million profit. More spectacularly still, 16 London Weekend Television senior managers became paper millionaires overnight in 1993 with the conversion of previously unlisted management and listed preference shares into ordinary shares (Table 3.6), as they became the main beneficiaries of a share scheme set up in 1989. In all, this yielded £70 million for 54 former and current employees of the company (*Financial Times*, 27 August 1993).

For many managers a logical extension of increased shareholding has been a management buy-out, especially when 'their' company has been faced with closure. These too grew rapidly in the 1980s but fell sharply in the 1990s as the effects of recession bit deeply (Table 3.7).Clearly many buy-outs represent a

Table 3.5 Executives holding share options, 1987

Company turnover (£m.)	Percentage of:	
	Main board directors	Senior managers
1–40	62	21
40–150	76	28
150–300	88	20
300–1000	77	38
1001 +	97	70

Source: *Financial Times*, 28 November 1988

Table 3.6   The   main   beneficiaries   of   London   Weekend
Television's share scheme

Christopher Bland, chairman	£9.15m.
Greg Dyke, chief executive	£6.87m.
Ron Miller, sales director	£6.87m.
Brian Tesler, deputy chairman	£6.87m.
Melvyn Bragg, arts controller	£2.87m.
Nick Elliot, managing director, LWT Production	£2.87m.
Peter McNally, ex group director	£2.30m.
Robin Paxton, managing director, LWT broadcaster	£2.10m.
John Kaye Cooper, entertainment controller	£1.70m.
Marcus Plantin, ex programme director	£1.60m.
Philip France, market director	£1.60m.
Derek Hamment, sales director	£1.60m.
Sydney Perry, managing director, Granada/LWTI	£1.60m.
Mike Southgate, managing director, London studios	£1.60m.
Roy van Gelder, ex personnel director	£1.60m.
Barry Cox, director, corporate affairs	£1.60m.

Source: *Financial Times*, 27 August 1993

Table 3.7   Management buy-outs, 1967–91

	Number	Value (£m.)	Average value (£m.)
1967–76	43	n.a.	n.a.
1977	13	n.a.	n.a.
1978	23	n.a.	n.a.
1979	52	26	0.50
1980	100	40	0.40
1981	170	120	0.71
1982	190	235	1.21
1983	200	230	1.15
1984	190	260	1.37
1985	230	1030	4.48
1986	270	1230	4.56
1987	300	2820	9.40
1988	400	5074	12.7
1989	450	6450	14.3
1990	500	2830	5.7
1991 (1st 9 months)	250	1280	5.1

N.B. These data are estimates
Source: *Financial Times*, 5 July 1986 and 13 October 1988

form of small firm formation under new ownership but the average size of buy-out increased sharply until the early 1990s; October 1987 witnessed the largest (to date) management buy-out in the UK, with the sale of the MFI furniture group by ASDA for £715 million. Those who become new owners via management buy-outs − not all of whom would necessarily have previously been shareholders − undergo a transition that has profound implications for their class position and source of monetary income.

A parallel trend to the growth of management buy-outs in the 1980s involved the growth of buy-ins. The first significant buy-in was the take-over of the ailing Woolworths retailing chain by Paternoster in 1982. By 1989 the annual value of buy-ins rose to £3.9 billion, largely due to the £2.1 billion buy-in of Gateway by the Isosceles consortium. In these cases, however, the class implications are rather different since the new owners install fresh management teams rather than managing their new companies themselves.

Without doubt, however, privatisation has been the main mechanism for encouraging, and in some respects successfully attaining, more widespread share ownership and the growth of 'popular capitalism' (Table 3.8). Between 1983 and 1987 the proportion of the population owning shares rose from 5 to 23 per cent: shareholding became much more evenly spread over both age

Table 3.8   Britain's shareholder profile, 1983–87

(a) Total share ownership		%	Number (approx.)
	1983 (pre-BT)	5	2.0
	1984 (post-BT)	8	3.2
	1986 (post-TSB)	17	7.0
	1987 (post-Gas)	23	9.4
(b) Number of companies invested in		%	Number (approx.) millions
	one	56	5.4
	two	22	2.1
	three	9	0.3
	four	8	0.8
	five	3	0.3
(c) Percentage of shareholders in different socio-economic groups	1983	1987	83/87 change
Professional employers and managers	56	26	− 27
Intermediate and junior non-manual	26	34	+ 8
Skilled manual	12	26	+ 14
Semi-skilled and unskilled manual	6	11	+ 14
Total	100	100	

Source: *Observer*, 25 October 1987

groups and socio-economic groups. Forty per cent of shareholders in the newly privatised companies were manual workers, for example. By 1991 some 25 per cent of the population were shareholders, although this fell quite sharply to 22 per cent in 1992 as the impacts of recession became evident and individuals sold (or were forced to sell) recently acquired shares. Clearly the government has successfully convinced many people, via its massive advertising campaigns, of the merits of taking up underpriced shares. This has often been in monopolistic companies such as British Telecom or British Gas which have a direct impact on their daily lives. Syd has not been without influence.

On the other hand, mass share ownership remains a thin veneer rather than something that is deeply embedded in the fabric of the nation. Mr Major's government, like its predecessors, is acutely aware of the need to 'deepen' share ownership if 'popular capitalism' is to be firmly established. It still has a long way to go, however. In particular, the majority of shareholders hold shares in only one or two companies, mostly acquired via privatisation. According to estimates by the Confederation of British Industry, by the late 1980s there were only around 1 200 000 employee shareholders (cited in *Financial Times*, 4 May 1989). This is less then 10 per cent of potential employee shareholders – not least because many of those who acquired shares in this way subsequently sold them. The greatest volume and value of shares remain heavily concentrated in a small number of individuals and families. Moreover, despite the widening of the share-owning base, the proportion of shares that were personally owned continued to fall. Private individuals continued to be net sellers of shares; for example, net sales amounted to £19.8 billion in 1989, £7.8 billion in 1990 and £2.6 billion in 1991. In sharp contrast, in 1992 there were net purchases of £3.6 billion of equities, as the collapse of the housing market seemed to have a much more marked impact than years of Thatcherite rhetoric as to the merits of popular capitalism. It remains to be seen, however, whether this amounts to anything more than a temporary reversal, in very specific circumstances, of a longer-term trend.

Whilst wider share ownership marginally alters the source of monetary income for many people, great inequalities remain in share ownership, strategic decision-making power and access to unearned incomes. To some extent, the government would like to narrow these inequalities, although in practice its policies have had the opposite effect. Deepening share ownership and 'sedimenting' it more widely throughout the population is vital to securing the permanent establishment of the 'enterprise culture' and to bringing Mrs Thatcher's own cultural revolution to fruition. Mr Lawson, when Chancellor of the Exchequer, was keen to promote direct ownership of shares for political reasons, so that the investor (and potential Tory voter) is more closely involved in the capitalist economy. This eloquently illustrates the ideological and political implications of promoting 'popular capitalism'. Mr Major's government is equally under no illusions as to the importance of 'deepening' share ownership. As with the promotion of small firms, encouraging mass share ownership represents one aspect of Mr Major's vision of a classless society and a strategy for class restructuring in the UK in the 1980s and 1990s.

3.4 Working for a wage: wage labour and money incomes

Despite recent falls in the number of employees in employment and Mrs Thatcher's attempts to create an enterprise culture and popular capitalism, the vast majority of the UK population must work for a wage or depend directly upon the wages of others. There have been and still are great variations between industries and occupations in the ways in which people experience wage work, in their forms and levels of wage incomes, terms and conditions of employment, and the extent to which employees are subject to or exercise authority in the workplace.

3.4.1 The changing pattern of industrial employment

We begin by summarising the main points about these labour market changes in the period of One Nation politics. Total employees in employment fell from a peak in 1966, to a low point in 1973, and then rose somewhat sporadically to another peak in 1979. Mining and manufacturing employment declined significantly and consistently after 1966; industries were differentiated by the rate at which employment shrank. In contrast, service employment grew, both in the public and private sectors, though within this very heterogeneous category there was great variation. Service sector expansion was associated with declining male and growing female employment and declining full-time and growing part-time employment.

There are undoubtedly great, and changing, variations in wage levels within manufacturing and the services. However, as successive *New Earnings Surveys* reveal, in broad terms there had already been an important further shift towards a service-based economy over most of the post-war period, with a greater preponderance of poorly paid part-time jobs (typically taken by married women) in sectors such as distribution, professional and scientific services (education, health) and miscellaneous services. In part, this was encouraged by state policies towards employers' National Insurance contributions, taxation policies and the exclusion of part-time workers from basic 'fringe' benefits such as sickness benefit, holiday entitlement and pension rights. To some extent feminist demands for jobs that are more appropriate to the needs of people with child-care responsibilities, as well as trade union demands for a shorter working week and less overtime, also accelerated the growth of part-time work.

During the era of the Two Nations project, the labour market tendencies established over the preceding years have been both reinforced and modified as a result of government policies (Table 3.9). Between 1979 and 1983, as a direct result of government economic policies, full-time employment in manufacturing collapsed. This was mainly a loss of relatively well-paid jobs although in industries such as clothing and footwear manual workers are poorly paid. Consequently, the UK labour market became characterised by low-wage but relatively highly productive labour (see Figure 3.5) – and as such increasingly attractive to inward investing companies seeking to penetrate the European Community market. Service sector employment was, in aggregate, stable but with a further switch from full-time to low-wage part-time work. Overall, the number of people in employment fell by almost 9 per cent in four years.

This aggregate decline was partially reversed in the next six years. Full-time male employment in manufacturing fell only marginally – a slowing down that reflected the scale of the preceding 'shake out'. Female full-time employment grew much more. The major areas of growth were in the services, especially of part-time work for women. By 1987 almost one-quarter of employees in employment worked part-time whereas only one-sixth had done so in 1979. Employment then fell sharply in the early 1990s, with particularly heavy losses in manufacturing and in full-time employment. Part-time work continued to expand, however, though at a much reduced pace.

Service sector growth in part resulted from government policies to promote the City of London as a global financial centre. Almost one-half of all employment growth since 1979 has been in financial services. Much of the increase

Table 3.9   Changes in employees in employment, 1979–91, thousands seasonally adjusted

	December of:				
	1979	1983	1987	1989	1991
Total	22 670	20 670	21 474	22 302	21 363
Full-time	18 787	16 031	16 232	16 768	15 602
male	13 172	10 847	10 744	10 831	10 068
female	5 615	5 185	5 488	5 937	5 534
Part-time	3 383	4 639	5 242	5 534	5 661
male	n.a.	798	921	972	1 000
female	3 383	3 841	4 321	4 562	4 581
Service industries	13 328	13 337	14 672	15 242	15 180
Manufacturing industries	7 053	5 349	5 028	5 101	4 620
Other industries	2 289	1 984	1 774	1 969	1 563

Source: Training Commission (1988): Department of Employment (1992)

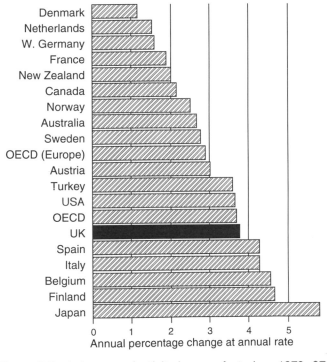

Figure 3.5 Labour productivity in manufacturing, 1979–87

Source: OECD

has been of part-time and poorly paid jobs (for example, in contract cleaning and catering), not least in the City itself. In this, it resembles much of the remaining service sector growth, concentrated in retailing, distribution, hotels and catering. This restructuring of the service sector, and the creation of a private sector service economy characterised by part-time, poorly paid jobs, were facilitated by the dismantling of Wages Councils. In addition, there has been revived growth in employment in personal services. The increased wealth of the new middle classes based on two-income professional households, led to demands for domestic cleaners, nannies, au pairs, and housekeepers, articulating new links between new middle and new working classes. This exemplifies the growing dichotomy within the service sector: some well-paid full-time jobs, but many more poorly paid ones, both part-time and full-time. Moreover, much of the growth in such service sector employment was associated with the increased significance of small firms as a source of waged employment (Tables 3.10 and 3.11). Companies employing less than 20 people created a net increment of 295 000 jobs between 1985 and 1987, as compared to only 20 000 by all larger companies (Department of Employment 1990). This trend subsequently continued in more muted form, with such firms

Table 3.10   Job generation by company size, 1987–90

Size	Net job creation (services)	As % of 1987 employment
1–4	357 (250)	29.4 (35.4)
5–9	166 (103)	10.7 (14.6)
10–19	92 (44)	4.7 (6.2)
20–49	76 (46)	5.8 (6.5)
50–99	85 (46)	7.4 (6.5)
100–499	123 (75)	6.2 (10.6)
500–999	55 (26)	9.8 (3.7)
1 000–4999	36 (36)	3.4 (5.0)
5 000–9999	14 (8)	2.8 (13)
10 000 +	125 (72)	3.7 (10.1)
Total	1 127 (708)	7.7

Source: Department of Employment (1990)

Table 3.11   Small firm growth, 1963–86 (firms employing 1–99 people)

	Number of enterprises	% share enterprises	% share net output
1963	58 166	88.7	11.8
1970	69 095	91.1	13.9
1979	84 229	93.9	14.6
1986	125 503	96.4	19.3

Source: Advisory Council on Science and Technology (1990)

creating almost 400 000 new service sector jobs between 1987 and 1990 – over 55 per cent of the total service sector increase. It seems highly likely, however, that this trend will have been reversed in the recession of the early 1990s.

These labour market changes had important repercussions on trade unions, with a great fall in membership. Between 1979 and 1985 manufacturing employment fell by 13 per cent. Trade union membership in manufacturing employment fell by 24 per cent, however, because job losses were concentrated in the heavily unionised manufacturing industries, such as shipbuilding, steel and engineering. 'New' manufacturing jobs were often in non-union plants as union membership was traded off against higher wages and enhanced fringe benefits. For example, 63 per cent of electronics plants in Scotland's 'Silicon Glen' and 86 per cent of high-tech health care companies in Scotland are non-unionised. More generally, employment gains have been concentrated in non-union service industries. Furthermore, there has been an unprecedented legislative assault on trade unions as one of the defining characteristics of the Two Nations project. As a result of these various changes, comparing the position in 1990 with that a decade earlier, there were fewer members of trade unions (a little more than 10 million), fewer employees covered by collective bargaining, fewer shop stewards, fewer closed shops and fewer strikes, according to the 1990 *Workplace Industrial Relations Survey*. The unions have not, however, been passive objects in this changing pattern of labour demand. Some have actively competed with one another for sole negotiating rights in one-union plants. But these changes undoubtedly have posed great problems of organisation for them in attempts to protect jobs, wages and working conditions, and in politically representing their members' interests. By the early 1990s, Gillian Shephard, Secretary of State for Employment, felt able to comment revealingly on relations with the trade unions in this way: 'There was a war in the 1980s but that is now over' (quoted in the *Financial Times*, 16 July 1992). With strike activity in 1991 at its lowest level since records began a century ago (Bird 1992), in a labour market characterised by high unemployment and low-wage flexible jobs for many of those in employment, there was considerable evidence to support her view.

3.4.2 *The changing pattern of occupations*

There have been important changes in the occupational pattern over a long period. There were four main ones in the 1970s (Brown, R. 1984): increased professional and managerial jobs, both for men and women; growth in routine clerical jobs, with a decline in male employment being more than offset by a growth in female employment; a decline in male jobs in manufacturing; and substantial losses of male jobs in unskilled labouring and in transport. The effects of these are clearly revealed in Table 3.12, which summarises the position in 1981. This is as near an approximation as it is possible to get to the start of Mrs Thatcher's period of office, using available statistics. The vast majority of employees – over 80 per cent – held occupations that lacked any significant degree of authority, though with important differences between men and women. Even so, there was considerable differentiation in the occupational structure of the wage-earning middle and working classes. Junior non-manual workers (mainly female) stood in a different position in the labour market to (mainly male) skilled manual workers, for example. Whilst the available data for 1991 are based on a different classification (Tables 3.13 and 3.14) they suggest a more sharply differentiated occupational structure than a decade earlier.

Table 3.12 Persons economically active, by socio-economic group, 1981
(percentages)

Socio-economic group (SEG)	Men	Women	Total
1. Employers and managers in central and local government, industry, commerce, etc., large establishments	5.5	2.1	4.1
2. Employers and managers in industry, commerce, etc., small establishments	8.7	4.3	7.0
3. Professional workers: self-employed	0.9	0.1	0.6
4. Professional workers: employees	4.5	0.9	3.1
5. Intermediate non-manual workers	7.3	14.4	10.1
6. Junior non-manual workers	9.5	37.3	20.3
7. Personal-service workers	1.1	12.2	5.4
8. Fore 'men' and supervisors: manual	3.6	0.7	2.5
9. Skilled manual workers	26.3	4.0	17.6
10. Semi-skilled manual workers	13.6	10.4	12.3
11. Unskilled manual workers	5.8	6.7	6.2
12. Own account workers (other than professional)	5.3	1.8	4.0
13. Farmers: employers and managers	0.7	0.1	0.5
14. Farmers: own account	0.7	0.1	0.5
15. Agricultural workers	1.2	0.5	1.0
16. Members of armed forces	1.6	0.2	1.0
17. Inadequately described and not stated occupations	3.5	4.2	3.8
Total	99.8	100	100
Total number	15 527 000	9 879 000	25 406 000

Source: Census of Population (1981), Economic Activity in Great Britain, Table 17, HMSO

Table 3.13 Occupational analysis of persons in employment by SOC (Standard Occupational Classification) major groups, spring 1991 (percentage)

	Men	Women	Total
1. Managers and administrators	17.8	10.1	14.5
2. Professional occupations	10.4	8.3	9.4
3. Associated professional and technical occupations	8.0	10.0	8.9
4. Clerical and secretarial	7.0	27.3	15.9
5. Craft and related	23.8	3.7	15.0
6. Personal and protective services	5.7	13.6	9.1
7. Selling	5.3	11.2	7.9
8. Plant and machine operatives	14.1	5.1	10.2
9. Other	7.6	10.6	8.9
10. Inadequately described/not stated	0.2	0.2	0.2
Total number	14 159 000	11 034 000	25 194

Source: Naylor and Purdie (1992)

Table 3.14 Occupational change, 1984–91

	Thousands		
	1984	1991	% change
Managerial and professional	6868	8571	+ 24.8
Clerical and related other non-manual	3546	3936	+ 11.0
Other non-manual	1779	2004	+ 12.6
Craft and similar occupations	3993	3861	− 3.3
General labourers	302	150	− 50.2
Other manual	6584	6671	+ 1.3

Source: Naylor and Purdie (1992)

3.4.3 Incomes, rewards and deprivations

Over the period of the One Nation project, occupational differences in incomes tended to narrow, although they remained of considerable magnitude (Table 3.15). Male income differentials between occupational groups have expanded dramatically in the years of Two Nations politics, however. Over the period 1973–79, occupational groups which had a fall in real earnings were all towards the top of the incomes distribution. In sharp contrast, between 1979 and 1986 these groups received the largest increases. More generally, non-manual occupational groups received greater relative real earnings increase than did manual ones. This difference continued to widen in the second half of the 1980s. This points to a growing differentiation between and within the middle and working classes in terms of wages. Despite more rapid growth in the 1980s, wages in many non-manual occupations (especially for women) remain far below those in manual occupations (especially men). The main point, however, is that the overall distribution has widened significantly in the 1980s. In 1979 a worker in the top 10 per cent of the income distribution earned, on average, 2.33 times as much as one in the bottom 10 per cent; by 1987 this had increased to 3.0 times as much.

As income inequalities have grown so sharply in the 1980s, we will look in greater depth at those occupations associated with particularly high and low remuneration. The Royal Commission on the Distribution of Incomes and Wealth (1976) revealed that, in 1974–75, 65 000 individuals had annual incomes of £10 000 or more, representing about 0.3 per cent of those receiving employment income. High-wage earners were concentrated in general management (55 per cent) and in professional and related occupations supporting management (including lawyers, company secretaries, accountants, marketing and advertising managers), administrative civil servants, local government officers and so on. Many of this group experienced a slight fall in income in the remainder of the 1970s but, especially in the private sector, generally

Table 3.15 Changes in earnings for occupational groups, 1973–86

	Average wage (£) 1973	% change 1973–79	% change 1979–86	Average wage (£) 1986
By gender				
Males – manual	157.1	5.0	5.7	174.4
– non-manual	190.0	1.0	22.4	244.9
Females – manual	82.6	20.5	8.0	107.5
– non-manual	104.2	14.9	21.7	145.7
Selected occupational groupings				
Professional, management and administrative	243.4	– 4.8	28.7	296.2
Managerial (excluding general management)	206.8	– 1.0	20.6	246.8
Clerical	142.9	2.6	16.7	171.0
Catering, cleaning and other personal services	123.6	5.7	8.7	142.0
Farming and fishing	117.1	4.0	6.4	129.5
Making and repairing (excluding metal and electrical)	166.9	– 0.8	7.0	177.2
Painting and assembling	157.1	3.2	3.2	167.4
Constructing and mining	159.8	4.9	3.0	172.6
Transport and storage	154.9	7.1	4.0	172.4

Note: Average wage is calculated in real terms with respect to 1986 levels, and refers to gross weekly and male earnings
Source: Adams et al. (1988)

experienced large wage increases in the 1980s (Reward Group 1992). They remain those in which incomes are highest, often very high indeed. By 1992 the average salary of managers had risen to £30 000 and that of company directors had risen to almost £69 000 (Remuneration Economics 1993). On average, almost 15 per cent of their pay is in the form of profit-related bonuses rather than basic salary, as Table 3.16 shows. For the very highest earners in company boardrooms – who receive astronomical salaries, as is shown in Table 3.17 – the performance-related payments assume much greater significance, although often these bear only a tangential relationship to actual performance. Increasingly, they are the key factor that enables boardroom base salaries to rise at around twice the rate of those of the workforce as a whole. In addition, however, the complex links that exist between directors on the remuneration committees of many major companies subtly serve to create a climate in which there is an inbuilt dynamic for directors' salaries to rise (*Independent on Sunday*, 24 November 1991; see also Table 3.18).

In contrast, selling, catering, and cleaning figure prominently amongst those occupations characterised by low incomes. These are precisely the sorts of jobs that expanded rapidly in the 1980s, concentrated in industries characterised by

Table 3.16 Remuneration of company executives and senior managers, 1979–89

Type of job	Average total money (£)	Percentage of holders of each type of job who receive the following:								
		Full use of company car	Subsidised private telephone	Help with housing	Life assurance	Free medical insurance	Share option scheme	Loans at low interest	Bonus	Bonus at % of recipients' average salary
Managing director	64 516	100.0	61.7	11.3	96.7	91.5	41.7	8.5	55.8	21.7
General manager	40 300	95.0	50.8	18.8	93.6	90.9	36.0	15.5	56.2	18.1
Financial heads	38 749	97.7	45.8	6.9	96.0	90.1	34.2	4.3	55.2	17.9
Marketing heads	38 012	96.6	43.7	11.3	96.2	86.1	38.4	10.0	54.6	17.0
Production heads	38 235	98.8	51.6	10.7	97.6	94.6	28.3	2.5	49.6	15.3
Purchasing heads	25 806	78.3	25.4	6.2	94.3	73.4	18.4	6.7	40.8	15.1
All executives, 1989	30 355	78.6	37.4	8.9	95.2	75.5	23.7	4.7	44.1	15.9
All executives, 1979	11 089	69.0	—	6.5	92.8	50.6	10.5	9.0	43.9	12.5

Source: *Financial Times*, 4 October 1989

Table 3.17   The highest paid company directors in the UK, 1988 (earnings over £500 000)

Sir Ralph Halpern	Burton Group	1 359 000[*]
Christopher Heath	Baring Brothers	1 339 219
Lord Hanson	Hanson Trust	1 263 000[*]
†	Robert Fleming	1 238 000
†	Anglo Leasing	1 205 000
John Gunn	British & Commonwealth	988 647[*]
Robert Noonan	Marrier Estates	935 463
Sir John Nott	Lazard Brothers	816 731[*]
Richard Giordano	BOC Group	782 300[*]
Herve de Carnoy	Midland Bank	748 458
Robert Bauman	Beechman	693 474
'Tiny' Rowland	Lonrho	656 251
Michael Slade	Helicar Bar	653 000
†	WCRS Group	622 000
George Davies	Next	561 152[*]
Maurice Saatchi	Saatchi & Saatchi	500 000[*]

Figures relate to most recent financial year.
[*] Chairman
† Highest paid director
Source: *Financial Times*, 5 October 1988

Table 3.18   Directors' and executives' salary increases, 1988–89

	Company	Old salary	New salary	% rise
Henry Wendt	Smith Kline Beecham	428 000	1 160 000	171
Lord King	British Airways	178 600	385 791	116
Jonathon Agnew	Kleinwort Benson	276 630	509 000	84
Christopher Levington	TI Group	409 088	715 097	75
Eric Parker	Trafalgar	296 296	480 000	62
Bill Brown	Standard Chartered	170 000	272 000	60
Peter Grant	Sun Life	128 125	205 000	60
Lord Blakenham	Pearson	299 000	465 000	55
Neil Shaw	Tate and Lyle	349 019	534 000	53
Sir Paul Girolami	Glaxo	400 000	600 000	51
Michael Hepher	Abbey Life	204 600	307 000	50

Source: *Observer*, 29 April 1990

a plethora of small, labour-intensive firms in competition with one another, with little unionisation and, at best, weak collective bargaining. This is a combination that is strongly associated with low wages. The Thatcherite emphases upon encouraging small firms, weakening trade unions, people 'pricing themselves into jobs' and creating a service economy are all integrally linked to the incidence and persistence of low pay. Together they form a potent recipe for the expansion of a low-wage, labour-intensive service economy. By 1991 nearly one in three employers were illegally underpaying their staff, with such employers particularly concentrated in food retailing, cafes and snack bars, restaurants, hotels and pubs. This was seen as related to a reduction from 177 in 1979 to 64 in 1991 in the government's Wages Inspectorate (Low Pay Unit 1992).

Wages are only one form of monetary reward for work, however. There are also other 'fringe benefits', very unevenly distributed between occupational groups. There were, however, marked differences between occupational groups in entitlements to holidays with pay, sick pay and private pension schemes throughout the decades of the One Nation project. Generally, manual workers had much less access to such benefits than did non-manual workers. Within the non-manual group, rights to these benefits increased with status and responsibility. In the 1980s, this gap widened. 'Fringe benefits' became an increasingly important way of distinguishing between employees. Many company executives and senior managers receive a wide range of such benefits: company cars or car allowances; subsidised lunches; subsidised private telephones; life assurance; free medical insurance (Table 3.16). For all such executives, 'fringe benefits' impinge on many aspects of their life-styles and the extent to which they remain 'on the fringe' is debatable. Whilst other non-manual workers received less in both the range and amount of such benefits, in general they remained in a more favourable position than manual workers.

Despite some slight reductions since 1945, a 'clear class gradient' remained throughout the period of One Nation politics in terms of incomes and rewards (Brown, R. 1984). Subsequently, in the Two Nations era, this gradient became steeper, with sharper differences between occupational groupings of employees, a direct consequence of the political economy of Thatcherism and Majorism.

3.4.4 *Further differences between wage earners*

Changing corporate strategies and government policies have widened income differences between occupational groupings in other ways. Such growing divisions reflect three related processes of change in the 1980s: the emergence of more sharply differentiated and multiply-segmented labour markets; the continued development of internal labour markets within big companies; and a growing dichotomy between core and peripheral workers in the labour forces of big and small companies alike.

Companies have increasingly recognised the importance of constructing a committed core workforce by using a 'responsible autonomy' (see Friedman 1977) managerial strategy, although perhaps only 1 in 10 of larger employers consciously think of a core–periphery dichotomy in their labour force (McGregor and Sproull 1992). An important mechanism in creating this commitment is to increase employee share ownership and to link pay to performance and profit. On average, in 1987–88, companies paid over 16 per cent more to 'above average' as compared to 'adequate' graduate employees within five years of recruiting them. These performance premia varied widely between sectors, from 7 per cent in construction to 21 per cent in technical and scientific services. Companies have begun to adopt profit-related wages across the whole range of their employees, not just senior managers and highly skilled employees in short supply. By early 1988 430 companies, covering 70 000 employees, had registered schemes for profit-related pay with the Inland Revenue in response to provisions made in the 1987 Finance Act for tax relief on 50 per cent of profit-related pay. The number of schemes then rose steadily as successive Budgets made them financially more attractive. The 1991 Budget further significantly increased the tax-free profit payments allowed under approved schemes. The number of schemes then rose by over 25 per cent in the last three months of 1992, from 3268 to 4149, whilst the number of participating employees rose by 24 per cent from 780 600 to 973 000. The impact of such schemes on labour market behaviour was therefore becoming more generalised as Majorism continued to promote the Thatcherite project of popular capitalism.

This growth in performance and profit-related payments, often related to the introduction of decentralised wage bargaining, not only further differentiated between core and peripheral workers but also created divisions within the former group. Moreover, such changes are also related to redefinition of working practices, intensification of work, increased demands for flexible working and so on (see Atkinson 1984; Hudson 1989b). Whilst producing divisions within the bulk of the core workforce, performance-related payments have also enabled the gap between directors and senior managers and the rest of the workforce to grow. In addition, senior managers receive 'fringe benefits' denied to other employees. These sharply differentiate their recipients from workers who receive performance-related wage payments but are excluded from the lucrative world of fringe benefits.

The occupants of the core workforce fill more secure niches in the labour market than do those in the peripheral workforce. There is such great variety in the terms and conditions on which waged work is offered in this, often hidden, world of peripheral workers, that generalisations can be dangerous. The UK's growing army of part-timers, temporary workers, homeworkers and the self-employed – the so-called 'flexible labour force' – expanded by 1.15 million (16 per cent) between 1981 and 1985. Of this increase, 828 000 (72 per cent) was recorded between 1983 and 1985 and over 700 000 (60 per cent) was of temporary workers. These trends have since continued, though at a slower pace. There was an increase between 1984 and 1987 of 91 000 (7 per cent) temporary workers and of 133 000 (9 per cent) workers with second jobs, mainly as employees. Subsequently, the rate of increase in numbers of temporary jobs slowed whilst that in second jobs accelerated (Table 3.19). Even so, these data must be treated as conservative estimates, as many workers may not declare

Table 3.19 Temporary and second jobs, 1984–91 (thousand)

	1984	1987	1991
Temporary jobs	1310	1401	1453
Second jobs	703	836	1075

Source: Naylor and Purdie (1992)

second jobs and this form of employment shades into the 'black economy'. Moreover, the growth of the flexible labour force is forecast to continue for the rest of the 1990s: for example, the Institute for Employment Research forecast a growth of some 1.4 million part-time jobs between 1990 and 2000, with 1.0 million of these taken by women (cited in *Financial Times*, 8 January 1993).

Casual and fixed-term contract workers differ in their personal characteristics and in the industries and occupations in which they are most concentrated. Casual workers are most prevalent in three industries: distribution and hotels; agriculture; other services. Fixed-contract workers are concentrated in other services and construction. In terms of occupation, 25 per cent of all casual workers had jobs in catering and cleaning. The remainder mostly work in sales or in professional posts in health, welfare and education. Contract workers are more evenly distributed but with a concentration in teaching. Thus the growth of a service-based economy in the 1980s has been closely linked to the growth of casual working, although casual employment has long been endemic in service industries such as retailing, catering, hotels, pubs and clubs. More surprising has been the re-emergence of casualised work in some branches of manufacturing, such as steel (see Beynon et al. 1994). Such particularly stark instances of the re-creation of casualised work revive memories of an earlier and harsher era.

Many companies have taken advantage of persistent high unemployment to recruit staff directly on a casual basis, often at very low wage rates. To some extent, they have been aided in this by legislative changes. The 1986 Wages Act removed about 500,000 workers below the age of 21 from the protection of Wages Councils, and confined the latter to setting a minimum hourly rate and single overtime rate. Moreover, this was a rate that fell steadily from 80 per cent of the national hourly rate in 1981 to around 65 per cent in 1990. A further Bill published in December 1992 proposed to abolish the remaining 26 Wages Councils along with minimum pay rates for 2.5 million poorly paid workers, many of whom were women (see Chapter 5, p. 152). In 1909, Winston Churchill, who established the Wages Councils, told his fellow Members of Parliament that: 'It is a serious national evil that any class of His Majesty's subjects should receive less than a living wage in return for their utmost exertions.' In 1992, Mr Major's government was taking a radically different view as it travelled further down the deregulatory path of Thatcherism.

Even before this draconian change became enacted, however, the preceding 1986 Act had marked effects. It removed casual workers' (along with new full-time employees') guaranteed access to premium rates on bank holidays. This increased the incentive to recruit young casual staff. As a direct result, there was an estimated 10 per cent increase in casual and temporary staff in the retailing sector over the Christmas 1987 period. Such staff were often paid little more than £2.00 per hour but this simply represents the seasonal expression of a more widespread practice of recruitment of cheap casual labour in retailing. More generally, in 1986 25 per cent of all casual workers were aged 16–19 years and a further 12.5 per cent were aged 20–24. Casual work is endemic amongst the young. For many it represents their only chance of waged employment in the UK of the 1980s and 1990s.

Casualisation is not the only way in which divisions between core and peripheral workers, and within the peripheral workforce, have been redrawn. Sub-contracting has expanded greatly. Manufacturing output rose by 35 per cent between 1979 and 1984 but services purchased by manufacturing companies increased by 56 per cent, indicating considerable growth in sub-contracting as the anatomy of the social division of labour was redrawn. Half of the increase in service sector employment between 1979 and 1985 resulted from increasing sub-contracting from manufacturing. A 1987 survey in the West Midlands revealed that 39 per cent of workplaces had experienced replacement of directly employed labour by contractors. Increasingly, sub-contracting is being institutionalised as a planned part of companies' production strategies, increasing competition between sub-contractors. As a result, wages and working conditions for those employed in such companies have deteriorated.

In branches of manufacturing such as clothing and service activities such as packing, homeworking has long been important but there is evidence that in the 1980s it grew further (see Chapter 5, pp. 144–145; also, for example, Baloo 1989). At the boundary homeworking shades into the 'black economy', though the latter is by no means confined to homeworking. Small-scale sub-contracting firms have made increasing use of 'off the cards' labour to cut costs and increase their flexibility in hiring and firing. There has also been some growth in 'informal' activities which provide services to those in formal employment. Electricians, joiners, painters and plumbers, themselves often already in formal employment or self-employment, have found increasing scope for 'off the cards' work as other people engage in house improvement or maintenance. By definition, 'black' work is not recorded in official statistics so that it is impossible to estimate its precise extent. But it has undoubtedly grown in the 1980s.

It is important, however, to note that there is evidence that the flexible use of labour by bigger employers may be rather limited (McGregor and Sproull

1992; Hunter and MacInnes 1992; for evidence of such strategies, see Beynon et al. 1994). On the other hand, this may simply confirm that the growing use of flexible labour has been linked to burgeoning small firm growth. There are, however, those who would question in other ways whether the distinction between labour market 'insiders' with stable jobs and 'outsiders' in poorly paid part-time and/or precarious ones was, is or remains valid. Burchell and Ruberry (1989) for example, argue that there are five distinct types of workers in stable segments of the labour market, who have quite different levels of job expectation and satisfaction. Primary workers are largely male, well-paid and of higher social class. Stickers were mainly female and expressed greatest satisfaction with most aspects of their jobs, although these had lower levels of remuneration and fringe benefits. Female descenders had either quit paid work completely or moved to lower paid, part-time jobs in response to domestic pressure. Young and mobile males were a small group who were the most optimistic about their chances of getting a better job. Finally, male descenders, most of whom had been sacked or made redundant at some time, had slid into poorer jobs – or out of work and into the ranks of the long-term unemployed. This clearly presents a different picture of segmentation, but still one with clear implications for incomes, working conditions and life-style. However one conceptualises forms of work and wage relations, the diverse forms of changing wage relations outlined above share one common feature; they refer to individuals and households finding waged work on some basis within the UK. For others, this has either proved impossible or, alternatively, better prospects and wages have been perceived in becoming temporary international migrant workers. For many professional workers, working abroad for a time has been and continues to be financially lucrative. Increasingly, however, they have been joined by construction workers or redundant skilled manual workers from chemical plants or steelworks. Such jobs abroad are usually offered on short fixed-term contracts. However, the high rates of pay – even after agents' fees have been deducted – make them attractive, especially to younger men able to earn wages that were formerly unimaginable in the UK. This, then, represents an individualised response to the reality or threat of unemployment but it is an escape route that is denied to the vast majority, as we show in the next section.

3.5 On the dole

Following the mass long-term unemployment of the inter-war years, as the previous regime of accumulation collapsed into crisis, a commitment to 'full employment' was central to the post-war settlement and the regulatory mechanisms of One Nation politics. Between 1944 and 1975 governments of both parties sought to achieve this objective, though by varying means. At times, its pursuit came into conflict with other policy objectives, such as

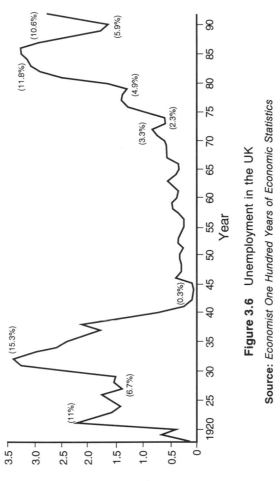

Figure 3.6 Unemployment in the UK

Source: *Economist One Hundred Years of Economic Statistics*

maintaining a satisfactory balance-of-payments position. The long post-war boom meant that these conflicts between policy objectives could effectively be masked, however. For most of the period between 1945 and 1970, unemployment rates in the UK were less than 3 per cent, with never more than 600 000 people registered as unemployed (see Figure 3.6). Following a sharp increase to 900 000 in 1972, unemployment fell in 1973–74 but there was then a fundamental change in governments' views on the priority to be given to 'full employment'.

In 1975 it became clear that the choices between competing government policy options had become harder and could no longer be fudged. No longer could the cracks be papered over. The Keynesian mode of regulation collapsed as international recession and deep structural weaknesses in the UK economy severely restricted the government's room for manœuvre. The April 1975 Budget ushered in the era of the Two Nations project as it confirmed that government economic strategy now centred on restraining the growth of public expenditure, cuts in real wages for most workers, and rising unemployment as deliberate policy choices. The Budget statement correctly forecast that registered unemployment would rise to over 1 million for the first time in 30 years because of the policies it contained; thus was the commitment to 'full employment' jettisoned.

Unemployment fell somewhat in the final year of the Labour government, but it began to soar after the election of Mrs Thatcher's government in 1979, reaching well over 3 million. Unemployment became a much more widespread problem in the UK than in other major capitalist countries (Table 2.1). Registered unemployment began to decline in the mid-1980s from its earlier giddy heights, but the fall owes much to the 28 changes in the definition of unemployment. From 1982, for example, only those claiming unemployment benefits, as opposed to all those fit and able to work, were counted. This alone removed 190 000 from the register. Even allowing for this downward massaging of the totals, registered unemployment remained at a very high level – around 2.3 million in June 1988. This considerably underestimated total unemployment. MacInnes (1989), for example, calculates that the real level of unemployment in June 1988 was 3.5 million – almost 50 per cent above the registered level. Even before the major change of definition in 1982, the Manpower Services Commission estimated that the actual number of unemployed exceeded the registered figure by 25 per cent. Whilst registered unemployment then fell rapidly, as the economy boomed, part of the fall was again due to a series of changes in 1988 and 1989 which removed 185 000 from the numbers registered.

Despite these changes, the probabilities of the unemployed successfully finding a job remained much lower in 1989 than they had been a decade earlier. Using data from the *Labour Force Surveys*, Payne and Payne (1993) show that in 1979 44 per cent of men who had been unemployed 12 months earlier had subsequently found work; by 1989 this had fallen to 32 per cent.

Whilst an improvement on the 25 per cent recorded in the depths of the 1981/82 recession, this still represented a serious decline in the chances of the unemployed finding paid work. By the early 1990s unemployment was again rising sharply. As registered unemployment approached the politically sensitive 3 million mark in early 1993, there were again suggestions that it was manipulated downwards; as one commentator put it, 'For two consecutive months the official count of unemployment has fallen. The trouble is, however, no one really believes the figures' (*Financial Times*, 20 May 1993).

During the long One Nation period, the incidence of unemployment was unevenly distributed between members of social classes, occupational groups, ethnic minorities, age groups, men and women, and between residents of different areas (see Hawkins 1978). This sort of uneven distribution is endemic to capitalist societies. Some of these aspects of inequality are explored in later chapters; here we focus upon the unequal impact of unemployment upon members of different classes and how this altered in the years of Two Nations politics.

The marked class bias in the incidence of unemployment widened further in the 1980s (Table 3.20). Manual workers (especially men) were more likely to be unemployed, and less likely to secure another job because of a lack of vacancies, than non-manual workers. Thus a growing proportion of long-term unemployed was of manual workers, especially unskilled males, permanently surplus to labour demand (except for that created by temporary job schemes). This growing pool of long-term unemployed – by February 1992 almost three-quarters of a million people had been unemployed for one or more years – is seen by some as part of an underclass (Morris 1993), more or less solely dependent upon government welfare payments as a source of income.

This is but one aspect of class and occupational inequalities. There is also an increasing flow of people on and off the unemployed register. This involves hundreds and thousands in any given month and is linked to the growth of casualisation, temporary contracts and sub-contracting. They

Table 3.20 Unemployment rates by occupation, 1979–92

	1979	1984	1989	1992
Professional		2.2	1.4	3.1
Intermediate	3.1	3.8	2.5	4.3
Skilled non-manual		6.4	3.8	6.4
Skilled manual	1.9	8.7	5.1	11.4
Semi-skilled	10.4	11.2	7.3	13.5
Unskilled		13.6	9.7	14.6

Note: excludes people unemployed for more than three years

occupy particularly precarious positions in the labour market and form a large disadvantaged group within the working class, disproportionately susceptible to unemployment. As a result of the uneven incidence of unemployment, 3 per cent of the labour force account for 70 per cent of unemployment weeks.

These groups are also disproportionately dependent upon state transfer payments for money incomes. There is a long history of state involvement with and inadequate provision for the unemployed. It can be traced back to the New Poor Law of 1834 which created two of the most powerful realities within the working-class experience of welfare: the means test and the workhouse. Its abolition in 1948 was linked to the introduction of a National Insurance scheme to provide unemployment benefit and maintain working-class living standards in short periods of unemployment between jobs in a 'full employment' economy. In fact, means-testing lingered on, for the new social security system involved two systems. Payments as of right were provided to those who had bought a certain number of National Insurance stamps. These payments could be in the form of retirement pensions or to replace earnings lost through sickness or unemployment. To cater for those ineligible for such payments, a National Assistance Board (NAB) provided means-tested benefits. Because it believed that means-testing caused considerable non-take-up of benefits, the Labour government in the 1960s changed the name of the NAB to the Supplementary Benefits Commission (SBC). This was an attempt to dissociate the image of the institution from the Poor Law of the past and give the impression that it would in fact supplement other forms of benefit. In practice, supplementary benefit continues as an alternative for those who never were or have ceased to be eligible for unemployment benefit. Already by the end of the 1970s 62 per cent of the unemployed in the UK were ineligible for unemployment benefit. This proportion has subsequently risen in parallel with youth and long-term unemployment.

The system of benefits assumed added significance within the parameters of the Two Nations project. The cutting edge of Thatcherite policy was to encourage the market to undermine state welfare and so recipients of unemployment benefit had, in some visible way, to be made worse off financially. They also had to be stigmatised as 'welfare scroungers', which served to divide them from those in work. In keeping with Mrs Thatcher's predilection for Victorian values, the legacy of the 1834 Poor Law lived on. In practice, this led to a series of changes that made the poor still poorer. In April 1981 earnings-related supplements for all short-term benefits (unemployment and sickness benefits, widows' and maternity allowances) were abolished. In addition, the statutory link between earnings and long-term benefits, such as pensions, was abolished and these were only increased in line with inflation. From July 1982 the Inland Revenue began to tax all benefits, including unemployment and supplementary benefits. This adversely affects those intermittently employed, for example, as casual labour. As a result of these 1981–82 changes, benefits were cut by £2200 million between 1979 and 1983 whilst the well-off and the rich received £2600 million in tax cuts – a clear indication of Thatcherite priorities.

Within the supplementary benefit system, there is discrimination against the long-term unemployed. Long-term sick, elderly or disabled claimants, receive a higher rate of benefit – but not the long-term unemployed. They are stigmatised as the 'undeserving poor', unemployed from choice rather than necessity. This is certainly one of the bleakest aspects of the Two Nations project. Even so, despite the real squeeze on the value of unemployment benefit, unemployment growth resulted in increased social security costs as a proportion of public expenditure. This in turn helped increase public expenditure as a proportion of GDP. Despite a decline from 1983–84, public expenditure in 1984–85 absorbed a greater percentage of GDP than in 1979–80 – in strong contrast to the declared aims of government economic policy. This was undoubtedly one reason for the changes in the social security system, as proposed in 1985, replacing supplementary benefit with income support. It lead to 1.4 million claimants being better off but 1.7 million being worse off. By the early 1990s, with Government borrowing soaring to an annual £50 billion, pressures to reduce this again translated to radical proposals further to emasculate the social security system, for example, via targeting single mothers as the new 'undeserving poor'.

Because of the costs to public expenditure, and for other reasons, the government has shown great interest in reducing registered unemployment by a plethora of temporary training and/or employment schemes. It has been very successful in this. At their peak in 1988 520 000 were absorbed by such schemes, though by 1991 this had fallen to 408 000 (Naylor and Purdie, 1992). These schemes originated in the activities of the Manpower Services Commission and the launch of the now defunct Job Creation Programme in 1975. By the early 1990s numerous schemes had come and gone, with varying objectives.

Questions have been raised about the adequacy of the training on offer and the provision of places relative to the numbers unemployed. Despite claims by the Manpower Services Commission (now the Employment Training Service) that quality of training was seen as a crucial strategic issue, suspicions persist that the commitment to retraining the unemployed in new 'high-tech' skills remains a token one. For example, the Community Programme, since its inceptionin 1982, has been structured to provide part-time, poorly-paid manual work. Like similar schemes, it is more concerned to shuffle existing low-paid jobs between a pool of unemployed, some of whom are at any one point in time employed in this way: eight months after leaving, for example, 55 per cent of participants in Community Programme schemes were again unemployed. The successor to this scheme, Employment Training, fared even worse; with training in England and Wales devolved to 82 employer-led Training and Enterprise Councils from 1990, 70 per cent of trainees over the previous twelve months once again became unemployed in 1992 (Unemployed

Unit, 1992). The main emphasis in government economic policy is on producing an expanding low-wage, low-productivity service economy, alongside a booming international financial services sector which can recruit key skilled employees on a global labour market if the need arises. While this remains so, there is little scope for large-scale, high quality (re)training programmes to provide highly skilled workers able to find well-paid secure jobs in manufacturing and services.

For the long-term unemployed, then, the future is one of dependency upon welfare payments, interspersed with spells on government temporary job schemes. In either case, they are, to borrow Pugliese's (1985) evocative phrase, 'clients of the welfare state' (or at least what is left of it) consigned to a future of minimal incomes. The long-term unemployed still bear the burdens of recession and are excluded from the benefits of renewed growth.

Although evidently aware of the political dangers of long-term unemployment, the government remains wide open to the charge that it is managing rather than resolving Britain's unemployment crisis. Governmental ambivalence reflects the actual gains as well as the potential danger that unemployment presents to it. For maintaining a 'managed' mass of unemployed – and the fear of those in employment that they might join it – provides a potent mechanism through which radical Thatcherite policies can be pursued. In Mr Lamont's infamous words in February 1992, when Chancellor of the Exchequer, mass unemployment was 'a price worth paying'. This deliberate creation of an 'underclass' of permanently unemployed, dependent upon state transfer payments in one form or another, is perhaps the most pernicious aspect of class restructuring in the UK in the 1980s and 1990s.

In this chapter we have examined the way in which class relations have been redefined in various ways as part of the political-economy of Thatcherism and how this is reflected in the distribution and sources of income and wealth. At one end of this process is the 'underclass' of long-term unemployed, created and maintained by state policies. It is simultaneously managed by part of the new middle class and separated from the working class. Its existence provides a context in which there is intense competition in the labour market as mass unemployment encourages divisions within the working class. These extend far beyond a simple non-manual/manual divide and allow a redefinition of the divisions between classes. For example, managerial authority can be (re)asserted in the workplace whilst growing income inequalities provide a material basis of increasingly differentiated life-styles. Earning a wage now tends to be a much more precarious process than it once was; the trend is strongly away from full-time regular jobs with predictable wages. For many, it has involved a switch to no job at all, for others to precarious employment. The Thatcher government encouraged these trends via its policies, informed by a view which was admirably summarised by Mr Norman Lamont, Financial Secretary to the Treasury in 1986. Mr Lamont asserted that the suggestion that employees need a guaranteed income to cope with household budgets rested on a 'misconception'. It is a misconception that the government has assiduously sought to eradicate via its policies and not without success. What must also be acknowledged is the political success of Thatcherism and Majorism in blurring perceptions of class boundaries, whilst leaving the fundamental structures of power and property ownership in the UK, if anything, reinforced. The extension of private property ownership, via council house sales, privatisation, share option schemes and so on has above all else conveyed the image of a mass property-owning democracy. Yet, in reality, wealth has become increasingly unequally distributed, as an already privileged élite (Standsworth, 1984) has further enhanced its privileges.

4

Divided by class II: consumption and life-styles

4.1 Introduction: class, consumption and life-styles

In 1957 Harold Macmillan (later Lord Stockton) remarked at a garden party in Bedford: 'Let us be frank about it. Most of our people have never had it so good.' This phrase, subtly modified to eliminate the reference to distributional inequality within a 'One Nation' political project, became a leitmotif for much of the post-war period. There has been a more or less steady increase in average per capita real disposable income and consumer spending although, since 1973, there has been more variation around this trend (Figure 4.1). Along with the growing number of two-income households, changes in work practices, shift patterns and increased leisure time and paid holidays, this has helped change consumption norms, the division of domestic and waged labour, and household life-styles. In contrast, the relative decline in the UK's position in the international economic order in recent years has been reflected in newspaper headlines such as 'UK living standards fall in world league'. One indication of this is that, in 1981, only Denmark and Germany of the UK's European Community partners would have seemed more expensive to a UK visitor but, by 1992, only Greece and Portugal would have seemed cheaper (CSO 1993). It remains to be seen whether the fall in 1991 is simply cyclical or whether it heralds a further fundamental change in the UK's place in the world.

As shown in Chapter 3, however, incomes remained unequally distributed around this rising average trend throughout the years of the One Nation political project. Since then income inequalities between classes have widened further as an integral part of the Two Nations project. These changing inequalities are related to both stability and change in class structure: stability in the reinforced position of the landed aristocracy and industrial and financial bourgeoisie, change in the recomposition of both middle and working classes, and the emergence of an 'underclass' (see Chapter 9) of permanently unemployed. In the 1980s and 1990s the gap in living standards between those in employment and the unemployed has taken on an increased significance. These changes reflect the effects of economic restructuring and employment

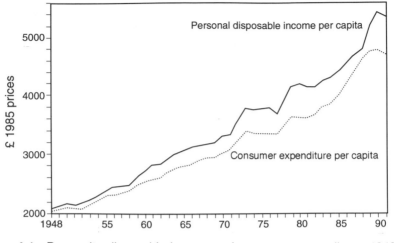

Figure 4.1   Per capita disposable income and consumer expenditure, 1948–91

Source: CSO, *Economic Trends*

change, taxation policies and cuts in welfare benefits that are central to the politics of Two Nations.

In capitalist society, living conditions and standards fundamentally depend upon money incomes and the capacity to buy goods and services in the market. Living standards are not reducible to monetary incomes, however, for there are important contributions – such as clean air, visual amenity, community, and attachments to people and places – that cannot be bought or sold. The resurgence of 'green' and place-specific politics reflects this, as is illustrated vividly by the fierce battle amongst local pressure groups over the location of the rail links from London to the Channel Tunnel entrance in Kent. Nevertheless, in an economy organised around commodity production, purchasing power in the market is crucial. Moreover, changes in tastes and new forms of consumption can influence what is produced – whilst producers seek to influence the pattern of demand.

Not surprisingly, there have long been great variations in consumption patterns, living conditions and standards. Equally unsurprisingly, as successive *Family Expenditure Surveys* reveal, these have increased over the last decade, both directly because of widening income differentials and indirectly, as those on higher, more secure incomes have drawn more and more upon easily available credit. By 1987, there were 13.1 million Visa cards and 11.4 million Access cards in circulation; in 1975 there had been 'only' 3.3 million and 3.1 million, respectively. Despite small falls in 1990 and 1991, associated with a switch in household behaviour from spending to saving in the face of recession, total consumer credit rose threefold from 1981 to reach £54 billion by 1991. By 1992 the personal debt to income ratio was at twice the level of a decade earlier. This dramatic rise was not attributable to a surge in conspicuous consumption, individual recklessness or gullibility, however. As the National Consumer Council (1992) stressed, the main cause of rising debt was an unexpected drop in income – not least because of rising redundancies and unemployment. Moreover, whilst the relatively affluent can secure access to bank loans and credit cards, poorer people, perceived as a bigger credit risk, of necessity have recourse to less formal and more expensive sources of credit, such as money-lenders.

Growing differences in living standards are not just a product of widening income and credit inequalities in the 1980s and 1990s, however. Divergent life-styles also reflect a more general change in political philosophy, expressed in decreasing public sector service provision and a growing reliance upon the market in shaping the distributions of services. Partially removing the provision of educational and health services from the sphere of the market had been a central element of the post-war consensus and the One Nation project. This was decisively reversed in the 1980s, with more and more emphasis on private provision through the market. At the same time there were increasing costs at the point of consumption for those educational and health services that are, as yet, still provided through the public sector. For example, a prescription that in 1979 cost 20p, in 1993 cost 475p.

In the remainder of this chapter we examine the patterns of inequality between classes (usually defined in terms of socio-economic or occupational groups) in four crucial areas that shape the quality of people's everyday lives; education; health; housing; consumption patterns and life-styles. We conclude by examining class variations in political allegiances and voting patterns.

4.2 Class and education

Education provides a crucial link between an individual's family background and his/her own life chances and class position (see Halsey et al. 1980; Burgess 1984). Access to different amounts, levels and qualities of education reflect parental social class. For most people, their formal education influences employment opportunities and class position, though for a few inherited wealth makes this relationship unimportant or irrelevant.

But how are these reciprocal links between generation, class and education to be understood? For some, the formal educational system is simply seen as a mechanism for reproducing class structures. It constrains the places of individuals within them to those occupied by their parents, grandparents and so on down the generations. For others, it is seen as helping reproduce class structures but facilitating the movement of individuals within these. For a few, formal education is perceived as offering a mechanism for progressively altering class structures themselves.

Greater equality of educational opportunity was an important element of

One Nation politics. No serious attempt was made, however, to abolish private fee-paying schools and the provision of education through the market for those able to purchase it. Likewise, no significant attempt has been made to abolish important qualitative differences between private and public sector provision of education. Nevertheless, state provision of, and public expenditure on, education was significantly increased at all levels from pre-school to higher education. This was intended to improve access to and equality of opportunity within the public sector. Equality of opportunity would provide a means to move more towards a more meritocratic, even egalitarian, society. What in practice happened in the decades of One Nation politics was rather different. Subsequently, with the ascendance of the Two Nations project, 'meritocracy' has been redefined in terms of ability to pay as 'merit' is rewarded through and reflected in the market for educational services.

One symptom of this is that the private sector, left substantially intact and *de facto* subsidised by the state (via tax relief on school fees) over the post-war period as the preserve of a small élite, began to expand in the 1980s. By the end of 1991, the Independent Schools Information Service claimed that independent schools had a 7.5 per cent share of the total school age population (compared to 2–5 per cent in the 1970s) and no less than 20 per cent of the 16–18-year-old group. There was particularly rapid growth in the second half of the 1980s. This was despite average fee increases that were well ahead of the rate of inflation. By 1989, average annual fees ranged from £6300 in senior boys' boarding schools to £2800 in preparatory day schools. These figures in themselves are powerful evidence of the effects of class and income differentials in generating inequalities in access to such schools. A survey by MORI for the Independent Schools Information Service revealed that of the 1989 entry, 58 per cent came from families with parents in professional occupations, compared to 7 per cent with parents in manual occupations.

Much of the increase in the 1980s resulted from parents who were dissatisfied with state educational provision. The MORI poll revealed that over 40 per cent of children entering independent schools in 1989 were from families in which neither parent had been similarly educated. The reasons given for this switch to the private sector are revealing: high standard of education – 34 per cent; state schools unsatisfactory – 22 per cent; discipline – 19 per cent; smaller classes – 17 per cent. Such views reflect an accurate perception of the situation; for example, whereas pupil : teacher ratios in the state sector remained around 19 throughout the 1980s, those in the private sector fell from 13 in 1981 to under 11 in 1991 (CSO 1993). Support for the view that state provision was inadequate also came from a seemingly unlikely source. Mr David Jewell, chairman of the Headmasters' Conference, suggested that a number of pupils at private schools were 'refugees' from the state system, adding that 'The underfunding has been a national scandal.' His female counterpart, Mrs Taliana Macaire, president of the Girls Schools Association, pointed out annual spending on each student for science instruction ranged from £24 to

£50 in the independent sector, as compared to £3 to £17 in the state sector (reported in *Financial Times*, 25 April 1990).

There is also strong evidence of recurrent class inequalities in access to and performance within state education at all levels. These inequalities have existed over the post-war period but widened further in the 1980s. At pre-school level, the 1979 *General Household Survey* revealed that well over half the children of professionals, employers and managers attended playgroups or day nurseries. They were much more likely to do so than children whose parents were in semi-skilled or unskilled occupations. This gap has subsequently widened. The 1993 Report of the Independent Commission on Education was strongly critical of inadequate levels of nursery provision. Whilst the numbers of children attending playgroups and nurseries rose, state provision fell. The largest increase was in children with registered childminders – up from 110 000 in 1981 to 273 000 in 1991 – as pre-school child care became effectively privatised, one part of the booming private service sector economy (see CSO 1993).

Differential access by class in turn tends to reproduce and widen differences in performance. Comprehensive schools were introduced in the 1960s at secondary level to replace the division between grammar and secondary modern schools. In conception – if not always in practice – they typified the spirit of One Nation politics. Many comprehensives stream pupils by academic ability, however, which tends to reproduce class inequalities. In addition, a failure to invest in education has led to many split-site comprehensives, cobbled together from existing schools. As a result, several of the objectives of comprehensive education have at best been partially attained in many schools.

Class inequalities have been magnified in two particularly important ways at secondary level. Firstly, there are enormous differences in the proportions of pupils staying on beyond minimum leaving age: 70 per cent of those whose parents are professionals, employers and managers compared to 27 per cent of those whose parents are manual workers. This is only the most striking manifestation of a more general process, however. Throughout the pupil's school career, there is a persistent class difference in survival and achievement rates. As parents' social class increases, the percentage of pupils without any formal educational qualifications decreases and the percentage with O levels (or equivalent), A levels and degrees rises. There is a marked class division in the proportions who survive in, and obtain formal qualifications from, the educational system. While there are also gendered and racialised divides (see Chapters 5 and 6), these are linked to rather than replace class differences. This class divide has been maintained, even increased, in the 1980s as successive *General Household Surveys* reveal.

Changes in the organisation and management of schools have further exacerbated this division. They lead to increasing differentiation between schools when, for example, parent governors in middle-class areas articulate their demands more effectively than those in working-class areas. In practice, streaming is being reintroduced as articulate middle-class parents seek places for their children in 'good' comprehensive schools. Schools are also prone to be more receptive to unproblematic and motivated pupils from 'good' family backgrounds, in response to the publication of 'league tables' of results. Furthermore, the devolution of financial management to individual schools has amplified tendencies to concentrate particular sorts of pupils in particular sorts of schools (see, for example, Smithers and Robinson 1991). This is especially so as schools that opt out of local authority control are more generously funded by central government.

Access to higher education shows a similar pattern of class inequality. The Robbins Report noted that children born in 1940–41 whose fathers had a professional background had a 33 times greater chance of entering higher education than those whose fathers were semi-skilled or unskilled manual workers. Although the situation has in some respects improved since then, with expanded state provision, considerable inequalities remain. There have been and still are powerful pressures which militate against children from working-class families going on to higher education. There are often material pressures to leave school before the sixth form to add to household incomes. Those who do stay on may find that working-class culture is not tuned to the needs of children striving for academic success. It is expressed, for example, in the absence of their own rooms and peace and quiet for doing homework. Such an environment may mean that academic ability is not translated into examination results. Even the most direct attack on class inequalities in access to higher education, via the creation of an Open University, brought no radical change. The situation continues to be that children of middle-class origin have a greater chance of becoming university graduates than those from the working class.

Class inequalities in access to universities widened in the 1980s (Table 4.1). The expansion of higher and further education after 1983 largely benefited children from professional and managerial homes who accounted for almost 70 per cent of the entry of 1989, compared to 62 per cent in 1977 (Smithers

Table 4.1 Social class of UK candidates accepted for universities (percentages), 1979–84

	Percentage accepted	
Social class	1979	1984
Professional, etc. occupations	19.8	22.1
Intermediate occupations	38.0	48.2
Skilled occupations, non-manual	21.1	10.1
Skilled occupations, manual	14.7	12.4
Partly skilled occupations	4.5	6.2
Unskilled occupations	0.9	2.1

Source: derived from UCCA statistics

and Robinson 1991). It is difficult to escape the conclusion that this at least in part reflects the effects of rising unemployment, concentrated on the working class, and the shrinking real value of the student grant, which has pushed a higher percentage of maintenance costs on to students or their parents. The switch to student loans and an admissions system in which as Lord Chilver, the Chairman of the University Funding Council, put it 'the student values education so highly that he or she is prepared to commit resources to it' can only widen class inequalities in access (quoted in the *Times Higher Educational Supplement*, 14 October 1988). The elimination of the binary divide between polytechnics and universities and pressures – for a while – greatly to increase numbers in the early 1990s did not result in a more socially equitable pattern of access but did instead diminish the unit resourcing of higher education.

In summary the educational system continues to be riven with class inequalities. They condition who gets access to what sort of education and how well children from different social class backgrounds perform in attaining formal educational qualifications. Thereafter, the type of education they receive influences the occupation that children enter on leaving the formal educational system. In this way inequalities in access to and performance within the educational system both reflect and help reproduce class structures within the UK.

Undoubtedly, access to 'top jobs' in UK society is closely constrained by class and educational background. Class structure and education are mutually reinforcing. The ruling élites (Church, armed forces, judiciary, Civil Service, Parliament, industry and business) are overwhelmingly drawn from the products of a very few public schools and universities, predominantly Oxbridge (see Miliband 1969). They continue to play a pre-eminent role in élite recruitment. The link between a select few public schools and the Oxbridge universities is particularly important in this respect. Public schools educate a small (though growing) minority of children in the UK but have usually provided 60 to 80 per cent of those holding these élite positions. In some instances, the role of the public schools has remained enormously influential and, sometimes, has increased. For example, in 1939 64 per cent of army officers of the rank of major-general or above had attended public schools, compared to 86 per cent in 1970. In other instances, there seems to have been some decline in their importance. For example, in 1939 84 per cent of under-secretaries and higher grades in the Civil Service had attended public schools, compared to just over 60 per cent in 1970. The trend for non-public school, non-Oxbridge educated people to rise to senior positions continued in the 1980s, exemplified when the Treasury's two most senior officials – Sir Peter Middleton and Sir Terence Burns – both fell in this category. It seemed that meritocratic principles were continuing to make progress, at least at these very high levels. An interesting twist to this theme is that there have also been changes in the Conservative Party. Whereas between 1918 and 1974 75 per cent or more of Conservative MPs attended public schools, by 1983 this had fallen to 63 per cent. This change is in fact symptomatic of the changing class basis of the Conservative Party, which Thatcherism both grew out of and reflects. It is symptomatic of Thatcherism's attacks on 'them' (as opposed to 'us'), on a patrician Conservative One Nation politics, reproduced through the old boy network of public schools and Oxbridge, and the alternative emphasis on self-advancement and reward based on labour and consumer markets.

Educational background and shared experiences have also been important in the social construction of industrial and financial élites in the UK. The City of London has constantly sought to erect non-economic barriers to entry by establishing exclusive associations. These gradually assumed a distinctive social character based upon the most prestigious public schools. More generally, over a long period, there was a broader trend towards the growing significance of a public school and Oxbridge education amongst directors of both industrial and financial companies. For example, in 1906 about 37 per cent of finance directors attended both a public school and Oxbridge whereas in 1970 52 per cent did so. This re-emphasises the very powerful and long-established connection between the educational system and the ruling élites at the pinnacle of the UK class structure, but the system has been subject to some changes.

In one sense, one of the seemingly few progressive aspects of the Thatcherite years was an 'astonishing change in the class and educational background of today's industrial leaders' (Hannah 1992). Both public school and Oxbridge declined sharply in importance as sources of chairpersons of major companies (Table 4.2). Whether this was caused by the politics of Thatcherism or owed

Table 4.2 Educational background of the UK's industrial leaders,[*] 1979–89 (percentages)

	1979	1989
(a) Secondary education		
Top public schools	18	2
Other public or fee-paying	40	22
Top grammar schools	8	16
Other grammar schools	10	24
Other maintained schools	18	30
Educated abroad	6	6
(b) University education		
Oxford	10	22
Cambridge	28	10
London	8	8
Birmingham	4	10
Other UK universities	6	16
Overseas universities	6	6
No university education	38	28

[*] Chairman or Chairwoman of top 50 companies, excluding banks and other financial institutions
Source: Hannah (1992)

more to new patterns of ownership and corporate organisation, or to changes set in motion in the 1960s, which emphasised the importance of technological skills, remains a matter for debate. In some respects, reform of the City via deregulation and the 'Big-Bang' in 1986 can also be seen as an attempt to shake up the network of 'old school tie' linkages in the City.

Channelling products of select schools and Oxbridge to key positions of control and power in the UK society nevertheless remains one key aspect of a more general process whereby occupational opportunities are differentially allocated on the basis of educational and class backgrounds. The small trickle of children of working-class backgrounds, educated in state schools, who graduate through Oxbridge to positions of decisive power serves in practice to legitimate a profoundly unequal system. It creates the illusion that anyone from the working class can transcend his or her class origins. This is manifestly not the case, for differential education and formal qualifications do influence the distribution of occupations. For example, people in professional occupations tend to possess higher educational qualifications more frequently than do junior non-manual workers; skilled manual workers tend to possess those educational qualifications that can be obtained in schools and colleges; and 'unskilled' manual workers possess few formal qualifications of any type.

These differentials tended to widen in the 1980s and 1990s, as successive *General Household Surveys* show, with growing unemployment heavily concentrated amongst the formally unqualified. For example, a study by the Manpower Services Commission in the late 1970s revealed that over 50 per cent of unemployed young people had left school without any qualifications whilst most of the remainder had poor CSE grades. One response to this has been the creation by the state of a variety of temporary employment/training schemes for young people, such as YTS and YOP. By 1983–84 25 per cent of all 16-year-old school-leavers were engaged in such schemes. Access to them often depends upon the same criteria as are used in recruitment to permanent jobs: those with some formal educational qualifications are taken in, those with poorer or no qualifications are not.

Educational qualifications continue to be a key to the transition from school to work and from school to youth training schemes as well as into employment or unemployment. It is significant in this context that there have been cutting criticisms of vocational training policies for those aged under 18 years, with claims that they are in danger of producing a certificated, semi-literate underclass (Jarvis and Prais 1988). The Training and Enterprise Councils in England and Wales, and their Scottish counterparts, are supposed to guarantee places for all school-leavers. However, they do not always do so and there are also criticisms of the quality of training they provide and the types of skills that this transmits. In contrast, affluent upper- and middle-class parents can buy access to additional courses for their children to boost their competitiveness in the labour market. This is, however, now more likely to involve enrolment in a Berlitz language school or a prestigious secretarial course than a spell in

Swiss finishing schools. Moreover, as access to higher education expanded whilst labour demand fell – with a record 12.9 per cent of those who graduated in summer 1993 still unemployed in December 1993 – the ability to acquire such extra skills may well become increasingly important in securing employment.

Differential access to education both reflects and reproduces class inequalities. In the immediate post-war period, most men went into an occupation that was the same as, or similar to, that of their father. For most women, waged work was still seen as a temporary prelude to marriage and a life of domestic labour. Subsequently, there was some alteration in this pattern, although the working class remains largely self-recruited. A limited amount of long-range mobility via Oxbridge offered an important avenue for a small number of individuals from the working and lower-middle classes. For most, however, opportunities for mobility between classes have been more restricted. Perhaps the most significant change has been the growth of the service class. Only about 25 per cent of the service class (approximately defined as professionals, managers and employers) has been self-recruited and indeed it was recruited from all other classes in roughly similar proportions – providing opportunities for many women in the process.

Many commentators would argue that the main reason for these changes lay in the expansion of and improved access to the educational system over the last 40 years or so. But in fact class inequalities in opportunity in schools have been remarkably stable. Tawney's comment in 1931 that 'the hereditary curse upon English education is its organisation along class lines' remains as valid now as then. Others argue that changes in educational provision since 1944 have merely facilitated changing patterns of service class recruitment. This suggests that patterns of occupational change have been more important in producing mobility than has the educational system. Educational changes helped meet the changing labour demands of capitalist production in the UK as the growth sectors of the economy altered. Changes in schools in the 1980s – such as a core curriculum, 'opting out' and the increasing emphasis upon inculcating the enterprise culture in schoolchildren – are part of a policy to restructure state educational provision in schools to bring it more into line with the needs of the Two Nations political project.

For many years it was argued that equality of opportunity should be a central educational goal (see, for example, Blackstone 1979) but this goal is unattainable without first achieving a greater degree of equality in society itself. Equality of opportunity can no longer be seen as the principal mechanism through which to move to a more meritocratic society, let alone an egalitarian one. In an era in which society is becoming more unequal and government policies strongly encourage this tendency, abandoning even the goal of equality of opportunity, class divisions in access to and performance within the educational system can only widen further.

4.3   Class, health and health care

Few would deny the importance of good health, yet persistent class differences remain in health conditions, in the incidence of different diseases and in mortality rates. Such evidence is certainly not new, but it was most effectively marshalled in the politically controversial 'Black Report', which the Conservative government attempted to suppress (Townsend and Davidson 1982). This report revealed marked class inequalities in health conditions, perhaps most dramatically in differential death rates. It is worth quoting (355–60) on this point:

> . . .at birth and in the first month of life, twice as many babies of unskilled manual parents (Class V) die as do babies of professional class parents (Class I) and in the next eleven months four times as many girls and five times as many boys. A class gradient can be observed for most causes of death. . .if the mortality rate of Class I had applied to classes IV (semi-skilled manual) and V during 1970–2, 74,000 lives of people under 75 would not have been lost.

Differential class experiences of ill health and premature death continue throughout life. Moreover, despite the creation of a universally available National Health Service – perhaps the key institution of the One Nation project – class differences increased between the 1950s and the 1970s. Possibly the single most important finding of the Black Report is the lack of improvement, and in some respects the deterioration, in the health experience of semi-skilled and unskilled workers and their families relative to professionals during the 1960s and 1970s.

Such differences have, at a minimum, persisted or even widened during the 1980s – and are likely to have done so further in the 1990s. The most salient finding of the 1987 *Health and Life-style Survey* was marked class inequalities in the experience of ill health and in the incidence of disease. In some respects the health of the lower occupational classes has deteriorated against a backdrop of general improvement in the population as a whole. Managers and executives may be more prone to stress-related ulcers and cardiac complaints but middle-aged men in the lowest income groups are three times more likely than those with the highest incomes to report frequent illness. One expression of this is that a disproportionate number of older applicants for the Job Release Scheme in the mid-1980s were low-paid, semi-skilled and unskilled workers. This relates to a broader point: the growing significance of increased unemployment in widening health inequalities within the Two Nations project. The unemployed are more likely to suffer from ill health than those of the same age who are in employment. Detailed longitudinal studies reveal evidence of increased ill health associated with the threat of redundancy, redundancy itself and subsequent unemployment (for example, see Beale and Nethercott 1985).

There is undoubtedly a growing divide between the health conditions of those in and out of work and, more generally, growing class inequalities in health conditions in the last decade or so.Why should such inequalities exist – and why should they have widened recently? In so far as they reflect more hazardous working conditions associated with some occupations, then labour market changes should have narrowed differences. On the other hand, persistent and widening differences in incomes impose differential constraints on living conditions in terms, for example, of housing or consumption patterns, nutrition and environmental conditions; these generate widening inequalities in health conditions.

This raises broader issues about government policies towards health inequalities to which we return below. First, however, we focus upon the more specific issue of class differences in access to health care. This must be seen in the context of the creation and evolution of the National Health Service (NHS). The original goal of the NHS was to guarantee equality of access to health care, irrespective of income or class position. Prior to the NHS, there was a diverse system of health care provision, strongly class-biased, with access to facilities determined by capacity to pay. The NHS inherited those facilities. From the outset it was characterised by tensions between the need for public investment to modernise inherited facilities and build new ones, and pressures to limit public expenditure. Nevertheless, in the three decades following its establishment, public expenditure on health care increased enormously, if unevenly and intermittently, but without removing class inequalities in access to care. Health care is regressively allocated; those in greatest need receive least. The Black Report spelled out the reasons for this. The relatively educated, affluent middle classes are able to influence the organisation of health care services within the NHS to meet their own perceived needs. Class differences in access to NHS health care reflect a 'social inverse care law', with the middle class in a more favoured position than the working class, who are less able to use its services effectively (for example, see Phillips 1979). The reduction in NHS provision relative to growing needs in the 1980s and 1990s has exacerbated this situation and reinforced the social inverse care law.

Differential access to NHS care is only one facet of class inequalities. Private sector provision was not abolished with the creation of the NHS – indeed, in important ways the NHS presupposed a continuing private sector. The option of private sector health care has remained for those who can afford it. Furthermore, in the last decade or so, private sector provision has expanded as the emphasis on market provision became more prominent. In the early 1970s there were about 4500 (out of 36 000) beds in private hospitals and nursing homes for acute cases, with about another 4500 private beds in NHS hospitals. Most of the private institutions were non-profit-making charities and trusts, such as Nuffield. From 1977 private sector developments were influenced by the expectation that the Labour government would eliminate pay beds in NHS hospitals. This led to rapid growth in the provision of private beds for acute care, especially around London: by 1979, there were around 6600.

Private health care continued to expand (Mohan 1988). Acute beds in private hospitals increased from 6600 in 1979 to over 10 000 in 1985; the number of hospitals rose from 149 to 201. This growth was concentrated in the 'for profit' sector which increased from 61 to 106 hospitals and from 1900 to 4400 beds, in response to very high rates of return. In 1981, these were estimated at 15–30 per cent, on a turnover of £330 million. This led to increasing investment by multinational capital in health care provision in the UK. Companies such as American Medical International (with 12 hospitals and 1200 beds), Hospital Corporation of America, Humana, and St Martin's Property Investment (owned by the Kuwaiti Investment Office) expanded their activities. It was a very selective investment, avoiding areas of medical care where the need for investment was high and/or profitability was low, and was concentrated around the location of greatest purchasing power, London.

As well as growth in acute care, there has been an increase in private sector sheltered and nursing homes for the elderly, a reflection of greater longevity among those able to afford such facilities. These doubled to 5100 between 1981 and 1984. They are projected to go on rising as the population ages and as the number of elderly in long-term care outside the NHS rises at 6000–7000 a year for the foreseeable future.

There undoubtedly has been selective widening of access to private medical care through perks such as BUPA membership for senior managers (Table 3.16). By 1989 75 per cent of company executives' medical insurance policies were wholly paid by employers. State policies (via tax reliefs, hidden subsidies to cut private sector costs and so on) have also helped in this tightly defined broadening of access. Despite such tinkering at the margins, access to private health care remains strongly class biased, powerfully rationed by capacity to pay. A slightly larger minority of people now have access to private sector care whilst standards of provision have declined for the vast majority reliant on an NHS constrained by government expenditure restrictions. The gap between the privileged few and the rest of the population has increased. By the early 1990s, however, there were growing difficulties in the private sector as the recession hit individual and corporate spending on private health care and insurance, a sharp reminder of the limits to private provision.

The policies of successive Thatcher and Major governments exacerbated the class inequalities summarised as the social inverse care law. The then Secretary of State for Social Services, Patrick Jenkin, summarily dismissed the recommendation of the Black Report for reducing health care inequalities: 'I must make it clear that additional expenditure on the scale which could result from the report's recommendations – the amount involved would be upwards of £2 billion a year – is quite unrealistic in present or any foreseeable economic circumstances'. This stance could perhaps be defended in the context of a deep national economic crisis in the early 1980s, albeit of the government's own making. Subsequent attitudes towards expenditure on the NHS cannot even be justified in this way. NHS expenditure has increased in the 1980s and the

1990s, but there is widespread agreement that it has not matched the growing need for medical care. Priorities became crystal clear in 1988, when the government preferred further tax cuts for the wealthy (on a scale not dissimilar to the £2 billion figure mentioned by Mr Jenkin) and a £15 billion repayment of the National Debt, rather than boosting NHS funding. Mrs Thatcher's administration increasingly regarded the NHS as a rump organisation to provide minimal medical provision for the unemployed and poor. The structural inequalities that generate the social inverse care law were deepened by a government that displayed no commitment to the equitable provision of health care.

The original goals of the NHS have clearly been rejected. It can no longer credibly be maintained that there is equality of access to health care in the UK. This is no longer a goal on the government's political agenda. Despite denials to the contrary, it is difficult to see any significant change in the position since Mrs Thatcher was succeeded by Mr Major. Yet this relict of One Nation politics – perhaps its most powerful symbol – cannot be lightly dismissed without significant political (and electoral) costs. Therefore, the emphasis is on cost cutting within the NHS via the generalised transformation of hospitals into independent trusts, the creation of an internal market for medical care services, and the encouragement of fund-holding general practitioners. This is part of a broader strategy of shifting the blame for inadequate service on to allegedly inefficient doctors who are incapable of managing their budgets, whilst setting up pseudo-profitability efficiency criteria as the guiding ethos of the health system. As a result the NHS increasingly becomes a commercial rather than a public service.

There has been, however, considerable confusion amongst government ministers as to whether there are class differences in health conditions and access to health care. For example, in March 1981, Patrick Jenkin, Secretary of State for Social Services, claimed that there was evidence to refute the claim that the working class suffered poorer access to health care. Other government ministers, notably Mrs Edwina Currie, subsequently conceded that the working classes do suffer from poorer health, whilst denying that this has anything to do with levels of NHS provision and class differences in access to medical care. Headlines such as 'Hospitals cuts axe 3000 beds' (*Financial Times*, 8 March 1988) are not significant for Mrs Currie, whereas they actually represent a widening of inequalities in access to care and health conditions. Rather than being a product of the social inverse care law, to Mrs Currie the poorer health of the working classes is a function of ignorance and a predilection of unhealthy foods such as fish and chips and sugary tea. As such, it is to be tackled by individuals changing their diets and life-styles rather than by government provision to narrow class differences in access to care. To some extent people could change to a healthier diet and life-style, but simply to blame the poor for their particular choice of cheap foods is to ignore the social processes that lead to low incomes and poverty in the first place. Class differences in health conditions go beyond class inequalities in access to health care, important though these are. A complex of social and economic factors affect health and all favour the better off. Consequently, reducing inequalities in health crucially depends on measures to reduce differences in material standards of living at work, in the home and in everyday community life (see Chapter 9). In particular, tackling class inequalities implies the general need for an anti-poverty strategy. This raises the question of the extent to which an attack on class inequalities in health conditions and care in the UK is possible. It is clearly incompatible with the existing pattern of class relations in the UK and with the government's promotion of privatised health care provision in which the market is the supreme allocator of resources.

4.4 Class, tenure and housing

Relations between class, incomes and housing are complicated. In general, those with higher incomes can afford to buy better quality dwellings in more desirable surroundings whilst many of the less affluent rent council housing. Some have suggested that tenure groupings represent 'housing classes' (for example, Rex and Moore 1967), others that owner occupation generates specific economic interests which are different from those of owners and non-owners of capital (for example, Saunders 1979). Yet others have been, correctly, critical of such views (for example, Elliott 1984). Location in the same tenure category can conceal enormous differences in housing experiences: that is, there are owner-occupiers and owner-occupiers, tenants and tenants, in terms of the size and quality of dwellings occupied. Class interests are not coincident with tenure, and tenure groupings do not replace class interests as a basis for social organisation and political practice. What is undeniably true is that homes represent a source of wealth for those who can afford to purchase a house (or houses) and for private landlords houses are a source of rental income. Home ownership has also acquired a broader political significance. The decades of One Nation politics were characterised by cross-party convergence on owner occupation as the preferred mode of tenure. This was carried over into the following years of the Two Nations project, but interwoven in new ways with themes such as privatisation and market provision.

There have been, over a long period, major changes in housing in the UK. Around 1900 90 per cent of households rented their dwelling from a private landlord. The remaining 10 per cent were owner-occupiers. The inter-war growth of owner occupation and the beginnings of local authority provision resulted in major changes. In 1947 60 per cent of homes were privately rented, 26 per cent were owner occupied, and 13 per cent were public sector rented. Since then, private renting has declined and owner occupation increased. Public sector renting grew after 1947 but has fallen in latter years, especially since 1979. By 1985 only 11 per cent of dwellings were privately rented,

27 per cent were publicly rented and 62 per cent were owner-occupied. By 1991, the comparable proportions were 7, 25 and 68 per cent as the trend away from renting and towards owner occupation continued.

The social class composition of each tenure group has also altered, but there is still a strong class differentiation in tenure. The 1981 Census of Population revealed that over 80 per cent of professionals, employers and managers were owner-occupiers whilst over 50 per cent of unskilled manual workers rented from a local authority. Moreover, there is a very marked class differentiation in second (and third) home ownership, which is also increasingly located abroad.

The benefits of wealth that owner occupation both confers and reflects also has a class basis. Because of owner occupation, intergenerational transfers of wealth have become increasingly important – though perhaps less so than seemed likely a few years ago. This reflects the early 1990s collapse of the housing market, especially in the South East. Older homeowners are also increasingly selling or transferring ownership of their houses prior to death to pay for residential and nursing care or provide extra income (Hamnett 1992a; 1992b). Mr Major's vision of 'wealth cascading down the generations', albeit down class-structured cascades, articulated as part of his vision of the 'class-less society' at the 1991 Conservative Party Conference, may well be more illusory than real.

Relationships between tenure, occupation and class have been further complicated, within the boundaries of the Two Nations project, as part of a more general Thatcherite strategy of promoting the virtues of Victorian self-help, allied to those of late-twentieth-century popular capitalism. Nevertheless, considerable class differences in tenure patterns remain. By 1985, for example, 87 per cent of professionals, employers and managers were owner-occupiers, as were 33 per cent of unskilled manual workers; but 58 per cent of unskilled manual workers rented from local authorities (LAs) as compared to only 4 per cent of the professionals.

Differences between furnished and unfurnished privately rented accommodation also interact with class, age and length of stay to produce markedly different groups of tenants. There are diverse groups of short-stay tenants including students, newly married couples, single person households and people who move in the course of their employment. For them, short-stay furnished lets are convenient, easy to enter and leave. In contrast, the unfurnished sector continues to be the domain of the longer stay, more elderly and low income households as the 1987 *General Household Survey* shows. They are effectively trapped in this sector, excluded from alternative tenures, and this is linked to the spatial concentration of multiply-deprived households in particular areas such as inner cities (see Chapter 9). There tend to be poor quality dwellings in this tenure. The 1986 *English House Condition Survey*, for example, revealed that the proportion of privately rented homes unfit for habitation or lacking basic amenities was five times higher than for privately owned or LA owned homes. But within the sector there are also very high quality dwellings in prestige locations, rented by the extremely affluent, members of the bourgeoisie and other people of property.

Mrs Thatcher's government viewed the decline of the privately rented sector with concern and tried to restore more attractive economics of landlordism via the 1980 Housing Act. It created new short-term (1 to 5 year) tenancies, after which landlords were assured of vacant possession. The changes were essentially cosmetic, in that privately rented tenancies fell from 13 per cent in 1980 to 11 per cent in 1985. As a result, fearing a permanent divide between owner-occupiers and the remaining LA tenants, the government announced plans in 1987 to allow LAs to subsidise construction of dwellings for private renting by housing associations and similar organisations. Once again, the government acknowledged a need for selective intervention despite its general ideological predilection for market solutions.

The extreme degree of social polarisation within the privately rented sector is absent within the remaining rump of LA housing. In the late 1940s public sector housing was seen as a key element in the emergent One Nation project, providing decent quality general needs housing for a wide social spectrum and eventually for a majority of the population. Public sector provision via LAs and new town development corporations subsequently increased, but later declined. Moreover, such housing increasingly became regarded as a 'second best' tenure for those unable to afford owner occupation. One particularly visible manifestation of this second best character appeared in the later 1950s and 1960s. Local authorities, faced with pressure to cut expenditure, switched to supposedly cheaper, system-built high-rise blocks to rehouse people from slum clearance schemes. This unpopular building form stigmatised council housing even further. In this, as in other respects, there were clearly divisive tendencies within the One Nation project. Neither Conservative nor Labour governments in the 1970s subsequently displayed much enthusiasm for providing good quality LA housing, placing increasing emphasis on housing associations.

The most serious attack on LA provision came in the 1980s, as part of the more general Two Nations assault on public sector provision. This assumed three forms. First, there were greatly increased sales of council houses (which we consider below). Secondly, there were very severe cuts in public expenditure on housing which meant the virtual collapse of council house building; completions fell from 100 000 a year in the late 1970s to less than 10 000 in 1991. This has reinforced the role of the residual stock as a low quality 'sink' for those unable to afford owner occupation. Furthermore, public expenditure restrictions resulted in 84 per cent of LA houses, in England alone, requiring repairs averaging £4900 each in 1985. Thirdly, since 1987, tenants have had the right to opt out of LA control and transfer their tenancies to a housing association or similar landlord. They have been encouraged to do so by the declining quality of their dwellings suffering from a lack of repairs because of expenditure restraints.

Growing restrictions on public sector provision were most starkly reflected in the growing numbers of homeless people on the streets of the UK's major cities, especially London (see London Housing Unit 1990). The number of homeless people doubled between 1979 and 1988 – to 370 000 (*Financial Times*, 29 December 1988) – and has since grown further. These are the people who live in some of the darkest corners of deprivation and disadvantage in the Divided Realm, and who suffer most acutely from implementation of the Two Nations project. But they are not the only victims of the cut backs in public sector expenditure on housing; there are, for example, also gendered and racialised implications (see Chapter 5 and 6).

Changes in the composition and size of the LA stock have had considerable implications for the class composition of this tenure. The *General Household Surveys* of the 1970s suggest that the LA sector was increasingly housing the poorer households. The evidence from the 1980s points to a continuation of this trend as a result of Thatcherite policies to reduce council stocks to a residual ghetto for the poor and unemployed. This, however, does not tell the full tale. There are still differences in quality within the remaining LA stock. Housing managers and officials continue to determine the rules of access and allocate households to dwellings in a situation in which need has generally outstripped supply. Local authorities have discretion in defining housing need and there is considerable variation in the criteria they adopt for positioning applicants on waiting lists. This determines which applicants are allocated dwellings. However, the quality of housing allocated depends upon housing managers' assessments of tenants: the better the grading, the better the accommodation. This is especially significant in relation to transfers within an LA's housing stock.

The meshing of allocation and transfer rules with the physical attributes of particular types of council houses produces a mosaic of different types of council housing areas. At one extreme are the better quality small-to-medium sized houses, especially the general needs dwellings of the 1940s and 1950s. These are allocated to the 'respectable' working class, typically stable white families with heads in full-time semi-skilled or skilled manual or clerical non-manual jobs. The stock of such houses is now much reduced through the selective selling-off of houses in the 1980s. At the other extreme are the 'difficult-to-let, difficult-to-live-in, and difficult-to-get-out-of' estates (see Taylor 1979). Often, but not exclusively, these are 1960s system-built blocks, 'sink estates' in which 'problem families' are deliberately concentrated by housing managers. The implications of such social segregation have become more serious since 1979 because of broader changes in labour markets and housing provision. We have already travelled a long way down the road to a situation in which state housing has become stigmatised welfare housing associated with the unemployed, the low paid, single mothers, black people and other minority groups, and in particular with the underclass.

In contrast, owner occupation has grown considerably in the UK over the post-war period. Owner-occupiers tend to have higher incomes and more wealth (often precisely because of owner occupation) than tenants. By the late 1970s 90 per cents of professionals and 80 per cent of employers and managers were owner-occupiers – but so too were many people from other occupational groups. The profile of owner-occupying households reflects the conditions of access to this tenure. These are structured by the interaction of state policies with the practices of financial agencies providing credit to owner-occupiers.

Given the purchasing power and choice, most people would opt for owner occupation. But this is not the point. Politicians and bureaucrats have created conditions which make this choice all but inevitable. State policies since the 1950s have aimed to make owner occupation a financially attractive proposition whilst house price escalation, especially in the South East, further enhanced this – at least until the early 1990s. Added to this, council house sales and the reduction in the public sector stock combined to push many lower-income people and households into owner occupation in the 1980s. Since owner occupation, for most people, necessitates borrowing money, the lending policies of the main credit agents – building societies, banks, insurance companies and LAs – are vital. Despite the growing share of mortgage business taken by the banks and insurance companies, reducing the building societies' 'share' of new mortgages to 55 per cent in 1987 from 85 per cent in 1984, building societies remain the main source of credit for house purchase.

The main determinants of whether a mortgage is granted are level of income, type of job and form of employment contract. Consequently, building societies favour non-manual salaried workers, though in the 1970s more unionised, especially skilled, manual workers became seen as credit worthy as they achieved better working conditions and more secure employment contracts. By the end of the 1970s absolutely more, though relatively less, manual heads of households were receiving mortgages than were non-manual ones. This trend continued in the 1980s with increasing council house sales boosting manual mortgagees whilst non-manual purchasers turned increasingly to banks and insurance companies.

Local authority mortgage schemes evolved to complement those of building societies, providing finance for lower-income purchasers of cheaper, older properties. However, the poorest householders seeking the cheapest houses have difficulty in getting LA mortgages. For them, the fringe banks and finance companies act as lenders of last resort, providing loans at punitive interest rates.

The combined effect of state policies and differential access to credit has been a regressive form of financing owner occupation. Public subsidies in the form of income tax and capital gains tax relief have helped owner-occupiers who, on average, have higher incomes than tenants. Furthermore, within the owner-occupied sector, the system of housing finance has given most to those who need it least; and it gave most in the 1980s. By the start of the 1980s owner-occupiers benefited by over £2000 million a year, a vast subsidy to the better off. Policies to increase council rents whilst raising the upper limits on mortgages qualifying for tax relief subsequently further increased the differential subsidy to the better off. By 1987, for example, 800 000 high earners escaped paying £270 million in tax above the standard rate, whilst total tax relief on mortgages was over £4500 million. It peaked at £8070 million in 1991/92. Whilst the higher rate relief was subsequently abolished, substantial mortgage tax relief remains. It still stood at over £6000 million in 1991/92, despite lower interest rates and the ending of higher rate relief (CSO 1993). It is a measure of the severity of the fiscal crisis facing Mr Major's government that in 1993 it announced further erosion of mortgage tax relief. It could be argued that the policies of the 1980s had pushed the property-owning democracy to its social limits; in this sense, there was little to be gained from seeking to increase owner occupation and little to be lost in eroding mortgage tax relief in the face of enormous pressures on government finances. It was a strategy with evident electoral and political risks.

As owner occupation has increased, so too has the diversity of owner-occupiers. There is a world of difference between the housing experiences of the landed aristocracy, the non-UK residents who bought up prestigious houses as UK prices collapsed in the early 1990s (see *Financial Times*, 13 February 1993), the residents of a suburban Bellway three-bedroomed semi, and those in old, run-down inner-city housing. All may be owner-occupiers but they live in social worlds that are, literally, classes apart. This takes on added significance in the context of the greatly increased sales of council houses to sitting tenants in the 1980s (over one and a half million to 1991). This has increased the divide between the remaining council tenants and owner-occupiers and exacerbated divisions between owner-occupying groups. Increased, but selective, purchases by sitting council tenants reflected the financial advantages of owner occupation, with houses generally sold at two-thirds of market price. They also reflected the perceived disadvantages of the authoritarian managerial practices of LAs as landlords. This provided space for proposals for tenants to opt out of LA control. More generally, it helped discredit the statist conception of socialism, that emerged in the late 1940s and subsequently became one element of the consensual One Nation project. In turn, this provided opportunities for market solutions, reinforcing the acceptance of aspects of Thatcherism and the Two Nations project amongst key sections of former Labour voters.

Even so, recent Conservative governments have recognised the political and social dangers of polarising housing provision around a private market for owner-occupiers and a rump public sector for an underclass of the unemployed and poor. It is in this context that the seemingly paradoxical recent government attempt to revive the privately rented sector (using public expenditure) must be understood. It is difficult to encourage the private rented sector in a market biased towards owner occupation. In these circumstances, the pill of public subsidy to private landlords was easier to swallow than the politically dangerous admission that market-led solutions to housing provision are iniquitous and divisive. At the same time, though, other government policy initiative sought to extend owner occupation at the expense of private renting. The 1993 Housing and Urban Development Bill, which would allow lease-holders to buy the freehold of their houses, was described by Sir George Young, the Minister of Housing, as 'an essential part of our policy on extending home ownership' (quoted in *Financial Times*, 25 February 1993).

Until recently, there was a popular perception that owner occupation was not only a desirable tenure in terms of tax efficiency but also one that offered a more or less guaranteed capital gain. With the easy availability of cheap credit in the latter part of the 1980s, house prices escalated rapidly, especially in the South East, as people increasingly borrowed larger mortgages in the belief that prices could only go in one direction. The recession and house price reversals of the early 1990s rudely shattered this illusion. More and more people who had bought at the height of the boom found themselves with nega-tive equity – mortgage debt exceeding the market value of their house. The numbers of both repossessions and people in arrears on their mortgage soared (Table 4.3). In 1991 repossessions exceeded 75 000, compared to less than 20 000 in 1988 and less than 3500 in 1980. The numbers of mortgages in arrears rose equally rapidly; there had been less than 10 000 people 12 or more months in arrears and less than 50 000 between 6 and 11 months in arrears in 1988 as compared to over 91 000 and almost 184 000, respectively, in 1991 (according to the Council for Mortgage Lenders).

The growing numbers of repossessions raised acute political problems for the government, puncturing the illusion that owner occupation was a one-way bet. For that reason, it put in place a rescue package with the mortgage lenders at the end of 1991, for the growing number of people 6 or more months in arrears - the point at which, historically, the lenders sought repossession. This rescue package had limited effect, however, since it was mainly directed at those within the social security network whilst about 80 per cent of those in

Table 4.3 Mortgage arrears, 1992–93

Period in arrears (months)	March 1992	March 1993
2	207 780	198 000
3–5	275 380	242 050
6–11	186 200	203 360
12 or more	103 880	156 740
Total arrears	773 240	800 150

Source: *Roof Magazine*, cited in *Financial Times*, 21 June 1990

arrears fell outside of it; typically, they were people in low-wage employment or families where only one partner was unemployed (*Financial Times*, 21 June 1993), concentrated amongst those converted to owner occupation by the 1980s 'right to buy' legislation. None the less, repossessions did begin to fall − to 68 000 and 60 500 by the years to March 1992 and 1993, respectively. However, this was largely because the mortgage lenders agreed to lower monthly repayments rather than repossess − otherwise it is estimated that repossessions in 1993 would have exceeded 120 000. These nevertheless remained at uncomfortably high and politically damaging levels. This combination of collapsing prices, growing arrears and high levels of repossession posed serious electoral and political threats to Mr Major's government − registered, for example, in a series of sensational Liberal Democratic by-election and local election gains in 1993.

4.5 Class, consumption and life-styles

Whilst average per caput income and consumption levels have risen strongly over the last 50 years (Figure 4.1), consumption patterns remain markedly unequal between classes, both inside and outside the home. These differences can be summarised as follows. Firstly, those in households headed by people in middle-class or white-collar occupations have higher consumption levels than those in manual employment. Secondly, expenditure on food and alcohol varies least between households and that on consumer durables and services varies most. Thirdly, the unemployed and economically inactive are relatively deprived, especially with respect to services and consumer durables. Spending on anything other than the necessities of food and shelter declines with the absence of a job. Fourthly, non-manual workers are most distinct in the extent to which they purchase consumer durables and services. Whilst such differences existed throughout the decades of the One Nation project, they were intensified in its Two Nations successor.

There are, then, important class differences in the ownership of consumer durables and domestic 'labour-saving' devices (the gender implications are examined in Chapter 5). These have, however, partially altered in recent years. In some cases, for example, there was almost universal household possession by the end of the 1970s: 92 per cent of households possessed a refrigerator, 97 per cent had a television set. In other cases, there has been considerable growth in ownership in the 1980s (Table 4.4). In this sense, the Thatcher years can be said to have witnessed decreasing class differences. But substantial minorities, concentrated amongst the poor and unemployed, still lack central heating, deep freezers, telephones and washing machines (Table 4.5). For some, the lack of consumer durables is a matter of choice but for many others it is a matter of necessity. Furthermore, these data reveal nothing about quality, for example, of the differences between an old black and white and

Table 4.4 Household ownership of
selected consumer durables, 1979–90

	% owning	
	1979	1990
CD player	—	21
Home computer	—	20
Video recorder	—	64
Deep freezer	40	81
Washing machine	74	87
Tumble drier	19	46
Dishwasher	3	13
Telephone	67	88
Microwave	—	50
Central heating	55	73
Car/van – one	44	44
– more than one	13	23
– in total	47	67

Source: CSO (1992)

a new 'high-tech' colour television set, or a brand new washing machine and one that is 20 years old. Such qualitative differences reflect income differentials and are class-related. The uneven growth in possession of these consumer durables reflects the interacting effects of two things. One is rising real incomes and access to credit for those in work (especially in households where married women work for a wage). The other is falling real prices, coupled with a second-hand market for those unable to afford the latest 'state-of-the-art' technology as a result of the fact that others can.

Ownership of new 'high-tech' and generally more expensive consumer durables (home computers, microwave ovens, videos) is much more restricted. Others - notably dishwashers – are 'older tech' but remain more expensive and so are not widespread. Price is a strong deterrent and ownership of these consumer durables remains heavily concentrated amongst the more affluent, often two-income middle-class households. As and when their price falls in real terms, they will doubtless diffuse across a wider spectrum of social classes but to date there has been an increasing class differentiation in their ownership.

Overall, then, over recent decades there has been a reduction in class inequalities of possession of several consumer durables that can have an important effect on the quality of people's daily lives but, in other respects, new class divisions have opened up (see Table 4.5). The pattern is a complicated and shifting one, not least because of competitive pressures which drive companies to seek both product and process innovations. However, to some extent, it

Table 4.5 Consumer durables and relations to social class, 1990

Percentage of households with	Professional	Employers and managers	Economically active			Economically inactive head of household
			Other non-manual	Skilled manual	Unskilled manual	
CD player	35	34	29	25	18	8
Home computer	45	35	30	24	2	5
Video	81	86	76	82	70	36
Washing machine	95	96	91	93	88	77
Tumble drier	65	67	53	54	44	28
Dishwasher	36	33	14	10	4	4
Telephone	98	98	92	86	71	84
Microwave	68	69	57	63	50	29
Car/van	98	98	82	82	51	40

Source: CSO (1993, Table 6.4 and Fig. 13.10)

reinforces the tendency towards a convergence across classes on an increasingly privatised life-style.

Another important aspect of life-styles centres on mobility. One indicator of this, albeit an imperfect one, is household ownership of or access to a private car. Household car ownership grew rapidly over the post-war period and, by the end of the 1970s, 44 per cent of households owned a car; 13 per cent had more than one. There were considerable class differences in household car ownership and in the quality of vehicles owned. For example, in 1979, 70 per cent of households headed by employers, managers or professionals had at least one car but only 9 per cent of those headed by unskilled manual workers had a car. By 1991 this pattern had altered little, the most significant change being the increase (to 23 per cent) of two plus car households, reflecting the redistribution of income to the affluent middle classes. This is a sharp reminder of how class differences in living standards have been increased as a consequence of deliberate income polarisation in the 1980s.

It is important not to confuse car ownership per household with personal mobility and access to employment opportunities and to leisure and recreational activities. This is especially so in one-car households. In these, for much of the time, all but one household member are in the same position as people in no-car households. This produces – *inter alia* – sharp intra-household age and gender differences in mobility. Public transport cut-backs in the 1980s and 1990s have served only to exacerbate such problems.

Differences in mobility are connected to those in leisure, recreation and holidaying behaviour. Although 70–80 per cent of all leisure activities are home based, many forms of non-home-based recreation and leisure require access to a car. For example, the most popular recreational activity revealed by the 1986 *National Survey of Countryside Recreation* was going for a drive, outing or picnic in the countryside. In all 54 per cent of people aged 12 or over undertook such activities, with strong class differences being reflected in car ownership. Holiday-making, both in the UK and abroad, has also become increasingly linked to car ownership and thus reveals strong class differentiation.

There are definite relationships between class, income and expenditure on different kinds of activities (Table 4.6) and also within these broad categories – for example, in terms of leisure activities (Table 4.7). Generally speaking, the lower the position of a household on the socio-economic scale, the larger is the proportion of its smaller income which is devoted to the necessities of food, housing and fuel, light and power. As income rises, so too does expenditure on a range of leisure activities and items, both in absolute and relative terms. In almost all areas of leisure the more affluent professionals and managers quantitatively do more and qualitatively do better than others. These differences in leisure expenditures and activities are indicative of significant variations in life-styles. For example, not only does spending on books, newspapers and magazines vary but there are also major differences in what

Table 4.6 Household expenditure: by socio-economic group of head, 1991

						Percentage of all expenditure				
Socio-economic group	Housing	Fuel light and power	Food	Alcohol and tobacco	Clothing and footwear	Household goods and services	Motoring and fares	Leisure goods and services	Other	Average weekly total expenditure (£)
Professional	17.8	3.2	15.4	4.1	5.8	13.3	18.5	17.7	4.2	400
Employer and manager	17.8	3.7	16.0	5.5	6.8	12.6	15.6	17.4	4.6	407
Other non-manual	18.4	3.9	16.2	5.7	6.8	13.5	17.9	13.0	4.6	307
Skilled manual	17.1	4.3	19.3	8.2	6.5	11.6	17.9	10.7	4.3	282
Semi-skilled manual	18.3	4.8	19.3	8.1	6.3	12.6	15.3	10.5	4.7	234
Unskilled manual	12.9	6.1	21.0	8.5	5.4	12.5	14.7	9.5	4.2	203
Retired	26.1	7.1	18.8	4.3	4.6	12.9	10.6	11.3	4.5	152
Unoccupied	17.7	6.0	19.6	7.2	6.2	12.8	14.0	11.9	4.6	204
Self-employed	20.3	4.3	17.7	6.3	5.9	13.5	14.0	13.6	4.3	339
All households	19.4	4.7	17.8	6.2	6.1	12.8	15.3	13.2	4.5	259

Source: CSO (1993, Table 6.3)

Table 4.7 Expenditure on selected leisure items in 1985 by gross normal weekly income of household

	Up to £100	Over £100 up to 150	Over £200 up to 250	Over £300	All households
Average weekly household expenditure on selected items (£ spent)					
Alcoholic drink consumed away from house	1.68	3.72	6.28	11.35	5.76
Meals consumed out	1.01	1.99	3.45	7.98	2.58
Books, newspapers, magazines, etc.	1.48	2.17	2.81	4.15	2.58
Television, radio and musical instruments	2.04	3.29	4.65	6.59	4.20
Holidays	1.13	2.70	4.24	12.34	4.98
Cinema admissions	0.03	0.05	0.11	0.17	0.09
Theatre, concert, etc. admissions	0.04	0.16	0.26	0.55	0.23
Subscription and admission charges to participant sports	0.11	0.34	0.48	1.55	0.61
Admission to spectator sports	0.02	0.08	0.15	0.23	0.11
Sports goods (excluding clothes)	0.03	0.07	0.24	0.85	0.31
Total weekly expenditure leisure	8.64	16.12	26.27	52.70	26.08
Expenditure on above as % of total	12.3	12.9	15.0	18.1	16.1

Source: CSO (1988, Table 10.18)

is purchased. For instance, few unskilled and semi-skilled manual workers and their families read either *The Times* or *Financial Times*. Despite the homogenising effect of mass ownership of televisions, this means that different classes receive quite distinct images of the world.

The greatest differences between income groups are in expenditure on alcoholic drinks and meals consumed outside the home, and on holidays. The middle classes and more affluent strata of the working class have the resources to spend more on food and drink outside the home. The more heavily home-based television and video life-styles of many of the less affluent and less mobile working class and unemployed (see CSO 1993, 142) are less a matter of choice than of necessity. These class differences are even sharper in relation to holiday-making. Since the early 1960s, there has been little variation in the percentage of adults taking an annual holiday – around 55 per cent. Most of those who do not take a holiday cannot afford to do so. For those who can and do choose to take a holiday, expenditure, frequency and location vary with class and disposable income. Some 80 per cent of professionals and managers took a holiday in 1991 – with almost 20 per cent taking three or more holidays – compared to 50 per cent of these employed in semi-skilled or unskilled manual occupation (CSO 1993). There are also considerable differences in the holidaying experiences of those who, in August, can afford to take a week in Torquay as opposed to two weeks in Torremolinos or three weeks in Thailand. The latter may also have a couple of weeks in Tangier in the spring, another two weeks skiing in Cortina d'Ampezzo in winter, and weekends in a country cottage somewhere in rural England in the intervening months (Williams and Shaw 1992) Once again, the considerable redistribution of income within the Two Nations project to the already affluent has exacerbated existing tendencies and helped sharpen class differences.

How then might we summarise the many class differences in living conditions and life-styles? At the risk of some over-simplification, we can recognise five broad groups in the UK in the 1990s:

(1) The small minority of the solidly Conservative upper class, the landed aristocrats and the major industrial and financial capitalists. They own considerable amounts of property in all forms and lead life-styles that are beyond the imagination of the vast majority of the population.
(2) The predominantly Conservative middle class, owner-occupiers with building society or bank mortgages, cars and a clutch of consumer durables. They lead mobile life-styles, actively participating in a variety of leisure activities and holiday-making at home and abroad.
(3) The affluent working class, skilled manual and intermediate non-manual workers. Many are now owner-occupiers as a result of council house sales, and share owners as a result of selling-off nationalised industries. Not infrequently, they have been converted to vote Conservative in general elections as a result. Typically they possess a car and a range of household consumer durables and take an annual package holiday in the Mediterranean.
(4) The rump of the semi-skilled and unskilled manual working class, mainly voting Labour and living in housing rented from an LA, sometimes with a car and few consumer durables, but with many unable to afford an annual holiday, particularly a foreign one.
(5) The underclass of the unemployed and impoverished, many not bothering to vote, subsisting on state welfare payments in poor quality dwellings on 'sink' council estates. They live on or below the boundaries of poverty in conditions of squalor that are beyond the imagination of the affluent upper and middle classes.

Although these class stereotypes are over-simplifications – not least because they ignore the interactions of class with gender and race – they do indicate the degree to which life-styles and living conditions in the UK have become both differently and more deeply divided along class lines as a product of prosecuting the Two Nations project.

4.6   Class and party politics

Rather than take a broad view of 'politics and power', which in a sense permeates all aspects of inequality in the UK, we focus here on the relationships between class and electoral and party politics. In particular, since the class composition of those elected to Parliament and of those in state employment was considered in Chapter 3, we examine which classes vote for which parties. The links between politics and class have been, and remain, complicated ones. Classes are the object of party competition, something in a way 'produced' by parties, as well as something pre-given. Classes are pre-given, however, in two senses. The relations of production are what they are at any given moment, whilst classes have a form and a content given to them by previous conflicts and struggles. But classes are constantly being 'reproduced' in new ways, both materially and ideologically, by policies and campaigns aimed at defining people in particular class terms.

For much of the population, party political choices are at best connected to class interests only in a loose sense. This was the case throughout the years of both One and Two Nations politics. Undoubtedly, in general terms, the Conservative Party represents the interests of capital against labour whilst the Labour Party was formed to defend the interests of labour against capital. Although political parties clearly express class interests, the ways in which they do so are complicated. Political parties formulate programmes for, and develop links with, numerous elements in society outside the class whose interests fundamentally inspire (or inspired) them. The election of Mrs Thatcher's first government in 1979 registered an important change in the relationship between class and politics, however, as expressed through the electoral process. This both reflected and enabled momentous political changes. Their significance is revealed by examining the basis of class support for Thatcherism, how this was constructed and how it has been maintained following Mrs Thatcher's departure from office.

This in turn requires a brief consideration of the links between party politics, voting and class in the UK in the post-war period. It seems reasonable to infer that the political loyalties of the owners and controllers of capital will have remained firmly with the Conservative Party. By 1986, for example, over 90 per cent of the political donations of £2.25 million made by British public companies was to support the activities of the Conservative Party; over £500 000 was given by only 10 companies. It is also clear, however, that there are wide discrepancies between the amount of money that Conservative Central Office admits to having raised and donations that can be traced through the accounts of the 1500 largest companies in the UK. According to Labour Research, this discrepancy amounted to at least £21.9 million between 1988 and 1991 alone, more than half the money donated (*Independent on Sunday*, 20 June 1993). In addition, there are substantial donations from abroad, transferred via various offshore accounts. Moreover, there is evidence of a positive correlation between corporate donations and directors and executives appearing in honours lists (see *Observer*, 3 July 1988). Of the top 100 companies, 42 had given money to the Conservative Party since 1980 – and of this number 28 (67 per cent) had directors or senior executives who had been awarded honours. Of the remaining 52, which made no donations, only 23 (40 per cent) had featured on honours lists. The replacement of Mrs Thatcher by Mr Major, committed to a 'classless society', has had no perceptible impact upon this relationship. Indeed, faced with a crisis in Conservative Party funding in 1993, Mr Major revived the fund-raising Downing Street dinner parties, much loved by his predecessor.

In a revealing comment upon the character of class power and the representation of class interests in state policy formation, a former Conservative Central Office official noted that: 'Donations get you on the inside track, they win you access to ministers, to ministerial advisers and invitations to No. 10. If an honour comes at the end of that process – that's not surprising because you have brought yourself to the attention of the most senior figures in the party' (quoted in *Independent on Sunday*, 20 June 1993). Even so, as the resignation of the Duke of Westminster from the Conservative Party in February 1993 shows, there is no automatic correlation of interest between even the most affluent and powerful and Conservative Party support. Clearly the Duke saw proposed leasehold reforms as striking at the heart of his own economic interests as well as more generally cutting across existing private property rights. As he put it: 'I cannot morally stay within a party which I fundamentally believe has ideologically gone off the rails' (quoted in *Financial Times*, 25 February 1993).

What, though, of the party political affiliations of those who depend upon being able to earn a wage as their source of income, whether 'middle' or 'working' class? There was a reasonably strong relationship between party political support, voting and class over much of the period of One Nation politics from 1945 until the late 1950s or mid-1960s, depending on one's interpretation of the electoral data. Manual workers tended to vote for the Labour Party, non-manual workers for the Conservative Party; in both cases about two-thirds of each group voted for 'its' party. Whilst all worked for a wage, type of occupation clearly correlated with voting behaviour, though far from perfectly. In this sense, the One Nation project was marked by a class cleavage in voting patterns. Even so, there was also considerable 'cross class' voting in this period. Between 25 and 30 per cent of manual workers voted Conservative whilst 25 per cent of non-manual workers voted Labour.

How, then, in the period to the late 1950s–mid-1960s were the programmes of the two major political parties constructed within the parameters of the One Nation project so as to both define 'core' classes of support and at the same time attract cross-class support? In part, the origins of this cross-class voting lie in the character of the political parties and the considerable consensus on economic and social policy that was integral to One Nation politics. It soon became clear that the post-war Labour government was committed to reforming rather than replacing capitalism and that succeeding Conservative governments accepted the goals of 'full employment' and the creation of a welfare state. Moreover, it seemed that Butskellite economic policies offered a route to more or less full employment and generally rising living standards, especially in the 1950s. Thus white-collar support for the Labour Party to some extent reflected the growth of the welfare state and, more generally, of social mobility as people moved into non-manual jobs but retained their parents' Labour Party affiliations. Conversely, working-class Conservative voting was associated either with a deferential culture, in which manual workers knew and accepted their place in the social order, or, conversely, with middle-class aspiration. More generally, the Conservatives projected themselves as the 'one nation' party. This emphasis on the precedence of shared national identity over class differences linked to strands that run deeply through Conservative politics, such as respect for law and order. Then as now this resonates powerfully with many working-class voters, sometimes tinged with racist overtones. Although indubitably an over-simplified view of the links between class and party politics, it nevertheless helps identify some important points about them.

From the late 1950s, however, these links began to alter. This process is referred to as dealignment. It involves two analytically distinct, though in practice related, elements. Partisan dealignment involved decreasing support for both major parties and growing support for other parties and/or growing abstention in general elections. It began with the resurgence in the Liberal vote in the late 1950s and developed further with the growing support for nationalist parties in Scotland and Wales and with the increasing complexities of party politics in Northern Ireland. It took a new twist in the Two Nations era with the emergence of the SDP, the formation of the Liberal–SDP Alliance and its transformation into the Social and Liberal Democratic Party, and some small-scale support for the Green Party. These partisan dealignments in the middle ground of party politics in the 1980s have been particularly important in enabling successive Conservative governments to retain power.

Class dealignment refers to the declining probability that any individual will vote for the party associated with his or her social class. Between 1964 and 1974 there was increasing white-collar support for the Labour Party, from people employed in the public sector, especially in welfare services. There were, however, no perceptible changes in working-class voting patterns in this period. In contrast, after 1974 there was a steady decline in the percentage of manual workers, especially skilled manual workers, who voted Labour. One expression of this was the falling percentage of trades unionists voting Labour (Table 4.8). The chief beneficiaries of this in the 1979 general election were the Conservatives (Table 4.9). This was undoubtedly crucial in bringing about the election of Mrs Thatcher's government.

This selective switch in working-class support to the politics of the 'new right' in 1979 clearly reflected the experiences of the preceding years of Labour governments, racked by economic crises. Simultaneously, people experienced mounting unemployment and increasing inflation. This was a combination that orthodox Keynesianism believed impossible, so that the credibility of economic policies based upon it was eroded. To some considerable extent it also reflected the impact of the public sector strikes during the 1978–79 'winter of

Table 4.8 Voting by trade union members in general elections, 1964–87

	% Labour	% Conservative	% Other
1964	73	22	5
1966	71	25	4
1970	66	28	6
1974 Feb.	55	30	15
1974 Oct.	55	23	16
1979	51	33	13
1983	39	31	30
1987	42	30	26

Source: MORI, cited in *Financial Times*, 10 October 1988

Table 4.9 Voting by occupational class (in percentages)

	Conservative	Labour	Alliance	Nationalist	Other/nonvoting
1979					
Professional	42.9	18.0	17.1	1.7	20.3
Administrative/managerial	50.0	13.0	10.2	1.3	25.6
Routine non-manual	39.5	19.9	14.7	1.7	24.3
Skilled manual	27.1	36.8	8.2	1.7	26.2
Semi-skilled manual	23.8	44.7	8.6	1.4	21.6
Unskilled manual	17.2	43.8	9.3	1.8	27.8
1993					
Professional	42.8	11.2	23.4	1.0	21.5
Administrative/managerial	48.8	9.7	18.9	0.6	22.0
Routine non-manual	37.5	17.0	17.4	1.0	22.0
Skilled manual	31.0	31.7	24.6	1.6	33.3
Semi-skilled manual	20.9	27.8	19.8	1.6	29.8
Unskilled manual	15.9	31.7	16.5	138	34.5
1987					
Professional	40.4	16.1	27.6	0.9	14.9
Administrative/managerial	49.7	10.0	18.8	0.8	20.7
Routine non-manual	36.1	20.2	17.4	1.5	24.8
Skilled manual	27.0	26.2	16.9	1.6	28.3
Semi-skilled manual	21.7	40.6	15.3	0.9	21.5
Unskilled manual	17.8	32.5	13.2	1.6	34.9

Source: Johnston et al. (1988)

discontent'. These revealed that the Labour government could no longer restrain working-class militancy via its close links with senior trade union leaders as unemployment rose and working-class living standards fell. The old grand compromise was no longer tenable in these circumstances. The Conservative election campaign was skilfully constructed to emphasise dealing firmly with the trade unions, reducing inflation and encouraging job creation in an enterprise economy. It was a campaign that was particularly successful in attracting working-class support to Mrs Thatcher's brand of Two Nations politics as the limits to the One Nation project became increasingly and painfully apparent.

Such an interpretation is fine in as far as it goes. However, the creation of a substantial, but selective, basis of working-class support for the politics of Thatcherism needs to be set in a broader context. From around the end of the 1950s, it increasingly became apparent that the class compromises of the post-war consensus were incompatible with capital accumulation and economic growth in the UK. Changing patterns of employment and occupations also weakened both major parties' hold on 'their' respective segments of the labour force. The middle classes were affected in contradictory ways by several changes. First, by the necessity of white-collar workers to unionise, the continuing dequalification of various traditional middle-class occupations, the encroachment of the working class on formerly middle-class preserves (such as access to grammar school education) and, especially in the 1970s, the effect of inflation. Such changes tended to polarise the middle classes, partly towards the Labour movement, partly towards anti-union and authoritarian positions. Thus many of the middle class remained attached to or were converted to Thatcherite neo-conservatism whilst minorities expressed support for the programmes of the Labour and Liberal parties in 1979 (Table 4.9).

By the 1970s the former bases of working-class political culture were under severe strain. The working class experienced the full impacts of deindustrialisation as the failures of consensus politics to promote economic modernisation and an internationally competitive manufacturing sector were revealed in collapsing manual employment and soaring unemployment. Mrs Thatcher shamelessly and successfully linked this to the issue of immigration (Chapter 6). This both weakened working-class faith in Labourism and loosened the bonds of a working-class culture constructed around a particular pattern of industries and employment. For some, it is this reduction in the extent of the traditional working class of manual workers, rather than class dealignment, which underlies the declining electoral fortunes of Labour. It is clear, however, that not only were the numbers of manual jobs and trade unionists falling sharply, but so too was the proportion of that shrinking number of trade unionists who were voting Labour (Table 4.8). As Leys' (1986 emphasis in original) remarks, with sharp insight:

> The loosening of the bonds of the old working class culture provided an opportunity to redefine the 'classes' of the workers most affected by these changes. The

working class did not 'wither away'. It began to break out of its traditional mould and became susceptible of being 'formed' again in new ways. The radical right ... realised this. The electoral victory of Thatcherism demonstrated the enormous importance of their perception that a fresh opportunity had arisen to create a new kind of 'conservative working man'. It was a struggle – not necessarily permanent, but a victory all the same – in the struggle between classes, about classes.

In the 1970s, then, as the One Nation project crumbled, the emphasis shifted from the maintenance of established class allegiances to the redefinition of classes and the articulation of new grounds for party allegiance. This move was initiated by the Conservative Party, which proved to be infinitely more adept and effective than the Labour Party in seizing the initiative and taking advantage of the changes.

This redefinition of the terrain was partly in response to the emergence of new social movements from the 1960s. These cut across conventional party lines, each concentrating on one issue or set of themes. These included equality for women, equality for ethnic minorities, preservation of the environment, nuclear disarmament and the creation of global peace. Although these issues cut across party and class boundaries, the people involved in the movements are far from being a cross-section of British society. The most prominent group is the so-called 'new middle class' – professional and technical-scientific workers, highly educated and, often, in state employment, along with mostly middle class housewives and students.

The key point about the emergence of these groups *vis-à-vis* the rise of the new right is that they are protest movements, challenging the parameters of established party politics and state policies. From this standpoint, the emergence of new and radical political forces in Britain may be seen as evidence of the collapsing hegemony of the dominant class, which had either to be reconstructed or succumb to the pressure of opposing social forces. The 'Thatcherite' themes of family, law and order, immigration, 'hard work' and the like appealed to popular reaction against these new movements, in language which tapped a large reservoir of traditional sentiment amongst ordinary people. By contrast, the Labour Party's emphasis throughout the 1970s was almost wholly on the economic issues of immediate concern to workers as workers (with a strong bias towards white male workers), and only secondarily on issues such as personal security, racial or sexual emancipation or the environment. In short, the Labour Party did not respond as positively to these new movements as the Conservative Party responded negatively. In fact, in different ways the Liberal Party (via its version of community politics) and the National Front and its successor, the British National Party (via racism) responded more strongly to these shifts than did Labour. Whilst the former in particular helped split the non-Conservative vote, the crucial point is that the political programme of the new right was constructed to redefine its class basis of support on a range of non-economic and seemingly non-class issues.

This not only helps explain why Mrs Thatcher's government was first elected in 1979, but also why it was subsequently re-elected in 1983 and 1987 and has succeeded in maintaining broadly the same pattern of class support (see Table 4.9). It also helps explain why, despite its coincidence with a deep and painful economic recession, the Conservative Party under Mr Major won the 1992 general election – albeit with a much reduced Parliamentary majority. Whilst the process of class dealignment may have halted, there is no evidence of a realignment on to the old One Nation model. Rather the Two Nations project has seen the establishment of a new and more complicated pattern of links between class and party political allegiance, though not necessarily permanently. Despite what in many ways is an appalling economic record, the Conservative Party had until 1989, by and large, retained the support of the working class at the same level as in 1979. There is as yet no analysis of voting in the 1992 general election along the lines of Table 4.9. Nevertheless, it is clear that although the Conservative Party lost working class votes – hardly surprising, as the election fell in the middle of a deep, long and painful recession – it retained enough support to win the election and confound most political pundits' predictions. Its retention of a substantial measure of working-class support reflects a combination of factors.

First, it reflects the uneven and divisive distributional effects of economic policies within the working class in the 1980s and 1990s. For example, this is seen in the sales of council houses to former council tenants and of shares to workers in newly privatised industries. This helps account for the appeal of the Two Nations project to what became an electorally influential minority. Secondly, there are many strands of Thatcherite and Majorite politics that are only tangentially related to national economic performance. Thirdly, one can add the effects of events such as the Falklands/Malvinas and Gulf wars in whipping up nationalist sentiment, or the 1984–85 miners' strike in mobilising opinion against the trade unions and for the maintenance of law and order. Fourthly, there was the split in the opposition vote between the Alliance (then the SLD and SDP) and Labour. Fifthly, there were the divisions within these parties which made them (and some of their leaders) appear as distinctly non-credible alternative governments.

There has been some switch of professional support to both the centre parties and Labour, especially in 1987 (despite the material benefits accruing to them from changes in taxation and so on), mainly in response to the authoritarian turn of Thatcherite policies. To a lesser extent, there has also been a parallel switch in support from clerical and related workers. But the manual working-class converts to Thatcherism of 1979 have held firm in the critical moments of 1983, 1987 and – to a lesser extent – 1992 despite some wavering in the intervening years. This coupled above all with the increasingly uneven geographical concentration of votes for Conservative and Labour, the lack of a parallel concentration in those for the SLD and SDP, and the 'first past the post' electoral system, combined to return Mrs Thatcher to power with vast Parliamentary majorities despite winning a minority of votes nationally. It also enabled Mr Major, contrary to expectations, to win the 1992 general election.

5

Divided by gender

5.1 Gender relationships in historical context: One Nation versus Two Nations politics

Some of the theoretical issues related to gender, patriarchy and class have been touched upon earlier (see Chapter 1). Here we are concerned with the changing form and intensity of gendered inequalities in the UK. Gender inequalities have deep roots in UK society. They were considerably influenced by developments in Victorian Britain when there was a growing differentiation between women's roles in the workplace and in the home. These social relationships were locked into structures in space and the built environment. In particular, the suburbs with their separation of home and work came, in the twentieth century, to represent the ideal of family life, even if only the middle and some parts of the working class could aspire to living there. Suburbanisation has substantial social implications, however: it is 'an obstacle to combining paid employment with domestic responsibilities, it marginalizes nonfamily households, it inhibits women from participating in adult (nonfamily) activities and it gives substance to an ideology of domesticity (Madigan et al. 1990, 629). The late Victorian trend of declining relative levels of female employment continued through most of the first half of the twentieth century with the exceptions of the two world wars.

To some extent these gender divisions have narrowed in the post-1945 period as structural changes in the economy lead to increasing, though selective, participation by women in waged labour. In addition, women's movements have also become better organised and more forceful in pressing their demands for societal reforms. They have forced some concessions both in state policies and in civil society, notably in formal legislation such as the Equal Pay Act of 1970 and the Sex Discrimination Act of 1975. The EC has also enforced some changes on successive reluctant Conservative governments in the 1980s and 1990s, especially with respect to equal pay. However, the gendering of relationships continues to remain firmly rooted in many of the institutions, laws and behaviour patterns of the UK.

Changes in the gender structuring of inequalities in the UK can, to a degree, be related to the periodisation of economic restructuring outlined in Chapter 2, although they have also had their own dynamic. In the era of One Nation politics, the model of capital accumulation was predicated on full employment, albeit full male employment. There was a strong commitment to economic growth during both the years of Butskellism in the 1950s and of corporatism in the late 1960s and early 1970s. In this growth context, there was also a pronounced increase in female employment, especially of part-time jobs. There was also the growth of state support for the family in the post-1945 period. A number of measures were introduced including child tax allowances and social security benefits, although these mostly assumed that women were economically dependent on men. As McDowell (1990, 173) writes of the influential 1942 Beveridge Report, 'it accepted women's traditional role in the family, arguing that married women's main task was to ensure continuity of care for men and children'.

One exception to this tendency was the child benefit measure introduced in 1977; this was an untaxed universal benefit paid directly to mothers. Somerville (1992, 98) writes that it was 'this measure and its subsequent increases that allowed the Labour Chancellor, Denis Healey, to claim to deliver "family budgets"'; it underlined the positive value attached to families rather than being a measure specifically aimed at the poor. Another exception was a series of improvements to maternity benefits, culminating in the 1975 Employment Protection Act. This made it illegal for employers to dismiss women simply because they were pregnant, and it also established the right to maternity leave and to return to a job within 29 weeks of giving birth. These were, however, rare exceptions, for the One Nation era was essentially concerned with class-based inequalities and paid scant attention to the gendering of inequalities. It is not without irony that the most important of these exceptions were introduced as the mainstream commitments of the One Nation project were being abandoned.

During the period of Two Nations political strategies, there was a shift in the gendering of inequalities. The Thatcher government introduced legislation to promote what it called individualism, and market deregulation; the latter included the weakening of trade union powers, the abolition of many Wages Councils, and the limitation of collective services. In theory, this legislation was designed to enhance labour market flexibility. However, in practice, 'without espousing a particular policy on women's employment', many of these policies such as 'the Employment Acts of 1980 and 1982 have been measures which have particularly disadvantaged women' (Lewis and Davies 1991, 20). The 1980 Employment Act significantly weakened maternity entitlements: small firms (with less than six workers) were exempted from some of the provisions of the 1975 Employment Protection Act. This Act was presented as a measure to promote small firm growth, but it reinforced gender inequalities in the labour market. Contributing to and encouraged by the shift to more flexible employment strategies, involving more casualisation and fragmentation, there was a sharp increase in female employment in the 1980s, both full- and part-time. A large part of this was poorly paid part-time jobs in the

service sector (Sassen 1991). Women's propo⟨rtion of⟩ [...]
ment increased even more sharply in response [...]
during this decade.

There has not, however, been a concomitan⟨t⟩ [...]
such as greater child care facilities – to support [...]
of waged labour. Instead, the Thatcher governm⟨ent's⟩ [...]
choice, market deregulation and 'the family' h⟨ave...⟩ [...]
causes of women. Indeed, in most respects they [...]
taged them, especially given the cuts in many are⟨as⟩ [...]
in the face of increasing female employment, the [...]
the family the centrepiece of its ideological promotion of 'traditional' or even
'Victorian' family values. This, however, has revealed 'the contradictions
inherent in an economy increasingly based on the exploitation of women in the
labour market, where they are constructed as secondary peripheral workers
working for "pin money", but continuing to rely on women's domestic and
unwaged labour to sustain the relations of social reproduction (McDowell
1989, 174). Partly in response to these contradictions, and unable or unwilling
to meet the full cost of providing allowances for married women to act as
'carers', the Thatcher governments never directly sought to limit married
women's labour market participation. Instead, they have used the spurious
argument of 'family' values to justify *de facto* real cuts in the welfare state.
Not surprisingly, then, the number of women living in poverty increased
sharply during the Thatcher years (Townsend et al. 1987).

Comments by leading Thatcherite figures on what they construed as traditional family values were revealing. For example, Keith Joseph saw working-
class lone mothers as producing problem children who would be 'denizens of
our borstals, subnormal educational establishments, prisons, hostels for
drifters', whilst Patrick Jenkin, a future Minister of State for Social Services,
argued that 'quite frankly I don't think mothers have the same rights to work
as fathers do' (both quoted in Somerville 1992, 99). Attacks by ministers on
single parents at the 1993 Conservative Party Conference, and threats of massive cuts in the welfare state in the mid-1990s, confirmed that much of the
rhetoric of Thatcherism lives on in Major's governments.

The overall assessment of the impact of the Two Nations project on gendered inequalities is that whilst essentially concerned with the restructuring of
class relationships, it also served to further disadvantage women because of
the complex links between class and gender.

5.2 Men and women in the labour market

5.2.1 Changing forms of participation

Women's participation in the paid labour force is conditioned by their role in
the domestic household. The analysis of such participation therefore involves

the form and social relations of production, as well as cultural changes affecting families. This is certainly not a creation of the century. As Hakim (1993) has shown, the female activity rates of were only reattained in the 1980s. In the intervening period they fell substantially and in 1951 the rate was 43 per cent for women compared to 96 per cent for men in the 15−59 age group (Figure 5.1). By 1991 the gap had closed to 87 per cent for men and 71 per cent for women. To some extent, however, these data exaggerate the narrowing of the gap. Female activity rates were seriously under-recorded in the first half of the twentieth century when the ideology of feminine domesticity and dependent wives was particularly strong (Hakim 1993, 100). The proportion of all women in paid jobs or seeking work increased during the years of Two Nations politics from 60 per cent in 1973 to 64 per cent in 1979, and then fell to 62 per cent in 1983 before rising sharply to 73 per cent in 1991 (Table 5.1; note that these data are calculated differently from those used by Hakim). There has, therefore, been a real increase in activity rates since 1945, and especially in the late 1980s. This has been linked to casualisation and deregulation of labour markets (see pp. 86−9).

The changing labour market participation of married women is particularly striking. In 1911 only 10 per cent worked outside the home; by 1951 this had increased to 22 per cent. By this stage the strategic requirements of two world wars had already led to greater participation by married women in the workforce. Thereafter, labour shortages during the 1950s and 1960s led to a rapid increase in women's participation rates (Hakim 1979). By the 1990s, linked to the growth of part-time work, more than one-half of married women had paid jobs.

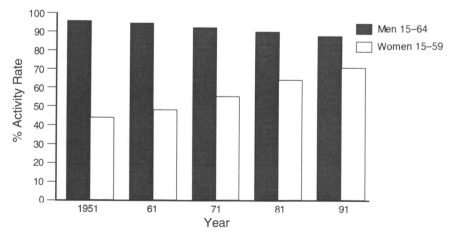

Figure 5.1   Male and female economic activity rates, 1951−91

Source: CSO (1992)

Table 5.1 Women's economic activities, Great Britain, 1973–91, women aged 16–59

Marital status and economic activity	1973	1979	1983	1987	1991
			(percentages)		
Single					
Working full-time	72	63	53	57	46
Working part-time	3	4	5	13	18
All working	76	6	13	9	10
Unemployed	3	6	13	9	10
Base = 100%					
Widowed, divorced or separated					
Working full-time	41	36	28	31	36
Working part-time	21	22	21	22	24
All working	63	59	49	53	61
Unemployed	3	5	8	8	7
Base = 100%					
Married					
Working full-time	25	26	25	30	34
Working part-time	28	33	31	34	33
All working	54	60	57	64	67
Unemployed	1	2	4	4	5
Base = 100%					
Total					
Working full-time	34	34	31	36	37
Working part-time	23	26	25	28	29
All working	58	61	56	64	67
Unemployed	2	3	6	5	6
Base = 100%					

Source: *General Household Survey*, OPCS, 1991

The changing role of women in waged labour was also related to the restructuring of production involving shifts to both the service sector and from skilled to semi-skilled manufacturing employment. It was also linked to the spatial reorganisation of production with, for example, assembly production being relocated in coal-mining areas which had large reserves of single and married women who had not previously been drawn into the formal waged economy (for example, see Massey 1984). In the era of One Nation politics, there was scant recognition of this changing role of women in the economy; women were reduced to a taken-for-granted source of labour for, first, the expansion and, later, the reorganisation of production. In the era of Two Nations politics the shift to more flexible forms of production in some industries led to further increases in female employment; this was underlined by the continuing decline of male-dominated forms of production, such as steel and coal, especially as their demise was part of the Thatcherite strategy for reshaping UK economic and political relationships. Gender relationships were not simply affected by the reorganisation of production but also contributed to the processes of restructuring. The existence of a reserve of cheap labour has influenced the overall development of the economy. For example, there is no inherent need for assembly tasks to be labour intensive but the availability of cheap female labour may make this more profitable than automation.

The state has also facilitated the feminisation of the labour force – to some extent. Whilst the Beveridge Report made no specific commitment to the full employment of women, the state has acted to subsidise some of the costs of reproduction, thereby facilitating as well as reacting to increased female participation in waged labour. Examples of such state intervention are increased schooling and collective caring provision. Even so, in these as in so many areas, the provision was partial and often inadequate. For example, the state provision of pre-school care in the UK is far from universal and has consistently lagged behind that in other major EU countries.

It is clear that access to most forms of paid work remains significantly gendered, and – in part due to limited state intervention – there are also important differences between women with and without dependent children. In the early twentieth century women working for a wage were almost exclusively young and single. There were high participation rates amongst the 15–25 group but very low rates in all other age groups. This changed in the 1960s, when growing participation by married women was central to the changing gender composition of the labour force. With married (and unmarried) mothers returning to work after child bearing and rearing, there were now double peaks in age-related participation rates. Subsequently, this pattern has again changed because an increasing number of women have returned to work between childbirths. Despite these tendencies, the domestic roles of women, and in particular whether they have responsibilities for caring for young children, are still the key to their labour force participation. Women without dependent children are more likely to be at work and more likely to be in full-time work than are women with dependent children; amongst the latter, 36 per cent were working part-time compared to 22 per cent working full time in 1991 (Table 5.2).

While single women have a higher level of labour market participation, this is also socially conditioned. There has been an assumption for many years that young unmarried women live at home and that, in effect, their parents will continue to subsidise their maintenance and other costs. This implicit assumption was made explicit in the era of Two Nations politics by changes made by the Thatcher governments to the social security system, especially the withdrawal of a range of benefits from 16–18-year-old men and women. Later in the life cycle, there is an assumption that married women's low wages are merely supplementary to the notional 'family' wage paid to men. These gender differences in jobs and pay became increasingly divorced from social reality

Table 5.2 Economic activity rates for women with and without dependent children, 1973–91

	Activity rates				
	1973	1979	1981	1987	1991
With dependent children					
Working full-time	17	16	15	18	22
Working part-time	30	36	34	37	36
All working	47	52	49	54	59
with no dependent children					
Working full-time	NA	NA	48	50	48
Working part-time	NA	NA	18	22	23
All working	NA	NA	66	72	72

for they ignored the growing proportion of households in the UK in which a woman was either the main or the only wage earner. The most obvious casualties of this social construction of employment are the many women who have access to neither a 'family' wage nor subsidised accommodation in a parental home. Unless they are one of the minority of women in relatively well-paid jobs, they are depressed into poverty.

5.2.2 Occupational segregation

Increased female participation rates – whether for women with or without children – do not equate with greater labour market equality. Women tend to have relative ease of access to only a few segments of the labour market. In 1992 50 per cent of women were in clerical and other intermediate and junior non-manual jobs, whilst a further 20 per cent were in semi-skilled manual and personal service jobs. This compares to only 46 per cent of women being employed in junior and intermediate non-manual jobs in 1975. This confirms the importance of structural change in the economy (shifts from manufacturing to services and within these sectors) in increasing participation rates. Yet there is also pronounced gendered occupational segregation of labour markets; while women provided more than three-quarters of the clerical workforce and of catering staff, they only constituted 8 per cent of managers. And over one-half of all men in the 1970s were in occupations in which they outnumbered women by a ratio of at least 9 to 1. There are, as might be expected, significant variations in the degree of segregation between different localities. For example, the proportion of men working in industries which were more than 90 per cent male-dominated was 66 per cent in Teesside but only 16 per cent in Cheltenham in the 1970s (Walby and Bagguley 1990, 65).

There is both vertical and horizontal occupational segregation between men and women: they tend to be segregated into different occupations and have different prospects for promotion within these. British Rail provides an example of both processes. In 1984 it employed only 8987 women compared to 140 530 men, that is less than 7 per cent of the total. Moreover women were disproportionately concentrated in lower-grade jobs. Well over one-half were in clerical jobs and only two had reached the grade of senior manager, compared to 589 men. The same pattern is evident in the Civil Service where in 1987 women constituted 76 per cent of administrative assistants but less than 10 per cent of higher-grade employees (Table 5.3). While some progress had been made between 1982 and 1987 in breaking down occupational segregation in the middle-rank posts in the Civil Service, the higher echelons continue to be largely male preserves. Thus in 1993 only 8.6 per cent of the top 1150 Civil Servants were women and there were no female Permanent Secretaries in the major departments (Whitehall Companion 1993). There are many other examples in areas where senior appointments exercise significant amounts of power. For example, in 1993 only 5 out of 91 High Court judges were women, while in 1992 there were no women Chief Constables in the police (Equal Opportunities Commission 1993).

Occupational segregation is the outcome of several linked processes. Women are legally excluded from some jobs such as on North Sea oil rigs and underground mines. But social processes of exclusion are far more important than the legal ones. The most important of these is the social definition of skills. Women workers carry into the workplace their subordinate status in society at large. The work of women is often labelled as being inferior or unskilled simply because it is undertaken by women. McDowell (1989, 176–17) writes that 'The supposed attributes of femininity such as caring, sympathy, and interest in people, persistence, attention to detail and manual dexterity

Table 5.3 Women civil servants, 1982 and 1987

	% of all civil servants	
Grade	1982	1987
Administrative assistant	81	76
Administrative officer	61	61
Executive officer	27	34
Higher executive officer	12	18
Senior executive officer	6	18
Grade 7 (principal)	7	8
Grade 6 (senior principal)	8	9
Grade 5 (assistant secretary)	4	8
Grades 1–4 (permanent secretary to directing grades)	4	4

Source: *Financial Times*, 25 February 1988

have been variously employed to explain women's concentration in servicing and caring jobs in the service sector, and in assembly work in the manufacturing sector.' In short, skill definitions are often no more than ideologically loaded classifications based on gender. The same argument holds with respect to part-time jobs. Some jobs, such as cleaning or catering, are socially constructed as part-time jobs because they are seen to be women's jobs; yet there is nothing in their nature which necessarily makes them part-time.

There are a number of mechanisms through which such social definitions are constructed. One of these is the emphasis placed on formal training. Unfavourable comparisons are drawn between the short formal periods of training in many women's jobs compared to, say, the traditional, long apprenticeships for many (male) jobs in manufacturing. Even if there was once any basis to such an argument, the decline of the traditional system of apprenticeships in the UK would have undermined it in recent decades. However, even the factual basis of the argument is questionable for the emphasis on formal training undervalues on-the-job training and skills learnt informally at home, such as sewing and cooking.

The largely male-dominated trade unions have also played a role in this social construction through frequent failures to support women's claims for jobs to be regraded. Until recently some unions also acted to thwart the entry of women into many better-paid and traditionally male-dominated industries such as shipbuilding. However, women have made some gains in the trade unions (Carter 1988). Firstly, the proportion of women who were in trade unions has increased and by 1979 stood at 39 per cent. Secondly, women have become more active in union affairs as has been evident, for example, in their prominent role in a number of NHS disputes, and more recently in the Timex dispute at Dundee. In general, however, women still tend to be less active than men in the unions. This can be explained by the tendency to be in part-time jobs and by the pressures arising from having to fulfil dual roles as wives and mothers. Thirdly, there is also some evidence that women are gaining better representation amongst the full-time officials and the national executives of unions. Even so, in the TGWU, which had 16 per cent female membership in 1985, women formed only 3 per cent of the national executive. Similar underrepresentation can be found in most major unions. Fourthly, and more positively, there are signs that women have gained a greater recognition for their concerns within unions. Thus sewing machinists at Ford had a long but ultimately successful campaign to get the TGWU to back their demands for pay parity with the majority of semi-skilled workers. These advances, however, have to be balanced against the declining overall numerical and bargaining strength of trade unions during the period of Two Nations politics.

There may also be indirect discrimination against women in firms' personnel practices. For example, a 1986 Equal Opportunities Commission report on British Rail found that a number of its employment practices discriminated against women. These included promotion based on length of unbroken

service, word of mouth recruitment and height requirements. Indirect discrimination still exists in many industries even though direct discrimination
has largely been made illegal.

The social expectation that women have 'dual careers' in which they combine paid jobs and domestic responsibilities also contributes to occupational
segregation. Taking responsibility for child rearing or caring for elderly relatives may mean that women are either not available for full-time work or can
only take jobs with fixed hours which fit in with their domestic roles. This may
exclude them from those management posts which require working flexible
hours or spending periods of time away from home. Single women are not
necessarily constrained in the same way but do suffer from general societal
expectations as to what constitutes suitable work for women.

These social constructions have strong associations with the ideology of the
family and the notion that men are the principal wage earners. Whilst that
ideology has been prevalent in the eras of both One Nation and Two Nations
politics, it has actively been promoted in the latter. The ideology of femininity
is also important. A selective emphasis on the glamorous aspects of femininity
contributes to the attraction of women to such jobs as receptionists and
hairdressers. This is encouraged by many employers. For example, when dis-
cussing recruitment, one manager of a branch of a high street bank stated that
(Collinson 1988):

> I think sex does come into it. Men would sooner be served by a pretty young
> thing, even at the risk of not getting quite the service that you would get from
> a keen young man. They are prepared to put up with that because they can stand
> there and ogle while they get paid the cash. Benefits in kind, isn't it?'

Whatever 'benefits in kind' there may be for individual women employees,
such stereotyping offers no benefits for women in general.

How then has occupational segregation changed between the periods of One
Nation and Two Nations politics? This is difficult to answer given the
problems of data inconsistencies (Walby and Bagguley 1990), and the fact that
the impact of government policies coexists with that of broader changes in civil
society including increasingly influential women's movements. Hakim (1992)
argues that there has been a greater decline in occupational segregation during
the 1980s than in the 1970s. This is, of course, in part a reflection of the run-
down of traditional male-dominated sectors of manufacturing, and the
increasing emphasis on flexible employment strategies. However, Hakim also
notes that there has been a sharp decline in vertical occupational segregation.
This suggests that increasing female participation in the labour market, combined with the impact of equal opportunities legislation, is having some effect
on the gendering of occupational opportunities. The most important aspect of
the labour market changes has been a feminisation of the service class in the
1970s and the 1980s (Walby and Bagguley 1990); this is related to the
increasing numbers of women with higher educational qualifications entering

the expanding service class. Despite these changes, there is still considerable vertical segregation in many economic sectors; only 8 per cent of top executives in British companies are women, leading to the conclusion that there is still a male-constructed glass ceiling blocking their promotion (Gregg and Machin 1993).

5.2.3 Part-time work

One particular feature of occupational segregation is the disproportionate number of women in part-time jobs, which tend to be low paid and (at least categorised as) low skilled (Beechey and Perkins 1987). Part-time working became more widespread towards the end of the Second World War but never exceeded 7 per cent at that time. Subsequently the number of part-time jobs has increased sharply and the vast majority filled by women. In 1992 44 per cent of women and 6 per cent of men were in part-time work (Equal Opportunities Commission 1993). For some women this may reflect a conscious lifestyle choice, whilst for many married women part-time work is a way of combining employment with a degree of flexibility to enable them to care for children or elderly relatives. But for many women part-time jobs may be the only paid work to which they have access. The decision to work part-time as opposed to full-time is also conditioned by the rules of the social security system. One of the ironies of the welfare state is that single mothers are least likely to be working part time; the system of state benefits and taxation makes full-time work the only viable labour market option for this group. Wages from part-time work – and sometimes full-time work – will simply not cover child care costs, for which there is no tax relief, and also compensate for the loss of benefits. In contrast to single mothers, mothers in two-adult households are far more likely to be in part-time work.

Not only do women predominate in part-time work but this work is concentrated in a few occupations (Figure 5.2). The vast majority are in the service sector and two-thirds are in just four types of jobs: catering, cleaning, hairdressing and clerical work. Within the manufacturing sector, women are similarly concentrated in low-paid and low-skilled part-time jobs. This underlines an important point: part-time work is more than a coincidental feature of occupational segregation; it is central to it. It is extremely rare to find a woman working part time doing the same job as a man.

It is not only responsibilities and basic wages (see following section) which vary between part-time and full-time jobs. Full-time posts are more likely to have more opportunities for earning overtime and bonuses. They are also more likely to have a whole series of fringe benefits such as sick pay, maternity leave or holiday pay. For those on low incomes these are more than fringe luxuries: they represent the difference between bare existence and some comfort, and between security and insecurity. Many employers also use part-time

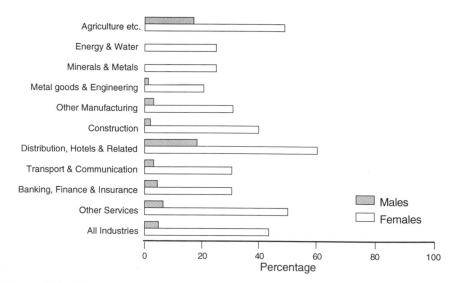

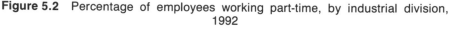

Figure 5.2 Percentage of employees working part-time, by industrial division, 1992

Source: *Labour Force Survey*

workers as a flexible buffer to absorb changes in their volume of business and to protect their 'core' full-time workers (see pp. 86–89) from the consequences of these. Instead, the consequences are borne by their part-time – and largely female – staff. Statistically this is seen in the facts that in 1992 57 per cent of temporary workers were women and that three fifths of these were part timers (Equal Opportunities Commission 1993).

5.2.4 Homeworking: a twilight area

Homeworking is another area in which there is occupational segregation between men and women. There are no precise data of the number of homeworkers in the UK but it is estimated that this exceeds 250 000. The majority are women and many work in or on the edges of the black economy. Homeworkers are a very diverse group. At one extreme are the professionals, some of whom are teleworkers using computers or advanced telecommunications in well-paid sub-contracting work (Castells and Henderson 1989). Homeworking offers them the advantages of flexibility and a comfortable working environment although there may also be difficulties of social isolation. Both men and women can be found in such jobs, many of which are in computing or publishing. At the other extreme are an estimated 130 000 child minders working from their own or other people's homes, often on a part-time and seasonal basis so as to fit in with school hours and terms.

There are also large numbers of homeworkers in manufacturing, especially in the clothing sector. According to a 1988 report by Birmingham City Council, *Homeworking in Birmingham*, there may be as many as 5000 such workers in that area alone. Amongst the many individuals highlighted is Saroj:

> Saroj's workplace is her home. She is usually to be found in the front room of the run-down terraced house in Handsworth, Birmingham. Small, dark and dusty, the room is filled with clothing material, an old sewing machine, a portable TV for Saroj's two and a half year old son to watch all day, and a budgie in a cage. Working as a seamstress Saroj sews pockets onto trousers, for which she gets paid 90p a pair. She works an average of 56 hours a week for which she earns between £20 and £25. All she knows about her employer is that he runs a small clothes manufacturing company at the cheaper end of the fashion market and that he employs about 30 other workers.

She is startling testimony that the world of sweat shops still persists in many British cities and has grown in the 1980s and 1990s as Victorian values reassert themselves in the labour market; it is a world mostly inhabited by women, many but not all of whom are Asians. Their labour market position is one of constraint not of choice: 'The Asian woman homeworker of the 1980s has the "free choice" of lousy work or no work at all' (Lewis and Davies 1991, 22). The contrast between the teleworker and the inner-city seamstress also emphasises the importance of locally differentiated labour markets offering very different work experiences to both men and women (see Chapter 8).

5.2.5 Women's pay and the feminisation of poverty

Given the extent of occupational segregation, there are of course considerable differences in men's and women's pay (Table 5.4). Over time there has been remarkably little change in the extent of the gendering of wage differentials;

Table 5.4 Women's earnings as a percentage of men's earnings in 1970–92. Average gross hourly earnings, excluding overtime, of full-time employees aged 18 and over

1970	63.1	1983	74.2
1975	72.1	1984	73.6
1976	75.1	1985	74.1
1977	75.5	1986	74.3
1978	73.9	1987	73.6
1979	73.0	1988	74.8
1980	73.5	1989	75.9
1981	74.8	1990	76.6
1982	73.9	1991	77.8

Sources: 'New Earnings Survey', report in *Employment Gazette*, November 1988, p. 570; *New Earnings Survey*, 1992.

full-time women workers have earned about three-quarters of the wages of full-time men workers since about 1976. There was a sharp increase in the mid-1970s, very much related to the passing of Equal Pay legislation at the end of the period of One Nation politics (Figure 5.3). Thereafter, there was a slight widening in the differential during the period of Two Nations politics, leastways until 1987. After 1988, however, there was a further narrowing of wage differentials. There are two main reasons for this. One is the decline of traditional sources of male-dominated skilled manufacturing jobs. The other reason is the feminisation of the service class; this has led to a narrowing of gendered inequalities in wages in non-manual employment in the second half of the 1980s.

This picture of narrowing differentials is in some ways deceptive for it is based on full-time employment. In contrast, the differential for all jobs – full-time and part-time – is much wider at 70 per cent in 1992; this is critical given the increasing share of part-time jobs in the labour market, which are over-whelmingly filled by women. It is also the case that there has been a narrowing of wage differentials in most of Europe during the 1970s and the 1980s and that the UK continues to have much wider differentials than virtually all other EC countries in both the service and manufacturing sectors (Table 5.5).

The gendering of income differentials is a product of several unequal relationships. Women are concentrated in low pay industries. For example, footwear and clothing are notoriously poorly paid sectors, and women constitute three-quarters of all manual employees in these industries. Many women in these and other industries are occupying posts which are below their real skill levels. This is frequently a problem for women returning to the labour market after having children, not least because, according to the Equal Opportunities

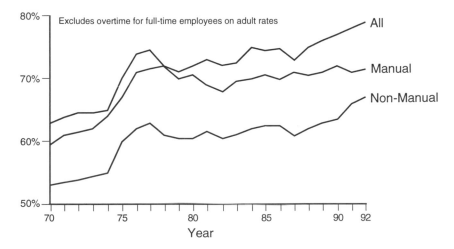

Figure 5.3 Women's earnings as percentage of men's (hourly earnings)
Source: Department of Employment, *New Earnings Survey*, 1992

Table 5.5 Male/female wage differentials in the EC, 1991

| | % difference between male and female earnings | | |
| | Manufacturing | | |
Country	Manual workers (hourly)	Non-manual workers (monthly)	Retail (monthly)
Belgium	− 26.2	− 35.5	− 26.8
Denmark	− 15.5	—	—
France	− 21.4	− 32.6	− 31.7
Germany	− 26.5	− 32.6	− 30.0
Greece	− 20.8	− 31.5	− 19.8
Ireland	− 30.2	—	—
Italy	—	—	—
Luxembourg	− 39.0	− 44.1	− 38.0
Netherlands	− 24.4	− 34.2	− 32.5
Portugal	− 29.5	− 30.8	− 19.7
Spain	− 22.6	− 35.2	− 36.2
UK	− 32.0	− 41.3	− 36.2

Source: *Commission of the European Communities*

Commission, only one-half of working women actually qualify for maternity leave with job guarantees.

However, the causes of gendered wage differentials extend beyond occupational segregation. There are also significant differences between male and female earnings even within the same occupation. According to the 1992 *New Earnings Survey*, female sales supervisors earn only two-thirds of the hourly rates of men and amongst footwear workers the figure is only 70 per cent. Elsewhere there are more egalitarian pay-scales; for example, female nurses and police officers earn over 90 per cent (but not 100 per cent) of the hourly rates of their male colleagues. A particular difficulty for working women is that these differentials are greatest where they have the greatest impact, that is in the lower-waged occupations.

Hourly rates do not measure the full extent of male–female inequalities, for men also have more overtime earnings. Amongst manual workers the proportion of women with overtime earnings is only about one-half of that for men. And although the gap closed somewhat in the late 1980s, men on average worked four times as much overtime as women (Table 5.6). By 1991 the average male full-time worker was earning £23 per week in overtime compared to only £5 for the average female.

Nor do the inequalities end there. Women have less access to fringe benefits which have become increasingly important as sources of real income. This is particularly evident in respect of occupational pensions. The 1942 Beveridge

Table 5.6 Levels of pay and hours for men and women, 1987 (1991)

| | Full-time employees on adults rates | | | | | |
| | Males | | | Females | | |
	Manual	Non-manual	All	Manual	Non-manual	All
Average gross weekly earnings (£) of which:	186 (253)	266 (376)	244 (319)	155 (159)	157 (237)	148 (222)
overtime payments	27 (35)	9 (11)	18 (23)	6 (9)	3 (5)	4 (5)
bonus, etc. payments	14 (15)	10 (12)	12 (14)	10 (10)	2 (3)	4 (5)
shift, etc. premium payments	6 (9)	2 (3)	4 (6)	3 (5)	2 (2)	2 (3)
Average total weekly hours of which:						
overtime hours	5.5 (5.3)	1.5 (1.4)	3.7 (3.3)	1.6 (1.6)	0.6 (0.6)	0.8 (0.8)

Sources: *Employment Gazette*, November 1987, p. 569; *Regional Trends* 1992, pp. 99–100

Report ignored women's pension needs, instead emphasising 'encouragement for voluntary action by each individual to provide more than that minimum for *himself and his* family' (quoted in Ginn and Arber 1993, 48; emphasis added). Women are disadvantaged in two ways: by their broken career spans and by occupational segregation and discrimination. As a result, whilst full-time men and women are equally likely to work for employers with occupational pension schemes, women are far more likely not to belong to these (Table 5.7). Again, however, it is the feminisation of part-time work which is the key differential for two-fifths of the employers of women in such jobs do not offer occupational pensions. As the size of pensions is based on levels of earnings and years of pensionable service, non-working divorced women are also disadvantaged because they have no legal claims on their ex-husbands' pensions. Finally, the official retirement age also gives men five more working years than women, although under pressure from the European Commission and the European Court this will be phased out in future.

One of the underlying assumptions behind the historically low wages received by women is the notion that men needed to receive a 'family' wage while women's wages were little more than an additional luxury. Even though this has never accurately portrayed historical reality, the notion persisted well into the twentieth century. Single women were particularly disadvantaged economically by this sexist assumption. The unequal pay received by women has, in a sense, increased in significance in recent years with increasing numbers of households having female-heads, whether single, divorced, widowed or separated. This has a direct bearing on their own welfare as adults and on the welfare of children raised in low-income, female headed households.

It has already been stressed that the ratio of male to female hourly earnings has been largely static in the 1980s. However, such figures conceal a far more worrying trend, the feminisation of poverty in the 1980s. A survey of living standards in London in the 1980s showed that the real earnings of men rose 9 per cent while those of women were static (Bruegel 1987). A particularly

Table 5.7 Pensions: the gendering of occupational schemes, 1991 (percentage belonging to current employer's pensions scheme)

	Men Full-time		Women			
			Full-time		Part-time	
	1983	1991	1983	1991	1983	1991
Present employer does not have pension scheme	22	21	24	20	40	39
Non-member of present employer's pension scheme	10	16	17	21	39	34

important cause of this was the growth of female part-time jobs. As a result there has been an increasing concentration of poverty in households headed by women. While only 20 per cent of all households were headed by women, they headed 62 per cent of all households in the lowest quintile of households ranked by income. Structural economic changes combined with the economic policies of Two Nations politics have increased the inequalities between men and women as well as between different types of households. This echoes the relative income redistribution from low to high income earners during the Thatcher governments' period.

There has also been a deterioration of women's position with respect to benefits. Gender inequalities were built into the welfare state from its inception, and so were present under One Nation politics. One of the key assumptions of the Beveridge Report was that working women had a similar career pattern to men which, of course, ignored their career breaks for bringing up children. The report also treated the family as a unit and made welfare provision for married women dependent on their husbands. This was seen for example in the way that separated wives received supplementary benefits rather than social insurance benefits; the underlying assumption was that women had been responsible for their own fates by allowing their marriages to fail.

Since 1979, however, the rights of women to benefits have been further weakened. Unemployment benefits are paid to those who are available for work. Since 1982 part of the test of availability has involved proof that adequate arrangements have been made for children and for dependants. Given the lack of state pre-school care facilities, this can be a major obstacle for many women. The Fowler Review had proposed to pay the new family credit through the pay-packet rather than directly to women, a move which would seriously have further undermined women's economic independence; however, sustained pressure led to this provision being dropped from the 1986 Social Security Act. Despite this 'victory', cuts in housing benefits, erosion of the value of child benefit and reductions in other welfare provision have disadvantaged women, especially those who are single parents. Media-generated controversy in the course of 1993 focused attention on a few 'home alone' children of single mothers who simply could not afford child care out of their low wages. This sharply underlined their vulnerability in the face of social welfare cuts and the low wages of Two Nations Britain.

5.2.6 The contribution and limitation of equal pay legislation

There have been some improvements in the legal provision of equal pay for women. The most significant landmark came at the end of the period of One Nation politics. The 1975 Equal Pay Act obliged employers to give equal pay and terms and conditions of employment to men and women employed on like work. This allowed individuals to claim like pay for like work and it certainly helped many people. The Act also contributed to some narrowing of income differentials in the mid-1970s (see Table 5.4; also Zabalza and Tzannatos 1985). However, it only allowed comparisons with men in the same occupations; this meant that many virtually exclusively female occupations, such as typists and secretaries, were excluded. By 1983 only 26 applications had been made under the Act to industrial tribunals and only 6 were upheld. In addition, many employers avoided complying with the Act, through actions such as moving all men or all women out of previously mixed occupations, or creating new grades so as to avoid direct comparisons of men's and women's wages. Therefore, whilst most women are receiving equal pay as defined by the Equal Pay Act, many women are not being paid in accordance with their skills.

The Act is flawed in that it has few positive provisions to break down occupational segregation. The main effect has been to remove overt sex discrimination in recruitment as, for example, in job advertisements. A small number of women have also gained entry to traditionally male-dominated jobs such as lorry driving or engineering apprenticeships. But the Act is essentially negative and there is no obligation for employers to create equal opportunities. Thus a 1988 survey of 21 large private companies, by the Labour Research Department, found that although all but one had an equal opportunities policy, only a minority had actually implemented measures to attract and retain women, especially working mothers. None had organised special nursery provision and only 7 per cent made specific payments towards child care.

The 1975 Equal Pay Act did not mark the beginnings of a major advance for women in the labour market. Whatever aspirations existed in this respect were to clash head on with the Thatcherite economic strategy for re-establishing UK economic competitivity on the basis of low wages and flexible labour markets. Mrs Thatcher's governments in the 1980s initiated no significant legislation to remedy the continuing disadvantages of women in the labour market. The few small advances that women achieved were mainly the result of external policy changes imposed on the UK by the European Community. In 1984 and 1986 the UK was compelled to change its equal pay legislation to comply with a 1975 European Commission directive that women workers should be paid the same as men for doing work of the same value.

Based on this legislation, there have been a number of legal judgments which have at least strengthened the formal pay position of women. The first of these concerned Ms Julie Hayward, a cook at Cammel Laird's Birkenhead shipyard. She won an appeal to the Law Lords for equality of pay to male shipbuilders. The Law Lords ruled that fringe benefits paid to women workers could not be used to justify paying them less. A second judgment concerned Ms Rene Pickstone, a packer at Freeman's, the mail order company; this prevented employers getting around the 1986 legal amendment by employing a token man in grades usually dominated by women. By 1993 only 23 claims in equal value cases had succeeded after nearly 10 years (*Financial Times*, 1 September 1993). This led, in the summer of 1993, to the Equal Opportunities Commission referring the UK government to the European Commission for not having implemented EC equal pay legislation. When challenged about its record, the government tended to emphasise the sheer increase of female employment opportunities in the UK. That has at least been consistent with its strategy for generating growth via low waged, flexible labour even if it has ignored the question of structural disadvantages in the labour market.

Despite some legislative advances, then, the benefits for women in the 1980s have been limited. Those who have probably benefited most are a small minority of highly educated and professional women, for whom there has been some long-term opening up of opportunities. Manual women workers have gained far less, especially compared to their gains in the 1970s; in a sense they are one of the groups which has paid the highest price for the Conservative governments' economic strategy.

At different times in the 1980s and the 1990s, there were indications that the pay and employment conditions of women (and men) in manual jobs were deteriorating rather than improving. Whilst this was partly due to employers finding loopholes in the Equal Pay Act, it also reflected the growing incidence of part-time working, and the rise of mass unemployment. Furthermore, legislative advances were not linked to increased provisions by either the state or the private sector for working mothers. A survey by the British Institute of Management in 1989 found that only about one-fifth of managers in the private sector considered that their companies had a coherent policy of commitment to equal opportunities. There were some improvements in the late 1980s when a number of companies announced plans to introduce crèche facilities and to give favourable treatment to mid-career breaks; however, these initiatives have tended to benefit better paid women in permanent, skilled and full-time jobs (Somerville 1992). Moreover, the stimulus to this was essentially economic – the increasing difficulties of companies in the South in labour recruitment. With the onset of the recession in the early 1990s, there has been less enthusiasm amongst employers for such measures.

The positive impact of the equal pay legislation also has to be seen in context of other government legislation, especially the abolition of most of the remaining Wages Councils in 1993. This important component of the Two Nations strategy removed minimum wages controls in several activities such as hairdressing and laundering in which there was marked occupational segregation. Thus some 80 per cent of the workers affected by the abolition of these councils were women. This was the culmination of a Conservative strategy which had seen the gradual whittling away of the number of councils, of their coverage of the workforce (under 21 year olds were removed from the Act's protection in 1986), and of their powers to set wage levels (see Figure 5.4). This is particularly important given that gendered wage differentials have been narrower in Wages Councils industries (Pay Equity Project 1993).

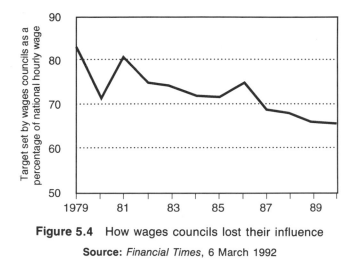

Figure 5.4 How wages councils lost their influence

Source: *Financial Times*, 6 March 1992

5.2.7 Men, women and unemployment

There has been no consistent policy actively to encourage the growth of female employment in either the period of One Nation or Two Nations politics. Nevertheless, employment growth has been more rapid for women than for men in recent decades. Between 1971 and 1990 the number of women in employment increased from 8.2 to 11.4 million, before slipping back to 11.2 million in 1993 following the economic crisis of the early 1990s. The gross figures are, of course, deceptive and take no account of the rapid growth of part-time work amongst women.

The growth of female employment also tends to obscure the growing incidence of unemployment amongst women. In absolute terms unemployed men still considerably outnumber unemployed women. However, the rate of growth for women in the late 1970s and the early 1980s was double that for men. Given the number of single women in the workforce and the large number of households dependent mostly or solely on a wife's/mother's earnings, increasing female unemployment had significant implications for deprivation in the UK. In the 1990s registered unemployment has again increased faster for men than for women; the differential is still substantial, being 14 per cent for men and 5.8 per cent for women in July 1993.

As a result of these trends, the experience of unemployment has become virtually universal amongst working women. According to one survey, 83 per cent of economically active women had been unemployed at some stage of their working lives (Martin and Wallace 1984). The duration of women's unemployment has also increased and in 1987 54 per cent of those currently unemployed had been so for at least six months (Table 5.8). In 1993 this figure

Table 5.8 Unemployment by sex and duration in 1987 and 1993 (percentages)

	Male		Female	
Duration of unemployment	1987	1993	1987	1993
Up to 26 weeks	35.5	39.3	45.8	52.1
27–52 weeks	17.4	20.5	21.8	21.5
1–2 years	16.2	19.7	14.3	14.8
Over 2 years	30.9	20.5	18.1	11.7
	100.0	100.0	100.0	100.0

Source: CSO (1988, 93)

was still 48 per cent for women, even if the corresponding statistic was higher for males. Nevertheless, these data do underline the growing feminisation of unemployment, which in turn is linked to the feminisation of poverty.

5.2.8 Social mobility and the persistence of inequality

Social mobility has already been discussed in general terms in Chapter 3, and here we look at its gendering (Dex 1987; Heath 1981). This issue is significant in understanding both the constraints on women during their own working lives and also on women's social mobility between generations.

Intergenerational marital mobility is sometimes measured by comparing the jobs of women's fathers to those of their husbands, although this is controversial in not recognising women's independent social status. The Scottish Mobility Study (see Abbot and Sapsford 1987) found that 42 per cent of married women had upwardly mobile marriages, whilst 37 per cent had downwardly mobile marriages. Of greater relevance is intergenerational occupational mobility; this has usually been measured – again controversially – by comparing the occupations of fathers and daughters. Any such analysis is made difficult by changing occupational definitions and by the need to take into account lifetime career developments. Nevertheless, the Scottish Mobility Study did find clear evidence that men are more likely than women to be upwardly socially mobile. The differences are greatest across the manual/non-manual divide. Relatively few daughters of manual fathers obtain non-manual occupations other than routine clerical-type posts.

Women are equally disadvantaged in terms of intra-generational mobility. They have far less overall occupational mobility than men and this is far more likely to be downwards. According to the Scottish Mobility Study three-quarters of men and women are downwardly mobile when they first enter the labour market, compared to their fathers' occupations. However, women are less likely to recover their positions at a later point in time. For example, amongst those with fathers in professional or semi-professional posts, 40 per cent of sons but only 12 per cent of daughters eventually achieved the same or higher status.

Apart from general discrimination in the labour market, the key to women's mobility is whether they have children. Childless women have far better opportunities to be upwardly mobile. For example, after having children 51 per cent of women return to work, but 37 per cent of these are downwardly mobile. They do not all recover their former positions, let alone achieve longer-term upward mobility. For many women the return to work is also accompanied by a shift to part-time working, with all that this implies in terms of reduced opportunities for future advancement.

5.2.9 Reprise: widening economic inequalities?

In concluding this section, it is necessary to emphasise that class interacts with gender in terms of both intergenerational and intra-generational mobility. Women achieved only limited advances in the labour market during the period of One Nation politics. However, there is evidence that in many respects their position remained static (e.g. equal pay) or even deteriorated (e.g. unemployment rates and the removal of minimum wage controls) during the period of Two Nations politics. The widening of many class differentials (see Chapter 3) only served to differentiate further the experiences of women in the labour market. This is epitomised above all by the boom in the City of London in the late 1980s; whilst hundreds of well-paid jobs were taken by women in the corporate financial sector, many more found employment in the increasingly unregulated low-wage army of caterers and cleaners who serviced them (Sassen 1991).

5.3 His and her schooling: the gendering of educational access and opportunities

5.3.1 Participation and qualifications

An assumption of One Nation politics was that the state had a critical role to play in facilitating a degree of social convergence. Whilst there were differences in the way this was interpreted by Labour and Conservative governments, there was also inter-party consensus that state-provided educational opportunities facilitated social mobility and a meritocratic order. There was a universalisation of access in the 1950s, but the 1963 Robbins Report was the most important educational landmark of One Nation politics. Unlike the Beveridge Report, it was not entirely gender blind; instead, it stressed that

Table 5.9 School-leavers' highest qualification, by sex, 1970/71 to 1989/90 (percentages)

UK	Boys				Girls			
	1970/71	1975/76	1985/86	1989/90	1970/71	1975/76	1985/86	1989/90
Percentage with:								
2 or more A levels/3 or more H grades	15	14	15	20	13	12	14	22
1 A level or 2 H grades	4	3	4	4	4	4	4	5
5 or more O levels/grades: A–C grades	7	7	10	11	9	9	12	15
1–4 O levels/grades: A–C grades	17	24	24	26	18	27	29	28
1 or more O levels/grades: D or E grades, or CSE grades 2–5	58	30	34	29	56	28	31	23
No GCE/SCE or CSE grades	—	21	13	10	—	19	10	7
Total school-leavers	100	100	100	100	100	100	100	100

Source: CSO (1988, 18, Table 3.12)

gender provided an additional dimension to class in underachievement in schools. The reforms initiated by Robbins did contribute to greater gender equality between boys and girls in their academic participation and achievements at school, although there continued to be a gendering of educational experiences, such as sex stereotyping of the curriculum. In the period of Two Nations politics, educational reforms such as the national curriculum, the opting out of schools, real expenditure cut-backs and devolved budgets for schools have had considerable social significance but little discernible impact in reducing gender inequalities.

There were important educational advances in the 1950s and 1960s with the universalisation of access and rising achievement levels. Between 1961/62 and 1973/74 the proportion of male school leavers with two or more A-level passes rose from 8 to 13 per cent whilst for girls the proportion increased from 5 per cent to 11 per cent. Subsequently the gap narrowed further to 14.9 per cent and 14.2 per cent by 1985–86, whilst by 1989–90 girls had overtaken boys (Table 5.9). By 1992 16 per cent of girls but only 14 per cent of boys had three or more A-level passes (*Financial Times*, 23 December 1993). In this respect there has been a real improvement in the position of women (Table 5.10). Some of the advances were made in the 1980s, but the foundations for these were laid in the educational reforms of One Nation politics.

After school, a larger proportion of girls proceed to some form of full-time education but this simple statistic is deceptive. To some extent, this can be explained by their disproportionate presence on vocational, sub-degree-level programmes, such as secretarial and nursing courses. This, in itself, reveals much about the gendered social construction of occupations. However, there have been steady improvements in girls' access to higher education, and in 1992 more girls than boys entered university, for the first time ever.

Gender divisions are equally strong in training. Whilst boys and girls are to be found in approximately equal numbers on full-time training courses, there are significantly more males on part-time or day-release courses. The expansion of government-sponsored training courses in the 1980s led to some equalisation of access to training (especially via the training credits scheme), leastways in terms of numbers. However, there is still strong streaming:for example, most students on clerical, shorthand and typing courses are women. Furthermore, unequal access persists in in-service training; for example, amongst clerical workers 60 per cent of women but 93 per cent of men receive further training.

Gender deepens educational inequalities which stem from social class. For example, amongst the children of fathers in professional occupations the greater tendency for sons to secure degrees is partly counteracted by the higher proportions of daughters obtaining other higher educational qualifications (Table 5.10). This is not the case amongst the children of skilled and unskilled manual workers where sons outperform daughters in obtaining all qualifications at A level or above. However, the differences are starkest at the lower

Table 5.10   Highest qualifications attained by men and women, 1990–91 (Persons aged 25–59 not in FT education) (percentages)

	Socio-economic group of father			
	Professional	Skilled manual	Unskilled manual	Total
Degree or equivalent				
Men	41	7	5	13
Women	24	4	1	7
Other higher education				
Men	15	12	5	13
Women	23	10	5	10
GCE A level				
Men	17	12	7	13
Women	14	5	1	6
GCSE O level grades A–C or equivalent				
Men	15	18	15	18
Women	22	23	16	24
Other				
Men	5	15	14	12
Women	10	13	11	15
No qualifications				
Men	7	36	54	31
Women	7	45	66	38
Total	100	100	100	100

Source: *General Household Survey*, 1991, Table 10.6

end of the scale of academic qualifications. Amongst those with no formal qualifications whatsoever, there is no difference between the sons and daughters of professional fathers but there is a striking difference amongst the children of unskilled fathers.

5.3.2   Educational Streaming

Whilst there has been convergence in participation in and success in obtaining qualifications from the educational system, there remains a form of gendered educational segregation in terms of the subjects studied. Thus in 1980 97 per cent of those taking O level cooking were girls, whilst the corresponding figures for French and mathematics were 59 per cent and 40 per cent, and for woodwork just 1 per cent. Such formal streaming of subjects as being 'suitable' for boys or girls is no longer practised. However, there is still strong social construction of the 'suitability' of subjects, and informal streaming by teachers and parents still occurs. At A level the differences are further exaggerated. According to the Equal Opportunities Commission, the ratio of boys to girls taking O level physics is about 2.5 : 1 but for A level physics it is 3.5 : 1. This gender streaming is extended into higher and further education courses: in 1992 a quarter of male but only 5 per cent of female undergraduates were taking engineering or technology courses (Figure 5.5).

Historically there has been a high degree of streaming in education and an opportunity was lost to rectify this in the immediate post Second World War period. The 1944 Education Act established secondary education for all and was pervaded by notions of equality in most respects − save gender. Instead, this Act was informed by the objective of relating girls' schooling to their future role as mothers. This notion that the primary responsibilities of women were as carers in the family setting, was reinforced by other social policies. For example, nursery schools set up during the war were shut down and women were encouraged to see their main responsibilities as home makers.

The streaming of aspirations and of learning experiences predates schooling. Streaming is strongly founded in childhood experiences in the home. The toys, books and games of boys and girls are different and contribute to socialisation into highly differentiated roles. Sex stereotyping is particularly strong in the

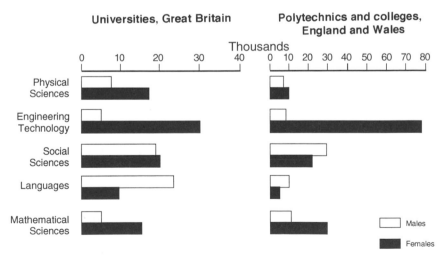

Figure 5.5 Subject choice in higher education, 1991–92

Source: Department for Education; Welsh Joint Education Committee; Welsh Office; Scottish Examination Board; Universities' Statistical Record

books produced for young children and these have and sometimes still do show boys and girls doing very different types of jobs and offering them heroes and heroines with very different characteristics. Later the organisation of schools further encourages stereotyping. This used to operate both through the range of subjects that were available in all-male and all-female schools, and in the types of subjects that were offered to boys and girls in mixed schools. Single sex and mixed schools streamed pupils in different ways; for example, all-girls schools offered a smaller range of science subjects than did mixed schools, but girls were more likely to select science options in the former than in the latter. These gendered institutional differences in education were only substantially reduced at the close of the period of One Nation politics. Since the 1975 Sex Discrimination Act it has been unlawful to discriminate between males and females in either education or training. Consequently, the degree of formal streaming has declined substantially. Nevertheless the influences of childhood socialisation and of informal streaming remain strong. The use of gender in mixed schools to categorise pupils, to organise their daily school activities and their play activities, all reinforce the differences between the sexes.

The importance of streaming and of schools' expectations extends into socialisation. Socialisation in schools is not only class specific but also gender specific. In working-class schools there is social pressure on males to conform to the stereotypical masculine qualities of strength, dominance and bravery, whilst female roles tend to be portrayed as submissive, weak and home centred. In middle-class schools the roles are portrayed differently but there are still strong gender differences: males are cast as the intellectual élite whilst for females there is more emphasis on being well dressed and well spoken. Gender stereotyping is sometimes more marked in private than in state schools. In private schools masculinity, leadership and initiative are emphasised for boys, whilst femininity and obedience are emphasised for girls. Consequently , the educational system – in all its various forms – can be said to have played an important role in socialising children into a view of the world that accepts and reproduces inequalities in terms of both class and gender.

Education is one of the keys to life chances and life styles. In the longer term inequalities in the subjects chosen at school, the levels of examinations taken, and the forms of post-school education all contribute to occupational segregation and income differences. However, whilst there has been greater female participation in sixth forms and universities, this will not necessarily eliminate such inequalities. A comparison of pay and educational qualifications reveals that, at all levels, women earn significantly less than men (Table 5.11). Whatever the hopes of educational reformers, and especially of the architects of the Equal Opportunities Act, it has become clear that equality of opportunity is unrealisable without first achieving a greater degree of equality in society itself (Blackstone 1980).

Table 5.11 Men's and women's earnings* and qualifications in the UK, 1991

| | Gross weekly earnings Percentages earning: | | | |
| | £120 or more | | £200 or more | |
Highest qualification attained	Men	Women	Men	Women
Degree or equivalent	98	98	80	64
Below degree level higher education	97	97	61	49
GCE A level or equivalent	96	93	49	19
GCSE O level grades A–C or equivalent	94	89	33	3
CSE other grades, etc.	95	84	24	5
No qualifications	92	73	22	4
Total	95	88	41	22

* Full-time employment only

Source: *General Household Survey*, 1991

The contribution of Two Nations politics to gender inequalities in education has been one of neglect, leastways in direct organisational and institutional terms. It could be argued that this, in itself, is a damning indictment given the persistence of manifold inequalities in achievements and participation. In addition, the indirect effects of other educational policies have been considerable. Expenditure cuts, decentralisation of budgets, and a national curriculum do not address issues of gender inequalities. Indeed, the harsh financial squeeze on resources can only make it more difficult to undertake any form of positive discrimination, whilst the suggestion that schools should 'specialise' contains an implicit assumption of a return to single sex schools. The promotion of 'Victorian values' and of the role of women as carers in the family, also engenders pressure for streaming.

5.4 Women in the domestic sphere: consumption, housing and leisure

5.4.1 Dual role or double responsibility?

Most women and men have dual roles in the labour market and in the domestic sphere, but there are important differences between their contents and implications, especially for married women. One Nation politics were initially founded on the assumption that the primary role of married women was in the home so that the implications of their dual careers were overlooked in such influential policy statements as the Beveridge Report. Towards the end of this period, there was some legal recognition of gendered inequalities via the Equal

Opportunities Act. However, these were not matched by changes in either social policy or in the domestic division of labour that were commensurate with the demands made on women by their dual roles. In the attempt to reshape both the conditions of production and civil society, as part of the strategy of Two Nations politics, the family has become the centre of two conflicting Conservative goals: the aim of producing a low-wage, flexible labour market, which requires particular forms of increased female participation in waged labour; and the aim of shifting the responsibility for care from the state to voluntary organisations and to women within families. On balance, the first aim has been prioritised by the Conservative governments, despite the passion generated at party conferences whenever 'family responsibilities' are mentioned (Somerville 1992). This portrayal of the dominant clash between the dual roles is, of course, an over-simplification, for in practice there are significant variations in the experiences of women, consequent upon their marital and class positions.

One of the most important recent changes in social organisation is that the proportion of women who live as part of a married couple, with or without children, has fallen sharply. Approximately one in six adults aged over 16 lives alone. There have also been changes in families: between 1971 and 1985 the proportion of families headed by married couples fell from 92 per cent to 86 per cent, whilst the share headed by lone parents, especially mothers, increased. Nevertheless, the majority of women at some time live in a household where they are called upon to fulfil the roles of wife and mother, perhaps in combination with working for a wage.

The dual role has not always been dominant. In the nineteenth century and the first part of the twentieth there was a growing separation between women's role in waged and domestic labour. Socially constructed expectations of behaviour followed from this. Men were expected to be competitive, outward-looking, calculating and unemotional, whilst women were 'the angels' at home. They were supposed to be warm and caring, providing unquestioned support to other members of the family. The Englishman's home may have been his castle but the bedrock for this was the emotional and material support provided by women. Whilst the sharp separation of domestic and labour market roles has subsequently been blurred, many attendant social attitudes survive. This is not simply a case of direct male dominance for many women have a deeply socialised sense of 'sacrifice' to the family.

The more stereotyped gendering of roles within the married couple household has become somewhat less common in the UK. Instead, there tend to be more companionable marriages, based on greater equality between male and female roles. Nevertheless there are still differences in these roles, especially in relation to the reproduction of labour power. However, only childbirth, by virtue of biological necessity, is necessarily specific to women. Virtually all other functions, such as child care or looking after a husband or dependent relatives, are social constructions.

In their roles as housewives many women enter into relationships of unequal exchange, in effect receiving maintenance payments in return for their household labour. The nature of the exchange is not always clear because work for the family is usually portrayed as being motivated by love. Whatever the emotional returns, the effect is to constrain women's lives. It also makes women without waged employment economically dependent on their husbands. The labour that they provide is essential to the functioning of the production system (McDowell 1993). As Castells (1977, 177–178) writes, the system only works because women 'repair their homes, because they make meals when there are no canteens, because they spend more time shopping around, because they look after others' children when there are no nurseries, and because they offer "free entertainment" to the producers when there is a social vacuum and an absence of cultural creativity'.

Class affects experiences of the dual role and, for married women, of the form of the unequal exchange of labour. Middle-class women are more likely to have the use of more and more effective labour-saving devices such as dishwashers (see Chapter 4). The middle-class wife may also receive help in the domestic sphere from servants or from a daily/weekly cleaner, who almost inevitably is a working-class woman. There was a rapid growth of domestic service in the 1980s – reviving images of the Victorian era – in households where both male and female partners were in paid jobs. This was typified at the height of the short-lived 1980s boom by Yuppies becoming Yuppeds – young urban professional people employing domestic staff. The domestic help may be employed directly and informally (often in the black economy) or via cleaning and maintenance companies. In either case, their salaries and job conditions are worlds apart from those of the people in whose homes they work. In this respect, they mirror the experiences of the cleaning and catering workers who service the City of London, the spiritual and material temple of Yuppiedom. Class, however, only modifies what are fundamentally gendered relationships. Both middle- and working-class housewives provide unpaid labour for their families. The middle-class housewife may not actually do much manual housework herself but she does undertake household management.

Since 1945 women – especially married women – have been drawn increasingly into the labour force. Whilst this increase was mainly on a part-time basis, in the late 1980s there was also a sharp increase in full-time female employment. As a result, many women have to work long hours in order to combine their dual roles. Their total workload may be far greater than that of their husbands. In addition, many women are called upon to provide unpaid assistance to their husbands in their businesses. This is often the case with shops, farms and other small businesses. Their assistance may involve helping out with routine duties, bookkeeping or other managerial responsibilities. The wives of businessmen – irrespective of whether they have their own careers – may also be expected to support their husbands' careers, for example by entertaining clients to dinner. In farming, the farmer's wife is expected to undertake all her domestic duties and to contribute to work on the farm. These contributions are rarely formally recognised in terms of wages or joint owner-ship of the business, except where partnerships offer tax advantages.

The way in which these dual roles are combined, mediated by class relation-ships, influences experiences of domestic work and leisure. The most obvious state policy impact on this in the period of Two Nations politics is the way in which public expenditure cut-backs, affecting public services, have increased the burden on women. At the same time, the redistribution of income between classes has meant that working-class women have been most severely affected.

5.4.2 Domestic chores, leisure and consumption

There are differences in the amount, form and gendering of the domestic divi-sion of labour between social classes. Amongst some segments of the working class, for example, household chores associated with the external appearances of houses tend to be raised to the status of obsessions. The same applies to the more marginal middle class whose anxieties sometimes approach a 'status panic' (Pahl 1984). Moreover, class-based differences in the domestic division of labour are not reducible to income, for they also incorporate regional and cultural elements. For example, in the North more time is spent on the prep-aration of food than in the South where there is more reliance on convenience foods (Hudson and Williams 1986). As a result men share in housework to varying degrees, but it remains overwhelmingly the responsibility of women, despite rising male unemployment and increased female employment.

Not only are there persistent differences in the amount of housework carried out but there are also increasingly subtle variations in precisely what is done by men and women (Table 5.12). Some tasks are still largely seen as appropriate to or even requiring men, such as house repairs, cutting the lawn or washing the car. With some shift in gender relationships, and the increasing involvement of women in waged labour, men are taking on more household tasks but in a highly selective fashion. They are, for example, increasingly likely to be involved in shopping or in washing up the evening dishes. However, they are less likely to prepare the evening meal or to do the house-hold cleaning and rarely – if ever – do washing and ironing. These variations cannot simply be explained by reference to whether or not wives are also in paid jobs. Even when women are in paid jobs, they are likely to do most of the housework, whilst there is rarely any genuine equalisation of the domestic division of labour even after men retire from waged labour. This is to be explained by socially constructed and deeply embedded views as to an appropriate household division of labour.

Child care is one of the most demanding of duties within the family and this is largely construed as a female role (Table 5.12). The nature of child care has

Table 5.12 Household division of labour in Great Britain, 1984

| | Allocation of tasks between couples Percentages* undertaken by | | |
	Men	Women	Shared equally
Household tasks			
Washing and ironing	1	88	9
Preparation of evening meal	5	77	16
Household cleaning	3	72	23
Household shopping	6	54	39
Evening dishes	18	37	41
Organisation of household money and bills	32	38	28
Repairs of household equipment	83	6	8
Child rearing			
Looking after the children when they are sick	1	63	35
Teaching the children discipline	10	12	77

* 'Don't knows' and non-responses mean that some categories do not sum to 100%

Source: Jowell and Witherspoon (1985)

changed over time. Women now have far fewer children but they tend to stay longer in a dependent phase of the life cycle (e.g. school). As a result of this extension of childhood, parenthood in the 1980s can be as long or even longer than it was in the past when families were larger. Other than for breast-feeding, there is no inherent reason why these responsibilities should fall upon the mother. They do so primarily because of the socially constructed character of motherhood. Women tend to be socialised from an early age to be mothers. Motherhood is not necessarily an unrewarding experience, even if it is also exhausting. Motherhood may also seem to be an attractive alternative to the drudgery of many forms of waged labour. However, the way in which the meaning of motherhood is constructed has resultant implications for women.

There are a number of ways in which motherhood constrains the life-style and life chances of the mother. It involves additional housework, thereby limiting available free time; for example, wives with one child do at least 40 hours of housework whilst those with two or three children do at least 70 hours (Oakley 1974). The range of facilities open to mothers with children is also limited. Many restaurants, pubs, hotels and other centres of leisure simply do not welcome children. Even where children are welcome — as in shops and swimming pools — it may be difficult for mothers to use these facilities without help if there are no crèche facilities. In this respect there may be distinct differences in the experiences of mothers who can and cannot afford to buy in help − whether this is a professionally trained nanny or a child-minding neighbour. There are also differences between those whose children are at boarding school and those whose children are at daily attendance schools. However, the most severely constrained are single parents or wives who receive virtually no support from their partners. Most mothers are also constrained by the spatial structures of society involving separation of suburban homes from services; this is particularly limiting where there is no access to a car and dependence upon public transport.

One of the major constraints on the lives of all mothers in the UK has been the consistent failure to develop child care facilities comparable to those in other Northern European countries. Child benefit allowances are paid to mothers but these do not include specific payments for purchasing child-care, to free mothers for at least part of the day. Nursery provision is also poorly developed. The early educational reforms of One Nation politics largely ignored this issue. However, the 1967 Plowden Report made a strong educational case for universal nursery provision. Demand for this was growing as a result of increasing numbers of mothers in waged labour. There were some advances in the last few years of One Nation politics and by the late 1970s over 50 per cent of all four-year-olds were in state-maintained nursery schools. However, only 15 per cent of three-year-olds were in state nurseries so that access was still largely dependent on social class. Instead, for working-class mothers the vacuum has been filled in part by child minding, often as part of the black economy. Amongst middle-class mothers there has been more emphasis on private nursery schools and on voluntary self-help groups. One of the legacies of Two Nations politics has been the failure to address the need to extend universal, free or low-cost nursery education, in the face of both public expenditure cuts and a particular Conservative Party ideology of the responsibilities of families − that is, of women (Somerville 1992).

Another significant, and potentially constraining activity, which may make demands upon women is caring for elderly relatives. About one half of families look after elderly relatives at some stage, and the larger part of the burden of care falls on daughters, or other female relatives. Again there is nothing in such care work which makes it inherently more suitable for women than for men. The state, via local authority social services departments, does provide some assistance both to elderly relatives living on their own and to those living with their families. Visits by nurses or by home helps can lighten the load. However, real cuts in public expenditure since 1975, as well as Conservative indications of further dismantling of the welfare state, suggest that the burden which falls on families, especially women, has increased and is likely to increase further.

As a result of this uneven division of domestic labour, there are important differences in the amount of leisure time available to men and women (Table 5.13). Amongst full-time workers, males, on average, have one and a half

Table 5.13 Men's and women's use of time in a typical week, 1985–92 (hours)

	Full-time employees				Part-time employees			Housewives	
	Males		Females		Males	Females			
	1985	1992	1985	1992	1985	1985	1992	1985	1992
Time spent on									
Employment and travel to work	45.0	48.9	40.8	43.7	24.3	22.2	21.1	—	0.41
Essential activities*	33.1	26.8	45.1	42.3	48.8	61.3	57.0	76.6	65.5
Sleep	56.4	49.0	57.5	49.0	56.6	57.0	49.0	59.2	49.0
Free time	33.5	45.5	24.6	33.0	38.5	27.5	41.0	32.2	53.5
Free time per week day	2.6	4.8	2.1	3.3	4.5	3.1	4.7	4.2	7.0
Free time per weekend day	10.2	11.3	7.2	8.3	7.8	5.9	8.7	5.6	9.0

* Essential domestic work and personal care. This includes cooking, essential shopping, child care, eating meals, washing and getting up and going to bed.

Sources: Leisure Fortunes, Summer 1986, The Henley Centre for Forecasting; CSO (1993)

hours more leisure time each working day. At weekends this rises to a three-hour difference. Even more striking is the difference between full-time male workers and housewives. Housewives have substantially less leisure time at the weekend than do full-time male workers and little more leisure time than part-time and full-time women workers. In addition, family holidays can involve a gendered division of labour with women tending to be more involved with pre-vacation preparation and with child care and (if self-catering) with cooking and other chores whilst on holiday.

Nor is it merely a question of the amount of time. Not only do husbands have more leisure time than do wives but its quality is different. Whereas wives have to snatch short periods of rest whenever they can and are 'on duty' during the evening, men tend to have solid periods of leisure when at home (Gregory 1982). In this sense, women's work in the home is integral to men's leisure. Furthermore, even when women are not physically working, the fact that they tend to assume the role of household manager means that they endlessly have to think of others.

Women's disjointed free time also restricts the leisure activities in which they can participate, especially given the geographies of services and housing. Many women are – or feel that they are – trapped in the home. Household chores or caring for elderly relatives or children may make it difficult to leave the home for any length of time. This again restricts the range of available leisure activities. In addition, housewives typically form part of the 'transport poor', lacking access to adequate transport at some part if not all of the day. This is less of a problem in two-car families but these are still relatively rare outside of the middle class and non-existent in the underclass. A perceptible increase in the climate of fear for women in recent decades also means that their patterns of mobility have become constrained whether they do or do not have access to car ownership (Valentine 1992).

These disadvantages in free time and leisure are not intentional outcomes of the strategies of Two Nations politics. However, cuts in existing services, such as pre-school facilities and school meals for children, and in community and hospital provision for sick and elderly relatives, have often tended to increase the responsibilities and the workloads of many women. Conservative Party ideology has also stressed the primacy of individual choice (to purchase care, second cars, etc.) allied with greater individual responsibility. In practice, this has often meant that women have had to assume more responsibilities and duties. The Two Nations strategy ignores the issue of how low-income families, or those which are dependent on the earnings of a wife, or a single mother, are to cope, let alone exercise any meaningful individual choice. Nor is this only a problem for a minority. The Royal Commission on the Distribution of Income and Wealth calculated in 1978 that, without the wife's earnings, three times as many families would be below the poverty line. Growing male unemployment in the 1980s has further exacerbated these problems. Furthermore, the emphasis on individual choice has gone hand in hand with the increasing abrogation by the state of its responsibilities to guarantee freedom from poverty, insecurity and unemployment. In sum, except for a privileged wealthy minority, there has been no real improvement in women's access to leisure in the Two Nations period.

5.4.3 'His' and 'her' consumption

Many of the inequalities which stem from the gendering of production and reproduction are carried over into consumption and the culture of consumption. Access to consumption is affected by both inequalities in waged labour and in the distribution of income within families. Traditionally, many men reinforced their positions as the principal wage earner in a family, by maintaining secrecy and strong control over their earnings. Even in the mid-1970s a number of surveys showed that only approximately one-half of all women knew how much their husbands earned. The very notion of a housekeeping allowance was based on the idea that there was unequal access to household income, and that the primary responsibility of wives was to support their husbands. One consequence of this was, and sometimes still is, that mothers and children may live in poverty even within relatively high-income households (Glendinning and Millar 1987). Whilst such familial situations still exist, the growth of female employment, and of female-headed households, has led to some changes. Despite this, however, women still tend to have either less direct access to consumption because of their lower incomes, or less control over their consumption, because of their positions of dependency within families.

The payment of family allowances directly to mothers was conceived as a buffer against child and female impoverishment within the family. These have, however, been victims of public expenditure cuts in the latter years of Two Nation politics. The real value of these benefits has fallen sharply, especially since child benefit allowances were frozen in the late 1980s. The family credit scheme provides some support for consumption in lower-income households but this has been more than counterbalanced by cuts in housing, clothing and other benefits.

Working wives can use their earnings to improve their personal consumption levels, as well as the living standards of their families. But this only underlines class differences amongst women. The lower the family income, the greater the proportion of the wife's earnings which is spent on general housekeeping and the smaller the amount that is available to her to spend on herself and her leisure. Even so women are not always guaranteed control over their own incomes. Consequently, there are many women – in or out of work, married or single – who are denied reasonable access to consumption even within prosperous households.

Because of their low pay, the consumption levels of women living alone, with or without children, are also more constrained than those of men living in similar circumstances. In this respect their lower levels of consumption are the end product of a long chain which originates in streamed education and training, and in the processes of socialisation. The resulting deprivation – both absolute and relative – is far more widely distributed than is commonly imagined, for one quarter of all households in the UK are headed by women. There are also lasting intergenerational implications because of the impact on the welfare of their children.

Unequal consumption is evident in several spheres. One of the most basic is in terms of food. In working-class households, for example, boys have been given priority over girls, and fathers ahead of their families when food was in short supply. Similarly, space within the home is not allocated equally; where there are conflicts, boys are often given priority. This may have implications for doing homework and, hence, for educational achievements. In this, as in so many respects, the fundamental inequalities stem from class differences in the availability of resources, but these are also gendered.

The most important gender differences in terms of consumption probably relate to housing. The distribution of men and women between housing tenures is highly uneven (Table 5.14). Households headed by men are far more likely to be owner-occupied than are those headed by women. In contrast, households headed by women are relatively more dependent on council-rented properties. Women are also far more likely than men to be living in unfurnished privately rented dwellings. The gendering of access to housing tenure is important because access to the 'exchange rights 'of owner occupation gives rise to fundamental differences in sources of capital gain, in obtaining credit, and in residential mobility (Madigan et al. 1990).

Whilst women's wages continue to be so much lower than men's, it will be more difficult for them to gain independent access to owner occupied houses. They will instead continue to be relatively dependent on the public sector. As

Table 5.14   Men's and women's housing tenure, 1985. By sex and marital status of head of household

	Males		Females	
	Single	All males	Single	All females
Owner-occupied, owned outright	16	22	23	30
Owner-occupied with joint mortgage	35	45	18	12
Rented with job/business	2	3	2	1
Rented from local authority/new town housing association	27	26	36	45
Rented privately unfurnished	6	3	11	9
Rented privately furnished	15	2	11	3
	100	100	100	100

Source: CSO (1988, 18)

such, they are amongst those most disadvantaged by the Thatcher governments' cut-backs in council house building. They also suffer from the residualisation of council housing whereby sales and a lack of new building have led
to a sharp deterioration in the quality of the remaining public housing stock.
The decontrolling of rents in the private sector has also increased the difficulties for many women, faced with having to pay full market rents for new
tenancies. Not all women, or even all low-paid women, will suffer from these
changes in housing conditions. At present separated women with children are
most dependent on council accommodation; approximately one-half of all
women whose marriages break down end up in council housing.

There are other class differences in women's access to housing. Until fairly
recently the ownership of the home in which a married couple lived was in the
name of the husband. In the last 20 years it has become common for building
societies to register properties in the names of both spouses. Since the passing
of the 1967 Matrimonial Homes Act, divorce courts have also tended to let
wives claim possession of at least part of the marital home, irrespective of
whether their names appeared on the property deeds. In this way there has
been a gradual improvement in the position of women, but it is largely confined to the middle class and the affluent fractions of the working class. Even
within this group there may be continuing difficulties in accessing good quality
housing. When marriages break down, women 'are less likely to be able to
remain as owner occupiers and more likely to experience a diminution in
housing quality and standard of living' (Madigan et al. 1990, 637). Mortgages
have to be paid, whilst the shared proceeds from the sale of a house may not
be sufficient to finance the purchase of new home for the wife. In this way,
the housing market position of women is fatally undermined by their weak
labour market position.

Women's weak housing market position is not in any sense a product of
Two Nations politics. But it is equally true that there was little positive action
to improve the position of women with respect to housing during the 1980s and
1990s. The principal emphasis of Thatcherism was on extending 'the property-
owning democracy'. Owner occupation has been extended but the ability to
purchase is based on the assumption of pooled family income. This may
benefit those women who are married or are cohabiting but it does little to
assist single women. They are also disadvantaged by the diminishing availability of council housing, following massive sales in the 1980s. One of the
grotesque travesties of the 1993 Conservative Party Conference was the sight
of a prominent member of the government blaming the lack of available
council housing on the priority being given to single mothers who, it was suggested, should be cared for and housed by their families.

The housing needs of women are also overlooked because present housing
construction policies have been conditioned by a presumption in favour of the
family. Local authority allocation rules and mortgage lending criteria similarly
tend to favour family occupation of dwellings. This favours the building of

family dwellings which, consequently, conditions the future possibilities for household occupancy by non-family groups (Rock et al. 1980). There is a hierarchy of social groups in terms of access to housing and it is probably headed by two-income middle-class households. At the bottom end are to be found single persons, especially those who are working class and, more generally, women.

The strategies of Two Nations politics have had a far from benign influence upon many of the developments in consumption which have been outlined. Public expenditure cuts have not been applied evenly across all areas of public policy. Instead they have fallen most heavily in the sphere of social consumption, that is, upon education, housing and some forms of social services. Women have been more affected than men by most of these cuts, and this is especially true of single parents and working-class women.

5.5　Men, women and political power

Women's battle for formal access to political power was, in a narrow sense, completed in 1928 when they secured the vote. However, in many senses the real battle has still to be won for despite – and perhaps because of – Mrs Thatcher having become Prime Minister, most of the positions of political power in the UK are held by men. This was symbolised by the total absence of women from John Major's first full Cabinet.

Parliament provides the most obvious stage on which to view the struggle for political power. What this shows is that after rapid initial gains, the proportion of women MPs then changed little over the next 50 years. For a long time, the high point in terms of the number of women elected to Parliament was 1964 (Table 5.15). In that year there were 28 female MPs and subsequently the number fell to 23 at the 1983 election. The number of women MPs has since increased sharply. By the time of the 1992 election, 60 women MPs had been elected, 9.2 per cent of the total. But this is still a long way from the notional 50 per cent of seats which should accrue to women if Parliament was not gendered. The Labour and Alliance parties are apparently more progressive in their selection of candidates and at the 1992 election had, respectively, 137 and 143 candidates. The Conservative Party was less receptive to female candidates and only fielded 63 candidates in 1992. However, all these figures are rather deceptive for women were disproportionately selected for seats for which the parties had no realistic hopes of victory. Labour has subsequently committed itself to selecting a minimum number of women candidates for winnable seats for the next general election.

Within Parliament there has also been little advance in women's progression into the Cabinet. All Cabinets since 1945 – until Mr Major's – have had at least one woman in them but again the high point came in the 1960s when, at various times, Harold Wilson appointed Barbara Castle, Shirley Williams and

Table 5.15 Women candidates in general elections, 1918–92

Election year	% of candidates	% of all MPs elected	No. of women MPs
1918	1.0	0.1	1
1922	2.3	0.3	2
1923	2.4	1.3	8
1924	2.9	0.7	4
1929	4.0	2.3	14
1931	4.8	2.4	15
1935	5.0	1.5	9
1945	5.2	3.8	24
1950	6.8	3.4	21
1951	5.6	2.7	17
1955	6.5	3.8	24
1959	5.3	4.0	25
1964	5.1	4.6	29
1966	4.7	4.1	26
1970	5.4	4.1	26
1974 Feb.	6.7	3.6	23
1974 Oct.	7.1	4.3	27
1979	8.4	3.0	19
1983	10.9	3.5	23
1987	14.2	6.3	41
1992	18.9	9.2	60

Judith Hart. In the 1980s the election of a Conservative government had mixed consequences for women. On the one hand it brought a woman to the office of Prime Minister but she, in turn, has not championed the cause of other women. Except for a brief period when Baroness Young was Lord Privy Seal, there were no other women in the Cabinet. The way in which Mrs Thatcher conducted her government also had ambiguous effects for women. It could be argued that her obvious toughness and competence may have reduced men's prejudices against women in power. However, the tendency to project her as 'the best man' in the Cabinet singled her out as a very atypical woman. In the Major governments, there were no women at all in his first Cabinet but Virginia Bottomley and others subsequently acquired relatively high profiles. All Cabinets have, however, remained bastions of male representation and power. If the government as a whole is considered, then there were still only 7 women in a total of 99, which was the lowest proportion in Europe in 1992 (Table 5.16). Women have made more progress, electorally, outside of Westminster. They form about one-quarter of all local government councillors in the UK and about one-sixth of Britain's Euro MP's. However, it is not without irony that the powers of local government have been severely constrained by male-dominated Conservative governments in the Two Nations period.

Women also continue to be seriously under-represented in most of the other

Table 5.16 Women in national governments in the European Union

Country	Date of formation of government	Total members of government	No. of women	% of women
Belgium	1992	16	2	12.5
Denmark	1990	19	4	21.1
France	1992	42	7	16.7
Germany	1992	53	9	17.0
Greece	1992	37	3	8.1
Ireland	1992	30	5	16.7
Italy	1993	62	8	12.9
Luxembourg	1989	12	1	8.3
Netherlands	1989	25	6	24.0
Portugal	1991	71	7	9.9
Spain	1991	18	2	11.1
UK	1992	99	7	7.0
EUR 12		484	61	12.6

Source: *Commission of the European Communities*

areas of the state. There are, for example, only 4 women amongst the chairs of the 40 largest quangos (*Financial Times*, 20 December 1993), few women in the upper echelons of the Civil Service, few women judges and until recently no female Chief Constables. Their under-representation in the legal services also contributes to the lack of confidence that many women have in the system of justice. There has been a series of court cases, especially with respect to rape, where elderly male judges have revealed strongly sexist attitudes in their summing up or their sentencing.

Beyond the realms of party politics, women have made some notable inroads in the political scene. The feminist movement has gained strength since the 1960s and especially since the first national meeting of the Women's Liberation Movement was held in 1970. The movement has sought more than just legal equality. It has tried to reduce the inferiority complex of women, which is bound up with many aspects of British culture. This general movement has spawned a number of smaller organisations, focused on more specific issues. One such group was Women In The Media which protested at the way women are portrayed by the media as well as their previous exclusion from jobs such as newsreaders. Another such organisation was the Women's Aid Federation which has campaigned for refuges for battered wives. However, it is in the 1980s that women have gained greatest prominence in the broader political sphere. Two very different milestones were the largely middle-class anti-nuclear Greenham Common movement, and the political mobilisation of women in the coalfields communities, along with miners support committees set up during the 1984–85 coal strike (see Loach 1985; Massey and Wainwright

1985). Although the direct 'victories' of these movements may have been limited, they were important as assertions of a greater self-confidence amongst women in terms of their capacity for effective political action.

It is appropriate to end this section by returning to consider how these broader women's movements have influenced the major political parties. There is a long history of special provision for women within the Labour Party. In the post-war period there has been a National Women's Advisory Committee and there have been statutorily reserved places for women on the National Executive. However, until the late 1960s the women's organisation was largely peripheral to the real centres of power within the party. Subsequently the Labour Party has strengthened its commitments to positive discrimination. For example, since 1986 there has been a formal party commitment to creating a post of Minister of Women's Rights, and it has also been obligatory to include at least one woman on every short list of parliamentary candidates. Even more significant is the decision by the Labour Party that there should be a minimum number of women candidates selected for winnable seats at the next general election.

In contrast the Conservative Party remains far more patriarchal. This is not to say that the Conservative Party has been untouched by feminist demands. For example, in 1983 Emma Nicholson became Vice Chairman (note the terminology) of the party with special responsibility for women. However, as with some of the other concerns of Mrs Thatcher, such as environmental issues in 1988, it was difficult to see this as little more than window-dressing on the 'doll's house' in the absence of any positive discrimination measures.

5.6 Reprise: the 'doll's house' still stands

Whilst overtly supportive of anti-sex discrimination legislation, recent Conservative governments have been resolutely opposed to all forms of positive discrimination. Indeed, the then Prime Minister, Mrs Thatcher, stated on Thames Television on 1 January 1981 that 'there is nothing more that you can do by changing the law to do away with discrimination. After all, I don't think there's been a great deal of discrimination against women for years.' Instead the Thatcher governments emphasised 'individualism' and individual initiative to overcome disadvantages. As such they did not recognise structural inequalities in UK society and were against policies to assist specific deprived groups, whether defined by sex, class or race. Under the Thatcher – and also the Major – governments there have been few initiatives to improve the position of women, other than under pressure from the European Commission or the European Court of Justice. Instead many of the government's policies, such as abolishing Wages Councils and reducing welfare, have seriously reduced the opportunities open to women and had detrimental impacts on their living conditions.

It is significant that in the 1970s the UK was at the forefront of legislation to give women and men equal rights, notably with the passing of the 1970 Equal Pay Act and the 1975 Sex Discrimination Act. Ironically, as gender inequalities came to be recognised, the era of One Nation politics was coming to a close. In contrast, as the Two Nations project took shape in the 1980s, the UK appeared before the European Court on sex discrimination charges more times than any other EC country. This is a telling statistic with respect to the priority given to gender issues. There is no evidence that women have yet been able to emerge fully from the 'doll's house'.

6

Divided by race

6.1 The division begins: immigration and the UK

Immigration into the UK has deep historical roots in slavery. There has also been a stream of immigrants from Ireland throughout the last two centuries. By the 1980s, for example, there were an estimated 1 million first- and second-generation Irish people in the UK. Since 1945 the UK has become a multiracial society with substantial ethnic and racial groups. This chapter concentrates only on the 'black' population of Britain, mostly of Afro-Caribbean or South Asian origin. These are by far the largest racial minority groups and their experiences provide insights into those of all non-white racial minorities with respect to education, jobs, housing and political power. Whilst we concentrate on these two main groups, this is not to deny their considerable national, regional, cultural and other diversities. Amongst Afro-Caribbeans there has been some reduction in diversity over time because the experience of living in the UK, and especially of racism, has led to pan-Caribbeanisation (James 1992), that is, a greater empathy for the cultures of the Caribbean as a whole. In contrast, there continue to be major differences within the South Asian group, especially between those of Indian origin and those of Pakistani or Bangladeshi origin. Finally, by way of introduction we wish to emphasise that we believe that race is essentially a social construction and not a natural division (see Jackson 1987).

The incorporation of non-white people into post-war UK society has passed through three main phases (Cross 1986), which can be related to the periodisation of broader political-economic changes set out in Chapter 2. The first is the 'pre-competitive' period 1948–62, which corresponded to the years of 'full employment and welfare state policies' (see pp. 28–31). This was a period of critical labour shortages in the UK, which could have undermined the post-war economic recovery. The strategy adopted to meet these shortages and to reduce labour costs was dual sourcing of workers from the rest of Europe and from the colonies. 'Traditional' immigration from Ireland was augmented by an estimated 460 000 workers recruited in war-torn continental Europe. There was also active recruitment in the Caribbean by companies such as London Transport, as well as a generally open-door policy towards immigration from the colonies. This inflow peaked in the early 1960s before the introduction of legislation to control immigration (Figure 6.1).

The 1962 Commonwealth Immigration Act marked the beginning of the second phase, the 'competitive' period 1963–76. This broadly coincides with that of 'modernization and the welfare state' (see pp. 31–34). The increasingly stuttering performance of the economy led to the rising level of structural unemployment, even though this was disguised for a time by cyclical variations. Ensuring a supply of low-cost labour faded as a priority as successive governments sought to increase national competitiveness via modernisation strategies. At the same time, rising unemployment fuelled the level and intensity of racism in the UK which eventually infected the party politics of the social democratic consensus. In a sense, the use of the terminology of One Nation politics for this period is inappropriate; there was already Two Nations politics in terms of racial issues. The 1962 Immigration Commonwealth Act, which severely restricted immigration, was a major symbol of this divide.

In this second period the main stream of immigration was from South Asia. The overall level of immigration fell with occasional fluctuations such as the

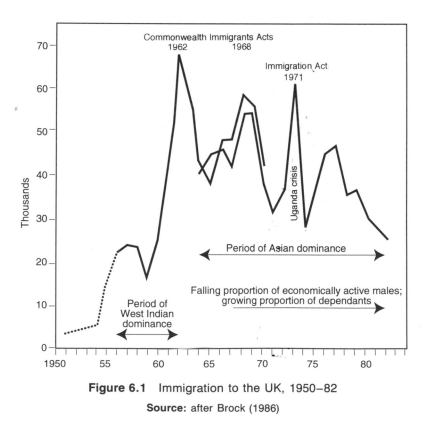

Figure 6.1   Immigration to the UK, 1950–82

Source: after Brock (1986)

arrival of some 27 000 Ugandan Asians in 1972. As a result of legislative changes, immigration was increasingly dominated by the arrivals of dependants, that is mostly women, children and elderly relatives; by 1979 they constituted 90 per cent of new arrivals from the New Commonwealth. Meanwhile, it had become increasingly clear that, in general, non-white workers in the UK were not making the transition in the labour force from being unskilled to being skilled workers. Instead, the labour market was becoming segmented along class, gender and racial lines. Large numbers of non-white workers — especially Afro-Caribbeans and those of Pakistani and Bangladeshi origin — were becoming part of the emerging underclass.

The third period of immigration, that of reduced levels after 1976, coincides with the era of Two Nations politics. Mrs Thatcher used immigration issues as an electoral device in her rise to power, and as unemployment inexorably rose, introduced further immigration controls in 1981 and 1987. The policies of Two Nations politics did not, otherwise, have a specifically racial dimension. However, public expenditure cuts, privatisation, deregulation and the attacks on trade unions, wages and working conditions impinged disproportionately on the working class, and especially, the underclass. Consequently, large parts of the non-white population of the UK have been disadvantaged by such policies. At the 1993 Conservative Party Conference, foreign 'scroungers' were castigated by Peter Lilley for living off the British welfare state: 'We have all too many home grown scroungers, but it's beyond the pale when foreigners come here expecting our handouts.' Immigration clearly still plays a vital role in party politics even if the role of race in domestic politics has changed over time. The early post-war non-white immigrants faced a double shock; the demystification of their views of the construction of UK society (James 1992) and the extent and the depth of racial hostility which they encountered. By the 1960s popular racism was taking root, especially in workplaces. It was fanned by the racist remarks of several MPs. Remarks such as that accredited to Conservative MP Martin Lindsay who referred to the 'future of our own race and breed' inflamed popular prejudices. Popular newspapers also presented immigration as a flood about to overwhelm British society.

Both Labour and Conservative governments made concessions to popular racism by passing a series of so-called Immigration Acts. The Conservatives began by passing the 1962 Immigration Act which the Labour Party opposed; it was a potent sign of the failure of the state to secure full employment even if this remained the accepted goal of all parties. After the 1964 general election Labour initially opposed further immigration controls. However, when it lost the safe Smethwick seat in a by-election to Peter Griffiths, a Conservative who had largely campaigned on immigration issues, Labour party strategists lost their nerve. The Wilson government then passed the restrictive 1968 Immigration Act. This was followed by the 1971 Immigration Act passed by the Heath government which further limited the issuing of work permits.

These Immigration Acts imposed increasingly strict barriers to the entry of immigrant workers whilst still permitting that of dependants. The legislation was inappropriately labelled because it was not really concerned with immigration. There were, for example, no restrictions on immigration from Ireland, and short-term guest workers were still welcome; indeed they were essential to the functioning of the economy. Rather these Acts were a racist response to popular prejudice and short-term political gains in the period of One Nation politics.

Immigration was only seen as a problem and immigration policies were only required when black people were involved. It was not a question of immigration as such, but of how social boundaries between black and white could be maintained to the advantage of white people. One means of achieving this was through the creation of two kinds of citizenship and two kinds of British passport holders. This was the principal objective of the 1971 Act, which restricted British nationality to patrials and to those who were registered citizens. Alternative citizenship – without automatic rights of residence – was granted to the (largely non-white) residual. This legislation, although not couched in overtly racialist terms, is not colour blind for the concept of patrials most severely impinged upon black and brown people. The 'Two Nations' of white and non-white were becoming inscribed in differing definitions of citizenship.

Towards the end of the period of One Nation politics, race and immigration again became a prominent party political issue. Both Labour and Conservatives stressed the need for strict immigration controls. However, their attitudes did differ as is indicated by the following quotes from the Parliamentary debate on immigration on 5 July 1976:

Roy Jenkins (Labour):
The British people occupy a largely urban, densely populated, industrialised island of limited size. ... Our imperial history, combined with the maldistribution of wealth and prosperity in the world has traditionally produced strong pressures to migrate to this country. These are basic facts. They necessitate both a strict limit on the amount and rate of inward immigration for settlement.

Winston Churchill (Conservative)
We cannot fail to recognise the deep bitterness that exists among ordinary people who one day were living in Lancashire and wake up the next day in New Delhi, Calcutta or Kingston, Jamaica. ... I believe that generous arrangements should be available to anyone who wishes to return to the country that he regards as his homeland.

More severe restrictions on immigration followed after the Conservatives were returned to power. From the late 1970s Margaret Thatcher increasingly associated herself with the issue of immigration, as part of her successful electoral strategy. In January 1978 she appeared on a *World In Action* programme on immigration and stated that 'people are really rather afraid that this country might be rather swamped by people with a different culture'. 'Culture' was a transparent euphemism for 'colour' in a blatant populist appeal to the white supporters of true blue Thatcherism. She then went on to promise a clear prospect of an end to immigration. Labour resisted the popular calls for further controls at this time, despite a rising tide of racism in the country.

Once the Conservatives had been returned to power, further immigration legislation followed. The 1981 Nationality Act broke new ground by depriving British-born children of immigrants of the automatic right of citizenship. There was a number of exceptions which, of course, tended to favour white rather than black or brown children. Then, in 1987, another Immigration Act was passed which was designed to make 'sensible and limited changes' to earlier legislation. What this really meant was that the right was taken away from every British man of marriageable age to bring his wife and children to the UK. The 1971 Act, which had provided that right, was undoubtedly sexist in that it did not extend the same rights to women. However, Mrs Thatcher's government's approach to equalization was to take these rights away from men! As usual the legislation had racist undertones; those with patrial connections (mostly white people) were excluded from these restrictions − for the real target of the legislation was young men of Asian origin. The 1987 Act was presented as an attempt to eliminate an anomaly, but in effect it replaced overtly sexist legislation with implicitly racist laws.

Over time the character of the South Asian and Afro-Caribbean communities in the UK has changed. Partly as a result of legislative changes, and partly because of the onset of economic recession in the 1970s and 1980s, the number of new arrivals has fallen (see Figure 6.1). It is becoming less and less accurate to describe these as immigrant communities. In 1983−85 the non-white population of the UK was estimated to be approximately 3.4 per cent of the total population and 40−50 per cent had been born within the UK. According to the 1991 Census, which for the first time asked about ethnic group rather than country of birth, 5.5 per cent of the population of the UK was non-white (Teague 1993). The largest non-white group, 2.7 per cent of the total, was from South Asia; 1.5 per cent considered themselves to be Indian, 0.9 per cent to be Pakistani, and 0.3 per cent Bangladeshi. In addition, 1.6 per cent considered themselves to be black; 0.9 per cent to be Black Caribbean and 0.4 per cent to be Black African. Therefore, the black and brown population of Britain is, in numerical terms, no more than a small minority. Yet it is a minority which is on the wrong side of many of the social divides in the UK.

The important issues for this chapter are to identify the precise nature of racial inequalities − in education, housing, politics, employment, income, etc. − in the UK and the ways in which these have changed over time. The framework for this is the economic periodisations that have been outlined, for ethnic minorities have made the transition from immigrant community to settled population at the same time as the post-war economic boom came to an end, and One Nation politics were superseded by the Two Nations project.

6.2   Race, employment and income

The relationship between class and race has been outlined in Chapter 1, and provides the framework for the following discussion. In our view class and race are interrelated and this influences labour market opportunities and constraints, incomes and unemployment for ethnic minorities. The experiences of different ethnic groups have tended to diverge during the post-war years, but some have remained markedly disadvantaged throughout this period, and all have been subject to some form of racial discrimination.

6.2.1   Race and employment in the UK

In the 1950s most black immigrants came to the UK as part of a replacement labour force. They occupied the less skilled, the dirtiest and the lowest paid jobs. Many of these were located in inner-city areas, thereby constraining the labour market opportunities of the following generation. This flexible and cheap source of labour was an invaluable ingredient in the moderate but sustained expansion of the UK economy in the 1950s and early 1960s, the period of 'full employment and the welfare state'. A similar role was played in other northern European countries by so-called 'guest-workers' from southern Europe and North Africa. In the 1970s the ethnic minorities, especially from South Asia, again played a role in the restructuring of the UK economy. They occupied many of the niches for casual and homeworkers in the emerging system of more flexible employment. To some extent, their availability in the labour market helped shape the new forms of employment relations.

Over time it became clear that non-white workers were, at best, making selective progress in the labour market. In part this was because the economic recessions of the 1970s and the 1980s reduced openings in the job market. However, there are other reasons including widespread discrimination, poor access to education for some groups and cultural alienation. The result is that, despite individual successes, and the overall economic advances of Afro-Asians and Indians, many black and brown workers have become trapped into the base of the hierarchy of jobs, income and status, forming part of the underclass.

Economic activity rates provide one indicator of labour market integration. In 1987–89 the highest rates were amongst Afro-Caribbeans, followed by Indians and then by white people, with substantially lower rates amongst Pakistanis and Bangladeshis (Owen and Green 1992). To some extent this reflects the gendering of participation rates, and the relatively small number of Pakistani and Bangladeshi women in waged work. During the 1980s, the activity rates of the main minority ethnic groups (with the exception of Indians) declined, whilst that of the white ethnic group increased. This may indicate a 'discouraged worker effect' (Owen and Green 1992, 13) in the face of perceived lack of job opportunities.

Table 6.1 Occupation by ethnic group and sex, 1971–86 (percentages)

	Males					Females				
	White		Non-white	Afro-Caribbean	South Asian	White		Non-white	Afro-Caribbean	South Asian
	1971	1984–86	1971	1984–86	1984–86	1971	1984–86	1971	1984–86	1984–86
Non-manual										
Management and professional	20	34	12	10	38	5	25	—	27	26
Clerical and related	18	11	17	11	11	55	40	—	31	32
All non-manual	38	46	30	21	49	59	65	51	58	58
Manual										
Craft and related		26		34	19		4			16
General labourers		2		4	2		—			2
Other		26		40	30		31			24
All manual	62	54	71	78	51	41	35	49	42	42
Total	100	100	100	100	100	100	100	100	100	100

Source: CSO (various dates)

The constraints on labour market access are indicated in Table 6.1. In 1971 white males and females were more likely than non-whites to be in non-manual jobs, especially higher paid and higher status ones. By the mid-1980s – for which period more disaggregated data are available – the pattern is more complex. Amongst males, South Asians were more likely than white workers to be in non-manual jobs, and in particular to be in managerial and professional jobs. Overlying this broad pattern there were also sharp differences between the more occupationally successful Indians and the less successful Pakistanis and Bangladeshis. Afro-Caribbean males were overwhelmingly in manual jobs. Amongst women, the white ethnic group had disproportionately more non-manual jobs, but both Afro-Caribbeans and South Asians were as successful as whites in securing managerial and professional posts. There was again, however, a sharp difference between Indians and Pakistanis/Bangladeshis.

Most ethnic minority groups have improved their occupational positions since the 1970s (Brown 1984), but these aggregate data exaggerate the change. Much of the growth, especially in managerial and administrative jobs, has been influenced by the shift to self-employment, which has been a central part of the Two Nations project. The fact that this is part of the strategy to lower production costs is reflected in continuing marked income disparities (discussed later). These disparities are reinforced by the poorer access of many non-white workers to fringe benefits, pensions, etc. by virtue of casual jobs or self-employment.

The aggregate data are also deceptive in that non-whites consistently underachieve within most of these broad occupational categories. They are, for example, appointed to supervisory posts far less frequently than are whites. Furthermore, most non-white supervisors are likely to be in charge of the work of non-white employees, reflecting the highly segregated nature of the labour market. This is particularly evident in shift-work, with much of the unpopular night-time work being done by non-whites. In the textile industry in Yorkshire and Lancashire nightshifts are often staffed almost entirely by South Asian workers. There are also important differences at the other end of the occupational scale. For example, whilst there are relatively large numbers of South Asian hospital doctors, they are concentrated into the least popular branches of medicine such as geriatrics. The existence of such qualitative job distinctions indicates that there is still strong occupational segregation along ethnic lines in the UK.

One area in which South Asians (but not Afro-Caribbeans) have made considerable progress is in self-employment. A 1982 PSI survey (see Brown 1984) found that, amongst Asians, 18 per cent of men and 14 per cent of women were self-employed compared to 14 and 7 per cent for whites. By 1987 21 per cent of South Asians as opposed to only 11 per cent of white people were self-employed (Srinivasan 1992). Two-thirds of such South Asians were in distribution, catering, repair and hotel work. Asians have not only gained access to self employment, but have also become small-scale employers; for example, they run retail and other businesses, including corner shops and restaurants. These may survive only through the long hours worked by the owners and their families, and therefore can be seen as a form of self-exploitation. Many such businesses initially relied on the ethnic community for their custom but their trade has become more widespread. The disproportionate numbers of South Asians in the petty bourgeoisie is partly accounted for by the lack of opportunities elsewhere, but it is also due to cultural factors, particularly the high status accorded to business entry and to financial success.

The economic progress of some South Asians – in particular of the Indians – is not to be denied and, in a way, it represents one of the successes of Mrs Thatcher's enterprise culture. However, the vast majority of South Asian workers are employees. Many – especially women – work in very low-paid jobs either in 'sweat shops' or as homeworkers. Moreover, Afro-Caribbeans have had a singular lack of success in becoming entrepreneurs. The Conservative Party's attempt to attract the electoral support of the ethnic minorities is, in reality, therefore, directed at one small segment, the middle-class South Asians. However, as Srinivasan (1992, 71) argues, this has not been successful because 'there is an ethnic impact on party affiliation'; the Asian petty bourgeoisie are more likely to vote Labour than Conservative.

6.2.2 Occupational segregation and discrimination

Many black and brown people came to the UK as replacement workers and they were drawn into those areas and industries which then had employment vacancies. They were therefore to be found in low-paid and low-skilled jobs in the health service, transport and some manufacturing industries in London and the larger cities. This does not mean that they were unskilled. The posts which they took were often less skilled than their previous white collar and craft jobs (Ramdin 1987; James 1992). Immigration was therefore accompanied by deskilling in the 1950s and the 1960s.

The labour market obstacles faced by immigrants – and their children – could not simply be overcome via the 'normal' educational, experience and qualifications routes of meritocracy. For black people generally do less well in the labour market than white people with similar qualifications. Amongst those with A levels or higher qualifications in the early 1980s, 84 per cent of whites compared to 75 per cent of South Asians had non-manual jobs (Brown 1984). The Afro-Caribbeans did even worse. Amongst those with no qualifications, the proportion of whites with non-manual jobs was four times higher than the proportion of Afro-Caribbeans. Racialised inequalities persist across all levels of educational qualifications.

Persistent inequalities in employment – beyond those to be expected because of differences in qualifications and previous training – are mainly accounted for by discrimination. This exists at the individual and the institutional levels, and in direct and indirect forms. Since the Equal Opportunities Act most forms of racial discrimination have been illegal. However, discrimination still persists in the UK in many indirect practices. It is underwritten by a colonial legacy and reinforced by the bitterness of race conflict over the four decades since large-scale post-war immigration began. Such racial hatred has served to segment labour markets and to weaken working-class collective action. In this sense, the division of the UK into Two Nations on the grounds of race has long been part of the fabric of capital–labour relations – both before and after the mid-1970s.

Many immigrants faced discrimination as soon as they had arrived. One immigrant from the West Indies in the 1950s described his experiences thus (Carter 1986, 32–33):

> I arrived on a Sunday night. On the Monday morning I was taken to the Labour Exchange to go through all the formalities. I remember very clearly the cold stare given to me by the man behind the counter when I told him that I was interested in a job as a tracer in a drawing office. The reason I chose that job was because I had done about three years of evening classes doing a City and Guilds course in architectural draughtsmanship. ... The job vacancy pages of the daily and evening papers were full of thousands of vacancies for this kind of job. But the Labour Exchange clerk paid no attention to my request and went straight to a filing cabinet labelled either manual workers or labourers.

Immigrants did not only face institutional discrimination. Discrimination was common amongst employers and amongst white fellow-employees. There are numerous examples of white workers refusing to work with black or brown people. In one notorious incident in 1955, white workers at the West Bromwich Corporation Transport Department went on strike against the employment of Indian trainee bus conductors. Official trade unions policies opposed racism but in practice the unions were usually passive whilst many local shop stewards were blatantly racist.

Black and brown workers continue to face discrimination in the job market (Policy Studies Institute 1993). For example, in test situations in which whites and blacks with equal qualifications or experience have applied for the same jobs, whites have been twice as successful. Furthermore, discrimination has not diminished over time. Surveys undertaken in 1974 and 1982 revealed that increasing proportions of Afro-Caribbeans and female South Asians had personal experience of discrimination when applying for a job (Brown 1984). As much as a quarter of the sample in the 1982 survey claimed to have experienced discrimination. Discrimination is greater at the lower end of the occupational hierarchy, with non-white unskilled manual workers experiencing most racial discrimination over jobs. This is a group that has disadvantage heaped upon disadvantage.

Whilst thus far this discussion has looked at broad racial inequalities in the labour market, these are of course gendered. For example, Jayaweera (1993,

384) writes that:

> Three decades after large-scale migration and in spite of a substantial number being British-born, these Afro-Caribbean women incorporate the ideal-typical characteristics of migrant labour in being condemned to do the dirtier kinds of manual work involving poor pay and shift work (often at night) that are rejected by indigenous workers. But additionally as women, they are segregated within this category, in domestic roles such as those of cleaner and kitchen hand, that involve menial labour, lower rates of pay and lower status than in the case of some male workers'.

For cultural reasons, and because of high male unemployment, married Afro-Caribbean women are more likely than white women to work full- rather than part-time, which is likely to further heighten their experience of racial disadvantage (Phizacklea 1982). In practice, many Afro-Caribbean women have not encountered any significant discrimination in their workplaces. However, when it is encountered this tends to be in critical areas such as training, which prevents them progressing to higher-grade jobs (Jayaweera 1993).

Racialised gendering is also encountered amongst South Asians, as Brah (1993) reports in the case of young Muslim women. She argues that in addition to discrimination, their labour market experiences are coloured by specific forms of patriarchal ideologies concerning the domestic roles of women. The timing of their migration was also important. Unlike the predominantly Indian immigrants of the 1950s and early 1960s who entered the labour market when it was still dominated by permanent and full-time jobs, their entry was during the recessionary 1970s when there was a shift to more flexible employment practices, greater casualisation and home-based employment.

6.2.3 Race and earnings

Occupational segregation goes hand in hand with unequal earnings, and both are linked to labour market segmentation and the form of capital accumulation in the UK. Black and brown workers provided much of the low-wage labour for economic expansion in the 1950s and the 1960s. Not surprisingly then, in the early 1970s non-white male non-manual workers earned 23 per cent less than white non-manual workers (Brown 1984). The differences were less amongst manual workers, but in skilled jobs non-whites still earned 11 per cent less than whites. For semi- and unskilled workers there were no significant differences, but this reflected the greater amount of shift-work done by black and brown workers rather than any genuine equality of pay. For women the picture was more complex, not least because non-whites were more likely to be in full-time jobs, but taking this into account, the usual racial differences emerge.

The reasons for inequalities in earnings are clear. Afro-Caribbean, Pakistani and Bangladeshi workers are more concentrated in low-pay industries and occupations, both manual and non-manual. Of even greater consequence is the failure of non-whites to gain promotion within particular occupational groups. Pirani et al. (1992, 32) have shown that there is a racial differential of about 33 per cent in gross incomes within occupational groups. The most important reason for this, they suggest, is 'direct and indirect discrimination at institutional level, manifest in the perception that ethnic minorities as less promotable than similar white employees' (p. 40).

There was little narrowing of income differentials during the 1970s and the 1980s. According to the 1982 PSI survey, white men earned about £20 more than Afro-Caribbean men and £18 more than South Asian men (Brown 1984). For women the differentials were smaller, being £4 less for South Asians and £3 more for Afro-Caribbeans. Whilst the differences are partly due to occupational segregation, they persisted across all the main occupational groups (Table 6.2). The real earnings gap is also larger than appears at first sight because the Indians have prospered compared to the Pakistanis and the Bangladeshis who entered the labour market later. In most cases wage differentials are greater for the 25–54 age group than for all ages, because young workers of all races tend to be paid similarly low wages when training.

Aggregate figures show that black women and white women earn approximately equal wages. However, controlling for age, white women have markedly higher earnings (Table 6.2). This confirms that black women are still failing to achieve higher-paid jobs in proportionate numbers. In contrast,

Table 6.2 Gross earnings by race and age, 1982. Full-time employees in Britain

| | Median earnings (£s) per week | | | |
| | All | | Aged 25–54 | |
	White	Black	White	Black
Males				
All males	129	110	137	115
Professional, etc.	185	152	187	171
Other non-manual	136	130	144	138
Skilled manual	122	112	127	115
Semi-skilled	111	101	115	104
Unskilled manual	100	98	117	111
Females				
All females	78	79	92	82
Professional, etc.	107	122	105	130
Other non-manual	82	86	99	97
Skilled manual	67	74	71	74
Semi- and unskilled manual	67	72	72	76

Source: Brown, C. (1984, Tables 111 and 113)

however, there are no major differences in earnings between black and white women in each separate occupational group. The large gender differential in pay between men and women leaves little scope for further disparities along racial lines. As most women are already earning minimal wages within any particular occupational group, there is little scope for further differences between black and white women. This combination of gender and racial inequalities is an important example of multiple deprivation, a theme to which we return later.

6.2.4 Race and unemployment: an unwanted inheritance?

The economic disadvantages of black people are further expressed in and compounded by higher unemployment rates compared to white people. In 1984 male unemployment rates were similar for whites and Indians, but were almost three times higher for Pakistanis/Bangladeshis and Afro-Caribbeans (Table 6.3). There was a similar pattern for women, but the ratio was only about two to one. During much of the 1980s it seemed that the most disadvantaged groups were paying the highest price for the strategies of Two Nations politics, as their unemployment continued to grow at above average rates. Ethnic minority workers were concentrated in those jobs most severely affected by recession; that is, traditional and marginal industries concentrated in the hard-hit inner cities. In addition the young age profile of the non-white community meant that disproportionate numbers first entered the labour market at a time of recession. Even if they obtained jobs, disproportionate numbers have been in these for short periods of time; they were, therefore, particularly vulnerable to the 'last-in-first-out' rule that often applies to redundancies. Over and above this, there is also persistent discrimination against black and brown people. By 1990 the unemployment rates of white people and of Indian people were virtually identical, whilst the rates for Afro-Caribbeans and Pakistanis/Bangladeshis were about double these. This pattern is broadly confirmed by

Table 6.3 Unemployment rates by gender and race, 1984 and 1990 (percentages)

	Males		Females	
	1984	1990	1984	1990
White	11	7	11	6
Afro-Caribbean	30	13	18	14
Indian	13	8	20	11
Pakistani/Bangladeshi	33	15	—	—
All	12	7	12	7

Source: CSO (1988, 1992)

the 1991 Census, which also reveals that there are much higher unemployment rates in some local labour markets; for example, 38 per cent of the Afro-Caribbean labour force in Liverpool and 45 per cent of South Asians in Tower Hamlets. As the recession became more generalised in the 1990s, there has been some convergence of unemployment rates.

Unemployment is even higher amongst young black and brown people. Whilst it is true that the immigrants of the 1950s and 1960s had faced considerable discrimination in the labour market, they did at least find jobs. This is far less likely to be true of their children, particularly in the period of Two Nations politics.

6.2.5 Black workers and the trade unions: reluctant support

Until, ironically, recent years, when their membership and power declined, trade unions' responses to racism have been muted. If unions do not represent the needs of ethnic minorities, it is not because they are not members of the unions. On the contrary, in the 1980s non-white workers were far more likely than white workers to be unionised. Only 35 per cent of white workers compared to 44 per cent of Afro-Caribbean workers belonged to unions in 1989–90 (Jones 1993); the proportions for Indian and Pakistiani workers are similar to those for whites, whilst Bangladeshis have a far lower membership rate, reflecting their positions in some of the more vulnerable sectors of the economy.

Whilst workers from ethnic minorities tend to support trade unions they do not necessarily obtain the support from the unions which they expect or to which they are entitled. Black and brown workers are poorly represented at virtually every level of trade union organisation, except for the actual membership. Despite the occasional well-known individual, such as Bill Morris, President of the TGWU, there are relatively few Afro-Caribbean or South Asian full-time officials, delegates to conferences or shop-floor representatives. The critical period was probably the 1950s and the 1960s when the unions were at the height of their power in an era of relatively full employment and larger-scale, centralised forms of production were in the ascendancy. This was when the unions could have fought and probably achieved substantial improvements for working-class ethnic minorities. That challenge was sidestepped. Ironically the unions have become more aware of the needs of their non-white members in the Two Nations era, at a time when their powers have been severely curbed by state legislation, declining membership and recession.

It has taken many years of struggle by black and brown workers to get the unions to take up their causes. There have been a number of hard-fought benchmark disputes through which black workers have gradually won better conditions. The first two of these were in the Midlands, at the Wolf plant in Southall and at Mansfield Hosiery Mills in Loughborough. In both cases

South Asian workers were frustrated by being allocated the least desirable jobs and the most unsociable shifts. Frustrated by a lack of support from local unions, they took unofficial action to remedy their complaints. Eventually, and with reluctant union support, they won their struggle. In this, as in many other similar instances, Asians rather than Afro-Caribbeans took the lead. This was not because the latter had no grievances – far from it. However, they tended to be employed in a more dispersed way through a variety of decentralised workplaces, unlike Asians who had a far stronger tradition of community-based job recruitment to large factories. Consequently, the grievances of the Afro-Caribbeans were less visible, less dramatic and less easy to organise around.

In the 1980s the focus of attention switched to London with the Grunwick strike. The largely Asian female workforce walked out in protest at the lack of union recognition at the factory, but their action was underlain by intense frustration with low wages and appalling working conditions. This was to be a landmark dispute because the small Asian workforce was able to win massive support from sections of the white working class.

Although awareness of the needs of non-white workers was emerging in the trade union movement in the 1960s and the 1970s, this intensified in the 1980s. In part Mrs Thatcher's government was responsible for the increased awareness, not least because its attacks on organised labour unified black, brown and white workers around common causes in a number of disputes. In contrast, however, the tensions stemming from the growth of unemployment at this time had the potential to divide the working-class, especially along ethnic lines. That it has not done so, leastways in the workplace, is in part due – almost perversely – to the way in which the Conservative government has repressed most forms of working-class resistance. At the same time, its wider immigration and other policies have undermined the influence of the National Front and other far right-wing groups.

6.2.6   Race and occupational mobility: unequal progress

Whilst non-white workers occupy some of the lowest rungs in the occupational hierarchy, and many groups seem locked into the underclass, others have improved their status and access to better jobs. One indicator of occupational mobility is the proportion of each ethnic group which was in the highest socio-economic category in 1974 and 1982 (Field 1986). The proportion of whites was constant but there was a twofold increase for South Asians and a fourfold one for Afro-Caribbeans. In the 1980s, ethnic minority and white employment in the service industries grew at similar rates, but there was a doubling of the numbers from ethnic minorities in managerial and administrative posts (Owen and Green 1992). The most remarkable change in recent decades has been the growth of the Indian middle class. According to Robinson (1988) there have

sons for this: continuing immigration of skilled Indian per-
ry into the labour market of British-educated second-generation
he upward mobility of earlier migrants. Therefore, there has
degree of upward social mobility amongst some sections of the
non-white population.

Rather than general upward social mobility, however, there has been
increased polarisation between and within ethnic groups. There has actually
been increasing relative concentration of non-white workers in semi- and
unskilled jobs. The proportion of South Asians – especially Indians – in this
category has fallen, but the proportion of whites has fallen even faster. In contrast, the proportion of Afro-Caribbeans in the least skilled and lowest paid
jobs has actually increased. Large numbers of non-white workers, especially
Afro-Caribbeans, are becoming increasingly locked into an underclass. There
is some upward mobility at the other end of the occupational hierarchy, but
this is largely limited to the Indian and Afro-Asian groups. As a result, the net
movement of all brown and black workers from manual to non-manual jobs
between 1974 and 1982 was only 3 per cent (Brown 1984).

The previous analysis was based on aggregate numbers in particular occupational groups at two different dates. Such an approach reveals little about
how individuals have fared. Longitudinal data are required for this purpose
and these have been used in a major study of the London labour market
between 1971 and 1981 (Hamnett and Randolph 1988). This shows con-
clusively that in the 1970s ethnic minorities there experienced more unemployment, and became relatively more concentrated in the lower rungs of the
occupational hierarchy. Black and brown workers became increasingly marginalised as jobs disappeared in many traditional industries. Nevertheless, the
experiences of ethnic minorities were far from homogeneous. Male South
Asian workers were moving into skilled manual work even though this has
been in decline. Afro-Caribbeans also made some gains, notably in obtaining
low-status clerical jobs in the rapidly expanding service industries. However,
Afro-Caribbeans were also the only group to increase in number in the
declining manual sector, and they also recorded the highest rates of
unemployment.

Employment provides a critical test of the degree to which ethnic minorities
have been integrated into UK society. The evidence suggests little if any
progress for these groups as a whole. Of course there are individual success
stories, and some Asian groups – especially the Indians – have prospered,
gaining entry to the professions or becoming small-scale business owners.
Nevertheless, many if not most second-generation black and brown children
are still getting the same types of low-pay and low-skill jobs as their parents
- if, that is, they get jobs at all. There has been some shift into the higher social
categories of jobs, but this does little more than reflect structural changes in
the economy. The most worrying feature is the way in which Afro-Caribbeans,

Pakistanis and Bangladeshis have remained firmly rooted at the bottom end of the occupational hierarchy and have shared least in upward social mobility. One of the keys to this is educational performance.

6.3 Education and race

Education is an important dimension of racial inequality in several ways: as a possible channel for social mobility, as an indicator of social integration, and as one of the more direct interfaces between the changing form of state provision and particular social groups. The aims of the educational policies of One Nation politics were centred on eliminating class-based disadvantages and advancing a notionally meritocratic society, even if this remained little more than an ambition of the social-democratic consensus. In practice, however, the educational policies of One Nation politics had in-built biases, and discriminated – albeit indirectly – against ethnic minorities.

Whilst the education of the first generation of immigrants had largely been determined before they arrived in the UK, education provided a potentially important route to social mobility for second and later generations. There is no simple and direct link between education and employment for any ethnic group, let alone South Asians and Afro-Caribbeans. For example, one study of young people in Leeds and Manchester found that the children of immigrants who have grown up in Britain, speak English fluently and have good educational qualifications, still have difficulties in obtaining jobs which match their qualifications (Martin 1980). Similarly, graduates from minority ethnic groups are more likely to be unemployed for longer periods of time than are white graduates (Johnes and Taylor 1989). In general then, educational qualifications do not necessarily remove barriers for ethnic minorities. Furthermore, as argued earlier, even if qualifications remove some barriers to entry to particular occupations, there are still considerable obstacles to progress within these. Education, in fact, may raise aspirations which are steadfastly difficult to fulfil in the face of individual and institutional discrimination.

6.3.1 Educational achievement and underachievement

The educational system of One Nation politics made few concessions to the particular needs of ethnic minorities. Not surprisingly, the 1981 Rampton Report found clear evidence of differences in educational performance between ethnic groups. Afro-Caribbean children were underachievers, whilst Asian children usually did at least as well as, and sometimes better than, white children. The differences can be summarised by a number of indicators:

(1) Only 5 per cent of Afro-Caribbeans compared to 20 per cent of South
    Asians and 23 per cent of all UK school-leavers had high grades in CSE
    and O level mathematics.
(2) Only 3 per cent of Afro-Caribbeans compared to 18 per cent of Asians and
    21 per cent of the UK groups had 5 or more O levels.
(3) Only 2 per cent of Afro-Caribbeans compared to 13 per cent of Asians and
    13 per cent of the UK groups had one or more A levels.
(4) Only 1 per cent of Afro-Caribbeans compared to 3 per cent of Asians and
    5 per cent of the UK group went on to university.

Whilst South Asian children as a whole outperformed Afro-Caribbeans,
their achievements were highly polarised. High achievements at one end of the
scale were offset by very poor results at the other. If all CSE or O level results
are considered, then South Asians performed less well than Afro-Caribbeans,
and both groups were outperformed by white children. The differences were
particularly acute for girls: one-half of young South Asian girls compared to
only one-fifth of Afro-Caribbean girls had no qualifications at all. The
Rampton Report therefore gave the misleading impression that all South
Asian children were achieving high-grade educational qualifications. This is
not the case. Those from working-class backgrounds, and from the Pakistani
or Bangladeshi communities, share the educational disadvantages of
Afro-Caribbeans.
   There are, then, considerable differences amongst South Asians (Table 6.4).
The young male Indian adult population is better qualified than young white
adults. In contrast, young male adult Pakistanis/Bangladeshis and Afro-
Caribbeans have less educational qualifications; 52 per cent of the former lack
any educational qualifications. The position of Pakistani/Bangladeshi women
is even worse for 68 per cent have no formal qualifications. In contrast, Indian
and Afro-Caribbean women have broadly similar qualifications to white adult
women (Tomlinson 1983). During the 1980s, there has been some convergence
in the educational qualifications of all ethnic groups. However, educational
achievements are still uneven amongst different ethnic groups and between
working-class and middle-class children. Any general closing of the divide
between non-white and white children has been matched by deepening divides
amongst the ethnic minorities.
   The reasons for the poor educational performance of children from some
ethnic minorities are complex. They include the barriers encountered in the
home, in the school curriculum and institutional organisation, social class, and
racial discrimination. None of these in itself provides a sufficient explanation
and not all the reasons apply equally to all ethnic groups. But together they
do explain the limitations of race-blind, and also location-blind, educational

Table 6.4 Highest qualification level by sex and ethnic group in 1984–86 (1988–90)

Highest qualification held by:	% of population aged 25–29							
	White		Afro-Caribbean/ Guyanese		Indian		Pakistani/ Bangladeshi	
Males								
Higer	17	(15)	6	(6)	24	(19)	12	(8)
Other	47	(57)	36	(58)	34	(51)	21	(40)
None	36	(29)	58	(30)	42	(30)	67	(52)
Total	100		100		100		100	
Females								
Higher	14	(13)	16	(16)	15	(13)	6	(4)
Other	36	(51)	30	(52)	29	(46)	14	(28)
None	50	(36)	54	(32)	56	(41)	80	(68)
Total	100		100		100		100	

Source: CSO (1988, 1992)

policies which fail to tackle the real roots of disadvantage.

The educational performance of all children is affected by the emotional and material circumstances of their home environments; the latter, in turn, is fundamentally affected by income. Children of Afro-Caribbean and Pakistani/Bangladeshi parents are doubly disadvantaged in coming from lower-income homes and being subject to racial obstacles. Right-wing politicians have argued that one of the supposed disadvantages of Afro-Caribbean children is the high incidence of single families in this ethnic group which, it is argued, contributes to a lack of emotional support. However, their disadvantages are rooted in the poverty of single-parent families. If the effects of social class are filtered out, there are no significant differences in the educational performance of Afro-Caribbean children in single- and two-parent families.

This is not to say that children from ethnic minorities suffer no disadvantages as a result of their home backgrounds. Some second-generation children are linguistically disadvantaged if their parents at home are unaccustomed to speaking the language of schools, 'standard English'. Large family sizes, poor living conditions and a lack of quiet working space may also contribute to poor educational performance. These multiple disadvantages are, of course, shared with many white children from underclass or poor working-class backgrounds. However, Afro-Caribbeans and Pakistanis/Bangladeshis are disproportionately represented amongst the low paid, the unskilled and the unemployed.

The type of school attended is also influenced by social class. Its impacts are expressed through both the neighbourhood effect (middle-class areas tend to have better schools) and the public/private divide. Because of income constraints, purchasing a private education is not a realistic option for most non-white parents, although it is becoming so for growing numbers of middle-class South Asians. As a result, the vast majority are unable to purchase the additional assistance provided by low staff–pupil ratios in private schools. Instead, working-class ethnic minority children are dependent on local state education. Given the residential distribution of their communities, this often means decaying inner-city schools. Low average ability levels and aspirations in many such schools militate against individual achievement.

The content and style of school teaching have been rooted in the history and culture of white Britain, and particularly in an ethnocentric view of colonialism. This has encouraged or reinforced racist ideas amongst white children and has also contributed to low self-esteem amongst black children. As a result, there was a campaign – which partly succeeded – for a more multicultural approach to education in the 1970s and the 1980s (Troyna and Williams 1986). However, the increase in multicultural and anti-racist education should not distract attention from the fundamental way in which class and race interact to produce educational disadvantage.

Racism also contributes to underachievement. This operates in a number of ways. There are some overtly racist teachers, whilst racism in the job market may discourage non-white children from pursuing educational qualifications. More significant than overt racism are the low expectations that many teachers have of non-white children, especially Afro-Caribbeans. Low expectations contribute to low self-fulfilment.

Many children do underachieve in the educational system but this does not apply to all individuals or, in equal measure, to all ethnic groups. Nor does it apply equally to males and females. Nevertheless, the broad class, home and school conditions outlined above do explain a large part of the educational disadvantage of ethnic minority children. These disadvantages tend to have a multiple character. Not least, inequalities in the job market and in schools feed upon each other and add to the cumulative disadvantages of many young people.

6.3.2 Race and education policy

The state education system of One Nation politics concentrated on eliminating (some) class-based obstacles to achievement and participation. Recognition that there were also specifically race based obstacles came late. Even then, the response of the state to racial disadvantage has been muted, leastways at the central governmment level; the response of local authorities has been more mixed and often more positive. The dominant ethos of educational policy in the latter years of One Nation politics is probably best represented by the views of the 1967 Plowden Committee. This argued that both non-white and white children in inner-city areas were equally disadvantaged; in other words there were specific class and location barriers but not racial ones. The policy response adopted was measures such as Educational Priority Areas and Educational Disadvantage Units. The Rate Support Grant was also weighted in favour of urban areas, while Section 11 of the 1966 Local Government Act addressed the educational needs of deprived areas.

In so far as there was an underlying philosophy to this approach, it was to avoid identifying race *per se* as a source of disadvantage. Instead, class or low income were seen as the major underlying causes. Consequently, the needs of immigrants rather than of children from ethnic minorities were emphasised. There was, therefore, a tendency to see the educational difficulties of non-white children as temporary, linked to the difficulties of transition to or assimilation in white UK society. This underestimated the persistent difficulties faced by second and third generations. It also meant that the issue of how to represent ethnic minority culture in the school curriculum was ignored.

Another failing of this approach was the uniform view taken of all non-white children, even though there are both high and low achieving individuals, as well as systematic differences between groups. In its most pernicious form this approach involved associating black children with the causes of educational disadvantage in some areas. It was a view which even crept into the Plowden Report, for it used the proportion of immigrants in an area as one indicator of educational disadvantage. The same argument surfaced in a far more political and blatantly racist form in west London in the early 1970s. Parents at two schools complained about the large numbers of 'immigrant' children in these. The Conservative Education Minister suggested that 30 per cent should be the upper limit for 'such' children in any one school and that dispersal policies might be necessary to achieve this. In practice, few local authorities ever practised this policy and it was abandoned in 1975.

By the late 1970s the context for policy formulation was changing. Parents in the ethnic minority communities began to demand multicultural education. Initially, assimilation of their children into British society through the educational system had been perceived as a route to better jobs and to upward social mobility, in keeping with the vision of One Nation politics. However, the educational and labour market experiences of the 1960s and the 1970s had been disappointing. Partly in response to this, and partly reflecting the growing self-assurance of these communities, there were now demands for a less Euro-centred education which recognised the values and the cultures of non-whites.

The Labour government in the late 1970s started to move in the direction of multiracial education. Its 1977 Green Paper stressed that there was a need to review an educational curriculum which was still firmly rooted in an imperial past. Conservative governments after 1979 initially showed little sign of responding to these pressures but the 1981 civil disturbances were to have a catalytic effect on policies. The Scarman Report pointed to links between school failures and unemployment with the 1981 riots. This led the Department of Education, in the same year, to issue guidance that schools should promote greater tolerance of other races and cultures, a small step towards multicultural education.

Local authorities reacted to this advice in various ways. Some simply ignored it whilst others, such as the Inner London Education Authority, set out to develop new curricula and other teaching resources. There was – probably inevitably – a backlash against multicultural education. This surfaced with a vengeance in Bradford. Ray Honeyford, headmaster of a school with a largely South Asian intake, argued in the Salisbury Review that an emphasis on multicultural education could lead to neglect of the needs of indigenous white children. The national publicity which this article attracted sharpened the political debate on multi-cultural education, but served to obscure the class issue of the disadvantages experienced by both white and Asian children.

What, if anything, has been the place of race and education in Two Nations politics? The fundamental answer is that this has not really been openly on the agenda. Mrs Thatcher's emphasis on individual responsibility and the denial of society did not recognise structural disadvantages, whether rooted in class or race. The most important legislative change in this period has been the 1988 Educational Reform Act (ERA) and the introduction of the national curriculum. At one level, this 'should vitiate those blatant forms of racist discrimination which have denied many black pupils access to the full curriculum' (Troyna 1990, 405). However, the same author (p. 414) argues that the claims of the ERA to provide a window of opportunity are misleading for 'entitlement cannot be genuinely offered within an institutional framework which sanctions the maintenance, reproduction and extension of inequality'.

There are three implications of the ERA which impinge strongly on racial inequalities in education (Troyna 1990, 412–413). Firstly, direct grant maintained schools become entirely independent of local educational control. Five years after acquiring this status, they can apply to the Secretary for State to change their admissions policies; criteria such as exam performance, area of residence, and religion could be used, all of which have significant racial implications. Secondly, the trend towards formula-based funding, as part of the local management of schools initiative, will make it more difficult to give preferential treatment to schools in deprived areas; 'by equating equality of treatment with sameness in the allocation of budgets, the approach is bound to exacerbate inequality' (p. 413). And, finally, open enrolment in response to the emphasis on parental choice may well accelerate a trend towards racially segregated schools.

The conclusion must be therefore that whilst the educational policies of the 1980s and early 1990s were not overtly racist, they are likely further to disadvantage large parts of the UK's ethnic minority communities. The emphasis on parental choice (both within the public sector and between the public and private sectors) is unlikely to benefit the vast majority of non-white children. This is precisely because much of educational disadvantage is structural, linked to class, home and neighbourhood. The children of middle-class Asian or Caribbean parents may benefit from private education, but it is difficult to see how 'parental choice' will benefit most working-class children, let alone the children of ethnic minority parents who are locked into the underclass.

6.4 Race and housing: living in separate worlds?

Racialised access to housing predates Two Nations politics. Disadvantages accumulated within the framework of largely race-blind housing policies during the 1950s and the 1960s; however, they were not immune from the growing racialisation (and sometimes racism) of politics in the second half of One Nation politics or from discriminatory practices in the allocation of housing and residential spaces. Nevertheless, the forms of housing disadvantage have subsequently changed, because this has been a strategic area for the Two Nations project. Promotion of the property-owning democracy and the constraining of local authorities' roles as providers of rented accommodation were not explicitly racialised policies, but they had explicit class origins and implications. But the intertwining of race and class inevitably meant that Two Nations housing policies had differential racial implications (Smith 1989).

Immigrants, and later the second and third generations in some ethnic communities, were geographically concentrated in some of the poorest quality housing. This cannot be accounted for simply by class; even controlling for class, some ethnic minorities occupy poorer quality housing than do the majority white ethnic group. There are also persistent differences in the housing tenures of white and non-white families and of individual ethnic minorities. Again these go beyond any variations which could be expected simply on the basis of class, or even of gender (Peach and Byron 1993).

Racial exclusion or steering effects in housing are produced by a variety of mechanisms. As previously emphasised, the interventionism of One Nation politics in securing the conditions for the reproduction of capitalist relationships was essentially founded on class concerns. As such it failed to address many of the practices of racial disadvantage and discrimination of housing allocation. Instead, there was continuing considerable racial discrimination, overt as well as indirect, in both the public and private sectors. At the end of this period, legislation in the 1970s belatedly removed the more visible manifestations of discrimination. The removal of institutional discrimination does not, of course, guarantee the removal of more individual and informal forms of racism but it has assured better access to local authority housing for ethnic minorities, even if only to the poorer quality stock. Improved access secured at the end of the years of One Nation politics has, however, been followed in the 1980s by relentless policies to reduce the size of, and redefine the role of, public sector housing.

In the private sector racial exclusion has been achieved under both One Nation and Two Nations politics via the market mechanisms of supply and demand. Income differentials amongst ethnic groups, coupled with the higher prices for properties in areas with high positive externalities, have constituted social and racial filters to residential mobility. Class discrimination has thereby become linked to racial discrimination to produce a form of housing segregation which is not only legally untouchable but is also encouraged, and even legitimated, by the emphasis of Two Nations politics on market mechanisms and individual choice. In this respect, racial segregation symbolises the gap between the rhetoric of equal rights legislation and the realities of structural disadvantage. An even more powerful symbol is the racialising of homelessness; the rate of ethnic minority homelessness is about four times that of white homelessness in London (London Housing Unit 1989).

6.4.1 Divided ways: race and access to housing tenure

The failure of One Nation politics to recognise the specific needs of ethnic minorities, combined with labour market marginality, meant that early immigrants were disproportionately dependent on the private rented sector (Rex and Moore 1967). Later changes in state housing policies, the accumulation of money within ethnic minority communities, and the boom in housing construction in the 1960s led to some change in access to other tenures. By the early 1980s there were new patterns of ownership and renting. Afro-Caribbeans, in comparison to whites, were far more concentrated in council housing and housing association dwellings: the corollary to this was the smaller proportion of Afro-Caribbeans in owner occupation (Table 6.5). In contrast, South Asian households were more likely than white households to be in owner occupation – 72 per cent compared to 59 per cent. By the late 1980s a decade of Two Nations housing policies had left their mark; commodification had reduced the proportion of all ethnic groups living in council housing, and had contributed to increases in owner occupancy. There continued, however, to be marked differences between ethnic minorities.

Housing tenure is not, however, necessarily an indicator of housing conditions, as the 1982 PSI survey indicated (see Table 6.6). Amongst owner occupiers, Asians and Afro-Caribbeans were less likely than whites to be living in detached dwellings, and more likely to be in older properties lacking amenities. They were also more likely to be living at higher occupational densities – particularly in the case of Asians. The same pattern of inequality was to be seen in the local authority sector. Only in the privately rented sector was there some blurring of differences, as this became the 'last resort' for a large part of the underclass irrespective of ethnicity.

Table 6.5 The housing tenures of ethnic groups in 1982 and 1987–90 (Great Britain) (percentages)

	White 1982	White 1987–90	Afro Caribbean 1982	Afro Caribbean 1987–90	Asian 1982	Indian 1987–90	Pakistani/Bangladeshi 1987–90
Owner-occupied	59	64	41	47	72	84	67
Council rented	30	25	46	42	19	8	17
Privately rented	9	10	6	11	6	9	17
Housing association	2		8		2		
Total*	100		100		100		100

* 'Others' excluded so the columns do not add up to 100%

Sources: Brown, C. (1984, Table 29); CSO (1992)

Table 6.6   Housing conditions of ethnic households in 1982

	% in flats	% in detached or semi-detached houses	% in dwellings built pre-1945	% lacking exclusive use of both hot water and inside WC	% with >1 person per room
All tenure groups					
White	15	54	50	5	3
West Indian*	32	23	60	5	16
Asian	16	26	74	7	35
Owner-occupiers					
White	5	67	56	3	2
West Indian*	1	37	84	3	13
Asian	4	29	81	5	33
Council tenants					
White	27	39	27	3	5
West Indian*	54	9	34	3	20
Asain	54	11	35	7	43
Private tenants					
White	32	33	87	27	2
West Indians* and Asian	24	21	83	32	22

* Terminology used in original

Source: Brown, C. (1984, Table 35)

The class differences between South Asians and Afro-Caribbeans are simply not substantial enough to explain the sharp variations in their access to tenure. Housing differences are the outcome of varying combinations of labour market disadvantages, gendered access to housing (as we show below), discrimination and cultural constructions. Given their specific social constructions, cultural and financial barriers, each tenure form is considered separately.

6.4.2   Private renting: the last resort

Until the early 1970s private renting was the principal source of housing for the non-white population, especially immigrants. They lacked money capital to purchase property and were discriminated against by the access and allocation rules of public sector housing. There was still a relatively large — if dwindling — stock of privately rented dwellings available in the 1950s and the 1960s, especially in the inner cities which were also the principal labour market for immigrants. Housing disadvantage was therefore closely linked to labour market segmentation and the need to assemble replacement or supplementary labour in particular locations. The rented dwellings available were often of poor quality, with short and insecure leases. Even so, immigrants still encountered discrimination.

One response to discrimination was that non-white immigrants sought out non-white landlords, a process which contributed to class divisions within the black community (Rex and Moore 1967). Whilst this provided an immediate response to the housing needs of immigrants, it could not offer a long-term solution to their needs and satisfy their aspirations. Furthermore, over time the squeeze on private renting by the policies of both One Nation and Two Nations politics, and persistent demolition programmes in inner cities, have reduced the stock of such dwellings. Within the residual stock, there seems to have been some reduction in the reported level of discrimination. In the 1960s a series of controlled experiments was undertaken whereby whites and blacks of similar incomes and ages telephoned for advertised rented flats or rooms. Discrimination against Afro-Caribbeans occurred in 62 per cent of the test cases. By the mid 1970s similar experiments found a discrimination level of 27 per cent against Afro-Caribbeans and Asians. Similar data are not available for the 1980s, but there is no reason to expect that discrimination no longer exists.

6.4.3 Council housing: administrative discrimination and commodification

Local authority provision developed, at various times, both to meet the general housing needs of the working class and to house the more disadvantaged (Gray 1976). Yet in the 1950s and much of the 1960s ethnic minorities were severely disadvantaged in their access to this sector. In 1961 only 2 per cent of Afro-Caribbeans lived in local authority dwellings (Peach and Byron 1993). Housing departments did not operate openly racist systems of allocation. Instead, there was indirect discrimination. In allocating priorities amongst applicants, they gave disproportionate weight to length of time on the waiting list rather than to housing need; this discriminated indirectly against immigrants who therefore failed to benefit from the expansion of social housing as part of the One Nation programme.

With time residential qualifications became less of a barrier for immigrants, especially the longer-settled Afro-Caribbeans, and ceased to be an obstacle for the second generations in the ethnic minority communities. As a result of these changes, and the collapse of the private rental sector and the effects of slum clearance schemes, by 1977 the proportion of Afro-Caribbeans in council housing – 45 per cent – surpassed that for the white population (Peach and Byron 1993). At a later date South Asians were also able to secure better access to council housing. In Blackburn, for example, only one Asian household a year was allocated a council tenancy between 1968 and 1972. By 1978 there were 56 allocations in a single year (Robinson 1980). However, the proportion of South Asians living in council houses remained far smaller than for white or Afro-Caribbean people. In part, this reflected a cultural preference for home ownership and, leastways for Indians, their increasing purchasing power compared to Afro-Caribbeans. Peach and Byron (1993) have also shown that the concentration of the Afro-Caribbean population in public sector housing can be explained in terms of social class and gender. Whilst the proportion of male household heads in council housing is very similar for Afro-Caribbeans and whites – controlling for class – there are disproportionately more black single, female-headed families in this sector. There is, therefore, class-differentiated, gendered and racialised access to this sector.

The removal of discriminatory practices in the compilation of council waiting lists still left scope for discrimination in the allocation process (Henderson and Karn 1987). This was evident in a comparison of the types of council dwellings occupied by the major ethnic groups (Table 6.6). Non-whites were twice as likely to be allocated flats than houses, and were four times less likely to be allocated semi- or detached dwellings. They were also more likely to be allocated pre-1945 dwellings. There are many other forms of unequal access. For example, ethnic minorities tend to have to accumulate more points on the waiting list before receiving their first offer of a council house. They are also less likely than white people to be given their first choice area of residence.

The inequalities described above had crystallised as being class based by the end of One Nation politics after the more blatant forms of racial discrimination had been eliminated. However, Two Nations housing policies have exacerbated the difficulties of access for ethnic minorities. Council house sales have led to a process of residualisation as better quality dwellings were sold to the better-off tenants. This left a residual of poorer quality dwellings for those in greatest need and with the least resources at their disposal. Poor non-white people – especially Afro-Caribbeans – were and are, therefore, in increasing competition with poor white people for a dwindling stock of poor quality council housing.

6.4.4 Owner-occupation: individual 'choice' and housing market discrimination

Given the race blindness of the housing policies of One Nation politics, and the exclusionary policies of private landlords and local authorities, in the 1950s and the 1960s the only real housing alternative to private renting was owner occupation – assuming that immigrants could secure sufficient capital and or a mortgage. To some extent, this was the preferred option of the South Asian community. Through hard work and savings, even relatively poor Asians managed to buy houses. Hence, by the 1980s, almost four out of every five South Asian households owned their homes. The emphasis on property-owning democracy and market solutions to housing 'problems', and on council house sales, in Two Nations politics further increased owner occupation, especially amongst the Asian community.

This does not mean that Asian families had unlocked access to large detached homes in leafy suburban lanes. Instead, their first purchase was often a low-price, short-lease, low-quality property. Given their labour market position, this was all that they could afford. As Phillips and Karn (1992, 358) state, 'Their route into owner occupation was often unconventional and costly, with first time buyers being deprived of any significant choice in either housing type or location.' There has subsequently been a marked improvement in the position of non-white owners as they traded up through the housing market in terms of price and quality. However, even in the 1980s they still occupied distinctly poorer quality dwellings than did white owner-occupiers (see Table 6.6). These houses continued to be disproportionately concentrated in the inner areas of large cities, although there has been some suburbanisation – into new nodes of ethnic minority concentration – in recent years (Robinson 1990).

Both race and class contribute to the locational concentration of ethnic minority owner occupation in the inner cities. Non-white families face more constraints than do white families in the same social class. For example, in Birmingham larger proportions of whites have been able to secure building society loans. Whites are also less likely to face building society refusals of their mortgage applications: the respective rates are 39 per cent, 51 per cent and 53 per cent for whites, Afro-Caribbeans and Indian families (Karn 1983). In part, this is because building societies generally do not favour lending on inner-city properties. This applies to both whites and non-whites in these areas but the latter are more likely to apply for mortgages on inner-city properties – either for cultural and community preferences or because these are the only properties which they can afford.

Yet, it is more than a question of the area of purchase. Non-white applicants are more likely to have insecure incomes or marginal jobs, which influences building societies' refusals to offer mortgages. Past discrimination against ethnic minorities has also led to fewer applications by those able to obtain a loan from another source. By the 1980s financial deregulation and greater competition was leading to changing attitudes amongst the institutions, whilst growing familiarisation with house purchase meant that ethnic minorities were making more use of mainstream financial institutions such as banks and building societies (Phillips and Karn 1992).

Another obstacle is the discrimination practised by estate agents, surveyors, valuers or other professionals (Sarre et al. 1989). Even in the 1970s – that is after the Race Relations Act – 12 per cent of non-whites in Birmingham were experiencing discrimination when they tried to buy homes (Karn 1983). Estate agents are particularly influential. Many try to steer black purchasers towards certain areas and properties – those which already have black residents. As recently as 1989 the Commission for Racial Equality successfully took action against three Oldham estate agencies which sought to steer Asians and whites to different parts of the city (Mullins 1990). White vendors have also been known to refuse to sell on racial grounds to black purchasers. One reaction to this has been the sidestepping of estate agents and greater reliance on informal information networks, which tend to be spatially restricted. As a result, whilst ethnic minorities, especially South Asians, have secured access to owner occupation, this has gone hand in hand with continued segregation in particular segments of the housing market and particular areas.

The commodification of council housing, combined with changes in financial markets in the 1980s, has benefited some individuals in the ethnic minorities. However, as Phillips and Karn (1992, 367) argue,

> completely outweighing these slight advantages, is the adverse impact that sales and neglect of housing rental production had upon ethnic minorities, particularly the very poorest, such as the Bangladeshis in London and Afro-Caribbean single parents. They figure disproportionately amongst the homeless and amongst those living in the worst conditions in bed-and-breakfast hotels and multi-occupied property.

6.4.5 Housing and segregation: racialised residential spaces

Britain's ethnic minorities are geographically concentrated; 57 per cent live in just two metropolitan areas, London and the West Midlands (Figure 6.2). There are ethnic minorities living in small towns and in rural areas but they are disproportionately concentrated in the metropolitan areas where 78 per cent live compared to 40 per cent of whites. Non-whites are also concentrated in the inner areas of these large cities. In the 1991 Census, more than one third of the residents in Brent, Newham, Tower Hamlets and Hackney belonged to ethnic minority groups, whilst outside of London the largest concentration relative to the white population was in Leicester (Teague 1993). This is not simply segregation along the lines of white v. black or even of South Asian v. Afro Caribbean. Instead there is segregation amongst Afro-Caribbeans according to islands of origin and between Asians according to religion, country and region of origin.

In a genuinely multicultural society concentration need not be undesirable *per se*. Instead, it could be the outcome of cultural preferences for living in close proximity to family, and to specialised shops, social and religious facilities. There are elements of this in the residential concentration of ethnic minorities in the UK. In addition, clustering tends to occur in the early stages of immigration for all groups, no matter what their ethnic or racial origins. Newly arrived immigrants usually rely on previous immigrants as their

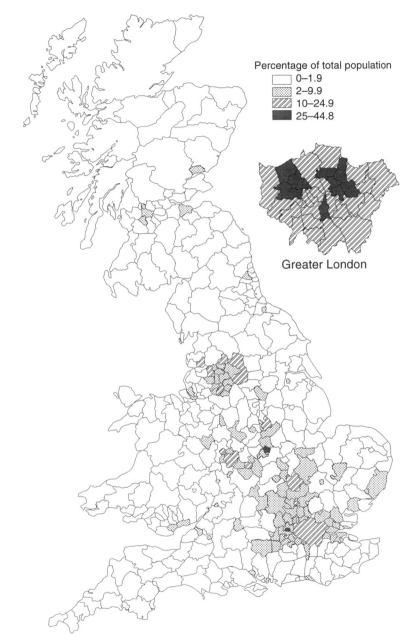

Percentage of total population
0–1.9
2–9.9
10–24.9
25–44.8

Greater London

Figure 6.2 Ethnic minority groups as a percentage of the total population, 1991

Source: OPCS, *Population Trends*, 1993

contacts in precarious, often informal job and housing markets; there are therefore advantages in concentration. Over time such residential segregation falls markedly for most immigrant groups; in the UK, for instance, this was the experience of the Italians and the Irish. However, it has not been the experience of non-white immigrants. There has been some suburbanisation in the 1980s but overall levels of concentration have changed little during three decades of immigration and settlement. Choice does not therefore explain the high levels of segregation in the UK. Instead we need to look at class.

Some residential segregation of the ethnic minority population is to be expected on the basis of social class. Immigrants tended to be replacement or supplementary labour in traditional, low-paid or unpopular jobs. Even in the 1990s, non-white families tend to be disproportionately working-class – and, indeed, to form part of the underclass. As working class families tend to be concentrated in particular residential areas, this alone would lead to ethnic segregation. However, this can only provide a partial explanation of non-white segregation. For example, only about one half of the spatial segregation of Afro-Caribbeans in London in 1971 could be accounted for by socio-economic characteristics (Lee 1977). Even this understates the point for the socio-economic characteristics of black people – such as their occupational segregation – are in part the outcome of racial discrimination. The same applies to black people's position in the housing market. Black people are concentrated in particular housing tenures, for reasons of class, gender and discrimination, which partly explains their residential distribution.

Whilst class and gender are important in explaining racialised segregation, Smith (1979, 156) argues that there is also a need to appreciate the politics of 'racial segregation'. She argues that after the Notting Hill riots, racial segregation came to be seen as a politically constructed problem. The riots were portrayed as the outcome of large numbers of non-whites being concentrated in small areas, rather than as a failure of capitalism or as a product of racism. Geographical concentration came to be seen as a cause of prejudice rather than as a consequence of discrimination. The response of the state in the 1960s was to introduce legislation to curtail the rights of settlement of non-white immigrants. The corollary of this was a failure to address effectively either the specific disadvantages of non-whites in labour and housing markets, or the disadvantages of all the poor residents of inner cities.

In the period of Two Nations politics the nature of segregation has changed once again. Firstly, 'the spatially selective effect of economic restructuring in recent years has meant that patterns of segregation increasingly restrict (rather than simply reflect) black people's labour market opportunities and their life chances in urban Britain' (Smith 1989, 161). This can only reinforce their housing market vulnerability. Yet the Conservative Party's emphasis on the 'sanctity of the market' has meant that policies to attack the roots of structural disadvantage – of which segregation is a potent symbol – have been elbowed off the policy agenda by those concerned to make market solutions work more effectively. This conceptualises racial segregation as no more than a passing phase of market adjustment.

It would be wrong to suggest that there have been no changes in the residential segregation of black people in the UK. Whilst there has been an increase in the segregation of Asians, there has been a decrease for Afro-Caribbeans in several large cities. This is mostly due to their changing relative positions within the housing market. In the 1970s Afro-Caribbeans gained better access to local authority housing – even if not equal access to the better quality dwellings. In the process of being rehoused by the council they have been dispersed, to some degree, and this has contributed to a decline in their segregation, albeit only within working-class areas. In contrast, South Asians have moved more into owner occupation. This has not led to any significant decline in residential segregation because the types of properties purchased – both through choice and constraint – tend to be in the inner city for the working class, whilst middle-class suburbanisation has been organised around new ethnic minority nodes.

Residential segregation remains one of the most potent symbols of the disadvantages faced by ethnic minorities in UK society. It is also an indicator of the continued inequalities between these ethnic groups. This is important because segregation mediates the distribution of society's material resources. It also contributes, along with racist practices, to the definition of racial groups, 'thus reproducing racial categories and racialising inequality' (Smith 1979, 152).

6.5 Race, politics and civil society

The relationship of ethnic minorities with the state, politics and the larger civil society are all major topics which cannot adequately be addressed in the space available here. Yet these are fundamental in understanding racial inequalities in the UK. Some insights into these larger issues are provided by considering a small number of related themes: these are the positioning of ethnic minorities in British politics, race relations legislation, racial attacks, and relationships with the forces of law and order. During much of the period of One Nation politics there was an inter-party consensus on race issues. Although this became strained at times during the 1960s and early 1970s, mainly with respect to immigration, it remained intact as there was broad agreement between Labour and Conservatives over integrationist aims. However, in the period of Two Nations politics there has been a break down of consensus because of the way in which Mrs Thatcher used immigration as an electoral issue and because of the attempts by the Conservatives to reconstruct the concept of nationality along narrowly and monoculturally British lines. It is against this background that rising levels of tension in the forms of racial attacks, strained relationships with the police and inner-city disturbances have to be seen.

6.5.1   The politics of race

During the 1950s there was broad consensus between Labour and Conservatives with respect to most issues relating to non-white people. While the 1962 Immigration Act strained the cross-party consensus it did not rupture it. The consensus was again put to the test in 1968 following Enoch Powell's infamous 'rivers of blood' speech. This inflammatory speech by a member of the Shadow Cabinet appeared to lend political respectability to an undercurrent of racism within the Conservative Party. Once race had been made an election issue, successive Labour and Conservative governments came under intense pressure to introduce stronger immigration controls.

The question of immigration control did, however, differentiate the parties. Labour adopted a more liberal stance than the Conservatives, although it did introduce the 1968 Immigration Act. Labour, for example, took positive steps to improve the legal infrastructure for integration during this period in the form of the Race Relations Acts (Banton 1985). As a result – and in the context of Powell's speeches – Labour was able to mobilise considerable support from the black community in the 1970 election. However, race had also become an issue amongst white voters. Opinion polls showed it to be one of their more important concerns. Consequently, 'it now seems certain that Powell made a major contribution to the decisive victory of his government and political rival, Edward Heath' (Layton-Henry and Rich 1986, 80).

The approach of the major parties to race issues was also shaped by developments on the far right, especially the growth of the National Front (NF). The NF was formed in 1966 but was a direct descendant of earlier right-wing movements such as the British National Party and the National Socialist Movement. In the 1970 election the NF fought 10 seats and it gained 3.6 per cent of the vote in these. The streak of racism in the Conservative Party surfaced in the willingness of some individuals to co-operate with the NF. This climaxed in the local Monday Club supporting the NF candidate in the 1972 Uxbridge by-election. This was too far outside the One Party framework of race and integration for the relatively liberal Edward Heath and the Conservatives expelled the Uxbridge Monday Club members. Therefore the One Nation consensus held, but only narrowly so in the early 1970s.

Immigration continued to be a contentious issue. In the October 1974 election the NF secured 9.4 per cent of the vote in Hackney South, and also received strong support in Leicester. Racial issues were again prominent in 1976, following press hysteria over the temporary housing provided for Malaysian Asian refugees. The NF capitalised on this and other issues and, in that year, secured 16.6 per cent of the vote in local elections in Leicester. However, this was to be its electoral high point. By the 1979 general election its share of the vote in the 303 seats it contested had fallen to 1.4 per cent. By the 1980s the NF was in political disarray and thereafter it fragmented.

In part the decline of the NF was due to its own political incompetence. However, it also reflected changes associated with Two Nations politics, and especially the way in which these were articulated within the Conservative Party. Edward Heath had been relatively liberal on racial issues. He had, for example, sacked Powell from his Cabinet and forbidden Tory candidates to exploit race as an electoral issue. Margaret Thatcher was to change this after she became party leader, and her nationalistic and populist approach was instrumental in undermining support for the Front.

Mrs Thatcher's leadership exploited immigration control as part of its electoral strategy. The critical turning point was a speech which Mrs Thatcher made in January 1978 on the *World in Action* programme, referring to the dangers of being 'swamped' by immigrants. There is no doubt that this interview harmed racial harmony in Britain. Bernard Levin commented in *The Times* that 'If you talk and behave as though black men were some kind of virus that must be kept out of the body politic then it is the shabbiest hypocrisy to preach racial harmony at the same time' (quoted in Layton-Henry and Rich 1986, 76). Following this speech there was a sharp rise in support for the Conservative Party for as Crewe (1983, 263) argued, 'there are votes for picking in fanning the flames of racial resentment'. The Conservatives entered the 1979 general election committed to tightening immigration controls and to introducing a new British Nationality Act. The tone of the debate, plus the abandonment of a commitment to liberalising conditions for immigrants already settled in Britain, marked abandonment of the post-war inter-party consensus on race.

Substantial swings to the Conservatives in the 1979 election in constituencies of previous NF strength suggest that Mrs Thatcher successfully attracted ex-NF voters (Layton-Henry and Rich 1986, 152). Therefore, Mrs Thatcher's election victory went hand in hand with the electoral eclipse of the NF, leastways during the 1980s. The 1981 British Nationality Act, which in effect further discriminated, albeit indirectly, against black immigrants, probably sealed the demise of the NF. The price of this, however, was that Mrs Thatcher's government lent further political respectability to thinly disguised racist politics. The British Nationality Act, which restricted the rights of citizenship of immigrants (mainly non-white) in the UK also opened up a new chapter in race relations. Saggar (1993, 46) argues that 'the locus of the race issue has shifted from matters to do with immigration numbers and towards a more subtle debate concerning ethno-cultural identity and nationhood'. The Conservatives advanced the notion of one nationhood as part of a Two Nations strategy, emphasising traditional ways of life and unity, most vividly illustrated by Norman Tebbit's 'cricketing test' of nationality. This is rooted in 'a nostalgic quest for patriotism rooted in a vision of national homogeneity which itself defines black people as outsiders' (Smith 1989, 167).

Ethnic minority populations are not simply objects of political intervention and the ideologies of the dominant political parties, however. They also have a potentially active role in British politics. For most of the post-war period, the nature of competitive two party politics — where the main contenders try to occupy the middle ground — has generally 'allowed the interests of discrete minorities such as black Britons effectively to slip between the cracks of democratic politics' (Saggar 1993, 38). However, by the late 1980s they represented approximately one in every 20 voters, and accounted for more than 10 per cent of the voters in 100 constituencies, and for as much as one-quarter or one-third of the electorate in a small number of seats. Not surprisingly then, there has been growing awareness in both parties of the relative importance of the black vote. This has been reinforced by more effective campaigning by the ethnic minorities themselves.

Traditionally, Labour has attracted the electoral support of ethnic minorities and in the 1960s regularly secured 90 per cent of the non-white vote. On narrow class grounds alone, it could be argued that the growth of a non-white middle class, and especially of small-scale Asian businesses, could have created a potential electoral constituency for the Conservatives. In practice, however, surveys in the late 1970s found that 95 per cent of Afro Caribbeans and 92 per cent of Asians were still intending to vote Labour (Crewe 1983). Mrs Thatcher, as Prime Minister, belatedly made attempts to develop this constituency. In particular, the second and third Thatcher governments, in comparison to the first one, tried to play down immigration and racial issues. However, this shift has been constrained by the party's continuing awareness of the electoral weight of the anti-ethnic minority vote.

Whatever the public pronouncements of the principal parties on racial equality, they have been slow to adopt Parliamentary candidates from ethnic minorities. It is difficult to escape the conclusion that the principal reason for this was an assumption that Asian and black candidates would be vote-losers. This, in turn, tends to discourage black candidates seeking nominations. The historical record makes dismal reading: there was one non-white candidate in the February 1974 general election, none in October 1974 and five in 1979. None were elected. It was only in 1987 that a critical breakthrough was achieved in Parliamentary representation. Four Afro-Caribbean or Asian candidates — all Labour — were finally elected as MPs. At the 1992 election their number increased to five. These were small but significant advances, given the difficulties of minorities in the British electoral and party systems. Throughout this time the Conservative Party failed to elect any non-white MPs or even to nominate them to winnable seats. The one exception to this was Cheltenham in 1992, which was winnable, but where the selection of a non white candidate unleashed a grassroots backlash which was both openly and implicitly racist. These electoral differences served to underline the widening divide between the Labour and Conservative parties on racial issues in the Two Nations era.

6.5.2 Race relations legislation

Within the parameters of One Nation politics, there was broad bipartisan consensus about the need to provide legal protection for ethnic minorities already living in Britain. In particular between the mid-1960s and the mid-1970s a series of Race Relations Acts made racial discrimination illegal. With hindsight these can be seen to be far in advance of the legislative frameworks in other major European countries if more limited than those in the USA (Anwar 1991).

The first important measure was the 1965 Race Relations Act. This established the Race Relations Board which was charged with seeking conciliation in cases of racial conflict, but the Act did not provide penalties for racial discrimination. At the same time, a number of reports provided convincing evidence of widespread racial discrimination (see Daniel 1965). This led to new and far stronger measures in the 1968 Race Relations Act: the Board was to seek conciliation initially but could then pursue legal actions against discriminating parties. The third important legislative milestone was the 1976 Race Relations Act. This established the Commission for Racial Equality which was to conduct strategic investigations into racial discrimination and had powers to issue non-discrimination notices. It was under this legislative umbrella that the notorious racist Robert Relf was imprisoned for distributing racist literature. This was the peak of the legislative achievements of One Nation politics.

The new legislative framework helped reduce some of the barriers faced by ethnic minorities. It was particularly significant in eliminating many instances of large-scale or institutional discrimination and some of the more blatant acts of individual discrimination. However, as with all legislation, it could not engender cultural changes or eliminate informal and subtle acts of discrimination. That all three Acts were passed by Labour governments is to the credit of that party, as are also the progressive policies and positive discrimination introduced by many Labour-controlled local authorities (Banton 1985). Nevertheless, until the late 1970s there was broad bipartisan consensus on the need for such legislation.

As part of the strategy of Two Nations politics, the Thatcher governments did not challenge this legislative framework but there was a marked failure to address the needs of ethnic minorities, partly camouflaged by the ideology of British nationality. Of course, urban aid has been directed at the inner cities but this is considered to be a problem of general deprivation, as well as a specific reaction to the civil disturbances of 1981, rather than a reaction to racial disadvantage. Given the Thatcherite emphasis on individualism, these governments could not recognise that there are structural racialised inequalities in UK society, especially given the electoral strategies adopted.

6.5.3 *Racial attacks and relationships with the police*

Ethnic minorities in Britain have been subject to racist attacks in both the two major time periods with which this book is concerned. In the years after the Second World War there was a series of attacks on non-white people. These took the form of collective violence. Amongst the most serious incidents were attacks on hostels housing Indian workers in Birmingham in 1949, attacks on immigrant homes in Camden Town in 1954, three weekends of violence against immigrant communities in Nottingham in 1958, severe riots against black people in Notting Hill again in 1958, and racial attacks in Dudley in 1962. This virtually marked the end of large-scale collective white violence against ethnic minorities.

It did not unfortunately mark the end of racist violence. By the 1960s 'Paki-bashing' was increasingly being reported in the press and the 1970s saw a sharp escalation of racially inspired attacks. Thereafter, the wave of racist violence intensified and the 1980s have seen a number of racist murders, as well as petrol bomb attacks on Asian churches and businesses. The true extent of racially inspired violence is unknown but as early as 1981 a Home Office Report estimated that there had been at least 7000 such attacks in the UK. In 1991 there were a reported 3400 racist crimes in London as a whole, and a growing number of racist murders of recently arrived refugees and of second and third generations. Almost as worrying as the escalation in violence has been growing disillusion amongst the black community concerning the ability of the police to stop such attacks. This, in turn, is linked to a general deterioration in relationships between the police and the black communities, especially young black people (Benyon 1986; Layton-Henry and Rich 1986).

Young Asian and black people have been represented in the press during the 1980s as being disproportionately likely to be involved in mugging and other violent crime in large cities. This image partly reflects the age structure of the ethnic minority communities, for violent street crimes are mostly undertaken by young people. However, even taking age into account, non-white youths are more likely than white ones to commit violent crimes. This has evoked a massive response from the police which many commentators consider to be disproportionate and provocative. It was linked to strong and pervasive racism within the police force (Cross 1986, 103). As Holdaway (1987, 145) writes, by the early 1980s 'a relationship between crime and black people, especially young black people, had developed in the police mind, and an association between "police and illegality" grew in the minds of black people'.

Particularly contentious was police use of Section 4 of the Vagrancy Act, the so-called sus-laws. This empowered the police to stop and search people in public places if they were considered to have intent to commit arrestable offences. It is a law that has consistently been disproportionately used against young black people. For example a 1982 survey in London found that

45 per cent of Afro Caribbeans aged 15–24 had been stopped during the previous year compared to 18 per cent of white people. This heavy-handed and sometimes racialised approach to policing has contributed to the alienation of young black people from the police, and to breeding a sense of profound distrust. In its most extreme form, this type of policing has involved massive police swamping of particular areas such as Lambeth and Lewisham with intensive stop and search procedures. Labelled 'fire-brigade' policing by Ramdin (1987, 476), this is the polar opposite of community policing.

Certainly not all, or even a majority, of the police are directly racist. However, substantial minorities of police officers hold generally hostile or suspicious views of non-white people, inevitably influencing the way in which they carry out their policing duties (see Benyon 1986). That in 1991 only 1370 out of 120 000 police officers in the UK were non-white, only adds to the problem. The tip of the iceberg of racism was revealed at the 1984 Police Federation Conference, when Peter Johnson, speaking from the platform, referred to 'our coloured brethren or nignogs'. Although the remark was quickly repudiated the damage had been done. Such racism constitutes one element in the inequality which exists in access to legal justice; others include the lack of black judges, barristers, etc. It is also important as one of the critical elements in a number of major civil disturbances in British cities in the 1980s.

6.5.4 Inner-city civil disturbances

A series of civil disturbances rocked Britain's inner cities in the 1980s. In part a product of the accumulated failures of One Nation politics, they were above all evidence of the simmering resentment against Two Nations politics. There were major outbreaks of violence in Brixton and in Toxteth (Liverpool) as well as other lesser disturbances in over 30 other cities in the summer of 1981. Two-thirds of those arrested during the major disturbances were non-white (Peach 1986) which led the popular press to brand them as race riots. However, the disturbances were anti-police rather than racial in nature. The Scarman Report on the major disturbances was unequivocal on this point for it saw their root cause as a spontaneous outburst of anger by young black people against the police (Holdaway 1982).

This is not to say that unemployment, poor housing conditions and general urban deprivation did not also contribute to the disturbances. Indeed, the Scarman Report confirmed that these were essential preconditions. But the outbreak of disturbances was highly selective. It did not include predominantly white areas of high unemployment such as South Wales or Tyneside, whilst Afro-Caribbeans were far more likely than Asians to have been involved. In other words, Afro-Caribbean relationships were the critical factor in influencing which areas experienced disturbances.

Violence erupted again in 1985. A night of violent clashes in Handsworth, Birmingham, ended in £10 million of damage to property and the death of two Asian brothers when their shop was set on fire. In September Brixton was again the focus. This time the disturbances were sparked when police, trying to arrest an Afro-Caribbean suspect, accidentally shot and seriously wounded his mother, Mrs Groce. However, the most serious violence was reserved for Broadwater Farm estate (in Tottenham). During a police raid on the estate, an Afro-Caribbean resident, Mrs Jarrett, collapsed and died. This was the prelude to a bitter confrontation, during which a police officer was hacked to death. The police were stretched to the limit of their resources and considered using plastic bullets and CS gas.

What had brought the UK's inner cities to the verge of full-scale riots, murder and the collapse of trust and respect between the police and young members of the ethnic minority communities? In part the roots lay in deprivation; for example, unemployment rates in Handsworth were 36 per cent at the time of the disturbances (Peach 1986). Young black and Asian people were also the subject of police harassment both as the result of legitimate attempts to crack down on street crime or drugs dealing and, sometimes, of racial prejudice and racism. Whatever the precise cause, the result was a deepening sense of resentment amongst young black and Asian people about living conditions, limited opportunities and racism. Lacking direct access to the formal channels of political power, they often felt that street action was their only form of political expression (Carter 1986).

6.5.5 Reprise: the bitter harvest of Two Nations politics

Neither inner-city deprivation nor racist attacks and harassment were products of the 1980s. Cities like Liverpool and Nottingham experienced racist attacks in the 1950s. The bipartisan One Nation consensus response had been to stress the need for racial harmony in the UK, combined with immigration controls. But 'by placing all other goals subordinate to the need to maintain peace ... the risk was that the underlying causes of conflict such as discrimination against black citizens, went unaddressed' (Saggar 1993, 40). In effect this is what occurred with the state responding only to occasional specific outbreaks of unrest, as in the inner cities. However, we would contend that, wittingly or unwittingly, Conservative governments in the 1980s greatly exacerbated the difficulties faced by ethnic minorities. In the run-up to the 1979 general election Mrs Thatcher cynically manipulated popular white racial prejudices, with respect to immigration. Moreover, the policies of the Conservatives in government have consistently disadvantaged low-income groups and the underclass in UK society, amongst whom ethnic minorities are disproportionately represented.

The dogmatic insistence on the primacy of market 'solutions' and the ideology of individual responsibility and enterprise has made successive governments in the Two Nations period blind to structural disadvantages. These were especially pronounced in the inner cities which experienced acute economic restructuring and cuts in public services. Yet for Conservative leaders such as Douglas Hurd the disturbances in places such as Handsworth were 'not a social phenomenon but crimes'. However, virtually all the objective evidence, including the report of the respected Scarman inquiry, identified the role of social and economic disadvantages and of racial tensions in these disturbances. In turn this was only the most visible manifestation of racialised disadvantages which permeated labour markets, education and housing, political power and the wider civil society.

The seeds of racial distrust and disadvantage were sown long before Mrs Thatcher's governments came to power. But the policies of Two Nations politics which sought radically to reform the UK economy and society unintentionally fertilised these seeds. This brought forth the bitter harvests which were reaped most spectacularly on the streets of London, Liverpool and Birmingham, but were in fact the legacy of most of the black citizens of a divided Britain.

7

Divided by region

7.1 Introduction: where you live matters

Pronounced inequalities between regions are endemic to capitalist development and nowhere is this more true than in the UK. Pre-existing patterns of
spatial inequality were radically reshaped from the earliest days of capitalism,
generating new contrasts in economic and social conditions between areas: for
example, between the cities and the countryside and between regions. From the
moment in 1928 when a Conservative government acknowledged that regional
inequalities constituted a political problem, spatially uneven development,
usually defined as a 'regional problem' but more latterly as an intra-regional
one (as we show in Chapter 8), has never been far from the political agenda.
Containing the regional problem within politically acceptable limits was an
important concern of the One Nation project. Even so, despite a long period
of state engagement with regional problems via regional policies, they have
been a persistent feature of the UK scene (see Hudson and Williams 1986). The
form of the problem, and the processes generating it, have certainly altered
somewhat, but the regional problem has persisted despite – some would say
because of – state policies.

In the 1980s, however, despite increasing governmental focus on urban
problems – or, again, perhaps because of it – the regional problem and, more
specifically, the growing divide between North and South re-emerged politically centre-stage as the Two Nations strategy took a clear spatial form. It
became a persistent focus of media attention as the following selection of
national newspaper headlines, all taken from the *Financial Times*, testifies:

South east increases lead in wealth (23 March 1984)
Prosperity gap widens between North and South (22 May 1985)
Job census figures will fuel concern over 'two nations' divide (5 January 1987)
North–South disparity confirmed (2 February 1987)
Regional wealth disparity 'growing' (18 February 1988)

Such newspaper headlines register a growing recognition of and interest in
the deepening divide between a booming South and a declining North. Broadly
speaking, the 'South' is defined as the standard regions of the South East,
South West, East Anglia (and on occasion the East Midlands) whilst the
'North' is defined as the remainder of the UK (Figure 7.1). Like most

Figure 7.1 Standard regional boundaries

newspaper headlines, those highlighting the growing North–South divide contain elements of truth, in this case substantial ones. At the same time they necessarily over-simplify more subtle patterns of spatial inequality in the UK in the 1980s (see Chapter 8). Furthermore, the recession of the early 1990s bit deeply into the economy of the 'South' and led to a dramatic narrowing, in some respects, of the North–South divide. This was again reflected in newspaper headlines, as the following selection demonstrates – taken again from the *Financial Times*:

South-east takes the brunt this time round (22 September 1990)
Recession hits south-east services (21 January 1991)
Golden triangle hits note of northern confidence (18 May 1992)

rtainly overstates the extent of recovery in the
perceived realignment in relations between North
Nations project; no longer was this seen as taking
onal expression. Indeed, the promotional phrases
of 'The Great North' conjured up images of a past
rth was the workshop of the world, a centre of rapid
or some at least. It remains to be seen whether the
South will again widen when national economic
ng, of course, that it does. As of 1993 it is not at all
clear as to what the future pattern of regional inequality will be.

The growing North-South divide was commonly represented, not least by
Mrs Thatcher's government, as a simple product of the operation of the
hidden hand of market forces. We wish to argue, strongly, that this is not the
case. On the contrary, the North–South divide was deliberately redefined and
enhanced as part of the political strategy of Thatcherism. The growing gap
between North and South and the Two Nations strategy were inextricably
linked. The North–South divide was also intimately connected to Thatcherism's electoral success. It remains equally intimately connected to the electoral prospects of Majorism. This was sharply brought home as the
Conservative majority fell sharply in the 1992 general election, by the wave of
Liberal Democrat victories in by-elections and local government elections in
1993 and by the attempt to paper over some of the cracks in the 'South' in the
1993 review of regional policy.

7.2 Unemployment, employment and incomes in the North and in the South

In many ways the most commented upon aspect of the growing divide between
North and South in the 1980s was the difference in unemployment levels and
rates. This revived memories of the 1930s, when sharp regional differences in
unemployment rates were central to the political recognition of the regional
problem. The war economy abolished such differences and over most of the
period of One Nation politics, these regional differences were confined within
a relatively narrow band. There were already wide differences in latter years
of the 1970s but these expanded in the 1980s (Figure 7.2) with unemployment
generally falling in the South and rising in the North, despite various adjustments to the count that had regionally specific effects, such as the removal of
miners accepting redundancy under the term of the Redundant Mineworkers
Payments Scheme. By 1990 registered unemployment in Northern Ireland
stood at almost 14 per cent whilst that in the South East (excluding London)
was a mere 3.1 per cent. As the recession of the early 1990s intensified,
however, regional differences narrowed sharply as unemployment rose more
rapidly in the South than in the North – but whilst the North–South gap

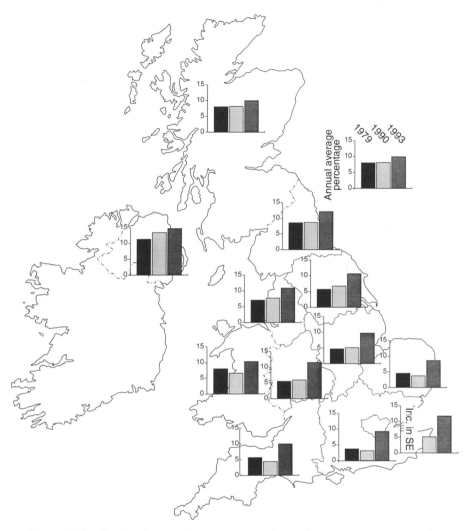

Figure 7.2 Regional unemployment rates (annual average percentages), 1979–93

Source: *Regional Trends*

narrowed, it certainly did not disappear (Figure 7.2). Again, long-term unemployment was most pronounced in the North.

Especially during the 1980s, the combination of a higher unemployment rate in the North and a higher vacancy rate in the South meant that people continued to migrate and increasingly to commute from North to South in a desperate search for work. This was despite enormous differences in house prices and housing markets. Between 1981 and 1991, for example, there was a net interregional, permanent in-migration of 610 900 into the South and a corresponding net loss from the North (Figure 7.3). Not all permanent migration into the South was work-related, however. Some, especially into the South West and the Channel coast of the South East but also Wales, was for retirement, contributing to the South West having (in 1991) the largest proportion – almost 22 per cent – of pensioners in its population. Other forms of migration into the South have also increased, however, including temporary short-term migration for work; there were an estimated 10 000 such long-

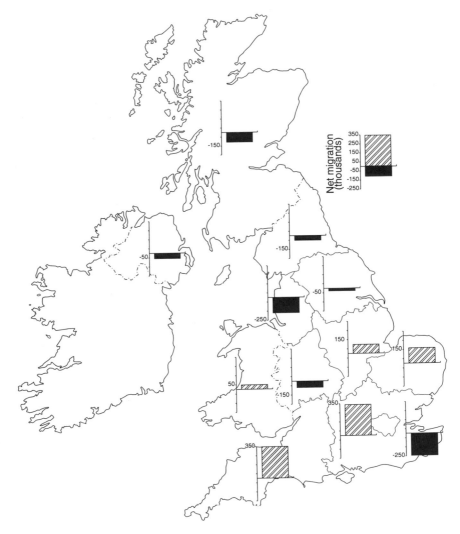

Figure 7.3 Net civilian migration (thousands), 1981–91

Source: *Regional Trends*

distance commuters in 1989. These differences in unemployment, vacancies and net migration are a reflection of the deepening employment divide between North and South in the 1980s (Figure 7.4).

At its simplest, this growing employment divide can be summarised as follows (see also Martin 1988). Between 1978 and 1989 employees in employment in the South rose by 572 000 but in the North they declined by 615 000. This massive difference was, above all, the result of the greater impacts of

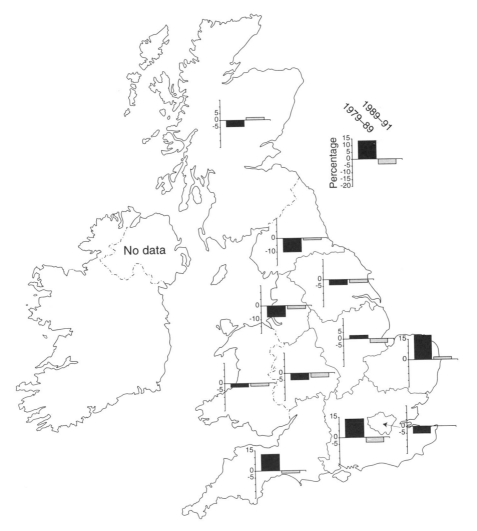

Figure 7.4 Total employment change (percentage), 1979–91

Source: *Regional Trends*

mining decline and deindustrialisation in the North and of the service sector growth in the South. Coal-mining job losses were almost exclusively concentrated in the North. Manufacturing employment there fell by 1 167 000, greatly exceeding growth in service sector employment, which in any case was mainly of part-time jobs (Figures 7.5 and 7.6). In contrast, in the South manufacturing employment fell by 422 000 but this was more than offset by service sector growth, although again much of this was of part-time jobs.

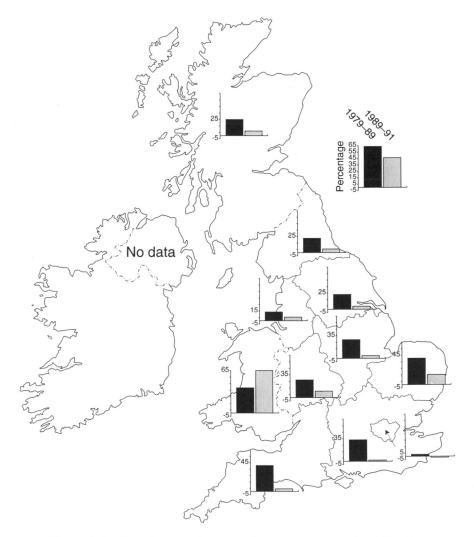

Figure 7.5 Part-time employment change (percentage), 1979–91

Source: *Regional Trends*

When an allowance is made for an estimated increase in self-employment, the regional divide widens further.

Between 1989 and 1991, however, the employment gap between North and South narrowed somewhat. Total employment fell by 429 000 in the South, compared with 228 000 in the North. Manufacturing employment fell by 268 000 in the South and 313 000 in the North. The dramatic change in the regional pattern of capacity utilisation in manufacturing between 1989 and

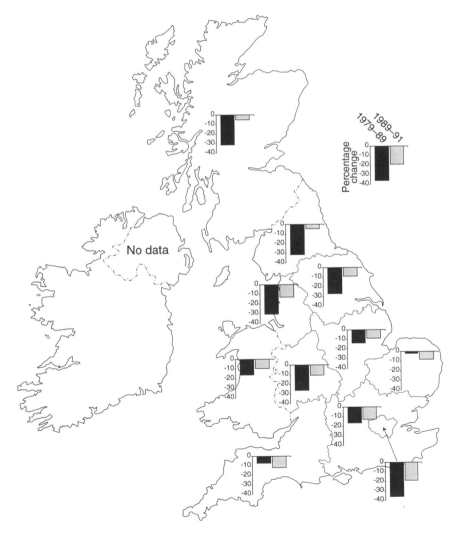

Figure 7.6 Manufacturing employment change (percentage), 1979–91

Source: *Regional Trends*

1992 (Figures 7.7 and 7.8) reveals the differential regional impacts of recession, with the South suffering badly. Whereas service sector employment (albeit almost all part-time) continued to grow in the North, it fell sharply in the South, especially in full-time employment. Thus whilst it is erroneous to regard the recession of the early 1990s as simply one of the service sector, the impacts of recession in services were most heavily concentrated in the South. Even so, by 1991 there were still more employees employed in the South than in 1978 whereas the North had suffered a substantial decline in employees in employment, a difference further magnified by differential growth in self-employment.

Sharply diverging patterns of economic activities in North and South were

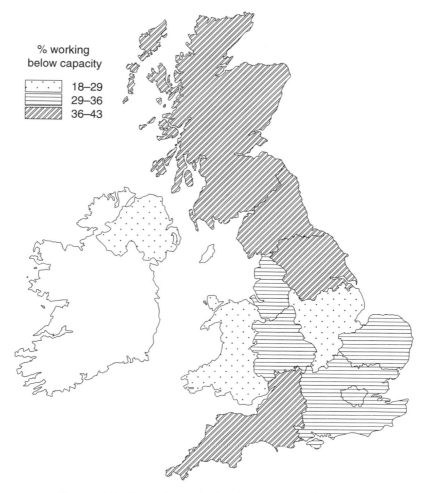

Figure 7.7 Capacity utilisation in manufacturing, 1989

linked to growing differences in regional output and productivity as well as labour market conditions. By 1991 (taking the UK as 100) gross domestic product per capita ranged from almost 117.0 in the South East to just over 75.0 in Northern Ireland. This was a slightly narrower gap than in 1989, when the South East stood at almost 120 relative to the UK average. However, it was far greater than in 1975, when the range had been from 112.9 to 80.0, for the same two regions. In 1975 only the South East had exceeded the national average whilst the West Midlands equalled it. By 1991, despite the impacts of recession there, both East Anglia and the South East exceeded the national average. All other regions fell below it and most of these had declined further

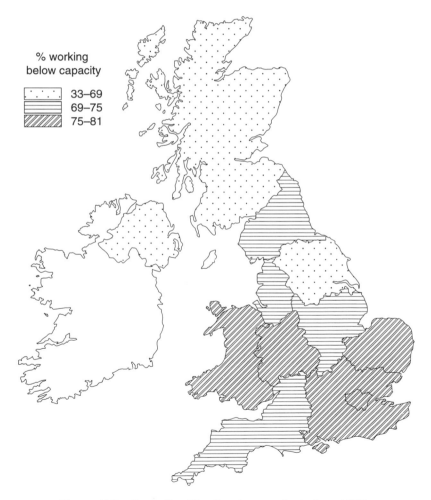

Figure 7.8 Capacity utilisation in manufacturing, 1992

relative to the national average. Above all, these changes reflect the continuing structural shift from a manufacturing to a service-based economy.

These numbers relating to aggregate employment and output reveal a growing quantitative division between North and South. What they hint at, but do not really reveal, is a growing qualitative differentiation in types of job, functions and economic activities. Such qualitative divisions have their origins in the changing intra- and international spatial divisions of labour that emerged during the 1960s. Broadly speaking, the South has reinforced its dominance in key growth sectors of both manufacturing and services and in the crucial control, decision-making and research and development (R and D) functions. By 1990 over 45 per cent of all the UK's graduates of working age were concentrated in the South East, attracted by the prospects of highly skilled and well-paid work. The large pool of such labour served as a powerful attraction for high-tech companies and activities, for R and D and head-quarters office functions. The North has been left with a concentration of declining industries and the routine occupations in both production and service sectors. This is easily demonstrated.

In the South East alone, with 27 per cent of national manufacturing employment and 39 per cent of service employment, there is a disproportionate concentration of jobs in 'high-tech' manufacturing activities and industries. This reflects the discriminating locational preferences of companies engaged in such 'high-tech' activities. Consequently 41 per cent of employment in advanced and 'high-tech' manufacturing and 55 per cent of that in R and D is found in the South East. The South East alone accounts for 54 per cent of government R and D establishments. In so far as a sunshine belt of 'high- technology' industry, typically based on new non-unionised small firms, is to be found in the UK, it is concentrated within the South in areas such as Silicon Fen (as Cambridge has become known) and around the M4 corridor and the M25 London orbital motorway.

Secondly, there is a disproportionate concentration of business (or producer) services employment in the South. The South East has over one-half of total national employment in this sector, closely linked to the role of the City of London. The historical pre-eminence of London in financial and money markets has been reinforced in the 1980s by a variety of interrelated changes: the growing importance of international finance; new markets such as those for Eurodollars; the influx of foreign banks; and deregulation of the Stock Exchange. Whilst its dominance has been weakened somewhat by growing international competition and the recession of the early 1990s, this has been a consequence of job loss rather than of relocation to other areas of the UK.

Thirdly, in so far as an 'enterprise culture' is being created in the UK, it is disproportionately concentrated in the South. The South East accounted for almost 47 per cent of all new business registrations between 1981 and 1989 (Figure 7.9). Moreover, throughout the 1980s, the rate of small firm creation was higher in the South than in the North. There are several reasons for this. The existence of numerous well-paid jobs and high incomes in the South East creates market opportunities for personal services, the main area of small firm growth. The concentration of R and D activities also creates market opportunities for small sub-contracting companies to emerge. In addition, the disproportionate presence of financial services in the South East creates a bias in favour of lending venture capital in what is perceived as a known, low-risk region. During the early years of the 1990s, however, the net rate of new firm formation nationally collapsed dramatically (to an increase of only 3000 in 1991). Whilst the South East held its share of the national total at 45 per cent

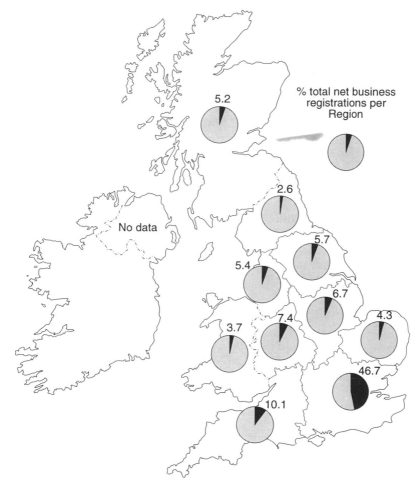

Figure 7.9 New firm formation, 1981–89

Source: *Regional Trends*

in 1991, by 1992 there were net business failures in the South East (outside of London) and the South West. The tide of bankruptcies rose as the previously favourable combination of circumstances favouring high rates of successful small firms formation in the South was rapidly reversed. Whether this is temporary or permanent remains to be seen.

In contrast to the South, the North tends to have a distinctly higher proportion of unskilled and semi-skilled labour in routine manufacturing and service jobs. These workers are more likely to be unionised and militant, at least to

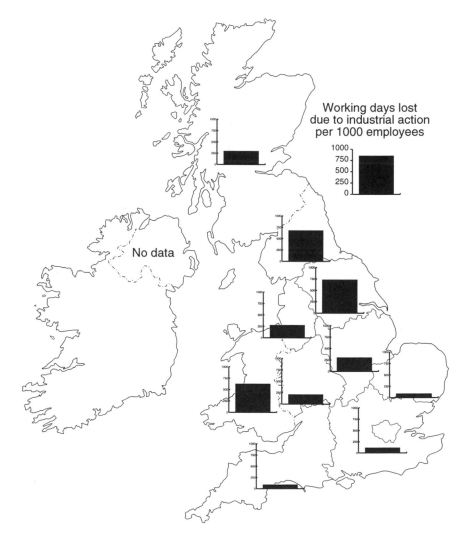

Figure 7.10 Industrial militancy, 1991

Source: *Regional Trends*

the extent that trade unions actually engaged in strike activity and other forms of industrial action in the 1980s and 1990s (Figure 7.10). In addition, there are relatively few new firms created in the North because there are considerable barriers to the growth of an 'enterprise culture' as a consequence of the previous cultural and political history of much of the region.

Changes in employment patterns are one important reason for the growing divide in incomes and wealth between North and South (Figure 7.11). For example, in 1980 average weekly household incomes in the South East and South West were £183.4 and £149.1 respectively. Only the South East exceeded

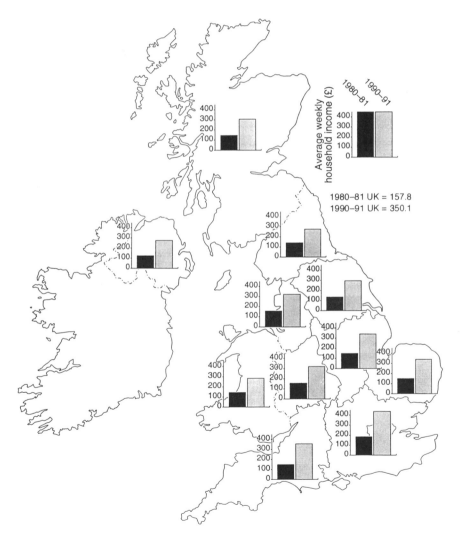

Figure 7.11 Average weekly household incomes, 1980–81 and 1990–91(£)

Source: *Regional Trends*

the national average of £157.8. At the other extreme were the North (£140.2) and Northern Ireland (£122.5). The average household income in Northern Ireland takes on an added significance in the context of newspaper headlines such as 'Northern Ireland poverty "second worst in Europe"'. It says much about regional division in the UK in the 1980s that the point of comparison had become Calabria, the most poverty-stricken region of the south of Italy. By the early 1990s, the interregional gap in the UK had widened further. Whilst only the South East (£434.1) and South West (£355.9) exceeded the national average (£350.1), average incomes in Northern Ireland (£274.1) and the North of England (£275.8) lagged far behind.

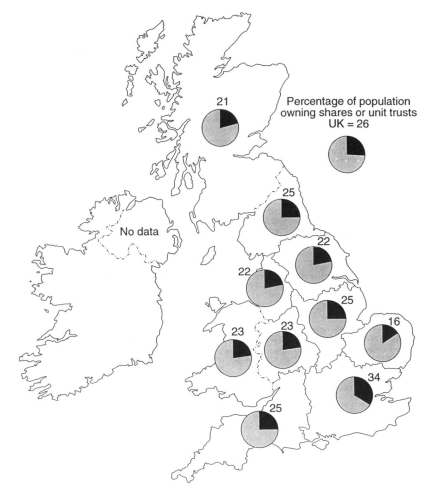

Figure 7.12 Popular capitalism, 1990

Source: *Regional Trends*

In general terms, these wide and growing regional income differentials reflect several factors. In part, they arise because of differing industrial and occupational mixes. Wage supplements to workers within the South East exacerbate these differences. During the boom conditions of the 1980s, companies in the South East paid up to 50 per cent more in allowances to try to recruit or retain staff in the face of chronic shortages of skilled labour. Such differences in remuneration continued in the 1990s, though in more muted

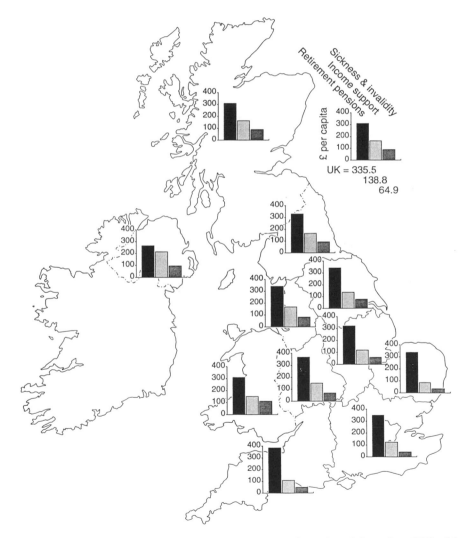

Figure 7.13 Government spending per capita on selected cash benefits, 1988–89

Source: *Regional Trends*

form. By 1993, for example, the average managers' earnings in the South East (outside of London) were £30700, compared to £24800 in the North (Remuneration Economics 1993). This also contributes to the more rapid growth of wages in the South East in particular.

There is much greater incidence of unearned incomes in the South, which further exacerbates the regional income divide. In the South West, this is related to the age structure of the population, with over 25 per cent of personal

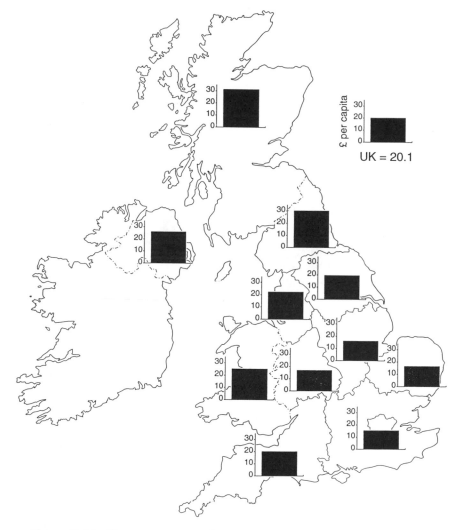

Figure 7.14 Government spending on unemployment benefit, 1988–89

Source: *Regional Trends*

incomes deriving from dividends, rents and pensions accruing to people of retirement age. For some in the South, however, dependence upon unearned incomes created severe problems in the wake of the problems of Lloyd's insurance business. For example, over 250 individuals associated with just one syndicate, Gooda Walker, and largely resident in Surrey and Sussex, lost at least £500 000 per head (*Financial Times*, 17 June 1993). Many of those affected were retired people and whilst they did not experience absolute poverty, they all suffered a sharp fall in living standards. Share ownership is also generally more prevalent in the South (Figure 7.12): 34 per cent of the adult population in the South East are share owners. In contrast, over much of the North less than 25 per cent of adults are share owners. This again is indicative of strong regional differences in receptivity to 'popular capitalism'. By the early 1990s, however, this had become very much a contrast between the South East and all other regions in contrast to the broader North–South divide visible in the mid-1980s (see Martin 1988).

In contrast, in the North there is a much greater dependence upon state transfer payments, notably unemployment benefits, supplementary benefits and retirement pensions (Figures 7.13 and 7.14). Dependence on state transfer payments other than retirement pensions is generally much higher in the North, with particularly high levels of benefit dependence in Northern Ireland. This contributed to Northern Ireland's unenviable position of being second only to Calabria in terms of poverty in the European Union.

7.3 Consumption, life-styles and living conditions in the North and South

Regional variations in households' expenditure patterns have been evident for many decades, including those of the One Nation project. Not surprisingly, they reflected differences in incomes. In the succeeding Two Nations era, these differences became more pronounced. Household expenditure in 1978–79 was highest in the then 'traditionally prosperous' South East and West Midlands, the only two regions to exceed the UK average. It was lowest in the North, South West, and Yorkshire and Humberside. By 1985–86 this pattern had altered significantly. Only in the South East (considerably) and East Anglia and the South West (marginally) did household expenditure exceed the national average. The greatest relative and absolute increases in income and expenditure occurred in the South East. As a result, there had been a considerable polarisation of household expenditure, around a North versus South divide.

There were also considerable regional variations in patterns of expenditure on goods and services. If anything, the 1980s have further reinforced these differences. This is certainly the case with respect to housing. By the mid-1980s expenditure on housing exceeded the national average (16.6 per cent) only in the South East (18.5 per cent), South West (17.2 per cent) and East Anglia (17.0 per cent). As these were the regions where household incomes were greatest, there were still more marked regional variations in absolute expenditure on housing. These regions are also those where owner occupation is highest. However, in general, the regional pattern of tenure differences remained unaltered throughout the 1980s and early 1990s, though owner occupation increased in all regions.

The most significant aspect of regional changes in housing markets in the 1980s was the differential growth in house prices (Figure 7.15). Average house prices in the South exceed those in the North for three main reasons. First, a given type of house costs considerably more in the South; for example, in 1986 a three-bedroomed inter-war semi varied in price between £24 000 in Northern

Figure 7.15 New dwelling price increases, 1981–89

Source: *Regional Trends*

Ireland and £73 000 in Greater London (see also Hamnett 1989b). Secondly, there is a bigger proportion of more expensive, larger and/or higher quality dwellings in the South. Thirdly, the housing stock grew more rapidly in the South. This increased average house prices as the pressure of demand pushed residential land prices into an upward inflationary spiral. Housing land increased in price in the South East (excluding London) from £166 400 per hectare in 1981 to £588 700 in 1990; the comparable figures for Greater London are £391 000 and £2 194 000. In East Anglia, prices rose even more spectacularly from £69 300 in 1981 to £524 100 in 1990. This is translated into the price of new dwellings. In turn, these influence the resale prices of existing dwellings as the land price per plot as a percentage of new dwelling price in the South East (excluding London) rose from 20 per cent in 1981 to 44 per cent in 1990 and in East Anglia from 14 to 45 per cent.

In these respects the North–South divide in the UK continued to widen until the early 1990s. The recession of those years then had a markedly regionally differentiated effect on housing markets (Figure 7.16). Whilst prices in the North at first generally continued modestly to increase, and then fell slightly, in the South the inflationary bubble of the late 1980s burst dramatically. Between the middle of 1990 and April 1992, house prices fell by over 10 per cent in the South East, East Anglia and South West but rose in the Northern Region (2 per cent), Scotland (5 per cent) and Northern Ireland (over 8 per cent), according to data from the Halifax Building Society (reported in the *Financial Times*, 29 June 1992). There was a growing number of repossessions and of people with negative equity (mortgages in excess of the market price of their dwelling) concentrated in the South. Whilst very serious for the individuals concerned, it is, however, important not to overstate the extent of a narrowing of differences in the housing markets of North and South. House prices remain at much higher absolute levels in the South and it is by no means implausible that the narrowing of the gap is a cyclical rather than a secular tendency.

There are then significant qualitative and quantitative divisions between North and South in housing conditions and provision, despite the impacts of the most recent recession. There is now not one housing market but two (Hamnett 1989a). The first is in London and the South East. The other is the rest of the country. This dichotomous housing market is of great significance for those reaching retirement age, who can realise considerable gains from selling a house in the South East and moving elsewhere. It is also significant for those who become long-distance commuters, working in the South but – unable to afford to reside there – living in the North.

The regional house price gulf is also of great significance for those without a job who wish to follow the advice proffered by Mrs Thatcher's former Secretary of State for Employment, Norman Tebbit, to 'get on their bikes' to search for work. As one commentator caustically noted, house prices varying from £51 000 for a starter home to £133 000 plus for 'four bedroomed luxury' in

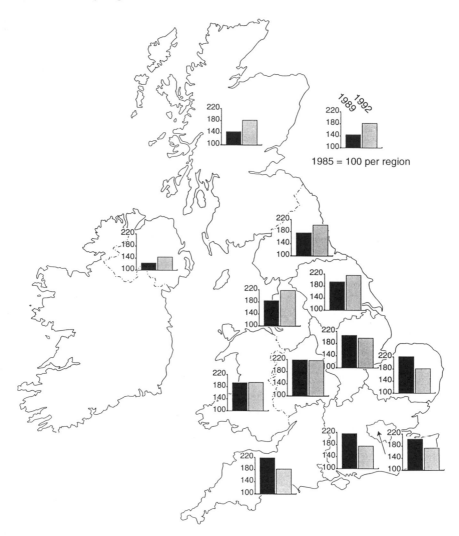

Figure 7.16 Changes in dwelling prices, all dwellings, 1989–92

Source: *Regional Trends*

Basingstoke held out 'not much promise – for a nurse from Skelmersdale or a cook from Middlesbrough' (quoted in the *Financial Times*, 23 February 1986). Differences in housing markets between the North and South make it prohibitively expensive for a family to come South to look for work. They also present a formidable barrier to attempts to solve regional unemployment problems via interregional migration, even more so as the recession has hit the South.

Compared to housing, the absolute and relative variation between North and South in other categories of household expenditure is generally less pronounced. This is particularly so in the case of 'basic' items such as foodstuffs, fuel, light and power and clothing and footwear. In a sense, expenditure on such items is both unavoidable and relatively income inelastic beyond a certain income level that enables needs for these items to be met. In so far as it does vary, such expenditure tends to be absolutely greater but relatively smaller in the more affluent South. This implies important qualitative variations in consumption of these 'basic' commodities because of income differences. In part, these differences reflect varying regional cultural traditions, and lend some credence to the persistence, in modified form, of a socially constructed North–South divide in tastes.

Interregional differences in expenditures on consumer durables and various services are rather more pronounced. Spending on these is higher in the more affluent South, both relatively and absolutely. Even so, falling real prices and slowly rising average real incomes over much of the North have resulted in a narrowing of the North–South divide in household ownership rates of some more basic consumer durables in the 1980s. By the early 1990s household ownership rates varied between regions over a narrow range for refrigerators (97 to 91 per cent), washing machines (91 to 84 per cent) and telephones (92 to 80 per cent) and at lower absolute levels for videos (69 to 56 per cent). Ownership rates tended to be both lower and more variable for more sophisticated and expensive consumer durables such as home computers (22 to 15 per cent) and dishwashers (18 to 7 per cent), but they were consistently higher in the South. Moreover, the North–South gap in ownership of these consumer goods has tended to widen over the last decade.

Regional differences in transport expenditure also increased in the years of the Two Nations project. One reason for this is greater spending on commuting, especially in the South East. There have been perceptible differences in regional car ownership levels since the 1920s and 1930s. By 1979, household car ownership was highest in the South West (65.4 per cent) and lowest in the North (50.9 per cent). By 1990 it had increased to a maximum of 77 per cent in the South East, outside of Greater London, but only up to 58 per cent in the North (Figure 7.17). Moreover, households having two (or more) cars are far more prevalent in the South. In part this is because of the concentration there of those in well-paid jobs which include a car as part of their remuneration.

It is important to remember, however, especially in the context of deregulation of buses in the 1980s, that household car ownership rates also reflect the (non)-availability of public transport. In both East Anglia and the South West there are rural areas that have wholly lacked public transport for more than two decades. For many households, in such areas, having a car is a matter of necessity. Household car ownership, especially in one-car households, should also not be confused with personal mobility.

There are significant regional variations in another sort of mobility: the

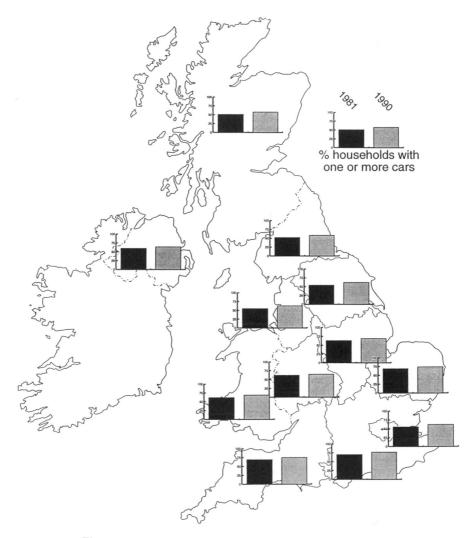

Figure 7.17   Household car ownership, 1981 and 1990

Source: *Regional Trends*

propensity to go on holiday. These have existed for many years but, in some ways, the North–South divide increased in the 1980s. In several regions in the North rather more households took no annual holiday in 1986 than in 1979. Residents of the South East took a disproportionate share of all holidays outside the UK in both years. The disproportionate number of people from the South East taking not just one, but two or more holidays a year, is decisively related to the regional distribution of incomes. Second home owners are also concentrated in the South East, enabling some of its residents to take frequent weekend breaks in their second homes in the far South West, Wales, the Lake District and other environmentally attractive areas. In a sense such regions provide a locale for consumption for those who generate their purchasing power in the South.

So far, we have concentrated on regional variations in private consumption, which directly reflect those in incomes. Increasingly, as an integral part of the Two Nations project, there has been a growing emphasis upon purchasing education and health services in the market, although this was again somewhat reduced by recession in the early 1990s. This redrawing of the private–public sector boundary has been particularly focused in the South. Almost one half of all private school places in the UK are located in the South East. This reflects regional variation in the ability to pay for education but, more significantly perhaps, the persistence of the public school system, which plays a crucial role in reproducing the class structure of UK society. The expansion to 10 000 acute beds in privately owned hospitals has also been heavily concentrated in the South East (see Mohan 1988). This is linked to the preponderance of executives and managers in this region receiving free health insurance as part of their remuneration package; 80 per cent of private treatment is paid for in this way (see Curtis and Mohan 1989). The growing significance of the private sector has sharpened the North–South divide in the amount and quality of provision of these services.

A review of the National Health Service revealed the continued existence of marked interregional variations in resource allocation (as well as intra-regional ones: see Townsend and Davidson 1982). The Resource Allocation Working Party (RAWP) was established to remedy this situation. Even so, at the start of the 1980s there were still marked regional variations in resourcing. The four Thames Regional Health Authorities and Oxford all had between 6 and 15 per cent above the level of resources calculated as necessary to secure equal access to health care for people of equal need. The remaining nine Regional Health Authorities (RHAs) were between 4 and 10 per cent below this level. There were also considerable regional and sub-regional variations in levels of provision of, and access to, medical facilities. For example, hospital waiting lists tended to be lower in the North than the South, although the pattern was a complicated one. Moreover, despite national norms, doctors' and dentists' list sizes were generally greater in the North than the South. Although this does not necessarily imply corresponding differences in quality of health care, it does suggest variability in ease of access to facilities.

During the 1980s, the Thatcher government attempted to narrow regional inequalities in public health care funding in line with the RAWP proposals. After 1983, for the first time, expenditure growth in 'underfunded' regions was to occur at the expense of real cuts in 'over-provided' ones. This has certainly resulted in a closer convergence of regional spending around the target norms of RAWP. The gap between the most overfunded and most underfunded regions fell from 25 per cent in the mid-1970s to 13 per cent in

1986–87, for example (Curtis and Mohan 1989). At the same time, however, given that needs increased more rapidly than NHS funding, there has been a deterioration in public provision of health care as regional convergence was achieved via differential cuts rather than differential growth and in a way that heightened intra-regional inequality (Curtis and Mohan 1989). For example, hospital waiting lists increased in 9 of the 14 English RHAs and in Northern Ireland, Scotland and Wales, although the pattern is more complicated than a simple North–South split. Nevertheless, differential provision of medical facilities is at least related to variations in death rates and health conditions, even if it does not cause them. Research at St Thomas's Hospital Community Medicine Department (reported in *The Sunday Times*, 27 March 1983) revealed that those areas in England with the highest probability of unnecessary deaths – people dying because of the non-availability of medical treatment that could prevent death – were the old industrial areas of the North. Probability of death is generally lowest in the South. The former tend to be areas with relatively poor levels of medical provision. The latter are relatively well-provided for. In this sense, whether you live in the North or South may literally still be a life-and-death matter in the UK.

Although less immediately dramatic in their impacts, regional variations in educational provision and participation have a profound effect on life chances. There were important differences in these throughout the One Nation project. In part, these reflected the concentration of private sector education in the South, and this has strengthened in the subsequent Two Nations era (see Bradford and Burdett 1989). There were also considerable regional variations in average levels of attainment in state schools, despite nominally equal levels of provision, which if anything have widened in the 1980s and 1990s. Children in the South are more likely to do even better in school exams. For example, by 1990/91 the percentage of male school-leavers with three or more A levels had risen to over 19 per cent in the South East (excluding London) and exceeded 15 per cent in the South West and East Anglia. In contrast, it exceeded this level only in two regions in the North (Figure 7.18). The publication of national examination league tables of GCSE results for English education authorities in 1992 confirmed the strong regional contrast (although this was overlain by powerful intra-regional contrasts). Every English county to the south of Birmingham, with the exception of Leicestershire and the Isle of Wight, was to be found in the top 50. Even so, these differences in schools examination performance understate the growing regional gap. More children in the South stay on beyond minimum school-leaving age, more take exams, and more go on to courses in further and higher education.

An important objective of the One Nation project and the post-war welfare state was to eliminate differences in access to, and levels of provision of, education and health services. Important regional differences remained, despite – and in part because of – the way in which state provision of these services was designed and implemented. Substantial cut-backs in state provision, as part of

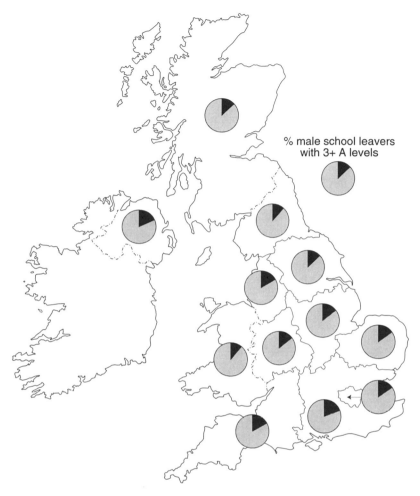

Figure 7.18 Educational attainment, 1990/91

Source: *Regional Trends*

a growing redefinition of the welfare state and a further shift towards privatisation and commercialisation of these services, has redefined and widened the North–South divide in the last decade as an integral part of the Two Nations approach.

7.4 Party politics: voting in the North and the South

A basic North–South, Labour–Conservative divide has been visible in UK politics throughout the post-war period. The consensus between 'one-nation' Tories, cast in the mould of Harold Macmillan, and Labour social democrats, on the need for government regional intervention reflected a shared perception of the regional divide and a shared awareness of the need to address the problems it posed. Even so, this division in the UK's electoral geography between a Conservative South and Labour North became increasingly challenged on an explicitly territorial basis from the 1960s. The re-emergence of the 'troubles' in Northern Ireland and the reawakening and reorientation of nationalist sentiment in Scotland and Wales thrust nationalism to the forefront of political debate. By the end of the 1970s, however, it seemed that nationalist demands in Scotland and Wales had largely been contained via the granting of greater administrative devolution within the UK state via the establishment of Development Agencies. The problems of Northern Ireland, however, remained no nearer to solution. Thus in the second half of the 1970s, there was a move back towards the Conservative/South and Labour/North division.

In the 1980s there were important changes in the pattern of national politics as the effects of the Two Nations project became increasingly evident. This was most notable in the emergence of the SDP and its subsequent saga of alliances and merger with the Liberals to form the SLD. There has also been a resurgence of nationalist politics, most markedly in Scotland. Nevertheless the party political North–South divide has been sharply reinforced as an integral – indeed necessary – part of the Two Nations project. There were marked shifts in the geography of voting over the period 1979–87 that, at the simplest level of generalisation, can be characterised as a dichotomous divide between North and South (see Johnston et al. 1988). Electoral support for the Labour Party both declined and became concentrated in its historical heartlands in the industrial North. The South, the location of most of the main beneficiaries of Mrs Thatcher's neo-right political economy of competitive individualism, showed its appreciation by voting more or less solidly Tory (Figure 7.19). In the 1987 general election 88 per cent of Parliamentary constituencies in the South (96 per cent if one excludes London) returned Conservative MPs as did 67 per cent of those in the two Midland regions. In contrast, over the remainder of the north of Great Britain, 67 per cent of constituencies returned Labour MPs. In terms of electoral geography, the UK had become two political nations. The third force of the SLD had been effectively frozen out, via a series of two-way contests with the Tories in the South and Labour in the North. Nationalist votes in Scotland and Wales became subdued as the nationalist parties declined to the point where they were little more than parties of protest, though they showed signs of revival in by-elections in 1988 and 1989. Northern Ireland followed its own tragic political trajectory but remained effectively marginalised.

This pattern of regional division was confirmed, though in more muted fashion in the 1992 general election. The Conservative Party, under Mr Major's leadership, won the election with a greatly reduced majority but with Conservative support heavily concentrated in the South. The Conservatives were decisively rejected in Scotland as nationalist sentiment once again revived there. The Conservatives now hold less Parliamentary seats in Scotland than

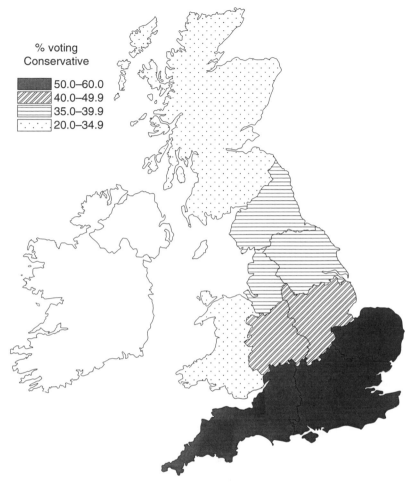

% voting
Conservative

50.0–60.0
40.0–49.9
35.0–39.9
20.0–34.9

Figure 7.19 Conservative Party support, 1987 General Election

they did after Labour's landslide victory in 1945. As the recession of the early 1990s increasingly made its effects felt in the South, there was a series of by-election defeats in previously safe Conservative constituencies (such as Christchurch) and in local elections, as electoral support switched from the Conservatives to the SLD. This raised serious questions as to the emerging map of electoral support for the major parties and as to the stability of the North–South divide in voting behaviour.

7.5 The political construction of regional inequalities in the UK in the 1980s and 1990s

Regional inequalities have long been a characteristic feature of life in the UK.

In this sense, the 1980s do not differ markedly from the years that preceded them. In another sense, however, they do differ radically. Before 1979, over a period of 50 years, governments had acknowledged that such inequalities were economically inefficient and socially divisive and had pursued policies to reduce them. After 1979, Mrs Thatcher's government pursued sectoral policies with strongly differentiated regional effects whilst cutting back on policies that formally sought to reduce regional inequalities. More generally, Thatcherism sought to polarise the UK socially via a Two Nations strategy that took a distinctive regional form. Moreover, this was a deliberate strategy to increase the magnitude of the North–South divide for electoral gain, whilst diverting attention from this via a plethora of cosmetic 'small area' policies. The North–South divide, and more generally spatial inequality, has been redefined as a result of a series of policy and political choices that were an integral part of the Thatcherite Two Nations project and which have survived Mrs Thatcher's departure as leader of the Conservative Party.

One element in this is the cut-backs in nationalised industry spending (see Hudson 1986, 1989c). These have been decisive in deindustrialising large swathes of the North as coal, shipbuilding and steel have been drastically restructured as a prelude to privatising the remaining rump of these industries. At the same time regional policy expenditures in the North have been drastically curtailed. The plethora of new 'small area' initiatives in no way compensates for this. Indeed, the urban aid programme was cut back by about 25 per cent in real terms between its peak in 1983–84 (after it was increased in response to the 1981 inner-city riots) and 1986–87. As automatic regional development grants were cut in the North, government spending on industry was increasingly channelled into selective schemes and into the South. Between 1981 and 1984, just under 25 per cent of selective industrial assistance – via support schemes such as those for microelectronics, fibre optics and robots – was given to companies in the South East alone. Much of the expansion of such sectors was a consequence of the concentration of government spending on defence-related production. This concentration increased in the 1980s: in 1977–78, 61 per cent of Ministry of Defence procurement expenditure was within the South and by 1985–86 this had risen to 64 per cent. Thus the widening of the 'gap' between North and South over much of the 1980s was in part a consequence of the remilitarisation of the British economy (see Lovering and Boddy 1988). As the impacts of the ending of the cold war began to be reflected in levels of military spending, however, the effects on the South (and more specifically particular places within it tied to the fortunes of defence industries) became increasingly apparent.

State support for the new 'enterprise culture' has, directly and indirectly, also been channelled to the South, especially the South East. This is exemplified by the disproportionate concentration of beneficiaries of the Business Expansion Scheme in the South East. In 1983–84, 63 per cent of investments supported by the Business Expansion Scheme were located there. This is because past patterns of social and economic development have meant that the most favourable preconditions for the successful implementation of policies to promote 'the enterprise culture' are generally to be found in the South East.

This favourable environment for the flowering of the enterprise culture in the South is further underpinned by other state policies and expenditures. In particular, both directly and indirectly, it is strongly reinforced by the concentration of state expenditure on defence and R and D into the South. But overlaying all these specific government policies that have both widened inter- and intra-regional inequalities, are the effects of the government's overall economic policy. This again has been sharply divisive both between North and South. The main thrust of economic policy, to reposition the UK in the international economy, centred around an expansion of internationally competitive financial services and a decline in manufacturing activities, has been a major reason underlying the growing North–South divide. The government can claim some success for its policy of promoting London as a major international financial centre; by 1990 there were no less than 494 foreign banks operating in London, well ahead of its main European rivals, Frankfurt and Paris (*Financial Times*, 7 February 1991). Expansion of financial services more generally has been overwhelmingly concentrated in the South, above all in London (see Thrift et al. 1987). Indeed, with 620 000 people working there in finance and business, London had the greatest concentration of financial employment of any of the world's cities (*Financial Times*, 8 July 1992). Conversely, industrial decline has been disproportionately concentrated in the North, often focused on specific communities as a direct consequence of the run-down of nationalised industries (see Chapter 8). The fact that this national economic policy resulted in disproportionately severe decline in the South in the early 1990s is not only indicative of a changing map of regional inequality but of a more profound national economic crisis.

The government's strategy simultaneously involved severe reductions in public expenditure to support industry in the North and a selective expansion of public expenditure to underpin growth in the South. As well as the redirection of state aid to industry to the South, there has been a considerable increase in other sorts of public expenditure to subsidise economic growth there. Provision and expansion of major international airports at Gatwick, Heathrow and Stansted, in conjunction with associated motorway developments such as the M11 and M25, are good examples. These have been crucial, both in relation to the South East's international role in financial services and business administration and in influencing the location of new 'high-tech' manufacturing. In addition, state investment in infrastructure itself results in considerable employment growth. The impacts of the Channel Tunnel in further redrawing the map of accessibility will further widen the North–South divide.

The political reconstruction of the North–South divide via differential tax relief and public expenditure was devastatingly revealed in George Rosie's television film *Scotching the Myth* (1990) – which revealingly has still to be shown on English networks. This showed the main target of state expenditure to be London and the South East; with almost all mortgage tax relief, 40 per cent of Civil Service salaries, the main government laboratories and research councils, practically the entire Ministry of Defence R and D budget, 60 per cent of the English roads budget, a rail subsidy as large as the annual budget of the former Scottish Development Agency, half of Britain's tax subsidy to company cars ... (see *Independent on Sunday*, 22 March 1992).

Furthermore, the regionally differentiated impact of recession led to further restructuring of state expenditure so as to channel more of it into the South. As the general impacts of recession in the early 1990s, as well as the specific impacts of changes such as cuts in defence spending, became evident, the government responded by making parts of the South eligible for regional policy assistance in 1993 (Martin 1993). It also adjusted its mechanisms for funding local government services, increasingly adjusting 'standard spending assessments' by 'area cost adjustments', supposedly to compensate local authorities in the South East for higher than average wage costs. The area cost adjustments rose from £418 million in 1988 to £1300 million in 1993. This led Mr Bruce Stevenson, Chief Executive of Cleveland County Council, to comment that the adjustment mechanism 'has in effect become a mechanism for moving sums of money from the rest of the world into the South-East ... [it is] a response to a political difficulty' (cited in the *Financial Times*, 3 March 1993).

7.5 Conclusions: the UK's map of regional divisions

By the late 1980s, there were deep regional divisions within the UK, and they were more sharply etched than they had been when Mrs Thatcher became Prime Minister. The North–South divide had widened with a vengeance. Divisions between the Two Nations were symbolised in those between the two regions. By the early 1990s, however, the magnitude of regional inequalities had been somewhat reduced as the effects of recession were disproportionately felt in the South. Overlaid on and intermeshing with this shifting pattern of regional inequalities, there were, however, other important changes in the map of inequality. Within cities, physical distances between affluent suburbs and gentrified inner-city areas on the one hand, and deprived local authority peripheral housing estates and decayed inner cities on the other, may have stayed the same. But the social distances between them grew markedly. Within rural areas there has similarly been a growing differentiation between the residential areas of the affluent middle classes and those of the remnants of the rural working class. It is at these more local spatial scales that the intermeshing and cumulation of structural disadvantages are most starkly visible. It is to issues such as these that we turn our attention in the next two chapters.

8

Divided within regions

8.1 Introduction: landscapes of disadvantage

Whilst the North–South divide is a major feature of the political and social landscape of the UK, it is not the only geographical dimension of the creation and reproduction of inequalities. As Balchin (1990, 102) argues, there is 'no interregional demarcation line separating the "haves" and the "have nots"'. Instead, there is a complex landscape of advantage and disadvantage with concentrations of poverty and unemployment in inner London and, indeed, in particular neighbourhoods in every town and city in the South. In contrast, there are the 'Northern highlights' (Breheny et al. 1987) in the North, towns and cities such as Harrogate and Edinburgh, which have performed more strongly in the 1980s and 1990s than the national economy.

These divides are particularly marked in the South where, behind the veneer of apparent affluence, there is considerable unemployment, homelessness and deprivation – and not only in inner London (Champion and Green 1989). In the late 1980s the economy of the South East grew at an unsustainable rate, mainly due to expansion in the service sector and Lawson's 1987 election winning budget. In contrast, 'The 1990s have ushered in the big freeze. ... Southerners already saddled with high rates of personal indebtedness, exploited what proved to be an unsustainable rise in house prices to borrow, spend and borrow more. The party ended with a cocktail of collapsing asset values and mounting job insecurity' (*Financial Times*, 7 December 1992). As a result, by the 1990s, East Sussex had a higher registered unemployment rate than most parts of Scotland and the northern region, whilst the 1993 review of regional policy included places such as Southend and Thanet in the list of assisted areas (Figures 8.1 and 8.2). The extent to which this new map of unemployment reflects cyclical or long-term structural disadvantages remains to be seen, but the misery of unemployment and debt in the midst of the once booming South is real enough. And it is important to realise that, even in the booming late 1980s, the very economic success of places such as Cambridge was predicated on the existence of low wages in sectors such as contract cleaning and catering. At the same time, the inflationary pressures generated in the local housing market by the economic boom made it increasingly

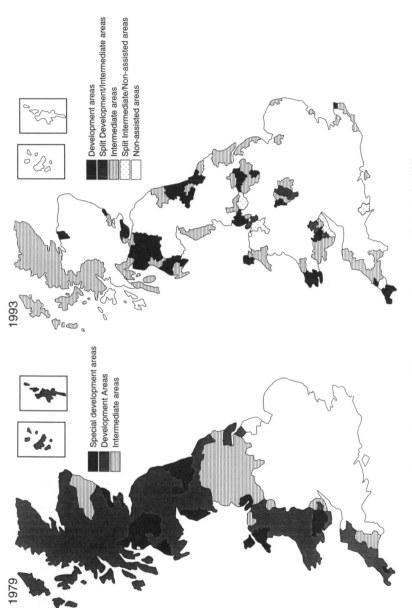

Figure 8.1 The UK regional policy map, 1979 and 1993

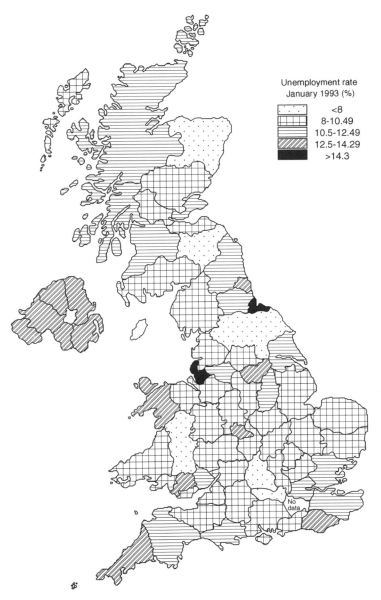

Figure 8.2 Unemployment rate by county, January 1993

Source: *Regional Trends*, 28

difficult for lower-income families to become first-time buyers (Crang and Martin 1991).

Whilst these landscapes of disadvantage are constituted as a complex mosaic, there are none the less some recurrent themes. There are contrasts between rural and rural areas, urban and urban areas, and urban and rural areas. It is, for example, possible to trace a social gradient from inner London through (mostly) increasingly prosperous suburban south London, out to the wealthy semi-urban fringe in Surrey Heath. This is essentially a graph of increasing material prosperity which is carved in the social landscape of the South East; it is characterised by the 1991 Census statistic which shows that whilst more than half the households in Surrey Heath had access to two or more cars, the equivalent figure in inner London was less than 10 per cent.

At the root of such social gradients lies a profound change in the role of metropolitan areas in the UK economy. Whereas in 1945 cities were still seen as dynamic centres of growth (for example, by the Barlow Commission), by the 1960s the largest cities were manifesting signs of economic decline especially in their inner areas (see Hudson and Williams 1986, Chapter 3). This was accompanied by, and compounded by, selective out-migration to the suburbs. At the same time, large disadvantaged segments of the population were effectively 'trapped' in inner urban areas which were losing their traditional employment bases and were characterised by poor housing conditions and deprivation.

There are systematic regularities in the landscapes of advantage and disadvantage within the regions of the UK, because these are rooted in - although not fully explained by – the material relationships of society. Given that these relationships have been reshaped during the shift from One Nation to Two Nations politics, intra-regional differences in the UK can be interpreted within this larger framework. To a large extent, the dominant influences are the same as those which shaped the North–South divide. For example, Champion and Townsend's (1990) study of different types of labour markets (see later in this chapter) found that this fundamental regional cleavage consistently resurfaced in their finer-grained spatial analysis. However, there were also distinctive intra-regional patterns of inequality – between suburbs and inner urban areas, and between small towns and metropolitan areas – which were reshaped by the strategies of One Nation and Two Nations politics.

In the late 1970s, and especially the 1980s, the funding priorities and programmes of One Nation politics were swept away to be replaced by 'new ones in keeping with the ideological imperatives of the "free market", and transformed the national policy matrix within which cities are governed and urban social relations are reproduced' (Gaffikin and Warf 1993, 67). The Two Nations economic strategy had a considerable impact on intra-regional differences, especially in the South East. The privileging of financial services, combined with deregulation of City markets and institutions, had a profound effect on the geography of the South East during both the boom and the bust phases of the late 1980s/early 1990s economic cycle. At the same time, the attack on local authorities' autonomy, and the switch from Keynesian 'managerial' planning to 'entrepreneurial' policies (Fainstein 1991; Gamble 1988), undermined the capacity of individual areas to develop effective, coherent strategies to combat unemployment and poverty via redistributive policies. This reshaping of central–local relations was especially marked in the largest cities following the abolition of the metropolitan counties and the GLC (Duncan and Goodwin 1985). As a result, there has been a 'shift in the priorities of local governments, which are increasingly less concerned with issues of social redistribution, compensation for negative externalities, provision of public services and so forth, and more enthralled by questions of economic competitiveness, attracting investment capital and the production of a favourable "business climate"' (Gaffikin and Warf 1993, 79). The effects of this – and especially of the lack of effective regional systems of social regulation – were particularly evident in the South East during the recession of the early 1990s (Peck and Tickell 1992). However, they were also evident in the redistributions which occurred within all of the UK's regions. The overall effect was that intra-regional differentiation became even more firmly shaped by central political strategies under Two Nations politics.

In the first edition of this volume we emphasised that spatial inequality has been redefined as a result of a series of policy and political choices that were an integral part of the Thatcherite project. Although these remarks were directed mainly at the North–South divide, they apply equally well to intra-regional contrasts, especially between older industrial districts and inner-city zones on the one hand as opposed to outer metropolitan and other semi-rural areas on the other. Thatcherite policies favoured the advantaged majority who socially and electorally dominated the latter types of areas. At the same time, the emphasis on 'entrepreneurial' policies, and the restructuring of industries such as coal and steel prior to privatisation, effectively abandoned older industrial districts and inner areas to increasing poverty and unemployment. This deliberately created the voting base which was to deliver four successive Conservative electoral victories. Therefore, when Mrs Thatcher celebrating her 1987 election victory referred to the fact that there was much to do in 'those inner cities', her words rang hollow. To a large extent the deepening crisis of the inner cities had been the price that her governments, wittingly or unwittingly, had been prepared to pay for electoral support in other parts of the UK.

8.2 Restructuring local economies

During both the One Nation and Two Nations periods, intra-regional economic changes have resulted from contrasting relative and absolute declines in the manufacturing sector and growth of the service sector. The productive bases of the principal cities and the older established industrial districts (including the coalfields) of the UK have been in relative and sometimes absolute economic decline for several decades. High rates of firm closures in these areas have not been matched by equivalent growth in new establishments (Elias and Keogh 1982). This is related to their industrial structures (a disproportionate dependence on sectors in national decline), an ageing capital stock reflecting a cumulative failure to reinvest, and the working out of new spatial divisions of labour in particular industries. For example, Massey and Meegan (1978) in their seminal study of electronic engineering, found that one half of job losses had been *in situ* (rationalisations and closures), whilst only one third had been due to direct locational transfers of production. In contrast, other locations – such as New Towns, outer metropolitan areas, medium-sized cities, and accessible rural areas – were more attractive to new investment. This was based on their increasingly favourable conditions of production: relatively young and non-unionised labour forces, lower costs of land and construction, access to the major motorway network, and favourable environmental conditions. In a way, therefore, the new intra-regional pattern of production was as much an expression of the new economic geography of the UK as was the deepening of the North–South divide.

As a result of the intra-regional reorganisation of production, there was a major redistribution of employment. Between 1960 and 1978 there were substantial employment declines throughout the UK urban and rural system (Table 8.1). These were especially severe in London and the conurbations and they increasingly impacted on outer as well as inner urban areas. The UK inner-city crisis, which entered the political agenda in the late 1960s and the early 1970s, was only the most obvious manifestation of the demise of the large cities as centres of productive employment. In contrast, the only employment increases were recorded in small towns and rural areas, especially in the more accessible locations.

During the 1980s there was little fundamental change to the urban–rural pattern of growth and decline, although the crisis of the old industrial areas of the UK deepened under the impact of the Two Nations strategy. In

Table 8.1 Manufacturing decline in urban areas in Great Britain, 1960–78

	% change in manufacturing employment, 1960–78
London	− 42.5
Conurbations	− 26.5
Free-standing cities	− 13.8
Large towns	− 2.2
Small town	+ 15.7
Rural areas	+ 38.0

Source: Hamnett (1985)

particular, the Thatcherite emphasis on removing protection (in various forms) from industry and opening up to international competition had a severe effect on sectors such as iron and steel, shipbuilding, textiles and cars; these tended overwhelmingly to be concentrated in the declining coalfields, the inner areas of the conurbations, and in particular towns and cities such as Luton, Corby and Bradford. However, the precise form and timing of economic change were influenced both by the shifting national pattern of restructuring as part of the Two Nations project and by the reshaping of the overall North–South divide.

The opening of the Thatcherite phase of the Two Nations project was marked by a deep recession in 1979–81, which destroyed 12 per cent of the UK's production capacity. This had particularly severe intra-regional effects, impacting deeply on large cities and older industrial areas; these were predominantly in the North with the exception of London. Between 1983 and 1990 there was strong national growth in jobs based almost entirely on the service sector which expanded by 18 per cent; this favoured medium-sized cities and more accessible rural areas, again predominantly in the South (Martin 1993). Growth rates were particularly marked in an arc stretching around London from West Sussex to parts of the East Midlands and East Anglia. Subsequently, the recession of the 1990s had a particularly severe impact on the service industries in the South East, and this affected almost all parts of the region; it was this which contributed to the apparent – and perhaps only cyclical – narrowing of the North–South gap.

It is only possible to analyse these employment changes in detail up to 1989. In this respect, Townsend's (1993a) work is invaluable in demonstrating the interrelationship between regional and intra-regional changes in the Two Nations project (see Table 8.2). London and the metropolitan areas of the North both suffered total employment declines. All other urban and rural zones had employment gains over the period as a whole, but especially the New Towns, mixed urban and rural areas and remoter, mainly rural areas. Growth rates in the North, however, consistently lagged behind those in the South. The key to the regional differential was not manufacturing; there was remarkably little difference in the incidence and scale of growth and decline in this sector for particular types of urban zones in the North and the South. However, there were marked differences in the service sector, as illustrated by banking and finance. All zones in the South had increases in excess of 19 per cent except London (although its share of higher-level jobs did increase) and the remoter rural areas. In the North there was financial service employment growth in only two zones. Even these increases seem to have been the result of intra-regional shifts, for there were large-scale decreases in non-metropolitan cities and in resorts, ports and retirement areas. Other analyses have confirmed that financial services growth in the North was generally patchy, and that only Edinburgh and Leeds clearly emerged as strong nuclei of growth (Leyshon and Thrift 1989). In other service sectors there was a more consistent pattern of

Table 8.2 Urban–rural employment changes in Great Britain, 1981–89

	% Change		
	Total (excluding agriculture)	Manufacturing	Banking and financial services
South			
Inner London	− 1.9	− 36.2	− 6.2
Outer London	− 2.6	− 34.4	− 3.5
Non-metropolitan cities	+ 5.4	− 22.2	+ 21.2
Industrial areas	+ 6.3	− 10.0	+ 35.7
Districts with New Towns	+ 17.9	− 11.1	+ 72.2
Resorts, port and retirement	+ 13.2	− 5.7	+ 19.4
Urban and mixed urban–rural	+ 17.0	− 6.2	+ 29.9
Remoter, mainly rural	+ 18.5	+ 3.6	+ 7.9
TOTAL	+ 7.9	− 15.5	
North			
Principal towns	− 6.8	− 31.6	− 24.4
Outer metropolitan districts	− 0.6	− 17.2	+ 1.6
Non-metropolitan cities	+ 2.8	− 14.4	− 20.4
Industrial areas	+ 2.1	− 6.8	− 6.0
Districts with New Towns	+ 9.3	− 1.0	− 5.9
Resorts, ports and retirement	+ 6.2	− 6.5	− 51.8
Urban and mixed urban–rural	+ 11.8	− 5.9	+ 3.8
Remoter, mainly rural	+ 14.6	+ 6.2	− 6.2
	+ 1.6	− 14.7	

Source: Townsend (1993)

decentralisation from the main urban cores to surrounding zones in all regions; this was due to the decentralisation of firms seeking out lower rents and suitable supplies of labour, and to consumer services following the out-movement of population.

In the course of the 1980s, therefore, there was a strong pattern of urban–rural employment shifts, but it continued to be mediated by the UK's dominant North–South cleavage. The distribution of unemployment also displayed similar geographical dimensions. Before 1979 high unemployment was already a feature of most of the UK's peripheral conurbations – especially Merseyside, Tyneside and Clydeside – as the limitations of the One Nation economic strategy were exposed. In addition, the coalfields and other traditional areas of manufacturing had also experienced high rates of structural and cyclical unemployment. This was reflected in the changing map of regional policy assisted areas (see Hudson and Williams 1986, 66–67). By the 1980s, however, the range of counties experiencing high unemployment rates had broadened considerably. The list now also included the metropolitan counties of the manufacturing heartland (the West Midlands, West Yorkshire and Greater Manchester), as well as the GLC, Cleveland and Derbyshire. However, as Champion and Townsend (1990, 132) stress, 'Ten years of additional "layers" of unemployment had changed the rank order in detail, with the effect of the coal and steel redundancies in South Yorkshire being one major example, but the main impression is of consistency', that is of the persistence of the North–South and the urban–rural divides.

The spatial effects of the 1990s recession were different from those of previous economic downturns, for they impacted on the South far more than the traditional industrial areas and leading cities of the North. Although unemployment still tends to be far lower in the South than in the North, many labour market areas in the former had unemployment rates above the national average. Amongst the more severely affected were the areas immediately adjacent to London such as Thanet and Hertfordshire, as well as part of the south coast and the Isle of Wight. It is the social and political pressures resulting from this new map of unemployment that led to the redrawing of the regional policy map in 1993 (Figure 8.1). As Martin (1993, 799) comments,

the rise in unemployment has been greatest precisely in the socio-spatial heartland of the Conservatives' electoral vote, the very part of the country that has formed the core of the Conservatives' political success in the last four general elections. Perhaps even more significant, some of the highest increases have occurred in areas encompassing marginal Conservative parliamentary seats.

The suspicion that the redrawing of the map of regional policy was largely a political exercise is reinforced by the fact that there has been relatively little change in the distribution of long term unemployment, with the North still carrying the brunt of this, whilst it is equally clear that the North has been the main loser in the redrawing of the map in 1993 as compared to that of 1979. However, even in this respect there are some areas of the South that clearly do have serious structural difficulties, notably the Medway towns, parts of the south coast and inner London (Figure 8.2). In other words, the new map of assisted areas can be seen as a cautious attempt by the Major government to respond to the limitations of the Two Nations economic strategy. It is ironical that these were precisely the types of areas which had seemed to benefit most from the regressive redistributional policies of Two Nations politics in the 1980s.

8.3 Housing: tenure and intra-regional locational access

The housing and planning policies of One Nation politics were worked out against the background of massive inter-war suburbanisation in the South, when over 4 million new homes were built mainly on the fringes of towns and cities. This was an accommodation of new life-style and consumption patterns, requiring low density residential development and space for home-based leisure. It was facilitated by low land prices, a virtually non-existent planning system and the availability of cheap capital and tax advantages for home ownership. This form of development was, however, flawed by an inherent contradiction: suburbs represented the social aspirations and savings of the expanding middle class but, at the same time, they threatened to destroy the traditional rural landscapes which had made such locations attractive.

In response to these pressures, the 1945–51 Labour governments laid down the foundations for a new urban policy: amenity was to be secured for individual and collective good via a mixture of containment of existing urban areas and controlled decentralisation. The essential mechanisms for this were negative land use planning controls and a programme of state-led investment in housing (see Mellor 1977; Hudson and Williams 1986). The showpieces of positive state intervention in housing were the New Towns but the main impact of this policy was the construction of 1.43 million local authority dwellings between 1945 and 1956. Conservative governments in the 1950s accepted the broad thrust of this approach but reduced the role of the state sector to that of a partner (to the private sector) with principal responsibility for providing homes for those in need. In this way a broad consensus was established which was not substantially changed during the period of One Nation politics. The net result was a continuous process of urban decentralisation, first of population but later of production and services, as the postwar economy expanded and developed.

Contrary to the initial vision of the One Nation period, the state did not take the leading direct role in the process of decentralisation, in the form of New Towns and overspill schemes. Instead, the initiative was taken by the private sector as the lead developer of owner-occupied housing estates in the outer urban areas. The public sector did play a role in decanting population from inner urban areas to new peripheral council housing estates, as part of slum clearance or urban 'modernisation' schemes. However, after the 1950s, an unequal private–public partnership became the One Nation model for housing construction in the UK. The main exception to this was in the inner urban areas, where the public sector was virtually the only substantial investor in housing, excepting some limited gentrification. The private rented sector was in continuous decline in all urban and rural areas.

The outcome of three decades of consensus One Nation politics was a sharply differentiated intra-regional distribution of housing tenures, with all that this implied for life-chances, life-style, mobility and wealth accumulation (see Chapter 4). The position at the end of this period is reflected in the 1981 Census data. Compared to the national average, the major cities had higher proportions of local authority dwellings and proportionately less owner occupation; this was especially marked in the Midlands, North and Scotland where there had been large-scale municipal rehousing programmes. There were also major differences between inner and outer urban areas (Table 8.3). Owner occupation and private renting were polarised, respectively, in outer and inner

Table 8.3   Housing characteristics of inner- and outer-urban areas in England and Wales, 1981

		% of households			
		Owner-occupied	Public rented	Private rented	With car available
Cities in metropolitan countries					
Birminham	Inner	44.0	34.6	21.4	38.3
	Outer	52.9	37.8	9.4	52.2
Liverpool	Inner	31.3	39.1	29.6	25.3
	Outer	45.7	39.9	14.4	45.3
Sheffield	Inner	33.7	49.6	16.7	37.0
	Outer	47.0	45.1	7.9	51.2
Manchester	Inner	26.3	54.4	19.3	29.9
	Outer	40.1	44.0	15.9	43.8
Leeds	Inner	39.8	37.2	23.0	34.9
	Outer	48.4	42.6	9.0	49.3
Coventry	Inner	66.2	19.2	14.6	51.8
	Outer	66.3	25.7	8.0	61.7
Bradford	Inner	55.8	25.8	18.4	31.9
	Outer	65.6	25.0	9.4	50.4
Wolverhampton	Inner	40.7	43.4	15.9	44.8
	Outer	46.2	48.5	5.3	59.0
Sunderland	Inner	58.9	26.4	14.7	44.6
	Outer	27.5	66.8	5.7	40.8
Newcastle upon Tyne	Inner	30.5	38.9	30.5	32.4
	Outer	35.9	52.1	12.0	36.9
Other cities in the North and Midlands					
Leicester	Inner	57.1	19.4	23.5	39.6
	Outer	46.0	44.9	9.0	53.1
Nottingham	Inner	35.2	42.0	22.8	35.0
	Outer	38.7	54.0	7.3	49.7
Kingston upon Hull	Inner	46.5	23.4	30.1	33.8
	Outer	35.2	55.2	9.7	45.6
Stoke-on-Trent	Inner	61.6	26.1	12.3	48.7
	Outer	53.6	39.2	7.2	54.7
Derby	Inner	51.8	26.1	22.1	39.4
	Outer	61.2	31.8	6.9	62.4
Other cities in the South and West					
Bristol	Inner	55.2	18.2	26.5	52.3
	Outer	54.0	38.9	7.1	63.3
Cardiff	Inner	60.9	12.4	26.7	42.8
	Outer	60.8	30.6	8.6	62.6
Plymouth	Inner	52.9	16.3	30.8	48.9
	Outer	55.5	32.1	12.4	63.2
Southampton	Inner	56.8	17.6	25.6	53.4
	Outer	52.6	37.9	9.5	60.9
Inner London		27.3	42.8	29.9	41.4
Outer London		61.9	23.2	15.0	64.0
Great Britain (average)		55.8	31.2	13.2	60.5

Source: Redfern (1982)

zones. The distribution of public sector housing was more variable, depending on whether individual councils had favoured inner-area renewal or investment in suburban estates.

As a result of these housing developments, the distribution of housing tenures has itself become a major barrier to geographical mobility at the intra-regional scale (as well as at the interregional scale). This follows from two essential facts: access to particular tenures, and sub-markets within these, is socially conditioned, above all by income and class (see Chapter 4); and the distribution of local authorities' housing stocks and their forms of management – especially their housing waiting lists – means that it is difficult for actual and intending tenants to move across local authority boundaries. Taken together these imply that there are availability, cost and quality hurdles as to who is able to live where.

Changes in housing policies, as part of the Two Nations political strategy, have changed the balance between housing tenures. The recommodification of council housing, together with limits on local authority building programmes, have contributed to new forms of intra-regional housing differentiation. Their precise forms vary both between and within regions. But the overall effect has been to further disadvantage the poorest segments of society. The availability of public housing has been severely reduced in all areas, and there has con-comitantly been a restriction on the potential residential mobility of the poorest elements in society. In short, the housing trap has closed further in the course of the Two Nations period. The two major tenures are now examined in turn.

A massive increase in owner occupation during the 1980s was a part of the Thatcherite political strategy of constructing a 'property-owning democracy' which provided an in-built electoral majority for the Conservatives. It also contributed, however, to sharp house price inflation. The concentration of the economic expansion after 1983 in the South, especially the boom in financial services, meant that there was a widening of inter- and intra-regional house price differences. Hamnett (1989) argues that changes, such as a 66 per cent rise in house prices in London 1983–86, amounted to a qualitative difference in the constitution of the owner-occupied housing market. Differences within regions were even greater than those between them: for example, in 1988 there was a £71 800 difference in housing costs between the most and least expensive parts of the South East, compared to a difference of only £59 700 between the South East and the northern region (Balchin 1990, 139). There were, therefore, real barriers to movements within many regions, as well as to interregional mobility. Despite this, however, there was a major political pay-off for the Conservative Party; rising house prices meant a windfall increase in the equity holdings of homeowners, and this was reflected in a greater inclination to vote for the party which had delivered these individual capital gains (Johnston 1987). The price for this was paid electorally by Labour and materially by first-time entrants to the spiralling housing market, and above all by those who aspired to but failed to gain access to this.

The government response to this housing market disruption – which its macro-economic policies and lack of effective territorial management had exacerbated – was to try and ease some of the pressures on the land market by relaxing controls on urban development in the outer metropolitan areas. Hence in the 1980s there was discussion about permitting private-sector development of 'new towns' and easing Green Belt and other controls. This, however, offended the middle-class conservationist and shire county elements of the Tory Party, hence underlining one of the contradictions for the government of its inter-class and intra-regional electoral base. The house price spiral was eventually halted and the development pressures in the outer metropolitan areas eased, but only as a consequence of the deep economic recession of the 1990s. This contributed to both an inter- and intra-regional convergence of house prices; for example, at the end of 1993 average house prices in London were recorded as being only £200 more than in the rest of the South East, reflecting change rates of − 0.6 and 3.5 per cent respectively in the previous quarter (Halifax Building Society regional house price index).

The Conservative strategy of recommodifying housing, via cuts in new public investment and intensified council house sales, has also had a differential intra-regional impact. The concentration of the council house stock in the largest cities has meant that this is where the impact has been greatest. For example, some 87 000, or 19 per cent, of the London council house stock was sold off between 1979 and 1985, at the same time as the private rented stock decreased by 17 000 (Balchin 1990, 143). Whilst the absolute numbers of sales in more rural areas were less dramatic, their impact was no less severe given the small stocks which were available anyway to meet housing need in such areas (Phillips and Williams 1984). However, it was the major urban areas which experienced the greatest change in their housing resources. It was also in these areas that the selectiveness of the sales was most apparent for they were left with the least attractive and poorest quality stock, concentrated in what Taylor (1979) has termed 'difficult to let, difficult to live in, and difficult to leave' estates.

Against this background of labour and housing market changes, there was growing spatial and social polarisation within the regions of the UK, especially in terms of an urban–rural divide. The ability to effect residential moves across any district boundary largely depended on being in or being able to enter the owner occupation market, whilst movements into particular areas – either those which were booming or which were especially prestigious – were barred to all but the more prosperous owner occupiers. In contrast, large numbers of people became even more firmly trapped in dwindling stocks of the poorest quality public housing or in the rapidly disappearing private rented sector. There were a number of highly visible symbols of these policies, none more distressing than the growing numbers of homeless people in the major cities; by 1988 there were 128 000 known homeless persons in the UK and 27 900 of these were trying to survive on the streets of London. Another symbol was the crisis of the inner cities where a substantial minority were caught between disappearing job opportunities and the housing trap (see Chapter 9). This selective intra-regional filtering of population is not simply a product of economic restructuring and housing market operations. Instead, it is also a mechanism which conditions access to the locations of jobs in new industries, to higher incomes and to a higher quality of life. As such it is a mechanism which contributes to the relative advantaging and disadvantaging of classes, ethnic and gender groups.

8.4   Intra-regional differences: worlds apart within regions

The discussion thus far in this chapter has concentrated mainly on urban–rural differences or inner–urban versus outer–urban contrasts. However, it is clear that there is a continuum, or a series of continua, along which areas can be located in terms of their economic structures, unemployment, housing conditions, and other criteria. Whilst there is not the space to delve into these in any great detail in this volume, we can provide a brief summary of some of the principal features of the four main types of areas, as identified by Champion and Townsend (1990): London and the other major cities, prosperous sub-regions, industrial areas and other rural areas (Table 8.4). In all four cases, their principal features have to be seen as the outcome of the interaction of their particular structures with the broader processes of change in the One and Two Nations periods.

8.4.1   London and the major cities

London, Manchester, Leeds, Liverpool, Glasgow, Birmingham and Newcastle were the dominant centres of accumulation in the UK economy in the nineteenth century. From the 1930s, however, the dominance of some of these cities began to wane, and this was a central feature of the second half of the One Nation period. Between 1960 and 1981 the six largest conurbations experienced a collective decrease of 1.2 million jobs, principally in their inner areas (Begg et al. 1986). However, employment decline had also become widespread in their outer areas. This was a result of the working through of restructuring processes, the poor conditions for new industrial investment and of planning constraints operated by both local authorities (development control) and central government (industrial development certificates and office development permits). Whilst they had employment gains in the service sector, these did not match job losses in manufacturing, so that the major cities came

Table 8.4 Population change, 1971–88, and employment change, 1981–87, by types of local authority districts

	Polpulation			Employment	
	1988 (000)	1971–81 (%)	1981–88 (%)	1987 (000)	1981–87 (%)
Large cities	10 865	– 10.4	– 2.4	5 452	– 4.2
London (South)	6 735	– 9.6	– 1.0	3 506	– 1.5
Other principal cities (North)	4 130	– 11.6	– 4.5	1 946	– 8.7
Prosperous sub-regions	22 182	+ 5.2	+ 3.2	8 465	+ 3.8
South	14 975	+ 6.1	+ 4.2	5 666	+ 6.1
North	7 207	+ 3.4	+ 1.3	2 799	– 0.5
Non-metropolitan cities	5 431	– 3.0	– 2.3	2 826	– 0.1
Districts with New Towns	2 821	+ 15.1	+ 5.1	1 079	+ 4.2
Resorts, port and retirement	3 611	+ 5.8	+ 7.2	1 105	+ 3.9
Urban and mixed urban/rural	10 319	+ 7.5	+ 4.4	3 455	+ 7.1
Industrial districts	16 021	+ 0.6	– 0.8	5 464	– 3.3
South	2 676	+ 4.8	+ 2.5	1 022	+ 1.1
North	13 344	– 0.1	– 1.4	4 442	– 4.2
Other metropolitan districts	8 572	– 1.4	– 1.5	2 888	– 4.6
Industrial areas	7 448	+ 3.2	+ 0.1	2 576	– 1.7
Remoter, mainly rural	6 419	+ 10.2	+ 6.1	1 897	+ 5.0
South	3 596	+ 11.4	+ 7.4	1 102	+ 7.2
North	2 823	+ 8.7	+ 4.5	795	+ 2.1
Great Britain	55 486	+ 0.8	+ 1.3	21 271	– 0.2
South	27 982	+ 2.1	+ 3.1	11 275	+ 3.1
North	27 505	– 0.5	– 0.6	9 996	– 3.7

Note: Due to rouding, certain items do not sum to column totals. 'South' companiese the South East, South West, East Anglia, East Midlands; 'North' the rest of Great Britain.

Source: Champion and Townsend (1990)

to experience high and persistent unemployment. Therefore, economic restructuring of the metropolitan areas had commenced quite early in the One Nation period, although their economic, housing and social crises were to deepen in the Two Nations period, as symbolised by the urban riots of the 1980s.

Their declining economic bases, and the attractions – socially constructed – of living conditions in the outer metropolitan and rural areas led to sharp population losses after the 1950s. After 1961 every one of the major cities, except Leeds, was to experience such losses. The scale of the losses was enormous with, for example, Glasgow losing one-fifth of its total population in the 1970s. The reasons for this were the erosion of the available stock of housing land by commercial and other developments, a lack of space, and the aspirations of the increasingly prosperous middle and skilled working class to new life-styles. Suburban and rural areas came to symbolise the good life that the 'haves' aspired to, whilst the large cities increasingly symbolised the terrain of the 'have nots'. The deterioration of the quality of life in the large cities, following the curtailment of public expenditure on services and amenities in the 1980s, reinforced this trend, and made even more critical the conditional access to residential mobility. The decentralisation of population had been an explicit objective of One Nation urban policy, but there had been an implicit assumption that the leading role of the state in housing provision, together with effective redistributional mechanisms, would open up near-universal access to what were in effect new spheres of consumption and – later – of production. What had not been anticipated was that decentralisation would be highly selective, socially, and would occur against the background of industrial collapse in the major cities.

In many ways the large cities were in the front line of the polarisation of UK society as part of the Two Nations strategy. It was not only that their economic bases were crumbling and that there was overheating in their housing markets, especially in London. There was also a deterioration in health provision, as funds were switched away from the major teaching hospitals, and in roads and in commuting conditions as transport expenditure was cut. Moreover, they displayed massive inequalities in close proximity with enclaves of wealth and advantage. Massey (1988, 15) for example, writing about London and the South East, argues that 'The richest region, in average terms, is the most unequal, and is getting worse'; the same applied in some degree to all the major metropolitan regions. These inequalities were starkest in the inner cities. For example, inner-city unemployment in 1951 was one-third higher than the national average, but by 1981 this had widened to 51 per cent, and the gap continued to increase in the following decade (Begg et al. 1986) (see Chapter 9). In addition, these areas have suffered from poor quality provision of collective services. For example, in inner London health care provision has been under pressure because of the relatively large numbers of local residents with special needs, such as the elderly and the very poor (Townsend and Davidson 1982). This has contributed to a marked geography of ill health in London; for example, Howe (1986) found that the standard mortality ratios for males from coronary heart disease varied from 122 in Dagenham to 51 in Sutton. It is not surprising that under these conditions, the principal cities of the metropolitan areas continued to experience large population losses, equal to − 5.4 per cent 1981–91 (Champion 1993).

With the deepening of the economic crisis in the 1980s and the 1990s many of the difficulties of the inner cities were exacerbated. At the same time, the problems of the largest cities became more generalised as peripheral housing estates – such as Easterhouse in Glasgow and Kirkby in Merseyside – also began to display the classic symptoms of urban deprivation and decay. Not surprisingly, all the metropolitan areas except London had average household incomes below the UK average in 1990; for example, Manchester, West

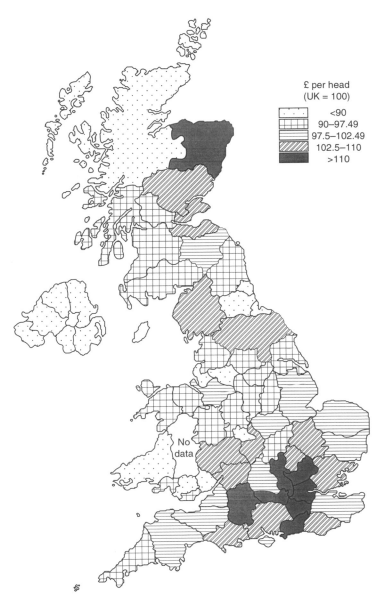

Figure 8.3 Household disposable income, 1990

Source: *Regional Trends*, 28

Midlands metropolitan area, Merseyside and Tyne and Wear all had levels which were only 85–90 per cent of the UK average (Figure 8.3).

8.4.2 Industrial areas

These are the remaining urbanised areas of the metropolitan counties in the North (Halifax, Sunderland, etc.), the coalfields and industrial districts such as Stoke and Luton, outside of the metropolitan areas. They are mostly but not entirely located in the North. Some, such as the coalfields of Wales and the North East, had experienced recurrent economic crises since the 1930s which persisted throughout much of the One Nation period. In other cities, such as Luton and Coventry, which had been seen as prosperous 'affluent worker' towns based on the car industry, it was the crisis in this industry in the Two Nations period which pushed them into their first major post-war crises. In other older established industrial districts – based on coal, steel, and traditional forms of manufacturing – the 1980s and 1990s were to witness a long slide into recession. Not least this is because they felt the full impact of the economic strategies of Two Nations politics: privatisation, public expenditure cuts, the devastation of the coal industry, and the insistence on 'market principles', cut a broad swathe through their economic structures. Many of these areas – such as Rhondda and West Hartlepool – have experienced substantial population losses through outmigration. However, the crises have also worked through their labour markets in the form of unemployment, and increased part time employment.

These areas tend to be characterised by high levels of deprivation, matching those in the inner cities in some respects. For example, Champion and Townsend's analysis of deprivation using the 1981 Census found that 23 of the 50 most deprived districts in the UK were industrial areas, with high rates of unemployment and poor housing conditions. This is not to say that these areas are uniformly deprived. 'Unemployment and housing conditions have led to increased social and political polarisation within industrial districts. The local map of unemployment was and remains predominantly a map of housing areas, with the highest rates evident in council estates and poor housing' (Champion and Townsend 1990, 215).

Whilst the economic recession of the 1990s impacted less heavily on these areas than on the South, it nevertheless added to already high levels of unemployment. In addition, individual areas such as Tayside suffered from closures in particular industries and defence cut-backs, whilst the coalfields of Yorkshire and the East Midlands were devastated by massive coal mine closures. They were therefore severely affected by the policies of Two Nations politics, especially by privatisation, cut-backs in expenditure on nationalised industries, and more generally by reduced public expenditure. Thus in January 1993, when average UK registered unemployment was 10.8 per cent, five of the highest county-level rates were to be found in Cleveland, Tyne and Wear, South Yorkshire, Merseyside and Mid-Glamorgan, all of which were industrial districts or based on metropolitan cities (Figure 8.2). These areas also had some of the lowest levels of household disposable income in the UK (Figure 8.3), reflecting both low pay and the absence of pay.

8.4.3 Prosperous sub-regions

Approximately two fifths of the UK's population live in what Champion and Townsend labelled prosperous sub-regions. They are in fact a very diverse set of areas encompassing shire counties, new towns, resorts, ports and retirement districts (see Figure 8.2). Although they are to be found in all regions of the UK they are essentially a feature of the South, with two-thirds being located in the South East, the South West, East Anglia and the East Midlands. Already relatively advantaged, they were favoured further by the regressive redistributional policies and the macro-economic growth strategies of Two Nations politics – leastways in the 1980s. For example, there was growth in excess of 7 per cent per annum in the outer South East, based on expansion in the high technology industries (especially in the M4 corridor and the Cambridge sub-region), manufacturing decentralisation from the principal cities and especially the expansion of producer and consumer services. Their ability to attract inmigrants meant that they dominated population growth in the UK. Between 1951 and 1971 they accounted for 82 per cent of national population growth, and this figure rose to 159 per cent in the period 1971–87 (reflecting negative growth elsewhere).

Whilst these were the increasingly prosperous areas of the UK, there were problems associated with this growth such as the social and environmental impacts of the urbanisation of the countryside, and strategic planning problems over the location of housing, retailing and transport. It is no coincidence that some of the most bitter clashes between environmentalist groups and developers during the 1980s and early 1990s were in this type of area. Twyford Down, the Winchester bypass, and the proposed 'new town' at Foxley Wood are only a few of the better publicised examples. These did cause the Conservative governments acute difficulties in balancing the competing interests of groups of its supporters in these areas. However, these were also the areas which provided the hard core of Conservative support in four successive electoral victories. Hence, the real shock for the Conservative Party of its by-election defeats in 1993 in Newbury and Eastbourne, places which had epitomised the 'haves' of Thatcher's divided Britain. These can be interpreted as votes of no confidence in economic strategies which by the 1990s had brought rising unemployment (Figure 8.2) to even these sub-regions.

8.4.4   Outer rural areas

The outer rural areas encompass much of Scotland, the northern Pennines, mid-Wales and the South West peninsula; they are therefore mainly but not exclusively to be found in the peripheral North. Economically, they have experienced a more or less continuous decline in their agricultural bases, have relatively limited industrial sectors and are increasingly reliant on the service sector, especially in their roles as locations for the consumption of leisure and tourism. In recent decades their lack of industrial bases and their strength in consumer services have meant that they have experienced relatively strong employment growth; for the same reasons they have not suffered as much as the prosperous and accessible rural districts in the 1990s recession. Employment growth has to some extent been fuelled by their above average population growth since the 1970s, attracting both economic and non-economic inmigrants. Between 1981 and 1991 they had a population growth rate of 7.6 per cent, the second highest in Great Britain, and well above the national average of 2.3 per cent (Champion 1993).

These rural areas are characterised by a high degree of social polarisation with some of the lowest-paid workers in the UK living alongside wealthy indigeneous and inmigrant families. The most disadvantaged families are those who have not been able to secure access to owner occupation. Instead they are dependent on a dwindling supply of council housing with many villages having only one or two or even no such dwellings available following the sales of the 1980s. Their only other alternative may be short winter lets or holiday accommodation, caravans or tied agricultural cottages (Phillips and Williams 1984). In addition, they also have experienced a run-down in collective services as education and health facilities have been withdrawn or centralised. Private sector services such as the village shop have also been in long-term decline. In overall aggregate terms these areas have some of the lowest levels of household disposable income in the UK, especially in Wales, Cornwall and parts of the North East (Figure 8.3).

8.5   Where you live matters

The North–South divide is firmly grounded in the economic organisation and the class structures of the UK, even if it is also formed by differences in housing markets, state intervention and in culture. It is in many ways an all-pervading influence when it comes to any analysis of the geographical dimensions of divided Britain. For example, Champion and Green's (1989) amalgamated index of prosperity (based on both static and change variables) in the local labour market areas (LLMAs) of the UK found that all 35 of the highest ranked places were in the South, even at this scale. They conclude (p. 95) that 'the main weight of evidence points to the north–south divide as the primary dimension in variations in economic health across Britain at the LLMA scale with a general tendency in the 1980s for a widening of this gap'.

In their updated analysis for the period up to 1989 (Champion and Green 1992) they also clearly identify an important intra-regional dimension to local prosperity, particularly outside of the South East, South West and East Anglia. This reflects the important differentiation between the old industrial districts and the principal cities, and the other parts of the other (mostly northern) regions. This is consistent with the identification of the 'Northern Lights' by Breheny et al. (1987). Using a quality of life measure, they argue that smaller towns − such as Hexham and Harrogate − offer a quality of life equal to or surpassing that enjoyed in much of the South, especially if their lower costs are taken into account. Therefore, whilst the North−South divide is a fundamental reflection of and influence on the quality of life in the UK, it also matters where you live within these regions. For some this is a matter of accident of birth but for others it is a matter of design − although one that can only be implemented if you have a strong enough foothold in the housing market and sufficient income. These − and therefore the class system and the gendering and racialising of opportunities − are keys to advantage and disadvantage. For there is a vast difference in all regions between living in an inner-city area or a sink council housing estate, and living in a semi-urban outer metropolitan area.

In the last two chapters we have shown that there is a distinctive geographical patterning of the divisions in the UK. In particular, we have drawn attention to the difficulties of the metropolitan regions and especially to those of their inner cities. This raises two important questions. Is deprivation something more than the accumulation of disadvantage across a number of dimensions of inequality; in other words is there a mutually reinforcing multiple deprivation and, perhaps, an underclass that it is difficult to escape from? And is multiple deprivation essentially a localised feature which is particularly associated with the inner cities, or is it endemic to UK society as a whole with a corresponding geographical distribution? We turn to these questions in the next chapter.

9

Divided and divided

9.1 Introduction

We have argued that there are a number of distinctive dimensions to inequality
in the UK. The most important dimensions are class, race, gender and location, but these are not the only ones. Age differences, for example, can be
deeply divisive in terms of access to the resources of society. That these dimensions are interrelated has become clear at several points in this volume. In the
last chapter, for example, it was argued that there are different types of urban
and rural areas in the UK. These have distinctive social profiles, and generalised structural advantages and disadvantages in terms of employment,
income, housing, education and other services. The structural disadvantages
of communities were especially evident in the principal cities and the old industrial areas. The spatial organisation of society is such that there is a clustering
of disadvantaged groups in particular areas. The inner cities are often
presented as the symbol of such spatial clustering of disadvantage, and this is
a theme which is examined in this chapter.

Whilst we have argued that there are areas characterised by multiple disadvantages, this does not imply that all individuals in such areas are similarly disadvantaged or that there are no disadvantaged people living outside of these
areas. Instead it is intrinsic to UK society that there are disadvantaged
individuals and groups. This system of disadvantage is class based and from
this stems the notion of multiple disadvantage because class has a profound
mediating effect on the dimensions of gender, race and location. In this
chapter we argue that the interrelationships between these individual dimensions of inequality assume a systematic form.

The systematic distribution of advantage and disadvantage exercises a considerable influence on the life chances of individuals and social groups. For
example, the probability of being unemployed is considerably greater for black
than for white people, for men than for women, and for those living in the
inner cities or the North of the UK. Therefore, it is of no surprise that one of
the groups with the highest probability of being unemployed is young, black
men living in the North or in the inner cities. There is no simple additionality
in this concentration of disadvantage. The separate dimensions can and do

frequently overlap and the effects are cumulative. Not least this is because class is so strongly associated with each of these cleavages in UK society.

Neither One Nation or Two Nations politics really addressed the issues of multiple disadvantage. The welfare state was initially constructed on the basis of class-based inequalities and with an overarching concern about high levels of (male) unemployment. Its policies were addressed at particular dimensions of inequality such as poor access to education or health, or the creation of a system of National Insurance for the unemployed. There was little recognition until the 1960s of many other dimensions of inequality or of the cumulative nature of disadvantages. This was a case of too little too late. By then state policies were being constrained by economic crises and public spending cuts which were the precursor, within the era of One Nation politics, of Two Nations policies. By 1981 there was not even a commitment to confront the deeper roots of inequality in the UK; instead increased inequalities were seen as necessary conditions for the success of the Thatcherite economic agenda.

There was no sharp break between the approaches of One Nation and Two Nations politics to multiple disadvantage. However, over time the increasingly astringent assertion of the responsibility of the individual, the dismantling or weakening of sections of the welfare state, and the castigation of many of the residents of inner-city areas as undeserving or criminal, made first the Thatcher governments and later the Major governments blind, at best, to the causes and the implications of multiple disadvantage. The first wave of attacks on the welfare state was seen in the late 1970s with the implementation of public expenditure cuts. Then, in the early 1980s came further retrenchment: the Supplementary Benefits Commission was abolished, as was the earnings-related supplement to unemployment benefit; two highly divisive Social Security Acts were introduced in 1980 and 1981; free school meals and transport were substantially cut back; and the real value of unemployment benefit was reduced. McCarthy (1986, 315) has powerfully summarised the impact of this period on those in poverty and deprivation:

> In three and a half years the Thatcher Government had increased stigmatisation, discrimination, dependency and anxiety. It had sown the seeds of a deep uncertainty for the future, not least with a second term looming, and given an impetus to privatisation and to declining standards in its relentless concern to reduce public expenditure and narrow the frontiers of State responsibility. In these three and a half years it presided over a near tripling of unemployment and a massive increase in the numbers of people and families dependent on an increasingly ramshackle and thread-bare supplementary benefit system.

As the Thatcher years unfolded so the gap in the approaches of One Nation and Two Nations politics to deprivation and poverty widened. A particular landmark was the comprehensive set of reviews of different parts of the welfare state which were launched by Norman Fowler in 1983–84. Presented as an attempt to update the increasingly piecemeal character of the welfare state, they were in reality informed by the aim of cutting public expenditure at the expense of the 'undeserving poor'. This was confirmed in the 1985 White Paper, on the reform of social security. It combined proposals to cut the benefits of pensioners and the unemployed, with increased selectivity, notably via the social fund.

The consequences of the first decade of Thatcherite policies were visible in the growth in the number of families receiving income support from 2.9 million in 1979 to 4.1 million in 1989 (data publicised by the House of Commons Social Security Committee, reported in *Financial Times*, 15 January 1993). In the 1990s, however, Conservative governments again returned to the theme of narrowing state commitment to the welfare state as part of their strategy to reduce public expenditure. The 1993 Budget was particularly significant in this; amongst the measures introduced were reductions in the period during which unemployment benefits could be claimed and alterations to future entitlements to pensions for women.

9.2 Multiple deprivation and areas of multiple deprivation

Multiple deprivation arises when an individual or social group suffers disadvantages in terms of a number of social dimensions. However, the term implies more than simple additionality; instead it suggests that these inequalities are linked and reinforce each other. The result is cumulative disadvantage which is greater than the sum total of the individual disadvantages.

The question immediately arises as to the composition of multiple deprivation. At one level multiple deprivation exists in the way in which it is experienced by individuals or social groups. It is obvious that not all individuals or social groups will view their disadvantages in the same way. Nevertheless there is a surprising degree of unanimity in the way in which people evaluate what constitutes the principal elements in the quality of life or well-being. One survey in the UK in the 1970s (see Knox 1976) found that the most highly rated components of social well-being were the following:

● your state of health
● family life
● housing conditions
● a stable and secure society
● job satisfaction
● financial situation
● neighbourhood quality

Whilst such surveys illuminate the perception of well-being, they do not explain the systematic variations in the distribution of multiple deprivation and social disadvantages. For this we need to revert to the analysis of the constraints on life-chances. Multiple deprivation arises from an inability to gain access to those resources which have the greatest influence on life chances: these are employment, housing and education. In turn, the ability to secure this access is influenced by social class, gender, race and location.

The most systematic empirical research on multiple deprivation has probably been carried out by Berthoud (1983) using special tabulations from the 1975 *General Household Survey*. Although somewhat dated, the results can be seen as a statement on multiple deprivation at the end of the period of One Nation politics. Berthoud's index of multiple deprivation is based on six main elements which are linked to the main dimensions of inequality which we have stressed. These are education (no qualifications), family (lone parents or separated or four or more children), housing (more than one person per room or lacking basic facilities), income (below 140 per cent of supplementary benefit entitlement), sickness (long-term illness or not working through sickness), and work (non-skilled manual, unemployed or low earnings).

Nearly one family in 11 experienced more than one-half of these problems and 50 000 experienced all six of them. Therefore, Berthoud saw the population falling into three groups. In the middle was a large number of persons suffering from one, two or even three disadvantages and who certainly face important inequalities. However, this was less significant than the polarisation between the one-quarter of the population who suffered from no disadvantages and the one in 11 who suffered from at least four. This polarisation has undoubtedly increased since 1975 as the analyses of the individual dimensions of inequalities have shown, especially the growing numbers in receipt of income support.

The results also showed that the larger the number of indicators in terms of which a family was deprived, then the greater the probability that it also experienced other problems; in other words, disadvantages were cumulative. The seriously disadvantaged were often multiply disadvantaged. Multiple disadvantage was most severe amongst those who experienced income, work or educational disadvantages (see Table 9.1). They were twice as likely to suffer

Table 9.1   The experience of disadvantage in the UK in 1975

Experience of specific problem	% experiencing four or five other problems
Income	65
Work	84
Education	71
Family	31
Housing	36
Sickness	36

Source: Berthoud (1983)

four or five other forms of disadvantage as are those who experienced specific inequalities in terms of the family, housing or sickness dimensions. This strongly underlines the class basis of multiple deprivation.

Berthoud's work is useful because the analysis was taken a stage further to consider the incidence of multiple disadvantage amongst particular social groups. Age emerged as an important criterion and the frail elderly were

Table 9.2 Vulnerability to multiple disadvantage, 1975

	% experiencing disadvantage
By age	
Up to 59	1
60–64	2
64–74	5
Over 74	8
By sex: non-married people under 60	
Men without children	19
Men with children	44
Women without children	31
Women with children	78
By occupation	
Professional/managerial	6
Other non-manual	11
Skilled manual	15
Semi-skilled manual	23
Unskilled manual	32
By region	
South West	19
West Midlands	19
South East	20
North West	22
Scotland	22
Yorkshire	24
East Midlands	26
North	29
Wales	29
East Anglia	30
By ethnic group	
White	22
West Indian[*]	41
Other non-white	26

[*] Term used in original
Source: Berthoud (1983, Table 7.1)

highly prone to illness, low incomes and poor housing. In the context of a marked ageing of the population, it was significant that those aged over 75 were eight times more likely to suffer from multiple disadvantage than were those aged less than 59 (see Table 9.2). There was also a high risk of disadvantage amongst children and in early adulthood, especially with respect to overcrowding and low incomes (in single-parent families). However, this was not as great as the substantial disadvantages of old age. Some of the disadvantages of old age may be unavoidable, such as sickness. However the experience of frailty is conditioned by that of class. The ability to buy private medical care or private home nursing can ease some of the difficulties associated with sickness. Low incomes and poor housing are also not inevitable in old age; much depends on the type of tenure occupied, on the availability of occupational or private pensions and on the accumulation of wealth. What this suggests is that poverty and multiple disadvantage are class-based, but that the symptoms are probably more painfully exposed in later life than they are even during the working life.

In Berthoud's analysis women were also more prone to multiple disadvantage than men, especially if they had children (see Table 9.2). Not least this is because the great majority of single parents are women, and lone mothers are especially vulnerable to multiple disadvantage. This constrains their employment possibilities and further exaggerates the inequalities that most women experience with respect to jobs and incomes. Again any such conclusions have to be modified to take into account the prevalent influence of social class. It is unusual for even single-parent, middle-class mothers to experience multiple disadvantage. They may well suffer from a number of social disadvantages but they do usually have the cushion of education and higher incomes (possibly in the form of a paternity contribution from a middle-class husband). Working-class single mothers often have no such cushion.

There was also a racial dimension to multiple disadvantage in Berthoud's analysis. Afro-Caribbean families were twice as likely as white families to suffer from this (see Table 9.2). Housing problems, low incomes and poor educational achievements were not only widespread amongst Afro-Caribbean families but they also tend to coincide. In very crude terms it means that they were almost as prone to multiple disadvantage as were the very elderly. Berthoud's analysis did not identify such a high risk of multiple disadvantage amongst Asian families. Whilst this was partly a function of the limited data available on race, it also reflected the considerable polarisation which existed between different sub-groups of Asian families, especially those of Indian compared to those of Bangladeshi origin. There is a growing number of middle-class Asian families whose experiences are very different from those of the multiply-disadvantaged majority of working-class Asians.

The discussion thus far has shown strong evidence of an association between social class and multiple disadvantage. Berthoud's analysis was based on occupational status rather than class but there was a strong inverse relationship between this and multiple disadvantage. Not only was this true of multiple disadvantage but also of every separate measure of disadvantage. Consequently 'no theory about the nature and causation of social disadvantage can be held valid without an explicit explanation of the role of social class' (Berthoud 1983).

The UK is a socially polarised country and, as was shown in the previous two chapters, this has strong spatial manifestations. As there are North–South class differences (as well as North–South unemployment differences), it is to be expected that there are regional variations in the incidence of multiple disadvantage. The greatest difference is between Northern Ireland and the rest of the UK, but there are inadequate data to consider this systematically. However, Berthoud's index did show that the lowest levels were in the South East, the South West and the West Midlands (but it is doubtful whether the latter would hold in the 1990s). In contrast, Wales, the North and East Anglia (but again probably not in the 1990s) had the highest levels. There are indisputable differences between North and South but inner cities are the locales with which multiple disadvantage or deprivation are usually associated.

9.2.1 The inner cities: the visible scars of multiple deprivation

Discussions of the UK's inner cities often invoke images of poverty, deprivation and physical decay. 'Inner-city problems' are not a creation of Two Nations politics for they certainly existed in the nineteenth century and more recently have been recorded and analysed in a number of reports dating from the 1960s. However, the civil disturbances in the inner cities in the 1980s, especially in 1981 and 1985, have brought these areas to greater prominence in the debate about poverty and inequality in the UK.

Spatial concentrations of poverty are more obvious than is poverty which is diffused throughout the population. But do geographical concentrations exacerbate the conditions in any way? It can be argued that geographical concentration represents an intensification of deprivation; the inhabitants of these areas experience collective deprivation. 'It is not a matter of multiple deprivation – of many people having many problems separately. It is rather an accumulated form of deprivation experienced by those living in inner city areas, psychic as well as material. Collective deprivation starts with inner-city residents' perception of their environment' (Davies 1981). The image and, often, the reality is of neglect and dereliction in the physical landscape. This is exacerbated by the widening gap between residents' awareness of conditions elsewhere in the city or society and the conditions which they see around them.

The emphasis on inner cities does not imply that only small numbers of people are involved, living in isolated pockets within the conurbations. Around the end of the era of One Nation politics, as many as 4 million people were living in inner city areas, approximately one in every 14 of the population (Smith 1979). A substantial proportion of the population live in areas where multiple deprivation is considered to be the norm, even if there are many individuals who are relatively well-off. They all suffer from the same poor environment, lack of jobs, and educational opportunities and services in these areas. Whether or not this leads to a self-reproducing culture of poverty is contentious; but it certainly leads to a collective awareness of living in a deprived area. The residents of these areas become categorised as impoverished and deprived in the eyes of the rest of the urban community, irrespective of their personal circumstances. This leads to disadvantage in terms of applying for jobs, houses or credit.

The most systematic study of urban deprivation in the 1980s used a number of indicators for Parliamentary constituencies in Britain (Sim 1984). This is a scale which allows inner and outer urban areas to be distinguished. Different types of deprivation are found in different parts of the UK (see Figure 9.1). However, there is considerable overlapping of different types of deprivation in inner London constituencies such as Brent, Hackney and Hammersmith. Glasgow also suffers from a marked overlapping of different types of deprivation. This does not necessarily imply that there is either multiple or collective deprivation in these areas but it suggests that it is likely. Other cities which feature prominently in this analysis are Liverpool, Manchester and Birmingham. Northern Ireland was not included in this particular study but there is ample evidence elsewhere. Belfast is not only the most deprived city in the UK but also, with the possible exception of Naples, in the European Union.

Although the inner areas of the conurbations are the locales which are most severely affected by deprivation, there are some notable concentrations in outer urban areas. Places such as Knowsley North in Merseyside have very high unemployment as do parts of outer Glasgow, and outer London areas such as Norwood and Ealing. Many of these areas are dominated by large council housing estates which were used to rehouse low-income families in the One Nation politics of the 1960s and proved unprivatisable in the 1980s and 1990s in the succeeding Two Nations era. This underlines an important point. There is nothing unique or timeless in the incidence of multiple deprivation in the inner-cities. Rather it is a particular spatial manifestation of underlying inequalities in UK society. The fact that it appears as an inner city problem is very much a reflection of the contingencies of the 1970s and 1980s. In other time periods the manifestation of multiple deprivation may be different. For example, in the 1930s it was more evident as a regional 'problem' and in the 1980s and 1990s it has become increasingly evident in outer urban areas.

At heart the crisis of the inner cities is economic. Structural changes in the UK economy in the post-war period have led to a decline in many of the traditional manufacturing industries in these areas. Many of the industries were dock-based as in Liverpool and London's East End. In addition there was also

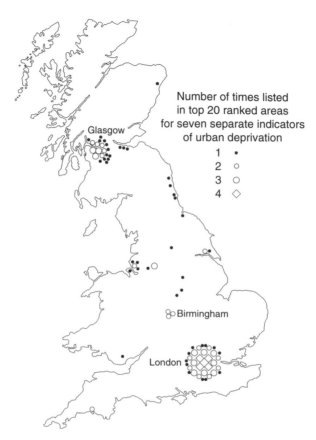

Figure 9.1 Parliamentary constituencies with high levels of urban deprivation

Source: Sim (1984)

widespread deindustrialisation in the inner areas of cities such as Birmingham, linked to the decline of car production and other traditional industries. At the same time there was a failure to attract new investment in growth sectors such as electronics. The ageing of industrial plant and a failure to reinvest were also important, as were changes in production technologies. Deskilling led to decreased dependence on unskilled workers and greater demand for cheap and flexible labour, which encouraged firms to seek out new labour reserves in other areas. The result was a high rate of plant closure and some out-movement of manufacturing firms.

There was some economic growth in the inner cities but it was primarily based on the service sector. Offices provided new jobs but these tended to be polarised between professional and clerical posts, with a semi-visible army of contract catering and cleaning workers in the background. There was also growth of jobs in warehousing and distribution but these were mostly poorly paid. As a result, there was a radical change in inner-city labour markets from the 1960s. This affected the number and types of jobs which were available, and the salaries which were on offer. In general, it meant that there were lower wages (compared to traditional skilled manual jobs), and rising unemployment. Better paid professional jobs were mostly taken by middle-class commuters, while inner-city residents were left with no or low-paid employment. Furthermore, unemployment was not spread evenly throughout the community. The most severely affected were young school-leavers, middle-aged and elderly men, the unskilled and black and Asian people. As a result, there was a large group of young people in the inner cities in the 1970s, 1980s and 1990s who were or had been unemployed for a substantial period of time. In absolute terms most were white but there was disproportionately high unemployment amongst black and Asian youth. This was an important contributory factor to the civil disturbances of 1981 and 1985.

Economic and social decline in the inner cities led to a high rate of outmigration. Many of those who could move out to the more prosperous suburbs with better job opportunities and more attractive environments did so (see Chapter Eight). In some of the more favoured inner areas – such as Islington in London – their places were taken by inmigrant middle-class families and individuals. This process of gentrification (Smith and Williams 1986) was particularly associated with the growth of Yuppies as a social expression of polarisation during the Thatcher boom years. The social changes have been particularly spectacular in East London's Docklands; one of the earliest and most prominent inmigrants was David Owen, one-time SDP leader, who bought a house adjoining the Thames in Limehouse. The arrival of such middle-class newcomers powerfully underlines the differences in life chances and wealth between them and the traditional residents of these areas. It also emphasises that inner-city 'problems' are firmly grounded in absolute and relative inequalities of wealth.

Outmigration was not an option for all inner-city residents. Instead poor access to housing – one of the most important aspects of their restricted life chances – meant that many families were caught in a housing 'trap'. High house prices and low incomes excluded many families from home ownership and they became dependent on renting. The stock of private rented dwellings is limited, declining and largely confined to older houses in inner cities. In addition, local authority tenants are mostly restricted to moving to other council properties located in the same municipality. In the metropolitan areas this means that they have few opportunities to move to the outer areas. Both sets of tenants are therefore restricted in their abilities to 'escape' the inner cities.

Social polarisation in UK cities has had serious implications for the distribution of multiple deprivation and for the life chances of those who live in these areas. The result has been that 'a pattern has emerged of a more unequal society as between a majority in a secure attachment to a still prosperous country and a minority in marginal economic and social conditions – the former moving into the suburban locations of the newer economy of a "green and pleasant land", the latter tending to be trapped into the old provincial industrial cities and their displaced fragments of peripheral council estates' (Halsey 1987).

The inner-city areas of collective deprivation are certainly not the creation of Two Nations politics but it is relevant to query whether the extent and the depth of such problems have increased or decreased in the 1980s and early 1990s. There is a lack of precise data to answer this question. However, the discussion elsewhere in this book has shown that inequalities have increased with respect to several of the separate dimensions of inequality. Homelessness has increased, the most desirable council house properties have been sold and real incomes have polarised. This has to be seen along-side diverging standards of provision in public and private health care and education. It is therefore impossible to escape the conclusion that multiple deprivation has increased as a consequence of the Two Nations project.

The factor which has contributed more than any other to an increase in mul-tiple deprivation is unemployment. Unemployment rates have risen in the UK in response to global economic conditions and deliberate government policy. This meant, for example, that the number of unemployed living in the inner cities increased considerably in the 1980s. It also meant that the proportion who were long-term unemployed (over one year) increased from 25 per cent in 1979 to 41 per cent in 1985; this subsequently fell to 33 per cent in spring 1993, although numerous changes in definitions cast doubt on whether there has been a real decline in the proportions unemployed. Unemployment, and especially long-term unemployment, are often at the root of multiple depri-vation and multiple inequality. In this respect the conclusion that inner-city multiple inequalities have increased is unavoidable.

Some concrete data to confirm this general conclusion are presented in a study of London (Low Pay Unit 1987). The extent of multiple deprivation in London was considerable even in the early 1980s. Furthermore the variations between the most privileged and the most disadvantaged areas of London were enormous; this is illustrated by a comparison of wards in terms of four indi-cators of deprivation (see Table 9.3). At one extreme are wards such as Spital-fields and St Mary (in Tower Hamlets) where one-fifth of the population are unemployed, between one sixth and one-quarter of households are over-crowded, three-quarters lack cars and less than one in 20 are home owners. In contrast, there are outer-London wards such as Selsdon and Cranham West where there is virtually no unemployment or overcrowding, almost everyone owns their homes and only one in eight households lack cars.

Given these differences, it is alarming that standards of living between the poor and the rich diverged in London more quickly than they had in the rest

Table 9.3 Multiple deprivation in London in 1981 (rank order of London wards) (%)

	Unemployed	Over-crowded	Not home owners	Not car owners
Most deprived				
1. Spitalfields (Tower Hamlets)	21.9	28.3	96.5	79.6
2. St Mary (Tower Hamlets)	19.5	16.5	95.2	74.0
Least deprived				
754 Selsdon (Croydon)	2.6	0.5	6.7	13.5
755 Cranham West (Havering)	3.2	0.9	4.1	12.4

Source: Townsend, et al. (1987)

of the UK in the 1980s. Not only was there divergence in relative terms but there was also a fall in the real spending power of the poorest quarter of the population during the first two Thatcher administrations. Between 1979 and 1985 the gross household incomes of the poorest tenth of London's population declined by 17 per cent. Even the gross household incomes of the poorest quarter of the population fell by 8 per cent.

The impoverishment of a large proportion of London's population was linked to high rates of unemployment. With 400 000 unemployed in 1986, London had the largest concentration of unemployment of any major city in the industrial world. This was not distributed evenly within London. Even at the level of the boroughs, unemployment rates varied from 5.9 per cent in Kingston to 22.7 per cent in Hackney (Low Pay Unit 1987). But at ward level some areas, such as Angell in Lambeth, had unemployment rates as high as 36 per cent. Moreover, the gap between areas had grown considerably during the Thatcher years. In 1979 the unemployment rate in the worst-affected ward was 2.4 times higher than in the least-affected ward; by 1986 this ratio had widened to 3.8. In other words, the probability of being unemployed was almost four times higher in parts of inner London than in parts of outer London. Social class and labour market position would again seem to be the keys to life chances and multiple disadvantage.

In the 1990s, the inner city areas may not have been as severely affected by the recession as some of the more prosperous areas of the South East, but the cyclical – and perhaps structural – rise in unemployment did come on top of already deep-set multiple disadvantages. In 1991, for example, more than 20 per cent of the population were receiving income support in Hackney, Hammersmith, Haringey, Islington, Lambeth, Lewisham, Newham, Southwark and Tower Hamlets in London. And in many instances these proportions were higher in 1991 than they had been in 1983 in the midst of an earlier economic recession (see Table 9.5).

9.2.2   *Deprivation need not be urban: the rural areas of the UK*

The publicity given to urban deprivation in the 1980s tended to obscure the fact that multiple disadvantages are not confined to such areas. The underlying roots of multiple disadvantage are to be found in the way in which society is organised, especially its class relationships. Multiple disadvantage is experienced by individuals and families and where they live influences the precise form of this rather than its root causes. This can be illustrated by considering rural areas although, it must be emphasised, we could equally well have looked at suburban areas.

Until the 1970s rural areas were usually portrayed as idyllic, pleasant, attractive and prosperous (see Phillips and Williams 1984, Chapter 1). This view was coloured by the romanticism which is attached to rural areas, which were often contrasted with the real and imagined horrors of urban areas. This romanticism is to be found in literature from the nineteenth century onwards, in government reports and in the popular press. It has serious consequences in two ways. Firstly, the seeming absence of poverty in rural areas reinforces the idea that multiple inequality is a specifically urban rather than an inherent feature of society. Secondly, it leads to there being hidden poverty and deprivation in rural areas. Because such areas are not seen to be experiencing the same degree or intensity of visible poverty as are urban areas, there is a mistaken assumption that there is no deprivation in the countryside.

Useful research on rural deprivation was undertaken on Scotland in the early stages of Two Nations politics (Millar 1980), using both area-level and individual household data (Table 9.4). Small-area data from the population census suggested that 4 per cent of multiply-deprived areas were found in rural areas but a household-level analysis showed that they contained about 14 per cent of all multiply-deprived households. Although not highly visible, multiple deprivation was widespread.

Many of the symptoms of deprivation in rural areas are similar to those observed in urban areas. The affected zones have experienced economic decline, population losses, reduced service provision, a lack of investment, the

Table 9.4   Multiple deprivation in Scotland in the late 1970s (%)

Area type	All Scottish households	Multiply-deprived households	Multiply-deprived areas
Major cities	37	61	65
Other urban settlements	40	25	31
Rural areas	23	14	4
Total	100	100	100

Source: Millar (1980)

operation of housing 'traps' and low morale. In addition, several other symptoms of deprivation are commonplace in rural areas. These include inaccessibility and isolation and a lack of infrastructure.

The most obvious form of rural deprivation is opportunity deprivation (compared to opportunities available elsewhere in the UK). This includes education, health and social services, jobs, shops and information. Closures of village schools and shops have actually led to a decline in the availability of such services in the post-war period. Even if the services are available, they are likely to be of poor quality, to be expensive and to lack choice compared to urban areas. The extent of the problem is considerable. In England and Wales alone there are some 3.3 million people living in settlements with less than 1000 population: of these some 1.4 million live more than 14 km from their nearest main town. Many of the difficulties result from central and local government policies begun in the One Nation era but subsequently intensified, which have sought to 'rationalise' service provision in the face of public expenditure restrictions and, sometimes, declining populations. The difficulties also result from mobility deprivation.

Mobility deprivation is the most distinctive form of rural deprivation. It can affect a community as a whole, as for example when a rail or bus service is withdrawn. However, depending on their access to private transport, some individuals are more affected than others. This is partly a matter of income and the ability to buy access to shops, doctors and leisure facilities in distant towns. However, this is only one dimension of transport poverty. For the 'transport poor' also include the elderly, housewives and young people who lack access to cars during all or part of the day. This reflects one of our earlier conclusions: class, income and unemployment may be the keys to multiple disadvantages, but these are most acutely experienced by women and by certain age groups, especially the elderly.

Given the emphasis on accessibility and isolation in rural deprivation, remote areas are usually characterised as being relatively deprived. However, severely deprived households also exist even in accessible and attractive rural areas, such as Sussex and Suffolk, which are normally characterised as the loci of middle-class individualised consumption. Individuals and households are deprived because of their positions in the class system and in the labour market, or because of their age or through being confined at home in one-car households. Living in the accessible countryside does not necessarily ameliorate these basic conditions. Indeed, the very presence of the new middle class with its individualistic and privatised consumption patterns can exacerbate the problem. Most obviously, they can outbid locals in the housing market. Furthermore, if they send their children to private schools or use private medical care, this may lead to a more rapid withdrawal of public services. There is, therefore, a direct link between the activities of the middle class and the multiple deprivation of some working-class households. This can be seen both in the overall division of income and in their competing interests within a given area.

9.2.3 *Multiple deprivation matters*

Multiple deprivation matters because a large number of people in the UK face a number of interlinked barriers blocking their access to improved life chances. It also matters because, judging from the evidence on class mobility, it may be transmitted between generations. The evidence on transmitted deprivation is patchy but largely unequivocal (Millar 1980). Low incomes tend to be transmitted between generations and this is linked to the way in which class conditions educational achievements and employment prospects. Children are seven times more likely to leave school without qualifications if their parents had only an elementary school education than if they had post-secondary-school education. Moreover, the inheritance of wealth – especially housing – is also a major channel for transmitting inequalities between generations. The expansion of home ownership in the post-1945 period, coupled with house price inflation in the 1970s and 1980s, has had a particularly strong influence in this respect. However, the collapse of house prices in the 1990s has dented this particular channel of wealth accumulation and transmission, although there are alternative means such as personal equity plans and trusts.

Class also influences the transmission of life chances in other ways. There is, for example, continuity in housing deprivation. Whilst 11 per cent of the adult children of parents living in houses lacking basic amenities also lacked such amenities themselves, only 4 per cent of the adult children of parents who had not lacked basic housing amenities did so. Mental and physical health are also influenced by intergenerational transmission for both social and genetic reasons.

There are no data on the intergenerational transmission of multiple deprivation or multiple disadvantage *per se*. The same individuals do not necessarily suffer from all these forms of disadvantage and it may therefore be questioned whether there is a strong degree of intergenerational transmission of multiple disadvantage. However, the way in which each of these indicators of deprivation is linked to social class – which is strongly transmitted between generations - makes it difficult not to assume that there is intergenerational inheritance of multiple deprivation. Those born into multiply disadvantaged households are themselves disproportionately likely to become multiply disadvantaged in adulthood. This reinforces the evidence that deprivation has strong roots in the structural inequalities in UK society.

Multiple deprivation also matters because of the way in which it is linked to the notion of an underclass. Conservatives have used this term to describe those who have become party to what they term the 'dependency culture'. In other words, the 'blame' for the multiple deprivation of inner city areas lies in the culture of the individual communities. Whilst this argument originated on the right wing of the Conservative Party, it has gained widespread adherence as part of the philosophy of Two Nations politics. For example, in November 1992 Kenneth Clarke in a lecture to the Tory Reform Group began by acknowledging that the existence of an underclass in decaying inner-city areas was one of the most formidable challenges facing Western democracies in the 1990s. He emphasised that even if there is economic growth 'it is not automatically the case that it will trickle down so that the inner city resident will get a fair share of it'. However, his response to this was straight out of the standard repertoire of the New Right: 'Public expenditure is not enough. Lateral thinking aimed at changing the culture of deprived groups and deprived areas towards the enterprise economy and active citizenship is required' (quoted in *Financial Times*, 25 November 1992).

Our understanding of the term 'underclass' is different, and we use it as a description of a part of society that has been trapped into structural poverty, long-term unemployment and deprivation (see Robinson and Gregson 1992). This is no accident of course but is a form of social closure which is the outcome of the organisation of society and economy (Rodger 1992). At one level the concept of the underclass has been useful as a means of attracting attention to the debates on poverty. However, we also agree with Robinson and Gregson's (1992, 44) hypothesis that in the 1980s, 'poverty has changed; something has happened to create a group of people trapped, isolated and cut off from the rest of society'. What has happened is of course the dismantling of parts of the welfare state, and the redistribution of income in favour of the advantaged. But equally important in the growth of the underclass has been rising unemployment and insecurity of employment, which Robinson and Gregson, and other commentators such as Morris (1993), believe are major – but not the only – pathways into poverty and multiple deprivation. Having thus become entrapped in the underclass, the prospects for escape appear even bleaker given the rise in unemployment, and changes in labour markets, in the 1980s and 1990s.

According to Cottingham (1982), people in the underclass share a number of experiences: severe income deprivation, unemployment, low skills, poor access to education and welfare services, ghettoisation in parts of the city, poor health, and a tendency to intergenerational poverty. There are also racialised and gendered dimensions with disproportionate numbers of women and people from ethnic minorities being found in the underclass. In other words, the underclass is an expression of the permanency – both structural and at the levels of individuals – of multiple deprivation in the UK. It is therefore all the more relevant to consider the policies which the state has adopted to ameliorate multiple deprivation in both the One Nation and Two Nations politics periods.

9.3 Multiple deprivation and state policies: remedies and gestures

Although the Beveridge report had not highlighted the need for state intervention to reduce or eliminate multiple deprivation, it recognised that there was a strong interlinking of different individual needs. Its target for the welfare state was the elimination of what it saw as five major areas of blight: want, ignorance, idleness, illness and squalor.

The response of the 1945 Labour government was to establish a number of new and revamped forms of social provision. These included income supplements and sickness insurance, the National Health Service, educational reforms, a large-scale public housing programme and macro-economic regulation of the economy to minimise unemployment. Although the full programme was not as comprehensive as that recommended by the Beveridge Report, it constituted a radical and impressive array of measures. It was, without doubt, the single most important landmark in the creation of the welfare state which was one of the cornerstones of One Nation politics. At the time it had no rival in Western Europe in terms of its scope and egalitarian tendencies. Even so, as we have argued earlier in this volume, it was limited in that the attack that it made upon class inequalities was gender and race blind in many respects, and had no prescription for attacking the multiple character of disadvantage.

In the 1950s and early 1960s there was no serious attempt to question either the legitimacy or the efficiency of the welfare state. Indeed, during two decades of economic growth and growing mass consumption, combined with a historical redistribution of wealth (see Chapter 3), there was an assumption that it was well on the way to eliminating poverty and deprivation, if not social inequalities. Furthermore, there was a broad Labour/Conservative consensus concerning the importance of these achievements. These were only really challenged in the 1960s when growing difficulties in the national economy became translated into stresses within British society, especially as the result of rising unemployment. There was, in effect, the 'rediscovery of poverty'.

The response of the Wilson government in the 1960s to the rediscovery of poverty, and to its essentially multiple character, was conditioned by the increasingly apparent crisis in the UK economy. In response to the pressures to reduce public expenditure, there was a growing lobby on the right in favour of greater selectivity in the welfare state, concentrating resources on those in greatest need. However, this implied greater reliance on means-testing and a move away from the principle of universalism. Selectivism had long been opposed by those in the Labour Party who had enduring and bitter memories of the harsh use of the means test during the inter-war years. As the main aim of such tests is to exclude applicants, the poor are more likely to be seen as the needy seeking charity rather than as individuals receiving their rights as citizens in a just society. The Labour Party at the time was still wedded to the Beveridge Report and unwilling to accept a substantial shift to greater selectivism, although we can note that it has returned to ponder this question in the 1990s. Instead Harold Wilson's government opted for the spatial targeting of policies. As poverty and deprivation had been identified as being particularly acute in urban areas in the 1960s, this led to the development of specifically urban policies. Any such approach implicitly, and wrongly, suggests that deprivation has a limited spatial distribution, although it has the political advantage of offering more tangible objectives for more visible policies.

Urban policy assumed a number of forms, all characterised by the concentration of additional resources on particular (inner) urban areas. Educational Priority Areas were introduced in 1968 along with the Urban Aid Programme. Area-based housing policies were also introduced: especially General Improvement Areas (1969) and Housing Action Areas (1974). The most important of these policies was probably the 1977 Policy for the Inner Cities. There were to be three tiers of special assistance to deprived urban areas, most notably seven inner-city partnerships in London, Birmingham, Liverpool, Manchester and Newcastle–Gateshead. This was important in two ways. First, the political weight attached to the launch of the programme underlined the considerable priority which was now attached to area-based policies. Secondly, the inner-city partnerships in the metropolitan areas were established as joint ventures between local and central government. This was to be a portend of a more radical attack on local autonomy by the Thatcher administration.

How are we to evaluate area-based policies? On the one hand they are preferable to greater selectivism. Welfare provision is still seen as a matter of social rights. It reaches deprived individuals by virtue of their being resident in a priority area, not because they as individuals have been subject to means-testing. In practice, however, area-based policies were often inspired by the objectives of limiting public expenditure whilst allowing governments to appear to be active in combating poverty. This approach was epitomised by Michael Heseltine's high-profile appointment as Minister for Merseyside. In short, area-based policies were an effective means of legitimation for the state. More fundamental was the implicit assumption that multiple deprivation was a localised and geographically concentrated phenomenon. This is patently misleading; there are deprived people living outside of priority areas whilst there are non-deprived people living within them. Indeed, deprivation is so widespread that, in order to delimit areas which encompassed even one-half of all deprived people, it would be necessary to include almost one-half of all the areas in the UK. Above all, this exposes the weakness of trying to tackle structural inequalities via area-based policies.

9.3.1 Deprivation, inner cities and Two Nations politics

At first sight the area-based policies of the Thatcher governments could be seen as a continuation of those which had been developed by previous Tory and Labour administrations. It can be argued that if the political rhetoric of Thatcherism is stripped away then the most obvious of the 'urban' policies of the 1980s – such as Enterprise Zones – are continuations of the policies of the 1970s. Such a judgement would be profoundly wrong: there has been a decisive reshaping of inner-city policies within the framework of Two Nations politics.

Inner cities have been profoundly affected by two of the major ideological planks of Thatcherism, individualism and deregulation. These are translated into a belief that the 'problem' of the inner cities is the lack of individual self-help and initiative. Except for Keith Joseph, no government minister has tried to relate this explicitly to the idea of the culture of poverty, which implies that individuals are socialised into low expectations and failure. Instead Mrs Thatcher's governments emphasised the need to remove constraints on individual initiative. This is associated, at an ideological level, with arguments about the need to reduce public intervention and to allow free enterprise and market forces to revive the inner cities.

It is within this context that Conservative area-based policies must be seen. The most important of these are the Enterprise Zones, Freeports, Urban Development Corporations (UDCs), and City Challenge. Enterprise Zones were heralded by Geoffrey Howe in 1978 as 'embodiments of laissez faire whose success in regenerating run down industrial and inner-city areas would help win the political "debate", against the alternative strategy of more state intervention as the solution to the UK's decline' (Anderson 1990, 471). When they were eventually implemented in 1981, they were presented as special economic areas which offered less regulated environments for firms. Planning controls were reduced in these areas, although – contrary to earlier conceptions – most health, safety and other regulations remained in force. There was also no abandonment of state intervention; instead, there was a benevolent financial environment with, for example, firms being excluded from paying rates during their first 10 years of operation. Freeports provided special zones where imported goods could be processed and then re-exported free of customs duties; six were set up in the 1980s.

UDCs were initially designated for Merseyside and London Docklands, and a further eight were established later. These strongly interventionist and non-elected agencies were initially charged with redeveloping derelict industrial areas and later with encouraging employment in them. They were given special exemption from many forms of local government control and planning legislation, the administration of which were transferred to the UDCs themselves. The City Challenge initiative was announced in 1991, and 11 authorities were chosen as 'pacemakers' in the first round in 1992, followed by a further 20 in 1993. This differs from previous initiatives in that there is greater emphasis on partnership between local and central government, and between the public, private and voluntary sectors. There are also organisational differences in the simplification of the grant scheme and the devolution of greater power to the executive of the programmes. It is too early to pass judgement on this particular initiative but it is already clear that it is flawed. First, it does not represent increased government commitment to the inner cities for the money made available has been top-sliced from existing programmes. Secondly, it uses the mechanism of a competition between authorities as a means of allocating resources to meet urban needs (Parkinson 1993). In a sense, therefore, it represents a further extension of Two Nations notions of enterprise and competition, and equally of a nation divided by the state into winners and losers, rather than assessed in terms of need.

Each of these programmes can be criticised in terms of its specific objectives but the extent to which these have been achieved is also debatable. They have all been designed to create deregulated economic environments for private enterprise. It is assumed that this will lead to economic growth the benefits of which will percolate down, eventually, to all members of the community in the form of increased opportunities for individuals. This makes a number of assumptions about the types of jobs created and the type of labour which is demanded by these firms; it is probably not the multiply-deprived who live in the inner-cities who benefit. These policies also represent a shift away from the previous attempt to tackle inner-city problems via an array of social and economic policies. In other words, there is even less explicit recognition of structural inequalities than there had been in the area-based policies of the 1970s. Instead, the Thatcherite response to the problems of inner city areas was to incorporate these within its low-wage and flexible labour market strategy for the economic revival of the UK. This is illustrated by the neglect of, for example, race-based disadvantages. Munt (1991, 199) comments that, 'the emphasis on economic objectives, together with the failure to identify the specificity of the racial dimension, had a finite effect in tackling what are multi-dimensional urban problems. Race-related expenditure within individual programmes had been more incidental than intrinsic to urban policy.'

In our view these initiatives, especially the UDCs, are probably better conceived of as attempts to bolster speculative property development than as specific policies to deal with multiple deprivation in British cities. Property-led regeneration may achieve physical redevelopment but its 'trickle-down' employment impact is limited. The process is also heavily dependent on the vicissitudes of the property market. This was clearly illustrated by the stalling of the redevelopment process in London's Docklands following the collapse of the UK property market in the early 1990s (see Figure 9.2). In so far as the real importance of these initiatives was symbolic and ideological, the failure of many of the property schemes in the Docklands in the 1990s reflected the general bankruptcy of Two Nations urban policies.

Perhaps the most telling statistical indictment of the inner-city policies of Two Nations politics was the report produced by the Policy Studies Institute (1992). It concluded that while there had been some improvements, the gap between deprived areas and the rest of the UK had actually widened in some respects. It catalogued a bleak list of increasing social divides between deprived urban areas and the rest of the country (see Table 9.5):

● the worsening of pupil–teacher rations against the national trend

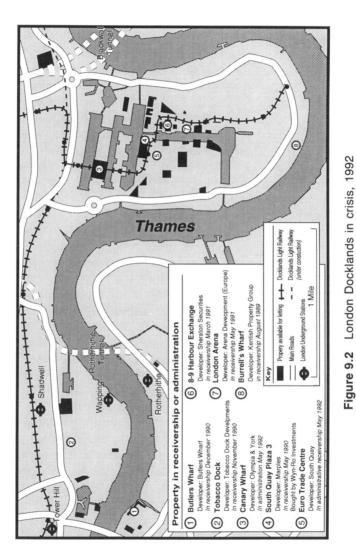

Figure 9.2 London Docklands in crisis, 1992

Source: Cluttons 'Docklands Office Survey'

Table 9.5 The patterns of poverty, 1983–91

	Unemployment ('000)		Income support (% of estimated population)		Homelessness (per 1000 households*)	
	1983	1991	1983/85	1989/91	1983	1990
Scotland						
Clydebank	4.0	2.8	—	—	1.3	4.6
Glasgow	75.7	39.8	—	—	1.8	3.1
Inverclyde	8.0	5.7	—	—	1.1	1.1
Monklands	9.7	5.4	—	—	0.9	1.1
North West Region						
Blackburn	9.5	6.7	—	—	0.5	3.5
Burnley	6.2	3.8	—	—	1.0	1.1
Knowsley	21.1	12.7	32.9	33.8	2.1	1.3
Liverpool	56.2	40.0	34.4	36.2	—	2.6
Manchester	43.6	32.4	22.2	32.0	0.9	13.8
Preston	9.0	6.2	—	—	0.8	1.7
Rochdale	14.5	9.4	22.0	16.2	0.5	3.5
Salford	19.0	12.3	25.0	22.3	1.9	1.2
West Midlands Region						
Birmingham	94.3	66.9	22.2	23.9	3.5	4.1
Coventry	27.9	17.5	23.1	19.3	0.8	1.3
Sandwell	28.3	17.6	25.6	20.2	0.3	1.1
Wolverhampton	22.7	15.3	24.7	21.9	1.1	—
Wales						
Blaenau Gwent	6.4	3.4	—	—	1.3	2.3
Rhondda	5.3	4.0	—	—	1.9	0.4
Northern Region						
Middlesbrough	16.1	9.7	—	—	1.1	3.5
Yorkshire and Humberside Region						
Bradford	30.9	23.1	21.3	18.5	1.1	2.2
Kingston upon Hull	23.6	17.8	—	—	0.7	—
East Midlands Region						
Leicester	22.1	16.7	—	—	1.6	3.3
Nottingham	21.6	19.0	—	—	1.7	4.1
Greater London						
Brent	15.3	16.2	15.4	18.5	4.9	3.1
Greenwich	13.3	13.3	19.4	18.8	1.5	4.0
Hackney	18.6	18.4	29.5	32.4	3.0	6.4
Hammersmith and Fulham	10.7	10.1	20.8	20.0	3.4	4.7
Haringey	15.5	18.0	23.1	27.2	5.8	6.2
Islington	14.7	14.2	28.4	26.5	7.4	7.1
Kensington and Chelsea	8.5	6.3	17.5	15.9	3.3	2.0
Lambeth	23.0	22.1	27.4	28.9	3.9	6.4
Lewisham	15.7	17.3	21.5	22.1	5.5	3.2
Newham	15.9	16.9	27.4	27.3	3.4	3.4
Southwark	18.2	18.8	29.0	27.6	3.8	2.7
Tower Hamlets	15.8	14.3	34.7	32.6	3.2	3.4
Wandsworth	15.3	14.7	20.8	18.1	1.6	2.2

*Households accepted as homeless by local authorities in second quarter of year

Source: Policy Studies Institute (1992)

- people from deprived areas were less likely to be on Employment Training schemes and were more likely to remain unemployed after leaving these
- the proportion of families qualifying for income support was greater in1989/91 than in 1983/85
- premature death amongst adults and infant mortality rates were higher than elsewhere in the UK
- unemployment had remained the same or had risen in two-thirds of the deprived areas
- the proportion of the population who were homeless had risen in virtually every single authority

Enterprise Zones, Freeports and UDCs also have in common the fact that they bypass traditional local authority influence on development and public expenditure within their areas. This has to be seen in context of the systematic attack on local government autonomy under the Thatcher administration. It is part of the process of restructuring of the state itself, of political centralisation which removes one of the checks by local communities on executive power. This is seen most starkly in the way in which the London Docklands Development Corporation has often proceeded to redevelop east London in the face of strong opposition from Labour-controlled local authorities. This is a struggle not only between central and local power but also between the interests of developers and the local community.

These are not the only instruments of centralisation, and centralisation has not been the sole prerogative of Conservative governments. There were substantial cut-backs in public expenditure and a move to reduce local authority financial autonomy under the Labour government in the 1970s. In particular, cash limits and the curtailment of Rate Support Grant supplements were imposed on local authorities in 1975. However, Conservative governments have been far more active in their attack on local autonomy. Quite apart from a stream of political rhetoric aimed at 'wasteful' (Labour, especially 'Loony Left') councils, metropolitan county councils and the GLC have been abolished. In addition, financial limits have been imposed on borrowing and spending, and these have been reinforced by 'rate-capping', a system of financial penalties. Some of the major victims of these cuts and centralism have been local authority expenditure on housing, education and special community programmes. Yet these are essential in any attempt to tackle urban poverty.

Cuts in local authority expenditure to counter poverty have been matched by cuts in many of the programmes directly controlled by central government. The most important of these are the social benefits administered by the DHSS, and the most significant development has been the 1988 reform of benefits. The National Association of Citizens' Advice Bureaux considered that by November of that same year, more than 80 per cent of claimants had become worse off. In particular, changes in housing benefits and in the loss of free school meals exceeded whatever gains most families had obtained via the family credit scheme.

By 1989 the government was exploring the possibilities for further shifts from public to private provision of welfare benefits. Ministers emphasised that there was a moral obligation on those who had benefited from government economic policies to support voluntary and charity groups. At the time individual donations to charity totalled only about £1.5 billion, less than 1 per cent of total household disposable income. There would have to be an enormous shift in individual donations if the charities were to be able to compensate, significantly, for past or planned reductions in public expenditure on welfare. Even if such a large-scale transfer of resources to the charities did take place, this would represent a shift away from providing benefits as of right to having to apply for charity. There would also be no guarantees about the ways in which these resources would be used. The priorities and resource allocation of the charities would not necessarily adequately reflect the needs of the multiply-deprived living in the inner cities. More recently, the 1993 Budget which further cut the entitlements of the unemployed and the disabled, amongst others, was yet another blow to the poorest and most deprived members of society.

If we look beyond welfare and urban policies, then the policies of Two Nations Conservatism are seen to have been even more damaging to the inner cities. Mrs Thatcher's government in the early 1980s deliberately used unemployment as a policy instrument, to weaken the power of labour and to combat inflation. The cost in terms of unemployment was felt especially

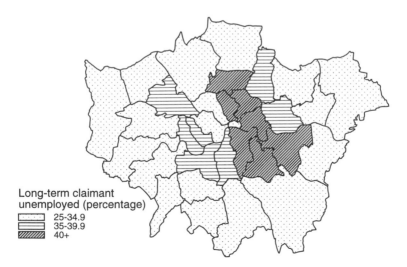

Figure 9.3 Long-term unemployment, London boroughs, January 1993

Source: *Regional Trends*, 1993

strongly in the inner cities. For example, unemployment rates in excess of 40 per cent were common in most of inner London compared to less than 35 per cent or even 30 per cent in large parts of outer London (Figure 9.3). Whilst economic growth recovered in the later 1980s, especially in 1986–88, unemployment continued at high rates in the inner cities. Given that there is such a strong association between unemployment and multiple deprivation, it is an unavoidable conclusion that Thatcherite economic policies increased the misery of the inner cities. In the recession of the early 1990s they were again in the front line of both economic restructuring and of new strategies to limit public expenditure.

Combating multiple disadvantage and addressing the needs of the inner cities are not high in the priorities of Two Nations politics. The emphasis on individual initiative either made the government blind to the many real structural inequalities in UK society, or has allowed it deliberately to ignore these. The main thrusts of government policies have been directed towards individuals, both in terms of means-testing individual benefits and in terms of increasing market opportunities for individuals. Beyond this, Two Nations politics have had little to offer the inner cities or the amelioration of multiple deprivation except attacks on the welfare state, and a narrow interpretation of the virtues of citizenship.

10

Divided forever and for ever?

10.1 Introduction

It has been demonstrated, we think beyond any reasonable doubt, that UK society has become more deeply divided in the era of Two Nations politics, particularly since 1979 as a result of Conservative policies. Moreover, these growing divisions since 1979 are a deliberate rather than an inadvertent consequence of those policies. In claiming this, we are not arguing that the creation of inequality was an end in itself; instead, it was explicitly and implicitly linked to the goal of creating an enterprise culture and a minimalist state whilst increasing choice (for the better off). We also do not deny that prior to 1979, there were already deep divisions in UK society. Nor do we wish to suggest that existing inequalities have simply been widened. Rather, the dimensions of division have been selectively reworked, redefined and magnified at one and the same time. Divisions by class, gender, race and space are more pronounced than they were in 1979 but at the same time the pattern of inequalities has been altered.

The question that we must now consider is this: is the future inevitably one of persisting, even deepening, divisions? To begin to answer this question, we need to look at three time horizons: the immediate future under the present Conservative administration, in other words under Majorism as opposed to Thatcherism; the medium-term outlook beyond the next election; and the longer-term outlook in terms of the possibilities of achieving the fundamental redistributions necessary to bring about a markedly more egalitarian UK. In a sense, all these questions are linked by a single issue: to what extent are divisions structurally inscribed in UK society, and to what extent have they taken a particular contingent form because of the specific policies and politics of the Two Nations stratagem?

10.2 The immediate future

In the conclusions to the first edition, we had posed the question of to what extent would a change of Prime Minister, and a switch from Thatcherite policies, produce a less divided, or perhaps a differently divided, society? Writing in 1994 it is possible to give a preliminary assessment in response to this question, after the first three years of Majorism. This will provide a perspective on the likely reshaping of a divided Britain in the near future.

The proverbial greyness of the Major administration makes it difficult to pinpoint clearly the differences – if any – between it and its predecessor, except for a less autocratic style of leadership. An argument can be made that Majorism is different from Thatcherism in substance and not only in presentation. For example, a number of the 'wets' in the Cabinet have been prepared to criticise the policies of the Thatcher years, including some of its basic tenets. David Hunt, for example, in a speech to the Tory Reform Group in 1993, argued that Conservatives should recognise 'the moral and social inadequacies of *laissez-faire*'. There has also been some increase in real spending on government services such as health and education, although the suspicion remains that this has been inspired mainly by electoral considerations rather than any renewed commitment to these services. Some support for this position can also be found in the Prime Minister's public utterances, as revealed in his defence of the ill-fated 'back to basics' campaign. Initially conceived as a rallying cry to unify the 1993 party conference, it subsequently boomeranged as an indictment on the sleaziness of the Conservative Party in both personal and public life. Joe Rogaly (*Financial Times*, 11 January 1994), for example, argued that it had become 'the defining slogan of a morally bankrupt government'. Yet when John Major sought to defend his campaign on *Breakfast with Frost* in January 1994, he argued that is was designed to meet the fears of ordinary people about unemployment, rising crime, and lower standards in education. Surely, it can be argued, the government of a Prime Minster who expressed such open concern for the problems of social disintegration is markedly different from those of the Thatcher years?

However, in essence, Majorism is no more than Thatcherism without its glorification of strong government. Ex-Cabinet Minister Ian Gilmour (1992), for example, has argued that the three central policies of the Thatcher governments were the poll tax, monetarism and privatisation. The poll tax was rejected by Major but there was no alternative for any leader given its enormity as an electoral liability. The Major government is not monetarist, but neither were Thatcher's after the early 1980s. But the central tenet of the Thatcher years – privatisation and market testing – remains intact. This is evident in the devastation of the rump of the British coal-mining industry and in the persistence with the privatisation of British Rail, despite widespread objections inside and outside the Conservative Party. There is also the much-heralded Citizen's Charter, which is essentially an instrument in the creation of a Britain of consumers making choices in markets and quasi-markets. This has been linked to continued market testing in local and central government. Elsewhere, Virginia Bottomley has been playing down the 'market' element of the health service reforms but without fundamentally altering these policies. The conclusion, therefore, is that in the absence of any alternative vision of the UK's future, Major is plodding along the same privatisation and market forces route as his predecessor. Like her government, his administration also lacks a coherent view of the limits of markets as economic and social steering mechanisms and, therefore, of the necessary role of government in both economic management and in creating a just society.

The future prospect, therefore, is for further privatisation of nationalised industries and public services, at knock-down prices, which will reinforce the illusion of a people's capitalism through widening the veneer of personal share ownership. The virtues of the enterprise culture and the promotion of small firms will continue to be glorified under Major as under Thatcher. There is likely to be a still greater, though ever more selective, reliance on the market as the mechanism through which goods and services are to be provided. Not all of the public sector will disappear but there will be intensified pressures on the remaining rump of public sector industries and services to behave as if they were in the private sector. In practice, this will mean reducing to new depths the access to, and the quality of, provision of health and welfare services. A secondary agenda is that privatisation, and the hiving off, of services to quangos will destroy democratic control – both central and local – over these.

For the foreseeable future, therefore, and indeed for as long as the present Conservative leadership remains in power, the most realistic scenario is one of continuing, indeed widening, inequalities. It is a future of 'more of the same' – if less stridently asserted – and therefore of unremitting divisiveness. The core politics of both Thatcherism and Majorism revolve around creating social divisions, rewarding those who succeed through the market, and punishing those who do not. There is nothing in the first three years of Majorism to make us expect that this will not continue to be the case.

The depths of the early 1990s recession simply mean that the 'punishment' of unemployment is more widely distributed both socially and geographically. Similarly, whilst the fiscal crisis of the 1990s – ironically a product of the Thatcher years – has meant that there have been generalised income tax rises, the taxation system remains highly favourable to higher income groups. Moreover, indirect tax increases, such as the imposition of VAT on domestic heating, have reinforced the regressive character of the UK tax regime. At the same time, the fiscal crisis has given urgency, bordering on desperation, to the government review of public expenditure. The autumn 1993 Budget further restricted the entitlement to unemployment benefits, and there is the likelihood of further cuts in this sphere, especially in universal schemes such as state pensions. There is little doubt that it is the poor and the unemployed who will be made to bear the most painful costs of the fiscal crisis heightened by the Conservatives through mismanagement and short-term electoral stratagems.

The changes outlined will further widen class differences in income, wealth, health and living conditions. The processes of class reformation and of a redefinition of the boundaries between classes will continue for such changes are central to the Two Nations project. Capitalism, by definition, requires a working class and the specification of this class, who is seen to be in it and who is not, is a matter of vital political concern. One of the central aims of the Two Nations programme has been to reform the working class as one that is passively subservient, and that bows with little protest to the changing demands of capitalist production. This helps re-create conditions for profitable accumulation within the UK. Both government policies on trade unions and on benefits (especially the elimination of the rights of young people) and prolonged recession during most of the 1980s and 1990, have meant that the government has largely fulfilled its aims in terms of labour market regulation and functioning. The decline in full-time male manual employment and the creation of part-time jobs, casualisation and home-working have all redefined class boundaries, at the same time as increasing the numbers of people living in both absolute and relative poverty (Chapter 3). The emphasis by the Major government on labour market flexibility as virtu-ally the only strategy for enhancing UK competitivity in world markets makes it likely that class differences in material well being will continue to widen.

It is equally difficult to foresee any significant reduction in ethnic or gender inequalities. Not least, this is because they are strongly related to, though they are certainly not reducible to, those of class. The government preaches the virtues of 'family' life and caring, whilst its economic strategies favour increasing part-time and full-time working by women. This inevitably means an increase in the demands made upon women in dual roles, especially given the cut-backs in the welfare state. The most tangible support that government could provide in such circumstances is extension of the UK's paltry nursery provision. However, despite repeated demands by such eminent bodies as the Royal Society of Arts, the Major government has refused to countenance expenditure on such provision.

Ethnic divisions also remain marked, even if they have changed in shape in the Two Nations years. There are now Asian and black MPs in Parliament but none in the Conservative Party, and ethnic minorities generally are poorly represented in positions of power in local and national government. Britain's ethnic minorities – especially Indians – have made selective educational and employment advances in the 1980s. However, it remains true that the majority of some large minority ethnic groups – such as Pakistanis and Bangladeshis – are still trapped in poor housing, low incomes and unskilled jobs. Such labour market segmentation contributes to the Conservative strategy of basing economic growth on low-cost labour.

These are not the only inequalities in UK society. With an ageing popula-tion, inequalities between different age groups will probably widen. The elderly are already more subject to multiple deprivation than any other social group. Such age divisions will continue and become more complex. Ageism will join sexism and racism as one of the defining dimensions of the divided society in the 1990s and into the twenty first century. This has been under-scored by growing concern in the Major administration about the future size of the pensions bill, especially given the tax relief provided to those who have taken out private pension plans. In a future in which an increasing proportion of the population is not only elderly, but frail and elderly (Benington and Taylor 1993), and in which pensions fail to grow in line with earnings, there is the prospect of even sharper social divides; the intertwining of class and age – most marked in access to private and occupational pensions – will become increasingly influential. It will therefore add another dimension to 'the private affluence and public squalor' (Walker and Walker 1987, 133) which has been the hallmark of the 1980s and the 1990s.

There is no doubt either that spatial inequalities will become more pronounced. This is because the spatial segregation of UK society is another integral part of the Two Nations project. The precise form of this has changed over time, but it has variously involved effectively ghettoising not just small areas of cities but whole swathes of the 'North' in a geography that separates the haves from the have-nots. The regional dimension was strongest during the 1980s. Not least, by creating two political nations, the 'North' and the 'South', Thatcherite policies created a new social and political landscape which made a massive contribution to Mrs Thatcher's electoral successes (Hoover and Plant 1989). The importance of this and other social divisions was underlined by a MORI opinion poll taken immediately after the 1987 general election. Few voters expected her to improve welfare services, reduce unemployment, or narrow the gap between rich and poor. What they did expect were more tax cuts and continuing low rates of inflation. These expectations appealed strongly to the affluent majority (in the South), many of whom were willing to accept the consequences of greater inequalities.

In the 1992 election the security of the Conservative electoral base was challenged by growing middle-class unemployment, especially in the South East and, for a time, seemed unlikely to deliver a fourth successive electoral victory. In the event, the Conservatives were re-elected albeit with a reduced majority. The 'North–South' divide did weaken, with Labour making advances in the South and the Conservatives performing better than expected in the North, especially Scotland. The SLD vote continued to be diluted over the national territory whilst pockets of nationalist support remained confined to the Celtic fringes. However, the key to the 1992 election was that:

> The Conservatives, despite losing some ground, were still too far ahead in key 'southern' constituencies in 1992 and the opposition parties still had too large a gap to close for sufficient seats to change hands and force a change of government. Herein lies the major answer to the puzzle of 1992: how could the Conservatives win, given that they were defending their record during a deep recession? They won not because of their record, but despite it, because of the large reservoir of support which they had built up over the previous thirteen years: their record over the 1987–92 period depleted that reservoir, but did not drain it and so . . . the seesaw tipped back, but it has not yet levelled out (Johnston and Pattie 1992, 1504).

At the time of writing, the Major government is already almost half-way to the last possible date for the next general election. Given the fiscal constraints on the government, and the policies already in place – including those announced in advance for taxation – it has little room to manœuvre, even if it had the will and the capacity to change tack effectively. Government hopes are presumably based on there being sufficient economic recovery to restore the 'feel good' factor in British politics, which means effectively in the South. In other words, the Conservative strategy is based on reassembling what Galbraith (1992) terms 'the contented majority'; under the British electoral system this need only be just over 40 per cent of those who actually vote, which is well short of a majority of the total population. If this fails to materialise, and middle-class and skilled manual unemployment remains high, then the Conservatives may jettison their leader in a last desperate attempt to win the election. But it is highly unlikely that he or she would have any more room to manœuvre than John Major has. In other words, the immediate future continues to be one of 'more of the same'.

10.3 Medium-term political alternatives?

At some point in the future, the Two Nations strategy may cease to be the dominant political philosophy. However, its legacy will persist, for the changes that have already been wrought over the last decade and a half penetrate deeply into the fabric of society. At best, they will take many years to reverse.

Nevertheless, although to some it has at times appeared as a seamless web, the Two Nations strategy has been riddled with contradictions. For example, one has only to consider how the government stridently proclaims the need for a market-driven energy policy. Yet in practice it selectively intervened to prevent market forces eliminating nuclear power stations, although it continues to refuse to do so on behalf of coal production! More fundamentally, the Two Nations strategy is supportable only if the 'contented majority' believes that it will continue to guarantee its quality of life; that means both economic prosperity, and guaranteeing minimum levels of services and social order. What it is unlikely to accept is paying high taxes to support the poor (even though the level of welfare benefits has been reduced) and yet see a real threat of social disintegration. Consequently, one could argue that the Two Nations stratagem will collapse under the weight of its own internal contradictions (Gamble 1983; Galbraith 1992). It might then be replaced by a new dominant political viewpoint, just as the One Nation strategy was ushered in in the 1940s in response to the failures of the 1930s. Just what this alternative might be is far from clear. Presumably it would bear some resemblance to the doctrines of former 'One Nation' consensus Tory politics. It is difficult to anticipate the possibility of anything radically to the left of this, given that the social and electoral cleavages in the UK in the 1990s are very different from those of the 1940s. Even so, such a modest change as this would surely usher in an era of narrowing inequalities in terms of all the main dimensions of division?

There is definitely some evidence to support such a claim if one examines the historical record. Over the post-war period inequalities in incomes and wealth became more muted. There was greater public sector provision of health and educational services, which removed their provision from ability to pay for them, whilst other parts of the welfare state provided some sort of a safety net for the old, the sick and the unemployed. But even here, although they were 'unintended', there was evidence of widening class divisions in access to and benefits from public sector provision of education and health care. There was also evidence of deep-rooted multiple disadvantage amongst the poor and unemployed.

Despite a long period of regional and then urban policies, spatial divisions did not disappear. It is salutary to recall that, despite the proclaimed good intentions of Conservative and Labour governments alike to tackle the 'regional problem', public expenditure per capita in the South East in 1978 was well above the national average. Although comprehensive data on the regional distribution of public expenditure are not available for the 1980s and 1990s, there is no doubt that the selective concentration of public expenditure into the 'South' has increased further. But the point that we wish to stress here is that the polarisation between 'North' and 'South' was already heavily underpinned by public spending policies before 1979. This is a point with profound implications for any serious attempt to narrow, if not eliminate, the 'North/South' divide, especially given that the convergence of the early 1990s may well turn out to be cyclical. The prospects for narrowing intra-regional differences also remain depressingly pessimistic.

More generally, there is an abundance of evidence that points to the persistence of inequalities – between classes, between ethnic groups, between men and women – even in the era of consensus, mildly socially-democratic reformist policies and politics. In part, such divisions remained because of, rather than despite, the implementation of avowedly reformist policies. The actual effects of policies often diverged from their intended ones. Therefore, the return of a version of One Nation politics – even if all else is equal – would not guarantee the elimination of inequalitites.

However, as has been argued throughout this book, not all else is equal either in the international environment or in the social and economic structures and the political culture of the UK. In the era of One Nation politics, international competition was generally much less pronounced in world markets, the internationalisation of capital was yet to reach the heights that it was to attain in the 1980s, and the national economy seemed to be much more closed than it was subsequently to become. In short, there still appeared to be a basis for managing the economy on broadly Keynesian lines. Since 1979 much of this basis has been quite deliberately demolished by government policies. For example, restrictions on the movement of capital have been abolished. The subsequent further increase in the internationalisation of what could once reasonably be regarded as UK-based capital has made it much less amenable to influence, let alone control, by government. Deregulation and privatisation have also resulted in important areas of the economy being placed beyond the reach of direct government influence. Such changes have been reflected in and compounded by national economic policy. This is based on engineering a further switch from an economy based on manufacturing and productive activity to one based on services. But within the service sector, internationally competitive financial services centred on the City of London are juxtaposed with domestically oriented low-skill, low-productivity and low-wage service activities. In another sphere, the Major government did withdraw from the exchange rate mechanism, but this only modified the limited degree of autonomy available to the government, for the pound is still susceptible to speculative pressures in international currency markets. Therefore, it is difficult to see how many of these changes could be reversed, except over a fairly long period.

Even with this qualification, the prognosis is not a promising one. For postwar consensus politics were based on attempting to influence, not control, private capital. They were not very successful then. The environment in which 'influence' could be exerted is now much less promising than it was then. For example, privatisation has removed many sectors of the economy from direct state intervention. The possibilities for 'control' over the dominant multinational conglomerates are also even less now than they were in 1979 and even then they were limited.

The changes in the international environment should not be underestimated. It can be argued that under increasing competitive pressures from the newly industrialising countries, restructuring in Europe will lead to a deepening of labour market polarisation. On the one hand, there will be a highly skilled and highly paid segment especially in international services and some advanced technology sectors. In contrast, there will be large numbers of 'unskilled' people receiving no or low pay because their jobs have been deskilled or eliminated by technological change, and wages will have been forced down by international competition.

In some ways, our medium-term prognosis is even gloomier than has hitherto been painted. Two Nations policies have made the UK a more divided society and future generations will have to live with the consequences of this. The sale of public assets, inadequate investment in health and education, and council house sales have all lessened the possibilities for future governments to provide better facilities and opportunities for the poor and deprived. The enormous public sector deficits of the Major governments also circumscribe the potential for more radical policies by future governments. Furthermore, a polarisation of wealth and a reduction in inheritance taxes have made for even greater inequalities in the intergenerational transfer of wealth, especially housing (Hamnett 1992b). Therefore the foundations for deep divisions in the next and succeeding generations have already been laid in the 1980s and early 1990s. Given the electoral weight of the 'contented majority', it is unlikely that any government could realise a significant resource shift to the poor, without alienating a large element of their essential support amongst the affluent majority.

10.4 So is the UK divided for ever?

The short answer to this question is 'yes, for as long as UK society remains a capitalist one'. Materially and ideologically, Two Nations politics have both powerfully reinforced and altered the character of capitalism in the UK. For the forseeable future, we have to rule out the possibility of any significant move to the left, let alone a socialist revolution. Indeed, it is by no means obvious what a move to the left would mean at present. For the Labour Party has moved rightwards to occupy the space left by Thatcherism/Majorism, which itself continues its long march yet further right. In this sense, Thatcherism/Majorism has redefined the political terrain in a way that seemed impossible only a few years ago. It is conceivable that Labour may continue to reposition itself so as to be elected on a political platform which places it to the right of the Conservatives in the next election. This is not to say that the terrain cannot again be redefined to accommodate a socialist project that would attract sufficient support to result in a government with very different priorities from those of the Conservatives. But it is to say that such a transformation is beyond the present bounds of possibility.

So if the future is to be a capitalist one, and social inequality is endemic to capitalism, then the realm must remain divided. Class inequalities are structurally inscribed into capitalist societies. Capitalism simply cannot exist without the capital : labour class relation, however this is or seems to be mediated by the emergence of the 'middle classes'. Ethnic and gender divisions are not necesssary in capitalist societies in the same sense as are those between classes but they are closely related to the latter. Hence they are unlikely to disappear in the UK. There are strong links between racialised and gendered inequalities and class, for example. Similarly, locational divisions are not necessary in the same way as are those of class but capitalist development has served to widen existing divisions and create new ones. Cleavages along the planes of class, ethnicity, gender and location have become intertwined in complex ways which makes them all the more resistant to progressive change. This is not to say that the pattern of divisions will remain unaltered. It will not. Nor is it to say that, within the limits defined by capitalist social relations, there is not scope for progressive changes that would at least narrow some of the existing inequalities. There is. And it is important, politically and ideologically, that such possibilities be developed wherever there is a chance to do so. Not least, it will continue to demonstrate that there are alternatives and that, however unpromising the circumstances, these can be kept alive. There is scope, for example, for forms of co-operative development that prove that such alternatives *do* exist which could begin to lay the foundations for a more profound transformation towards a more egalitarian society. But for the moment, and indeed for the foreseeable future, such developments will at best nibble at the margins of inequality. The divisions will remain deep, in all probability becoming deeper. Divided Britain will remain divided.

References

Abbot, P. and Sapsford, R. (1987), *Women and Social Class*, London: Tavistock.

Abercrombie, N. and Urry, J. (1983), *Capital, Labour and the Middle Classes*, London: Allen Unwin.

Abercrombie, N. and Warde, A. (1988), *Contemporary British Society*, Cambridge: Polity Press.

Adams, M., Maybury, R. and Smith, W. (1988), 'Trends in the distribution of earnings 1973–86', *Employment Gazette*, February, 75–82.

Advisory Council on Science and Technology (1990), *Overcoming Barriers to Growth in Small Firms*, London

Allen, S. (1982), 'Gender inequality and class formation', in Giddens, A. and Mackenzie, G. (eds), *Social Class and the Division of Labour*, Cambridge: Cambridge University Press.

Anderson, J. (1990), 'The "new right", Enterprise Zones and Urban Development Corporations', *International Journal of Urban and Regional Research*, vol. 14, pp. 468–89.

Anwar, M. (1991), *Race Relations Policies in Britain: Agenda for the 1990s*, Coventry: University of Warwick, Centre for Research in Ethnic Relations, Policy Paper in Ethnic Relations No. 21.

Atkinson, J. (1984), *Flexibility, Uncertainty and Manpower Management*, Institute of Manpower Studies, Report 89, Falmer: University of Sussex.

Balchin, P.N. (1990), *Regional Policy in Britain*, London: Paul Chapman.

Baloo, S., (1989), *Homeworking in Thamesdown*, Swindon Law Centre, 26 Victoria Road, Swindon, SN1 3AW

Banton, M. (1985), *Promoting Racial Harmony*, Cambridge: Cambridge University Press.

Barclays Review, November 1987 and May and November, 1989.

Barnett, A. (1982), 'Iron Britannia', *New Left Review*, No. 134, pp. 5–96.

Beale, N. and Netherott, S. (1985), 'Job loss and family morbidity: a study of a factory closure', *Journal of the Royal College of Practitioners*, vol. 35, pp. 510–14.

Beechey, V. and Perkins, T. (1987), *A Matter of Hours: Women, Part-time Work and the Labour Market*, Cambridge: Polity Press.

Begg, I., Moore, B. and Rhodes, J. (1986), 'Economic and social change in urban Britain and the inner cities', in Hausner, V.A. (ed.), *Critical Issues in Urban Economic Development*, vol. 1, Oxford: Clarendon Press.

Benington, J. and Taylor, M. (1993), 'Changes and challenges facing the UK welfare state in the Europe of the 1990s', *Policy and Politics*, vol. 21, pp. 121–34.

Benyon, J. (1986), 'The spiral of decline: race and policing', in Layton-Henry, Z. and Rich, P.B. (eds), *Race, Government and Politics in Britain*, London: Macmillan.

Berthoud, R. (1983), 'Who suffers social disadvantage', in Brown, M. (ed.), *The Structure of Disadvantage*, London: Heinemann.

Beynon, H. (ed.) (1985), *Digging Deeper: Issues in the Miners' Strike*, London: Verso.

Beynon, H. and Austrin, T. (1993), *Masters and Servants: Class and Patronage in the Making of a Labour Organization*, London: Rivers Oram.

Beynon, H. and Hudson, R. (1993), 'Place and space in contemporary Europe: some lessons and reflections', *Antipode*, vol. 25, no. 3, pp. 177–90.

Beynon, H., Hudson, R. and Sadler, D. (1994), *A Place Called Teesside: A Locality in a Global Economy*, Edinburgh: Edinburgh University Press.

Bird, D. (1992), 'Industrial stoppages in 1991', *Employment Gazette*, May, pp. 235–48.

Blackstone, T. (1980), 'Education', in Bosanquet, N. and Townsend, P. (eds), *Labour and Equality*, London: Heinemann.

Board of Inland Revenue (1992), *Inland Revenue Statistics 1991*, London: HMSO.

Bosanquet, N. (1980), 'Labour and public expenditure: an overall view', in Bosanquet, N. and Townsend, P. (eds), *Labour and Equality*, London: Heinemann.

Boyne, G.A. and Powell, M. (1993), 'Territorial justice and Thatcherism', *Environment and Planning C*, vol. 11, pp. 35–53.

Bradford, M. and Burdett, F. (1989), 'Privatisation, education and the North–South Divide', in Lewis, J. and Townsend, A. (eds), *The North–South Divide*, London: Paul Chapman.

Brah, A. (1993), 'Race and "culture" in the gendering of labour markets: South Asian young Muslim women and the labour market', *New Community*, vol. 19, pp. 441–58.

Breheny, M., Hall, P. and Hart, D. (1987), *Northern Lights: A Development Agenda for the North in the 1990s*, London: Derrick, Wade and Waters.

Broock, C. (ed.) (1986), *The Caribbean in Europe*, Loncon: Frank Cass.

Brown, A., (1962), *The Tory Years*, London: Lawrence and Wishart.

Brown, C. (1984), *Black and White in Britain*, London: Heinemann.

Brown, C.J.F. and Sheriff, J.D. (1979), 'Deindustrialization: a background paper', in Blackaby, F. (ed.), *Deindustrialization*, London: Heinemann.

Brown, R. (1984), 'Work', in Abrams, P. and Brown, R. (eds), *Urbanism and Inequality*, London: Weidenfeld and Nicolson.

Bruegel, I. (1987), 'Women: the feminisation of poverty', *Interlink*, p. 9.

Burchell, B. and Ruberry, J. (1989), *Segmented Jobs and Segmented Workers: An Empirical Investigation*', Working paper No.13, ESRC Social Changes and Economic Life Initiative, Nuffield College, Oxford.

Burgess, R. (1984), 'Patterns and processes of education in the United Kingdom', in Abrams, P. and Brown, R. (eds), *UK Society*, London: Weidenfeld and Nicolson.

Carter, A. (1988), *The Politics of Women's Rights*, London: Longman.

Carter, T. (1986), *Shattering Illusions: West Indians in British Politics*, London: Lawrence and Wishart.

Castells, M. (1977), *The Urban Question*, London: Edward Arnold.

Castells, M. and Henderson, G. (eds) (1989), *The City and Information Technology*, London: Sage.

Champion, A.G. (1993), 'Introduction', in Champion, A.G. (ed.), *Population Matters*, London: Paul Chapman.

Champion, A.G. and Green, A.E. (1989), 'Local economic differentials and the north–south divide', in Lewis, J.R. and Townsend, A.R. (eds), *The North–South Divide: Regional Change in Britain in the 1980s*, London: Paul Chapman.

Champion, A.G. and Green, A.E. (1992), 'Local economic performance in Britain during the late 1980s: the results of the third Booming Towns study', *Environment and Planning A*, vol. 24, pp. 243–72.

Champion, A.G. and Townsend, A.R. (eds) (1990), *Contemporary Britain: A Geographical Perspective*, London: Edward Arnold.

Collinson, D. (1988), *Barriers to Fair Selection*, Manchester: Equal Opportunities Commission.

Corrigan, P. (1984), 'Social welfare', in Abrams, P. and Brown, R. (eds), *UK Society*, London: Weidenfeld and Nicolson.

Cottingham, C. (1982), *Race, Poverty and the Urban Underclass*, Lexington: D.C. Heath.

Crang, P. and Martin, R. (1991), 'Mrs Thatcher's vision of the "new Britain" and the other sides of the Cambridge phenomenon', *Society and Space*, vol. 9, pp. 91–116.

Crewe, I. (1983), 'Representation and the ethnic minorities in Britain', in Glazier, N. and Young, K. (eds), *Ethnic Pluralism and Public Policy*, London: Heinemann.

Cross, M. (1986), 'Migration and exclusion: Caribbean echoes and British realities', in Brock, C. (ed.), *The Caribbean in Europe*, London: Frank Cass.

CSO (Central Statistical Office), various dates, *Social Trends*, London: HMSO.

Curran, J., Burrows, R. and Evandrou, M. (1987), *Small Business Owners and the Self-Employed: an Analysis of the General Household Survey data*, London: Small Business Trust.

Curtis, S. and Mohan, J. (1989), 'The geography of ill health and health care', in Lewis, J. and Townsend, A. (eds), *The North–South Divide*, London: Paul Chapman.

Daly, M., Campbell, M., Robson, G. and Gallagher, C. (1992), 'Job creation 1987–9: preliminary analysis by sector', *Employment Gazette*, August, pp. 387–92.

Daly, M. and McCann, A. (1992), 'How many small firms?' *Employment Gazette*, February, pp. 47–51.

Daniel, W.W. (1965), *Racial Discrimination in England*, Harmondsworth: Penguin.

Davies, H.W.E. (1981), 'The inner city in Britain', in Schwartz, G.C. (ed.), *Advanced Industrialization and the Inner City*, Lexington: Lexington Books.

Department of Economic Affairs (1965), *The National Plan*, London: HMSO

Department of Employment (1990), 'The growth of UK companies 1985–7 and their contribution to job generation', *Employment Gazette*, February, 92–8.

Department of Employment (1992), *Employment Gazette*, April, 191–9.

Dex, S. (1987), *Women's Occupational Mobility: A Lifetime's Perspective*, London: Macmillan.

Duncan, S. and Goodwin, M. (1985), *Central Control versus Local Autonomy: The Local Government Crisis in Britain 1979–84. Part 1: Centralising the Local Government System, 1979–83*, London: London School of Economics and Political Science, Department of Geography, Discussion Paper 13.

Dunford, M. (1990), 'Theories of regulation', *Society and Space*, vol. 8, pp. 297–321.

Dunford, M. and Perrons, D. (1986), 'The restructuring of the post-war British space economy', in Martin, R. and Rowthorne, B. (eds) *The Geography of Deindustrialization*, London: Macmillan.

Elias, P. and Keogh, G. (1982), 'Industrial decline and unemployment in the inner city areas of Great Britain: a review of the evidence', *Urban Studies*, vol. 19, pp. 1–15.

Elliott, B. (1984), 'Cities in the Eighties: the Growth of Inequality', in Abrams, P. and Brown, R. (eds), *Urbanism and Inequality*, London: Weidenfeld and Nicolson.

Equal Opportunities Commission (1992), *Women and Men in Britain, 1991*, London: HMSO.

Equal Opportunities Commission (1993), *Women and Men in Britain, 1993*, London: HMSO.

Eurostat (1993), *Rapid Reports: Population and Social Conditions. 1993–:10*, Luxembourg: Commission of the European Communities, Eurostat.

Eyles, J. and Woods, K.J. (1983), *The Social Geography of Medicine and Health*, London: Croom Helm.

Fainstein, S. (1991), 'Promoting economic development: urban planning in the United States and Great Britain', *Journal of the American Planning Association*, vol. 57, pp. 22–33.

Field, S. (1986), 'The changing nature of racial disadvantage', *New Community*, vol. 14, pp. 118–22.

Friedman, A. (1977), *Industry and Labour*, London: Macmillan.

Gaffikin, F. and Warf, B. (1993), 'Urban policy and the post-Keynesian state in the United Kingdom and the United States', *International Journal of Urban and Regional Research*, vol. 17, pp. 67–83.

Galbraith, J.K. (1992), *The Culture of Contentment*, London: Penguin.

Gamble, A. (1983), 'Thatcherism and Conservative Politics', in Hall, S. and Jacques, H. (eds), *The Politics of Thatcherism*, London: Lawrence and Wishart.

Gamble, A. (1988), *The Free Economy and the Strong State: the Politics of Thatcherism*, London: Macmillan.

Garrahan, P. and Stewart, P. (1992), *The Nissan Enigma*, London: Mansell.

Giddens, A. (1981), *A Contemporary Critique of Historical Materialism*, London: Macmillan.

Giddens, A. (1984), *The Constitution of Society*, Cambridge: Polity.

Gilmour, I. (1992), *Dancing with Dogma; Britain under Thatcherism*, London: Simon and Schuster.

Ginn, J. and Arber, S. (1993), 'Pension penalties: the gendered division of occupational welfare', *Work, Employment and Society*, vol. 7, pp. 47–70.

Glendinning, C. and Millar, J. (1987), *Women and Poverty in Britain*, London: Harvester Press.

Goldthorpe, J. (1982), 'On the service class, its formation and future', in Giddens, A. and Mackenzie, G. (eds), *Social Class and the Division of Labour*, Cambridge: Cambridge University Press.

Goldthorpe, J.H. (1983), 'Women and class analysis: in defence of the conventional view', *Sociology*, vol. 17, pp. 465–88.

Gough, I. (1979), *The Political Economy of the Welfare State*, London: Macmillan.

Gray, F. (1976), 'Selection and allocation in council housing', *Transactions of the Institute of British Geographers*, New Series vol. 1, pp. 34–46.

Gregg, P. and Machin, S. (1993), *Is the Glass Ceiling Cracking: Gender Compensation Differentials and Access to Promotion among UK Executives*, London: National Institute of Economic and Social Research, Discussion Paper 50.

Gregory, S. (1982), 'Women among others: another view', *Leisure Studies*, vol. 1, pp. 97–115.

Habermas, J. (1975), *Legitimation Crisis*, London: Heinemann.

Hakey, A.H., Heath, A.F. and Ridge, J.M. (1980), *Origins and Destinations: Family, Class and Education in Modern Britain*, Oxford: Clarendon Press.

Hakim, C. (1979), *Occupational Segregation*, London: Department of Employment, Research Paper No 9.

Hakim, C. (1992), 'Explaining trends in occupational segregation: the measurement, causes and consequences of the sexual division of labour', *European Sociological Review*, vol. 8, pp. 127–52.

Hakim, C. (1993), 'Notes and issues: the myth of rising female employment', *Work, Employment and Society*, vol. 7, pp. 97–120.

Halsey, A.H. (1987), *Social Trends*, vol. 17, London: HMSO, CSO.

Halsey, A.H., Heath, A.F. and Ridge, J.M. (1980), *Origins and Destinations: Family, Class and Education in Modern Britain*, Oxford: Clarendon Press.

Hamnett, C. (1985), 'Inner city decline', *Unit 18 D205 Human Geography Course*, Milton Keynes: Open University.

Hamnett, C. (1989a), 'The political geography of housing in contemporary Britain', in Mohan, J. (ed.), *A Political Geography of Britain*, London: Macmillan.

Hamnett, C. (1989b), 'The owner occupied housing market in Britain: a North–South divide?', in Lewis, J.R. and Townsend, A.R. (eds), *The North–South Divide: Regional Change in Britain in the 1980s*, London: Paul Chapman.

Hamnett, C. (1992a), 'The geography of housing wealth and inheritance in Britain', *The Geographical Journal*, vol. 158, pp. 307–21.

Hamnett, C. (1992b), *Inheritance in Britain: the Disappearing Billions*, London: Lifetime.

Hamnett, C. and Randolph, B. (1988), 'Ethnic minorities in the London labour market: a longitudinal analysis', *New Community*, vol. 14, pp. 333–46.

Hannah, L. (1992), 'Human capital flows and business efficiency: sense and nonsense in the Wiener thesis', lecture delivered at the Centre for Economic Performance, London School of Economics, 2 November 1992.

Hartmann, H. (1978), 'The unhappy marriage of Marxism and feminism: towards a more progressive union', *Capital and Class*, vol. 8, pp. 1–33.

Harvey, D. (1988), *The Condition of Postmodernity*, Blackwell, Oxford.

Hawkins, K. (1978), *Unemployment*, Harmondsworth: Penguin.

Hayek, F.A. (1988), *The Fatal Conceit*, London: Routledge and Kegan Paul.

Heath, A. (1981), *Social Mobility*, London: Fontana.

Held, D. (ed.) (1983), *States and Societies*, Oxford: Martin Robertson.

Henderson, J. and Karn, V. (1987), *Race, Class and State Housing*, Aldershot: Gower Press.

Hogarth, T. and Daniel, W.W. (1989), *Britain's New Industrial Gypsies*, London: Policy Studies Institute

Holdaway, J. (1992), 'The Scarman Report: Sociological aspects', *New Community*, vol. 9, pp. 366–70.

Holdaway, S. (1987), 'Themes and issues in police/race relations policy', *New Community*, vol. 14, pp. 142–51.

Hoover, K. and Plant, R. (1989), *Conservative Capitalism*, London: Routledge.

Howe, G.M. (1986), 'Does it matter where I live', *Transactions of the Institute of British Geographers*, New Series, vol. 11, pp. 387–411.

Hudson, R. (1986), 'Nationalised industry policies and regional policies: the role of the state in the deindustrialization and reindustrialization of regions', *Society and Space*, vol. 4, pp. 7–28.

Hudson, R. (1989a), *Wrecking a Region: State Policies, Party Politics and Regional Change in North East England*, London: Pion.

Hudson, R. (1989b), 'Labour market changes and new forms of work in old industrial regions: maybe flexibility for some but not flexible accumulation', *Society and Space*, vol. 7, pp. 1–28.

Hudson, R. (1989c), 'Rewriting history and reshaping geography: the nationalized industries and the political economy of Thatcherism', in Mohan, J. (ed.), *The Political Geography of Contemporary Britain*, London: Macmillan.

Hudson, R. (1992), *The Japanese, the United Kingdom, automobile industry and the automobile industry in the United Kingdom*, Discussion Paper No. 9, Change in the Automobile Industry: An International Comparison, University of Durham.

Hudson, R. (1993), 'Spatially uneven development and the production of spaces and places: some preliminary considerations and a case study of Consett', in Hauer, J. and Hoekveld, G. (eds) *Moving Regions*, Utrecht: Netherlands Geographical Studies.

Hudson, R. and Plum, V. (1986), 'Deconcentration or decentralization? Local government and the possibilities for local control of local economies', in Goldsmith, M. and Villadsen, S. (eds), *Urban Political Theory and the Management of Fiscal Stress*, Aldershot: Gower.

Hudson, R., Rhind, D. and Mounsey, H. (1984), *An Atlas of EEC Affairs*, London: Methuen.

Hudson, R. and Williams, A. (1986), *The United Kingdom*, London: Harper and Row.

Hunter, L. and MacInnes, J. (1992), 'Employers and labour flexibility: the evidence from case studies', *Employment Gazette*, June, pp. 307–45.

Income Data Services (1990), *Flexibility at Work*, IDS Study No. 454, 193 St John Street, London EC1V 4LS.

Ingham, G. (1982), 'Divisions within the dominant class and "British Exceptionalism"', in Giddens, A. and Mackenzie, G. (eds), *Social Class and the Division of Labour*, Cambridge: Cambridge University Press.

Jackson, P. (1987), 'The idea of race and the geography of racism', in Jackson, P. (ed.), *Race and Racism: Essays in Social Geography*, London: Unwin and Hyman.

James, W. (1992), 'Migration, racism and identity: the Caribbean experience in Britain', *New Left Review*, No. 193, pp. 15–55.

Jarvis, V. and Prais, S. (1988), *Two Nations of Shopkeepers: Training for Retailing in France and Britain*, Discussion Paper 140, National Institute for Economic and Social Research, 2 Dean French Street, London SW1.

Jayaweera, H. (1993), 'Racial disadvantage and ethnic identity: the experiences of Afro-Caribbean women in a British city', *New Community*, vol. 19, pp. 383–406.

Jessop, B. (1989), *Thatcherism: the British Road to Post-Fordism?*, Essex Papers in Politics and Government Number 68, University of Essex, Colchester.

Jessop, B., Bonnet, K. and Bromley, S. (1990), 'Farewell to Thatcherism? Neo-Liberalism and "New Times"', *New Left Review*, No. 179, pp. 81–102.

Jessop, B., Bonnet, K., Bromley, S. and Ling, T. (1988), *Thatcherism: a Tale of Two Nations*, Cambridge: Polity Press.

Johnes, G. and Taylor, J. (1989), 'Ethnic minorities in the graduate labour market', *New Community*, vol. 15, pp. 527–36.

Johnston, R.J. and Pattie, C.J. (1992), 'Is the seesaw tipping back? The end of Thatcherism and changing voting patterns in Great Britain 1979–92', *Environment and Planning A*, vol. 24, pp. 1491–505

Johnston, R.J., Pattie, C.J. and Allsop, J.G. (1988), *A Nation Dividing?* London: Longman.

Jones, T. (1993), *Britain's Ethnic Minorities: An Analysis of the Labour Force Survey*, London: Policy Studies Institute.

Jowell, R. and Witherspoon, S. (eds) (1985), *British Social Attitudes*, Aldershot: Gower.

Karn, V. (1983), 'Race and housing in Britain: the role of the major institutions', in Glazer, N. and Young, K. (eds), *Ethnic Pluralism and Public Policy*, London: Heinemann.

Keegan, W. (1984), *Mrs Thatcher's Economic Experiment*, Harmondsworth: Penguin.

Knox, P.L. (1976), *Social Priorities for Social Indicators: A Survey Approach*, Occasional Paper No. 4, Department of Geography, University of Dundee.

Kolinsky, M. (1981), 'The nation-state in western Europe: erosion from "above" and "below"?', in Tivey, L. (ed.), *The Nation State*, Oxford: Martin Robertson.

Lash, S. and Urry, J. (1987), *The End of Organized Capitalism*, Cambridge: Polity Press.

Layton-Henry, Z. and Rich, P.B. (eds), (1986) *Race, Government and Politics in Britain*, London: Macmillan.

Lee, T. (1977), *Race and Residence*, Oxford: Clarendon Press.

Lewis, J. and Davies, C. (1991), 'Protective legislation in Britain, 1870–1990: equality, difference and their implications for women', *Policy and Politics*, vol. 19, pp. 13–25.

Leys, C. (1986), *Politics in Britain*, London: Verso.

Leyshon, A. and Thrift, N. (1989), 'South goes north? The rise of the British provincial financial centre', in Lewis, J. and Townsend, A. (eds), *The North–South Divide: Regional Change in Britain in the 1980s*, London: Paul Chapman.

Lipietz, A. (1986), 'New tendencies in the international division of labour: regimes of accommodation and modes of regulation', in Scott, A.J. and Storper, M. (eds), *Production, Territory, Work*, London: Unwin Hyman.

Loach, L. (1985), 'We'll be here right to the end . . . and after: Women in the miners' strike', in Beynon, H. (ed.), *Digging Deeper: Issues in the Miners Strike*, London: Verso.

London Housing Unit (1989), *One in Every Hundred*, London: London Housing Unit.

London Housing Unit (1990), *London Needs Homes – the Real Cost of Housing in London*, Bedford House, 125–33 Camden High Street, London NW1 7JR.

Lovering, J. and Boddy, M. (1988), 'The geography of the military industry in Britain', *Area*, vol. 20, No. 1, pp. 41–51.

Low Pay Unit (1987), *Poverty and Labour in London*, London: Low Pay Unit.

Low Pay Unit (1992), 'It's a crime', *The New Review*, No. 17, 27–9 Anwell Street, London EC1R 1UN.

McCarthy, M. (1986), *Campaigning for the Poor: CPAG and the Politics of Welfare*, London: Croom Helm.

McDowell, L. (1989), 'Women in Thatcher's Britain', in Mohan, J. (ed.) *The Political Geography of Contemporary Britain*, London: Macmillan.

McDowell, L. (1993), 'Space, place and gender relations: Part 1 Feminist empiricism and the geography of social relations', *Progress in Human Geography*, vol. 17, pp. 157–79.

McGregor, A. and Sproull, A. (1992), 'Employers and their flexible workforce', *Employment Gazette*, May, pp. 225–34.

MacInnes, J. (1989), *Regional Trends in Employment and Unemployment in Britain 1986–8*, Centre for Urban and Regional Research, University of Glasgow.

Mack, J. and Lansley, S. (1985), *Poor Britain*, London: George Allen and Unwin.

Madigan, R., Munro, M. and Smith, S.J. (1990), 'Gender and the meaning of the home', *International Journal of Urban and Regional Research*, vol. 14, pp. 623–647.

Mama, A. (1986), 'Black women and the economic crisis', in Feminist Review (ed.), *Waged Work: A Reader*, London: Virago.

Marshall, G., Newby, H., Rose, D. and Vogler, C. (1988), *Social Class in Modern Britain*, London: Hutchinson.

Martin, I. (1980), 'Racial equality', in Bosanquet, N. and Townsend, P. (eds), *Labour and Equality*, London: Heinemann.

Martin, R. (1988), 'The political economy of Britain's North–South divide', *Transactions, Institute of British Geographers*, NS, vol. 13, No. 4, pp. 389–417.

Martin, R. (1993), 'Remapping British regional policy: The end of the North–South divide?', *Regional Studies*, vol. 27, pp. 797–806.

Martin, R. and Wallace, J. (1984), *Working Women in the Recession: Employment, Redundancy and Unemployment*, Oxford: Oxford University Press.

Massey, D. (1984), *Spatial Divisions of Labour: Social Structures and the Geography of Production*, London: Macmillan.

Massey, D.B. (1988), 'Uneven development: social change and spatial divisions of labour', in Massey, D. and Allen, J. (eds), *Uneven re-development*, London: Hodder and Stoughton.

Massey, D. and Catalano, A. (1978), *Capital and Land: Landownership by Capital in Britain*, London: Edward Arnold.

Massey, D.B. and Meegan, R.A. (1978), 'Industrial restructuring versus the cities', *Urban Studies*, vol. 15, pp. 273–88.

Massey, D. and Wainwright, H. (1985), 'Beyond the coalfields: the work of miners' support groups', in Beynon, H. (ed.), *Digging Deeper: Issues in the Miners' Strike*, London: Verso.

Mayer, M. (1992), 'The shifting local political system in European cities', in Dunford, M. and Kafkalas, G. (eds), *Cities and Regions in the New Europe*, London: Belhaven.

Mellor, J.R. (1977), *Urban Sociology in an Urbanized Society*, London: Routledge and Kegan Paul.

Miliband, R. (1969), *The State in Capitalist Society*, London: Weidenfeld and Nicolson.

Millar, A.R. (1980), *A Study of Multiply Deprived Households in Scotland*, Edinburgh: Scottish Office.

Ministry of Agriculture, Fisheries and Food (1988), *Farm Incomes in the United Kingdom*, London: HMSO.

Minns, R. (1980), *British Capitalism and Pension Funds*, London: Heinemann.

Mohan, J. (1988), 'Restructuring, privatization and the geography of health provision in the UK', *Transactions, Institute of British Geographers, New Series*, vol. 13, pp. 449–65.

Morris, L. (1993), 'Is there a British underclass?', *International Journal of Urban and Regional Research*, vol. 17, pp. 404–411.

Mullins, D. (1990), 'Housing and urban policy', *New Community*, vol. 17, pp. 114–22.

Munt, I. (1991), 'Race, urban policy and urban problems: a critique on current UK practice', *Urban Studies*, vol. 28, pp. 183– 203.

Nairn, T. (1977), *The Break-up of Britain*, London: New Left Books.

National Consumer Council (1992), *Credit and Debt*, London.

Naylor, M. and Purdie, E. (1992), 'Results of the 1991 Labour Force Survey', *Employment Gazette*, April, pp. 153–72.

Oakley, A. (1974), *The Sociology of Housework*, London: Martin Robertson.

Offe, C. (1975), 'The theory of the capitalist state and the problem of policy formation', in Lindberg, L.N., Alford, R., Crouch, C. and Offe, C. (eds), *Stress and Contradiction in Modern Capitalism*, Farnborough: D.C. Heath.

Ormerod, P. (1980), 'The economic record', in Bosanquet, N. and Townsend, P. (eds), *Labour and Equality*, London: Heinemann.

Owen, D. and Green, A. (1992), 'Labour market experience and occupational change amongst ethnic groups in Great Britain', *New Community*, vol. 19, pp. 7–29.

Pahl, R.E. (1984), *Divisions of Labour*, Oxford: Basil Blackwell.

Parkinson, M. (1993), 'A new strategy for Britain's cities?', *Policy Studies*, vol. 14, pp. 5–17.

Pay Equity Project (1993), *Narrowing the Gender Pay Gap*, London: Pay Equity Project.

Payne, J. and Payne, C. (1994), 'Recession, restructuring and the fate of the unemployed: evidence in the underclass debate', *Sociology*, vol. 28, 1–20.

Peach, C. (1986), 'A geographical perspective on the 1981 urban riots in England', *Ethnic and Racial Studies*, vol. 9, pp. 396–401.

Peach, C. and Byron, M. (1993), 'Caribbean tenants in council housing: "Race", class and gender', *New Community*, vol. 19, pp. 407–423.

Peck, J.A. and Tickell, A. (1992), *Local Modes of Social Regulation? Regulation Theory, Thatcherism and Uneven Development*, Manchester: University of Manchester, School of Geography, Spatial Policy Analysis Working Paper 14.

Phillips, D. (1979). 'Public attitudes to general practitioner services: a reflection of the inverse care law in intra-urban primary health care', *Environment and Planning A*, vol. 11, pp. 815–24.

Phillips, D. and Karn, V. (1992), 'Race and housing in a property owning democracy', *New Community*, vol. 18, pp. 355–69.

Phillips, D. and Williams, A.M. (1984), *Rural Britain: A Social Geography*, Oxford: Blackwell.

Phizacklea, A. (1982), 'Migrant women and wage labour: the case of West Indian women in Britain', in West, J. (ed.), *Work, Women and the Labour Market*, London: Routledge and Kegan Paul.

Pirani, M., Yolles, M. and Bassa, E. (1992), 'Ethnic pay differentials', *New Community*, vol. 19, pp. 31–42.

Policy Studies Institute (1992), *Urban Trends 1*, London: Policy Studies Institute.

Policy Studies Institute (1993), *Britain's Ethnic Minorities*, London: Policy Studies Institute.

Poulantzas, N. (1975), *Class in Contemporary Capitalism*, London: New Left Books.

Poulantzas, N. (1978), *State, Power, Socialism*, London: New Left Books.

Pratt, G. (1989), 'Reproduction, class and the spatial structure of the city', in Peet, R. and Thrift, N. (eds), *New Models in Geography*, vol. 2, London: Unwin and Hyman.

Pugliese, E. (1985), 'Farm Workers in Italy: agricultural working class, landless peasants or clients of the welfare state', in Hudson, R. and Lewis, J. (eds), *Uneven Development in Southern Europe*, London: Methuen.

Radice, H. (1984), 'The national economy – a Keynesian myth?', *Capital and Class*, vol. 22, pp. 111–40.

Ramdin, R. (1987), *The Making of Black Working Class Britain*, Aldershot: Gower.

Rampton Report (1981), *West Indian Children in our Schools*, London: HMSO, Cmnd 8273.

Redfern, P. (1982), 'Profile of our cities', *Population Trends*, vol. 30, pp. 21–32.

Remuneration Economics (1993), *Management Remuneration Survey 1993*, Survey House, 51 Portland Road, Kingston upon Thames, Surrey KT1 2SH.

Reward Group (1992), *Reward Management Salary Survey*, Stone Business Park, Stone, Staffordshire.

Rex, J. and Moore, R. (1967), *Race, Community and Conflict*, London: Oxford University Press.

Rex, J. and Tomlinson, S. (1979), *Colonial Immigrants in a British City: a Class Analysis*, London: Routledge and Kegan Paul.

Robinson, F. and Gregson, F. (1992), 'The "underclass": a class apart?', *Critical Social Policy*, No. 34, pp. 38–51.

Robinson, V. (1980), 'Asians and council housing', *Urban Studies*, vol. 17, pp. 323–31.

Robinson, V. (1988), 'The new Indian middle class in Britain', *Ethnic and Racial Studies in Britain*, vol. 11, pp. 456–73.

Robinson, V. (1990), 'Roots to mobility: the social mobility of Britain's black population 1971–1987', *Ethnic and Racial Studies*, vol. 13, pp. 274–286.

Rock, C., Torre, S. and Wright, G. (1980), 'The appropriation of the house: changes in housing design and concepts of domesticity', in Weskle, G.R., Peterson, P. and Morley, D. (eds), *New Space for Women*, Boulder, Colorado: Westview Press.

Rodger, J. (1992), 'The welfare state and social closure; social division and the underclass', *Critical Social Policy*, vol. 35, pp. 45–63.

Rowthorne, B. (1983), 'The past strikes back', in Hall, S. and Jacques, M. (eds), *The Politics of Thatcherism*, London: Lawrence and Wishart.

Royal Commission on the Distribution of Income and Wealth (1976), *Report No.6*, HMSO, London.

Rubinstein, W.D. (1981), *Men of Property*, London: Croom Helm.

Saggar, S. (1993), 'The politics of "race policy" in Britain', *Critical Social Policy*, No. 37, pp. 32–51.

Sarre, P., Phillips, D. and Skellington, R. (1989), *Ethnic Minority Housing: Explanations and Policies*, Aldershot: Avebury.

Sassen, S. (1991), *The Global City*, Los Angeles: University of California Press.

Saunders, P. (1979), *Urban Politics*, London: Hutchinson.

Sayer, R. and Walker R. (1992), *The New Social Economy*, Oxford: Blackwell.

Scase, R. (1982), 'The petty bourgeoisie and modern capitalism: a consideration of recent theories', in Gidden, A. and MacKenzie, G. (eds), *Social Class and the Division of Labour*, Cambridge: Cambridge University Press.

Scott, J. (1986) *Capitalist Property and Financial Power*, Wheatsheaf, Brighton.

Shanks, M. (1977), *Planning and Politics*, London: Allen and Unwin.

Short, J.R. (1982), *Housing in Britain: the Post-War Experience*, London: Methuen.

Sim, D. (1984), 'Urban deprivation: not just the inner city', *Area*, vol. 16, pp. 299–306.

Smith, D.M. (1979), 'Inner city deprivation: problems and policies in advanced capitalist countries', *Geoforum*, vol. 10, pp. 297–310.

Smith, N. and Williams, P. (eds)(1986), *Gentrification and the City*, London: Allen and Unwin.

Smith, S. (1989), 'The politics of "race" and a new segregationism', in Mohan, J. (ed.), *The Political Geography of Contemporary Britain*, London: Macmillan.

Smithers, A. and Robinson, P. (1991), *Beyond Compulsory Schooling*, Council for Industry and Higher Education, 100 Park Village East, London NW1 3SR.

Somerville, J. (1992), 'The New Right and family politics', *Economy and Society*, vol. 21, pp. 93–128.

Srinivasan, S. (1992), 'The class position of the Asian petty bourgeoisie', *New Community*, vol. 19, pp. 61–74.

Standsworth, P. (1984), 'Elites and privileges', in Abrams, P. and Brown, R. (eds), *Work, Urbanization and Inequality*, London: Weidenfeld and Nicolson.

Taylor, P. (1979), '"Difficult to let", "Difficult to live in", and sometimes "Difficult to get out of"', *Environment and Planning A*, vol. 11, pp. 1305–20.

Taylor, P. (1992), 'Changing Political Relations', in Cloke, P. (ed.), *Policy and Change in Thatcher's Britain*, Oxford: Pergamon.

Teague, A. (1993), 'Ethnic group: first results from the 1991 census', *Population Trends*, vol. 72, pp. 12–17.

ten Tusscher, T. (1986), 'Patriarchy, capitalism and the New Right', in Evans, J. (ed.), *Feminism and Political Theory*, London: Sage.

Thrift, N. (1992) 'Light out of darkness? Critical social theory in 1980s Britain', in Cloke, P. (ed.), *Policy and Change in Thatcher's Britain*, Oxford: Pergamon.

Thrift, N., Danisk, P. and Leyshon, A. (1987), *Sexy Greedy: the New International Financial System, the City of London and the South East of England*, Working Paper on Producer Series No.8, Universities of Bristol and Liverpool.

Tomlinson, S. (1983), 'Black women in higher education – case studies of university women in Britain', in Barton, L. and Walker, S. (eds), *Race and Class in Education*, London: Croom Helm.

Townsend, A.R. (1983), *The Impact of Recession*, London: Croom Helm.

Townsend, A.R. (1993a), 'The urban–rural cycle in the Thatcher growth years', *Transactions of the Institute of British Geographers*, vol. 18, pp. 207–221.

Townsend, A.R. (1993b), *Business Services in the Economic Development of Edinburgh*, Durham: University of Durham, Department of Geography, Working Paper 1.

Townsend, P. (1980), 'Social planning and the Treasury', in Bosanquet, N. and Townsend, P. (eds), *Labour and Equality*, London: Heinemann.

Townsend, P. and Davidson, N. (1982), *Inequalities in Health*, Harmondsworth: Penguin.

Training Commission (1988), *Labour Market Quarterly*, July,Sheffield.

Troyna, B. (1990), 'Reform or deform? The 1988 Education Reform Act and racial equality in Britain', *New Community*, vol. 16, pp. 403–16.

Troyna, B. and Williams, J. (1986), *Racism, Education and the State*, Beckenham: Croom Helm.

Unemployment Unit (1992), *Survey Results in Working Brief*, 409 Brixton Road, London SW9 7DG.

Urry, J. (1981), *The Anatomy of Capitalist Societies*, London: Macmillan.

Urry, J. (1986), 'Capitalist production, scientific management and the service class', in Scott, A.J. and Storper, M. (eds), *Production, Territory, Work*, London: Unwin Hyman.

Valentine, G. (1992), 'Images of danger: women's sources of information about the spatial distribution of male violence', *Area*, vol. 24, No. 1, pp. 22–9.

Walby, S. (1986), 'Gender, class and stratification: towards a new approach', in Compton, R. and Mann, M. (eds), *Gender and Stratification*, Cambridge: Polity Press.

Walby, S. and Bagguley, P. (1990), 'Sex segregation in local labour markets', *Work, Employment and Society*, vol. 4, pp. 59–81.

Walker, A. and Walker, C. (1987), *The Growing Divide: A Social Audit 1979–1987*, London: Child Poverty Action Group.

Whitehall Companion (1993) London: Dod's Publishing & Research Ltd.

Williams, A. (1987), *The West European Economy*, London: Hutchinson.

Williams, A. (1991), *The European Communities*, Oxford: Blackwell.

Williams, A. and Shaw, G. (eds) (1992), 'Tourism research: a perspective', *American Behavioural Scientist*, vol. 36, pp. 133–143.

World Bank (1992), *World Development Report*.

Wright, E.O. (1978), *Class, Crisis and the State*, London: New Left Books.

Wright, E.O. (1985), *Classes*, London: London.

Wright, E.O. (1989), *The Debate on Classes*, London: Verso.

Zabalza, A. and Tzannatos, Z. (1985), 'The effect of Britain's anti-discriminatory legislation on relative pay and employment', *Economic Journal*, vol. 95, pp. 679–699.

Index

activity rates 30, 135–9
Afro-Caribbean 177–217, 275
agency and structure 5, 18
agriculture 38, 164, 268
alienation 14, 182
Alnwick 56
apprenticeships 141
area-based policies 36, 246, 287–92
aristocracy 55, 56, 58, 97, 116, 124
Asians 145, 177–217, 275, 279, 298
Atlanticism 34

balance of payments see current account
Bangladeshis 177–217
bankruptcies 69, 70, 230
Barlow Commission 252
Basingstoke 238
Bedford 30
Belfast 277
Beveridge Report 1942 134, 138,
    147–9, 150, 155–6, 161, 285–6
Birkenhead 151
Birmingham 145, 205, 214, 217, 262,
    277, 278, 287
'black economy' 87, 88, 144
'Black Report' 107, 108, 109
Blackburn 203
Bottomley, Virginia 173, 296
bourgeoisie 6, 17, 97, 113, 185
Bradford 198, 255
Brent 206, 277
Brighton 16
British National Party 14, 130, 210
British Nationality Act 1981 211
British Rail 140, 141, 296
British Telecom 41
Brixton 14, 215, 216
Broadwater Farm 216
building societies 205

BUPA 109
Business Expansion Scheme 246
Butskellism 29, 30, 127, 134
by-elections 118, 179, 210, 212, 220,
    267

Cabinet 172–3
Calabria 232, 235
Cambridge 2, 28, 249, 267
Camden Town 214
Cammel Laird 151
capacity utilisation,
    manufacturing 225–6
capital 5, 7, 40, 62
    multinational 23, 35, 38, 65, 109
capital accumulation 18, 34, 129, 133,
    187
    flexible 28
capitalism 26, 218, 297
    crises 17, 18–19, 21, 22, 26, 27, 28,
        34, 89
    disorganised 27
    restructuring 31
    venture capital 229
car industry 266
car ownership 121, 239, 252, 280
Castle, Barbara 172
Channel Tunnel 98
Cheltenham 139, 212
child care 135, 138, 145, 152, 163,
    164–5, 166
    'home alone' 150
Child Poverty Action Group 2, 24, 53
Church Commissioners 55
Church of England 60
Churchill, Winston 87, 180
Churchillism 34
Citizen's Charter 296
citizenship 43, 181, 294, 180

City Challenge 288
City of London 38, 61, 66, 76, 104, 155, 163, 252, 302
and 'Big Bang' 38, 66, 105
Civil Service 103, 140, 174
civil society 4, 13, 17, 18, 21, 142, 162, 209–17
Clarke, Kenneth 284–5
class 4–9, 16–7, 24, 29, 35, 75, 95, 241, 270, 297, 303
and consumption 118–24
and education 99–106, 193
and gender 157, 163
and health 107–11
and housing 111–18, 208
and party politics 125
and race 14, 203
middle class 6, 9, 17, 77, 97, 124, 129, 133, 163, 164, 166, 168, 192, 209, 212, 283
service 106, 142, 146
working class 6, 7, 9, 12, 17, 29, 95, 97, 124, 133, 164, 166, 191, 208, 275, 298
clothing industry 145, 146, 184
coal industry 6, 135, 255, 256, 266, 296, 300
coalfield communities 16, 174
Commission for Racial Equality 206, 213
Common Agricultural Policy 58, 59
commuting 44, 221, 239
long distance 15, 222, 237
company structures 67–75
Conservative Party 24, 125, 126, 129, 130, 132, 172, 175, 210, 211, 212, 260, 261, 267, 284
Conferences 135, 171, 179
consumer credit 98
consumer durables 118, 119, 239
Consumers' Association 24
consumption 118–24
and gender 168–72
'contented majority' 300, 302
conurbations 16
Corby 255
Cornwall 268
corporatism 30, 37
Country Landowners Association 25
culture 164, 174
and race 180–1, 197, 198, 206
deferential 127

culture of poverty 277, 288
currency crisis 30
current account 2, 30, 32, 36, 45, 47, 48, 67, 91
Currie, Edwina 110

Dagenham 264
deflationary policies 31–2, 36, 40
deindustrialisation 40, 45, 129, 224, 246
denationalisation 29
Denmark 97
Department of Economic Affairs 3
Department of Environment 3
deprivation 3, 128, 170
and gender 153
rural 282–3
urban 277
Derbyshire 257
deskilling 185, 278
devaluation 29, 32
Development Agencies 245
divisions of labour 4, 29, 97
domestic 10, 13, 133, 142, 161–9
dual careers 142, 298
spatial 228, 254
Docklands (London) 279, 288, 289, 292
domestic service 163
Dudley 214
Duke of Westminster 126
Dundee 141

East Anglia 61, 227, 235, 236, 237, 239, 242, 255, 267, 268, 269, 276
East Midlands 255, 266, 267
Eastbourne 267
ecological issues 18
economic crises 4, 29, 33, 34, 35, 36, 40, 109, 128, 247
Edinburgh 249, 255
education 11, 273, 284, 289
and class 99–106, 194–6, 197, 198
and gender 101, 155–61, 194
and race 14, 101, 193–9
binary divide 103
comprehensive schools 101, 102
higher 102–3, 106, 157
multicultural 196, 197
national curriculum 157, 198

education (*cont.*)
  nursery 151, 166, 298
  private 100, 196, 241, 242
  public schools 103, 104, 241
  qualifications 157–8, 170, 185,
    193–6
  regional variations 242–3
  state 101, 106
  streaming 158–61
Education Act 1944 159
Educational Disadvantage Units 197
Educational Priority Areas 197, 287
Educational Reform Act 1988 198
elderly 53, 274–5, 283, 298
electronics 254
élites 103, 104
Employee share ownership plans 70
employment 28, 75–81, 254–7, 262–3,
    273
  and gender 30, 134–9, 142, 153,
    182–4, 186
  and race 182–7
  casual 59, 87, 88, 92, 134, 136, 182,
    187, 298
  contract workers 87, 89
  core and peripheral workers 85, 86,
    144
  family 59
  part time 45, 59, 75, 76, 86, 134,
    138, 141, 143–4, 146, 148, 155,
    163, 298
  second 86
  self- 59, 68, 86, 184, 226
  shift work 184
  temporary 86, 88, 92
Employment Act 1980, 1982 134
Employment Protection Act 1975 134
Employment Training Service 94, 292
energy crisis 37
Enterprise Allowance Scheme 67, 69
enterprise culture 38, 43, 54, 67, 68,
    74, 75, 106, 129, 228, 231, 246–7,
    253, 295, 297
  and race 185
Enterprise Zones 287, 292
entrepreneurs 69, 185
environmental issues 44, 130, 267
Equal Opportunities Commission 141,
    147, 152
Equal Pay Act 1970 133, 176
Equal Pay Act 1975 150–1, 152
equality of opportunity 100, 106

Essex men and women 43
estate agents 205
European Court of Justice 149, 175,
    176
European Union 2, 18, 23, 30, 32, 37,
    76, 97, 133, 149, 151, 152, 235
Exchange Rate Mechanism 1, 48

Falklands War 9, 41, 131
family 13, 135, 138, 159, 162, 166,
    168, 195, 273
  'wage' 138–9, 149, 171
farmers 58
feudalism 5–6, 55
finance capital 35
financial deregulation 45, 205, 228,
    252
financial services 76, 247, 255, 260
Ford 141
Fordism 28, 34
foreign direct investment 45, 66, 67
Fowler Review 150, 271
Foxley Wood 267
France 6
Frankfurt 247
freedom 3, 4, 43, 44
Freeman 151
Freeports 292

gender 10, 13–4, 16, 29, 35, 68,
    133–176, 181, 270, 275, 303
general election 1, 28, 41, 127, 131,
    132, 179, 210, 211, 220, 245, 253,
    267, 299
General Improvement Areas 287
gentrification 279
gentry 58
Germany 19, 30, 66, 97
Gilmour, Ian 296
Glasgow 16, 256, 262, 263, 264, 277
Govan 15
Greater London Council 253, 257
Greece 97
Green Belt 261
Green Party 127
'green' politics 98
Greenham Common 174
Griffiths, Peter 179
Groce, Mrs 216
Gross National Product 29, 45, 94,
    227

Grunwick 191

Hackney 206, 210, 277, 281
Hammersmith 277
Hampshire 61
Handsworth 216, 217
Harrogate 249, 269
Hart, Judith 173
Hayward, Julie 151
Healey, Denis 134
health 107–11, 264, 284, 292, 296
  care access 108, 110
  internal market 110
  private sector 108, 109, 111, 275,
    280
  social inverse care law 108, 110
Heath, Edward 32, 179, 210, 211
Hertfordshire 257
Heseltine, Michael 287
Hexham 269
homeless 42, 200, 262, 280, 292
homeworkers 86, 88, 144–5, 182, 185,
  187, 298
Honeyford, Ray 198
household survival strategy 69
housing 235–8, 257–62, 273
  and class 111–18, 199, 204
  and gender 114, 170–2, 204
  and race 14, 114, 199–209
  conditions 200, 205, 275
  council house sales 7, 38, 42, 204,
    260–1, 261, 268
  market 8, 47, 68, 74, 112, 208–9,
    283
  negative equity 117, 237
  owner occupation 7, 30, 115–6,
    170–2, 200, 204–6, 258, 261
  prices 115, 117, 221, 236–7, 249,
    260–1, 283
  private renting 202–3, 258, 279
  public sector 23, 170–2, 200, 203–4,
    258, 260–1, 277, 279
  regional variations 235–8
  repossessions 117–18, 237
  'trap' 260, 279
Housing Action Areas 287
Housing and Urban Development Bill
  1993 117
housing classes 111
Howe, Geoffrey 288
Hunt, David 296

Hurd, Douglas 217

ideology 3, 40, 69, 74, 125, 142, 166,
  168, 212, 213, 216, 252, 288, 303
immigration 29, 30, 129, 130, 177–82,
  216
Immigration Act 1962 178, 179, 210
Immigration Act 1968 179, 210
Immigration Act 1971 179, 180
Immigration Act 1987 181
income 81–9, 119, 267, 273, 281
  distribution 24, 35, 81, 97, 164
  fringe benefits 85
  profit-related bonuses 82
  unearned 64
incomes policy 32, 37
Independent Commission on Education
  1993 101
Indians 177–217, 275
individualism 134, 168, 200, 217, 271,
  288
industrial capitalism 6, 59
industrial relations 45
Industrial Reorganisation
  Corporation 32
inflation 32, 38, 40, 47, 128
inheritance 284, 302
inner cities 112, 182, 189, 196, 203,
  205, 206, 209, 216, 248, 252, 253,
  254, 258, 269, 271, 276–82, 284
  riots 9, 14, 209, 213, 215–6, 263,
    270, 279
Inner London Education
  Authority 198
innovation 119–20
international competitiveness 31, 32,
  37, 67, 255, 301
international migration 11, 89
International Monetary Fund 36
Ireland 30, 179
Irish 177, 208
Isle of Dogs (London) 14
Italy 21
Italians 208

Japan 19, 30, 66
Jarrett, Mrs 216
Jenkin, Patrick 109, 110, 135
Jenkins, Roy 180
Johnson, Peter 215

Joseph, Keith 135, 287
judges 140, 174

Keynesianism 4, 34, 43, 91, 128, 253, 301
Kingston 281

labour 5
  flexibility 23, 38, 45, 79, 86, 87, 88–9, 134, 137, 144, 162, 182, 187, 289, 298
  guest-workers 182
  replacement 182, 185, 208
  unwaged 10
labour markets 7, 93, 108, 114, 283
  and race 14
  deregulation 136
  gendering 13, 135–55
  participation 11
  productivity 19, 33, 37, 67
  segmentation 12, 45, 50, 85, 89, 203, 298
Labour governments 36–7, 129, 179, 181, 197, 210, 213, 286
Labour Party 8, 24, 36, 42, 125, 130, 132, 172, 175, 212, 260, 286, 303
  Lib–Lab pact 70
labour power, reproduction of 10, 11, 162
Lake District 241
Lambeth 215
Lamont, Norman 49, 95
Lancashire 184
land prices 59
land use planning 258
landownership 6, 55–62
law and order 127, 130
Lawson, Nigel 74, 249
Leeds 193, 255, 262, 263
legitimation 43
  crisis 34
Leicester 206, 210
leisure 58, 121, 163–9, 268
Levin, Bernard 211
Lewisham 215
Liberal Party 118, 130
Liberals/Liberal Democrats 220, 245
life styles 97–9, 118–24
  privatised 121

Lilley, Peter 179
Lindsay, Martin 179
Liverpool 15, 190, 216, 217, 256, 262, 264, 277, 287, 288
Lloyds 'names' 59
local elections 118, 210
Local Government Act 1966 197
location 12, 15–6, 139
London 15, 16, 56, 98, 109, 149–50, 197, 206, 208, 214, 217, 228, 234, 237, 242, 246, 249, 252, 254, 255, 257, 260, 261, 262, 264, 277, 279, 280, 281, 287, 294
London Transport 177
long waves (development) 18
Loughborough 190
Luton 255, 266

Maastricht Treaty 48
Macmillan, Harold 30, 97, 243
Major, John 23, 74, 87, 109, 110, 118, 126, 131, 132, 135, 172, 175, 244, 257, 271, 296, 300, 301
Majorism 25, 40, 48–9, 85, 86, 96, 295–6, 297, 303
Malaysian Asian 210
management buy-outs 71, 73
Manchester 193, 257, 262, 264, 277, 287
Manpower Services Commission 91, 94, 105
Mansfield Hosiery Mills 190
market deregulation 38, 39, 43, 65, 67, 68, 88, 134, 135, 179, 287, 301
marriage 162
Marx 5, 17–18
mass consumption 30
Matrimonial Homes Act 1967 171
Medium Term Financial Strategy 40
Members of Parliament
  and gender 172
  European 173
meritocracy 103, 106, 155, 193
Mezzogiorno 7
Middlesbrough 15, 238, *see also* Teesside
migration 221, 238, 252, 279
  retirement 222
  temporary 222
Ministry of Defence 246

mobility 121, 165, 283
  personal 121, 239
modernisation 30, 178
modes of regulation 19, 22, 28, 30, 253
Monday Club 210
monetarism 40, 47, 296
monetary policy 39
Morris, Bill 190
motherhood 165
multinationals 45, 64, 301
multiple deprivation 36, 112, 189, 269–93
multiple disadvantages 14, 55, 186, 270, 271, 273, 275–6, 284, 300

National Assistance Board 93
National Front 191, 210–11
National Health Service 14, 28, 107, 108, 141, 184, 241, 286
  funding 110
National Plan 31
National Socialist Movement 210
National Trust 58, 60
National Union of Mineworkers 41
National Women's Advisory
  Committee 175
nationalisation 19, 28, 29
nationalised industries 23, 40, 247, 266, 297
nationalism 15, 244, 299
Nationality Act 1981 181
New Poor Law 1834 93
new towns 254, 255, 257, 267
Newbury 267
Newcastle 262, 287
Newham 206
Nicholson, Emma 175
North (of England) 233, 234, 237, 258, 276
North Africa 182
North East 266, 268
North–South divide 15, 218–248, 252–62, 269, 276, 299
Northern Ireland 15, 127, 220, 227, 232, 235, 236–7, 242, 244, 277
'Northern lights' 249, 269
Notting Hill 208, 214
Nottingham 214, 216
nuclear disarmament 130

nuclear power 38, 300

occupational segregation
  and gender 139–43, 151, 152
  and race 185–7, 188
One Nation politics 3, 24, 28–36, 41, 50, 54, 75, 81, 85, 89, 92, 97, 99, 100, 101, 103, 107, 110, 111, 113, 116, 118, 125, 126, 129, 130, 131, 133–5, 137, 142, 146, 150, 153, 155, 157, 161, 166, 176, 178, 179, 180, 181, 193, 196–7, 199, 203, 209, 210, 213, 215, 216, 218, 220, 235, 242, 252–5, 257–8, 263–4, 271–2, 276–7, 283, 285, 286, 301
Open University 102
Owen, David 279
Oxbridge 105

Pakistanis 177–217
Paris 247
party politics
  and class 125–32
  and class dealignment 127, 131
  and gender 172–6
  and political donations 125
  and race 179–80, 211–12, 298
  and regional variations 243–5
patrials 180, 181
patriarchy 10, 12, 175
patriotism 211
pensions 147, 148, 184, 297, 298
periodisation 26–7
personal equity plan 8, 70, 284
personal pension plan 8, 64
Pickstone, Rene 151
place 9–10
Plowden Report 1967 166, 197
'popular capitalism' 8, 43, 73, 74, 75, 86, 112, 235
police 140, 174, 214–15
Policy for the Inner Cities 287
poll tax 296
Portugal 97
poverty 1, 2, 3, 28, 50, 53, 110–11, 114, 118, 124, 195, 232, 272, 275, 276, 282, 285, 286, 292
  and gender 135, 149, 153, 169
Powell, Enoch 210, 211

power 5, 9, 13, 18, 35, 64, 126
  decentralisation 23
privatisation 8, 16, 23, 38, 41, 42, 43,
  44, 48, 62, 70, 73, 96, 131, 179,
  243, 246, 296, 297, 301
profits 7, 21, 30, 33, 37, 54, 55, 58,
  65, 67, 68, 71, 109, 298
property-owning democracy 260
public expenditure 21, 22, 29, 30, 31,
  36, 38, 39, 172, 179, 247, 248, 264,
  266, 271, 283, 292
public sector borrowing 2, 14, 21, 48

quangos 24, 174

race 9–10, 14, 16, 29, 35, 68,
  177–217, 270, 275, 289, 303
race relations 36, 210, 211
Race Relations Act 1965 213
Race Relations Act 1968 213
Race Relations Act 1976 213
Race Relations Board 213
racial discrimination 182, 186, 199,
  203, 204, 205, 208, 211, 213, 216
racial segregation 200
racism 12, 179, 180, 181, 190, 196,
  210, 214–5
Rampton Report 1981 193
rate 'capping' 292
recession 1, 15, 32, 40, 42, 47, 48, 69,
  71, 74, 89, 92, 95, 98, 109, 131,
  190, 219, 220, 228, 237, 238, 241,
  245, 248, 255, 298
  regional impacts of 226
redundancies 99, 107, 189
Redundant Mineworkers Payments
  Scheme 220
regimes of accumulation 19, 22, 28,
  30, 89
regional inequalities 30, 218–49,
  299
regional policy 15, 23, 40, 220, 245,
  246, 248, 249, 256, 257, 301
regulation theory 19, 26
relations of production 125, 136
Relf, Robert 213
rents 60, 62
residential mobility 170, 200, 260
residential segregation 206–9

Resource Allocation Working
  Party 241
restructuring 37, 49, 68, 97, 136, 138,
  150, 192, 253, 255, 263, 294, 302
Robbins Report 102, 155–6
Royal Commission on the Distribution
  of Wealth and Income 168
rural areas 16, 252, 253, 255, 261, 268

Scarman report 198, 215, 217
Scotland 15, 127, 154, 242, 245, 258,
  268, 282–3
second homes 240
self employed 9
Sex Discrimination Act 1975 133, 160,
  176
share ownership 8, 62–7, 235,
  297
  employee schemes 85–6
  institutional 64
  option scheme 70–1, 96
Shephard, Gillian 79
Silicon Fen 228
Silicon Glen 78
single parents 143, 171–2
Skelmersdale 238
slavery 177
small businesses 14, 38, 43, 64, 77, 84,
  89, 134, 192, 228–9, 297
Smethwick 179
social construction
  and gender 140, 159, 162
  and race 202
social democracy 27, 127, 301
social justice 18
Social Liberal Democratic Party 127,
  131, 244, 299
social mobility
  and gender 154–5
  and race 191–3
social polarisation 43, 113, 191, 246,
  261, 266, 268, 273, 279, 297,
  298
social reproduction 135
Social Security Acts 1980, 1981 150,
  271
social segregation 114
social structure 4–17
social well-being 272
socialisation and gender 160
socio-economic groups 9

South East 47, 48, 112, 115, 117, 220, 222, 227, 228, 229, 232, 234, 235, 235, 236, 237, 239, 240, 241, 242, 246–7, 248, 249, 252, 260, 261, 267, 269, 276, 281, 299, 301
South West 222, 232, 234, 235, 236, 237, 239, 241, 242, 267, 268, 269, 276
Southall 190
Southend 16, 249
state 17–25
  crisis of 29, 48, 67
  limits to interventionism 31
  'nanny' 39
  regulatory role 4, 17–22
  restructuring of the 24, 31, 33
  role of 10, 138, 295
strikes 41, 230
  miners' strike 1984–5 131
sub-contracting 88, 144, 229
suburbs 133, 166, 205, 208, 209, 252, 258
Suez crisis 31
Suffolk 283
supplementary benefits 94
Supplementary Benefits Commisssion 93, 271
Surrey 56, 235, 252
Sussex 235, 249, 255, 283
Sutton 264
Sweden 19

taxation 13, 19, 24, 30, 42, 43, 47, 48, 49, 50–1, 54, 60, 67, 70, 75, 98, 110, 116, 134, 297, 299, 300
Tebbit, Norman 211
Teesside 139, 257
temporary employment schemes 94
Thanet 249, 257
Thatcher, Margaret 23, 89, 91, 109, 110, 113, 118, 125, 126, 129, 131, 134, 135, 171, 172, 173, 175, 179, 181, 191, 209, 211, 216, 217, 220, 241, 246, 248, 281
Thatcherism 22, 25, 27, 32, 37–49, 54, 68, 70, 84, 85, 88, 93, 94, 96, 103, 116, 129, 130, 135, 151, 171, 181, 220, 253, 255, 260, 271, 296, 297, 299, 303
Timex 141
Torquay 124

Tory Reform Group 284, 296
Tottenham 216
tourism 45, 121, 123, 168, 268
Tower Hamlets 190, 206
Toxteth 14, 215
trade 33, 45
trade unions 24, 31, 37, 38, 39, 41, 43, 75, 84, 129, 179, 230
  and gender 141
  and race 186, 190–1
  non-unionised plants 78–9
  one-union plants 79
training 141, 157, 187
Training and Enterprise Councils 94, 105
Transport and General Workers Union 141
transport deregulation 239
'transport poor' 168, 283
Two Nations politics 1, 2, 3, 4, 13, 25, 28, 32, 36–49, 54, 66, 67, 68, 70, 76, 79, 81, 85, 91, 92, 93, 94, 97, 98, 100, 107, 111, 112, 113–14, 116, 118, 124, 125, 127, 129, 131, 133–5, 136, 137, 138, 141, 142, 146, 150, 153, 155, 156, 161, 162, 168–9, 171, 172, 176, 178, 179, 180, 181, 184, 186, 189, 190, 198–9, 203–4, 208, 209–11, 213, 215, 217, 220, 235, 241, 242, 245, 246, 248, 252–5, 263–4, 271–2, 277, 280, 282, 284–5, 287–94, 295–304
Tyneside 215, 256, 266 *see also* Newcastle

Ugandan Asians 179
underclass 7, 12, 14, 55, 95, 97, 115, 116, 124, 168, 179, 191, 192, 216, 284, 285
'undeserving' poor 94
unemployment 2, 3, 7, 28, 36, 40, 43, 48, 50, 53, 68, 69, 79, 87, 89–96, 92, 95, 97, 99, 103, 105, 106, 114, 115, 118, 124, 128, 129, 178, 191, 238, 249, 256, 257, 264, 266, 267, 276, 279, 280, 281, 285, 292, 293–4, 297, 299, 300
  and gender 11, 135, 153–4, 168
  and health 107, 110
  and race 189–90, 192

urban areas 16, 252, 254, 262–8
Urban Development
    Corporations 288–9, 292
urban policies 246, 258, 285–94, 301
USA 19, 66, 213
USSR 22
Uxbridge 210

Vagrancy Act 214
'Victorian values' 1, 13, 43, 93, 118,
    135, 145, 161, 220
voting behaviour 8, 9, 15, 126–9,
    131–2, 185, 257

wage bargaining 86
wages 29, 82–5, 87, 143, 179, 302
    and gender 145–52
    and race 187–9, 191
    fringe benefits 86, 143, 147, 184
    profit-related 86
    public sector 48
Wages Councils 77, 87, 134, 152,
    175
Wales 127, 215, 241, 242, 245, 266,
    268, 276
wealth, redistribution of 8
welfare benefits 2, 134, 138, 150, 166,
    169, 235, 264, 272, 292, 293, 297,
    298
welfare 'scroungers' 93
welfare state 2, 4, 7, 16, 25, 27, 98,
    43, 127, 135, 143, 166, 177, 243,
    268, 271, 272, 285, 286
    clients of 95
    selectivism 286
West Bromwich Corporation Transport
    Department 186
West Midlands 88, 206, 227, 235, 257,
    266, 276
Williams, Shirley 172
Wilson, Harold 179, 286
Wiltshire 61
winter of discontent 1, 37, 128–9
Wolf 190
Women in the Media 174
Women's Aid Federation 174
women's liberation movements 133,
    174
working practices 45, 67, 86

Yorkshire and Humberside 184, 235,
    257, 266
Young, Baroness 173
Young, George 117
Yuppies 43, 163